The Power of Group Attachment

The Power of Group Attachment provides evidence for the fundamental role that interpersonal and group attachment have played in our survival and evolution as individuals, groups, organisations, and species.

Arturo Ezquerro and María Cañete deliver a creative integration of updated theoretical knowledge, meticulous research and inspiring clinical work; they go beyond the consulting room, and draw on cross-cultural studies, to postulate that there is no such thing as individual or interpersonal attachment without group attachment. Their joint work enhances and brings closer together the fields of group analysis and attachment theory. Compelling narratives from group-analytic psychotherapy, for a broad range of problems (including trauma, suicidality, mood disorder and psychosis), demonstrate effective change from polarisation and hatred (idealising one's own group and denigrating other's) to working through conflict and accepting real differences between members, the hallmark of both therapy and healthy social life.

Original, scholarly, yet personal and accessible, the book is addressed to mental health professionals and managers as well as politicians and educators: it expands the reader's social and democratic consciousness at this crucial time when our world is descending fast into pathology, global warming, and vicious violence stemming from unresolved personal and collective trauma.

Dr Arturo Ezquerro: London-based consultant psychiatrist, psychoanalytic-psychotherapist, and group analyst; senior assessor and trainer, Institute of Group Analysis; honorary member International Attachment Network, and World Association of International Studies; former Head NHS Medical Psychotherapy Services for Brent; over a hundred publications in six languages, including *Encounters with John Bowlby* (Routledge).

Dr María Cañete: consultant psychotherapist, psychiatrist, and group analyst; trained at the Tavistock Clinic; senior trainer, Institute of Group Analysis; former director NHS group psychotherapy programmes, University College, St Charles, and Mile End Hospitals, London; published widely in English, German and Spanish, including *Group Analysis throughout the Life Cycle* (Routledge).

The New International Library of Group Analysis (NILGA)
Series Editor: Earl Hopper

Drawing on the seminal ideas of British, European and American group analysts, psychoanalysts, social psychologists and social scientists, the books in this series focus on the study of small and large groups, organisations and other social systems, and on the study of the transpersonal and transgenerational sociality of human nature. NILGA books will be required reading for the members of professional organisations in the field of group analysis, psychoanalysis, and related social sciences. They will be indispensable for the "formation" of students of psychotherapy, whether they are mainly interested in clinical work with patients or in consultancy to teams and organisational clients within the private and public sectors.

Recent titles in the series include:

Intersectionality and Group Analysis
Explorations of Power, Privilege and Position in Group Therapy
Edited by Suryia Nayak and Alasdair Forrest

Group Analysis
A Modern Synthesis
Sigmund Karterud

Tolerance - A Concept in Crisis
Psychoanalytic, Group Analytic, and Socio-Cultural Perspectives
Edited by Avi Berman and Gila Ofer

Advances in Group Psychotherapy
Living in the Passionate Bad Fit
Stewart L. Aledort, Edited by Lee Kassan

The Power of Group Attachment
John Bowlby Revisited from a Group-Analytic Perspective
Arturo Ezquerro and María Cañete

The Power of Group Attachment

John Bowlby Revisited from a Group-Analytic Perspective

Arturo Ezquerro, María Cañete

Routledge
Taylor & Francis Group

LONDON AND NEW YORK

Designed cover image: Getty | koratmember

First published 2025
by Routledge
4 Park Square, Milton Park, Abingdon, Oxon OX14 4RN

and by Routledge
605 Third Avenue, New York, NY 10158

Routledge is an imprint of the Taylor & Francis Group, an informa business

British Library Cataloguing-in-Publication Data
A catalogue record for this book is available from the British
Library

ISBN: 978-1-032-22293-6 (hbk)
ISBN: 978-1-032-22294-3 (pbk)
ISBN: 978-1-003-27195-6 (ebk)

DOI: 10.4324/9781003271956

Typeset in Times New Roman
by Apex CoVantage, LLC

Contents

4   Suicide risk: when group attachment is not enough, or is it?   145

ARTURO EZQUERRO

**5   Group cohesion versus group coherency through
an attachment lens**   184

ARTURO EZQUERRO

6   A case of perverse group attachment   207

ARTURO EZQUERRO

About the authors

Arturo Ezquerro, a London-based consultant psychiatrist, psychoanalytic psychotherapist and group analyst, is senior assessor and trainer at the Institute of Group Analysis, honorary member of the International Attachment Network, of the Spanish Society for the Development of Groups, Psychotherapy and Psychoanalysis, and of the World Association of International Studies. He is former Head of NHS Medical Psychotherapy Services for Brent, London (for which he received clinical excellence awards), regularly collaborates with the media and has over 100 publications in six languages, including *Encounters with John Bowlby* (Routledge), *Relatos de apego* (Psimática), *Group Analysis throughout the Life Cycle: Foulkes Revisited from a Group Attachment and Developmental Perspective* (Routledge), *Apego y desarrollo a lo largo de la vida* (Editorial Sentir), *Amor i desenvolupament a través del cicle vital* (Editorial Sentir). John Bowlby was his supervisor and his mentor at the Tavistock Clinic during the last six years of his life (1984–1990).
Email: arturo.ezquerro@ntlworld.com

María Cañete is a London-based consultant psychotherapist, psychiatrist and group analyst, who trained at the Tavistock Clinic and at the Institute of Group Analysis, where she is a senior trainer and seminar leader. She has substantial experience working in both public and private sectors, and developed a special interest in the psychotherapy treatment of psychosis and of older adults. She is a former director of NHS group psychotherapy programmes at University College Hospital (Islington and Camden), at St Charles Hospital for people over 65 (Central and North West London), and at Mile End Hospital for psychotic patients (Tower Hamlets). She has published widely in English, German and Spanish, including *Group Analysis throughout the Life Cycle: Foulkes Revisited from a Group Attachment and Developmental Perspective* (Routledge).
Email: maria.canete@ntlworld.com

1. An innovative volume that clearly shows how the attachment theory paradigm can be applied to the clinical realities and theoretical basis of group analysis. The group attachment formulation is so convincing that, indeed, I found myself wondering why no one had done it before! The distinction between group cohesion and group coherency and how this reflects the state and stage of the attachment dynamic is particularly illuminating. This academically sound yet readable book is strongly recommended for all mental health professionals and at all levels of experience and training.

Prof Jeremy Holmes MD FRCPsych: *Consultant Psychiatrist in Psychotherapy; Honorary Professor of Psychoanalysis, University of Exeter, UK.*

2. Once again, Arturo Ezquerro and María Cañete have gifted us a truly original work, expanding and integrating such vital components of mental health as group analysis, attachment theory, and many others besides. Drawing upon the work of the late Dr John Bowlby, whom I had the privilege of meeting many times, and who would, I know, have adored this book, the authors have demonstrated effective ways in which the enhancement of attachment structures can not only enrich group life and interpersonal relationships but also help us to prevent suicide. I recommend this text most warmly.

Prof Brett Kahr, *Senior Fellow, Tavistock Institute of Medical Psychology; Honorary Director of Research, Freud Museum, London.*

3. The deepest and widest exploration into the complexities of evolutionary group attachment processes I have come across. It gives a more than welcome new dimension to both attachment theory and group analysis. Drawing on a broad range of disciplines, the authors clearly demonstrate how groups, in clinical settings and in society, can bring out the best and the worst in us. The reader will find moving stories of therapeutic group connections that promote well-being and maximise survival and, also, poignant examples of *perverse group attachment*, which is at the basis of fanaticism, dehumanizing others, violence and, in extreme cases, genocide.

Dr Mauricio Cortina MD, *Psychoanalyst; Director of Attachment, Development and Human Evolution, Washington School of Psychiatry.*

4. In this engaging book the authors apply attachment theory to highlight the interconnectivity between individual and group dynamics. The result is a timely reminder of the creative and destructive potential that can emanate from the links between the two. This book is a clarion call to therapists of all persuasions to recognise the indivisibility of person and context, and to reflect on the significance of their interventions both inside and outside the consulting room.

Dr Christopher Clulow PhD, *Consultant Couple Psychoanalytic Psychotherapist; Senior Fellow, Tavistock Institute of Human Relations.*

5. A remarkable state-of-the-art study on healthy and therapeutic group attachment, as well as perverse group dynamics, which illuminates the paths back to sanity. It integrates contributions from different clinical disciplines and schools of thought in a very welcoming manner and, in consequence, serves as a good role model for badly-needed theoretical inclusivity. No doubt, Arturo Ezquerro and María Cañete have given birth to a genuine classic that will continue to attract readers for many generations to come.

Dr Estela Welldon FRCPsych, *Consultant Forensic Psychiatrist; Founder and Honorary President, International Association for Forensic Psychotherapy.*

6. Drawing on attachment theory, anthropology, sociology, psychoanalysis, developmental psychology, group analysis, neuroscience, literature and poetry, this book is a catalyst that injects a contagious passion for life and makes knowledge on mental health, attachment and complex group dynamics palatable and accessible. I recommend it to primary care professionals, their managers and their patients.

Dame Clare Gerada DBE, FRCPsych, *President, Royal College of General Practitioners.*

7. Emanating from a rare amalgam of cross-cultural, socio-political, anthropological and qualitative clinical-process research, this volume brings attachment theory and group analysis up to date. It goes beyond conventional studies to explore novel aspects of group affiliation and group attachment, and convincingly demonstrates the relevance of attachment dynamics in challenging situations within organisational life and service provision. As a critical developmental psychologist, I found this text enormously helpful and inspirational. It should be core reading for professionals and service managers alike.

Prof Erica Burman, *Developmental Psychologist; Group Analyst; Professor of Education, University of Manchester; Former Chair, Psychology of Women and Equalities, British Psychological Society; Marcia Worrell Mentoring Award (2023).*

8. A unique cross-fertilisation of John Bowlby's attachment theory and SH Foulkes's group analysis, which brings together innovative theoretical formulations and meaningful clinical interventions. The reader will embark on a fascinating journey from the birth of humankind, through increasingly sophisticated group configurations and organisational dynamics, to current evidence-based group-analytic psychotherapy. Beautifully written, this book is an awe-inspiring contribution to meet the challenges posed by contemporary mental health practice.

Dr Carla Penna PhD, *Psychoanalyst and Group Analyst; Former President, Brazilian Association of Group Psychotherapy; Visiting Professor of Medical Psychology, Federal University, Rio de Janeiro.*

9. Elegantly written, methodically researched and highly instructive, this book has succeeded in making explicit and accessible what has always been implicit but not always acknowledged: the centrality of attachment in group analysis. It distinctly shows how the group matrix can come to be a foundational secure base, from which multiple dynamics of interpersonal and group attachment relationships can be explored and understood. I was particularly struck by an original case study on perverse group attachment, a compelling narrative that includes a masterful and profound depiction of human frailty, socio-political complexity, and the tragic consequences of untreated personal and collective wounds.

Reem Shelhi, *Contemporary Psychoanalytic Psychotherapist;*
Group Analyst and Clinical Supervisor.

10. This a refreshing addition to group-analytic and attachment literature. It succeeds in making a strong, persuasive and much-needed case for the integration of attachment and groups, in therapeutic, organisational and socio-political contexts. It builds on a growing interest in the importance of group attachment, which is at the core of human evolution and survival. It should be essential reading for practitioners and students and, by application, offers an authentic theoretical basis to all those involved in group work in a wide variety of settings.

Revd Dr Anne Holmes PhD, *Group Analyst; Former*
Tutor IGA Foundation Course, Oxford.

11. An attractive and generous read about how humans have lived, developed and related to each other that goes back to our very beginnings, to our earliest and most powerful drives, motivations and contributions, within which attachment processes have been essential in both interpersonal and group contexts. In addition, the book provides a 21st century perspective on psychotherapy and organisational life, as well as on the influence that healthy (or otherwise) attachment experiences have on the different ways that teams employ to explore and work together.

Prof Erik de Haan, *Director, Ashridge Centre for Coaching,*
UK; Professor of Organisational Development, School of
Business and Economics, Amsterdam University.

12. According to the World Health Organisation, about one in four people worldwide have suffered or will suffer from a diagnosable mental health problem at one point in their life. In this fascinating and original book, Arturo Ezquerro and María Cañete provide us with a broad perspective that meaningfully explains how culture and socio-political circumstances influence and modulate mental illness, and how societal pathologies impact on individual vulnerability.

Rosa Montero, *Journalist and Novelist (translated into*
27 languages); National Prize for Spanish Literature (2017).

13. Wearing two hats, as a group-analytic psychotherapist with a background in education, I found this book provides a unique learning experience, as it delivers scholar and clinical knowledge in ways that are decidedly readable, personal and very engaging. I can strongly recommend it to professionals in both mental health and education, as well as to any interested member of the public.

Jacqueline Fogden, *Group Analyst; Psychotherapist; Former Headteacher.*

14. I have very much enjoyed reading this book – a tour de force! Moreover, I am in awe of the authors' erudition and their capacity to translate sophisticated concepts, as well as complex internal, interpersonal and group processes into plain English, which makes the text accessible, instructive and telling. I have found that this work has been written not only for the profit of mental health professionals, but also for the benefit of all enquiring minds.

David Chalom BDS, LDS RCS, *Former Dental Casualty Officer in Maxillofacial Surgery, London.*

15. As a journalist, exposed to both British and Spanish culture, I have to communicate complex affairs to large audiences simply. Looking after my language is an essential part of my job. I am impressed by *The Power of Group Attachment.* The book is eloquent and jargon-free, rooted in British empiricism whilst displaying Spanish creativity; it contains wisdom and, at the same time, touches your heart. Above all, it is an antidote against despair, a model of inclusivity and an injection of hope. Read it for joy, for instruction, to be a better person, a better professional and a better citizen.

Juan Cruz, *Journalist and Writer; Author of 42 books.*

16. Building on Bowlby's attachment theory, this pioneering project brings together updated findings from anthropology and cross-cultural attachment studies, and proposes a radical hypothesis that group attachment created humankind. The volume helps expand the reader's democratic consciousness in the context of real-life events and the life-long need for interpersonal and group attachment. Unlike other books written on group dynamics, this progressive text affords a fresh approach and develops a plausible narrative about the evolution of human group attachment as the maker of humankind.

Orit Badouk Epstein, *Attachment-based Psychoanalytic Psychotherapist, Supervisor, Trainer and Writer; Former Editor*, Attachment: New Directions in Psychotherapy and Relational Psychoanalysis.

17. This is a very welcome integration of group analysis and attachment theory, which puts *group attachment* firmly at the core of the evolution and survival of humankind. The theory is robust, illustrated and brought to life with extensive historical, group-analytic and anthropological context, alongside contemporary attachment and wider mental health research, as well as the authors' outstanding clinical work.

Debra Nash, *Psychotherapist; Group Analyst; Former Director of Training Group Analysis North, UK.*

18. *The Power of Group Attachment* is a rewarding read that explores widely and deeply themes that are highly relevant to both the attachment and group-analytic schools of thought and clinical practice; it enhances and brings up to date attachment theory and group analysis. Anyone who fears that complacency is the enemy of creativity in any therapeutic endeavour can be sure to find, in this book, a satisfying antidote.

Desmond King, *Consultant Clinical Psychologist; Group Analyst; Honorary Member, International Attachment Network.*

19. Arturo Ezquerro and María Cañete's book fills a gap in the attachment and group-analytic literature. Since therapy groups provide a relatively secure environment, it is only natural to use them to change people's attachment patterns. However, not enough had been written about attachment and group analysis, which are key mental health components. So, this is an important theoretical and clinical contribution to the mental health field, and highly recommended to students, experts and anyone who is interested in the field.

Dr Haim Weinberg PhD, *Consultant Clinical Psychologist; Author of ten books; Group Analyst, Israel and USA.*

20. This sequel and companion volume to the successful *Group Analysis throughout the Life Cycle* – which was Foulkes revisited through an attachment lens, is a *vade mecum* for Group Analysts, Psychotherapists and all those interested in Groups and Mental Health, revisiting Bowlby through a Group-Analytic lens. It does what Manfred Kets de Vries did for business leaders and Psychoanalysis; it provides, in straightforward language, a comprehensive framework to understand what is going on with the inner worlds of those who perform or seek to perform in the external world, resulting in a compelling, accessible and integrated approach. Indeed, in their readability and accessibility to the non-technical reader, these twin volumes do a great service both to Group Analysis and to Attachment Theory.

Prof Barry Curnow, *National Director of Training, Institute of Group Analysis, UK.*

21. The scope of this timely book is impressive, skilfully demonstrating the continued significance of the applications of attachment theory as a valuable means to thinking about group dynamics and analysis. It is a fascinating and engaging evidence-based read. Ezquerro and Cañete draw you in and present a meaningful and critical discussion of *mainstream* thinking, through which they invite the reader to make deep connections and enjoy the role attachment ubiquitously plays in our live. This is enticingly illustrated with captivating case studies. An essential reading for anyone wishing to understand the individual self together with the group self.

Dr Deborah Bailey-Rodríguez PhD, *Senior Lecturer in Psychology, Middlesex University, London.*

22. Attachment theory provides a powerful tool to decipher a world descending ever deeper into pathology and violence. As exploited by nefarious leaders, the evolutionary and universal need for group belonging and group attachment explains how the collective can act in ways unthinkable to individuals. Arturo Ezquerro and María Cañete give us a timely and necessary perspective.

Dr John Eipper PhD, *President of World Association of International Studies, USA.*

23. An important contribution to the specialist literature on the psychology of attachment and human development, and on the understanding of our complex social group nature. It includes a fascinating case study, exploring how attachment experiences as well as other psychosocial, cultural and political factors impacted on a press officer during the Spanish Civil War, who later murderer his two sons. A key learning point is made that confronting ghosts from the past can help heal deep wounds properly.

Jimmy Burns-Marañón OBE, *Author and Journalist; Chairman, British-Spanish Society.*

24. In this powerful and original book which will resonate in many branches of psychotherapy, psychology and broader mental health, Arturo Ezquerro and María Cañete work to fill a gap in the specialist literature, creatively exploring and developing the dialectical space between group analysis and attachment theory. At a time when group attachments appear to be intensifying and hardening, this book arrives as a timely exploration of a concept that carries great potential to help us make sense of the different ways (healthy, perverse or otherwise) in which we attach to our groups.

Peter Zelaskowski, *Psychotherapist; Group Analyst; Former Editor*, Group-Analytic Contexts.

25. In this original work, both scholarly and personal, Ezquerro and Cañete start from the premise that *group attachment created humankind*. Indeed, during the Pleistocene, collective child rearing enriched our capacity to think imaginatively about each other. The authors substantiate their argument with a deep exploration of the evolutionary processes of *group selection* (the group equivalent to Darwinian natural selection), key to the creation and survival of collaborative human organisations. Compelling narratives from group-analytic psychotherapy show effective change from idealising one's own group to accepting and integrating real differences between members, the hallmark of both therapy and healthy social life.

Dr Sebastian Kraemer FRCPsych, FRCPCH, *Family Therapist and Honorary Consultant Child and Adolescent Psychiatrist, Tavistock and Portman NHS Foundation Trust, London.*

26. I am delighted that Dr Ezquerro and Dr Cañete, have gifted us again the warmth and humanity of their approach in their work with people suffering from major psychiatric conditions such as psychosis, bipolar affective disorder, schizoaffective disorder and suicide risk, which indicates the complexity and value of their work. As always, their challenging and thought-provoking theoretical constructs are vividly brought to life and made clear by the jargon-free and receptive narrative of the clinical encounter.

Dr Paul Mallett FRCPsych, *Consultant Adult Psychiatrist; Former Medical Director, Central and North West London NHS Mental Health Trust.*

27. Arturo Ezquerro and María Cañete apply great theoretical and clinical mastery whilst deeply connecting attachment theory with group-analytic thinking, bringing together key group concepts, such us *cohesion* and *coherency*, with reparative attachment-based work on *group ruptures*. Their clinical-process research is a source of inspiration. And they go beyond the consulting room to also study historical figures, which brings a new dimension to the group-analytic and attachment literature. It is especially rewarding to follow their narratives and learn how multi-personal attachment becomes interpersonal and even transpersonal, as there are elements located in-between people rather than only having personal characteristics. I was touched by their statement:

"There is no such thing as individual or interpersonal attachment without group attachment".

Dr Robi Friedman PhD, *Consultant Clinical Psychologist; Co-Founder, Israel Institute of Group Analysis; Former President, Group Analytic Society International.*

To John Bowlby: teacher, supervisor, mentor and friend

Acknowledgements

John Bowlby and SH Foulkes are a large part of this book and its predecessor *Group Analysis throughout the Life Cycle*. In fact, whilst working on these twin volumes, they have both been present in our minds and in our writing. We wish they would have been professional partners during their life time . . . Anyway, we have endeavoured to integrate their distinct and, yet, complementary work. And, we know, they would have been delighted to see attachment theory and group analysis connecting up and growing.

Our joint project has also benefited from what we learned from our tutors, teachers, trainers, analysts, supervisors, colleagues and trainees in the UK, Paraguay and Spain, including John Padel, Horacio Etchegoyen, Andrés Rivarola, Vicente Madoz, Agustín Carrizosa, Peter Bruggen, Anton Obholzer, Caroline Garland, Sandy Bourne, John Steiner, Sheilagh Davies, Marcus Johns, Adele Mitwoch, Harold Behr, Norman Vella, Malcolm Pines, Robin Skynner, Julio Ayala, Alfredo Gazzano, Morris Nitsun, Efigenio Amezúa, Tony Kaplan, Peter Shoenberg, Brigid MacCarthy and Jane Marshall.

We are especially grateful to colleagues and friends who have read the manuscript or significant parts of it: Danny Allen, Lisa Steele, Jeremy Holmes, Brett Kahr, Mauricio Cortina, Clare Gerada, Barry Curnow, Peter Zelaskowski, Anne Holmes, Estela Welldon, Carla Penna, Christopher Clulow, Erica Burman, Reem Shelhi, Rosa Monero, Juan Cruz, Erik de Haan, David Chalom, Jacqueline Fogden, Orit Badouk Epstein, Debra Nash, Desmond King, Haim Weinberg, John Eipper, Deborah Bailey-Rodríguez, Paul Mallett, Jimmy Burns-Marañón, Sebastian Kraemer, Robi Friedman and Emilio Butragueño. Coming from a wide range of disciplines and professional backgrounds, they have gifted us insightful and stimulating comments and endorsements, from which we have learned. They remain a motivating force.

We are deeply indebted to Paul Preston and Cheri Marmarosh, who have respectively written a generous and powerful preface and afterword. Their contributions have enhanced the overall content of the book.

This project also owes a great deal to the work of Susannah Frearson (Routledge's Editor for Mental Health and Psychoanalysis) for her generous and invaluable assistance, particularly during the process of preparing and delivering the manuscript, and to Earl Hopper (Editor of the International Library of Group Analysis) for his ideas, encouragement, responsiveness and accessibility as a secure base to us both.

Finally, we wish to thank our patients for seeking help, then and there, and for trusting us to accompany them during their healing journey. Without them, this book would not have been possible.

London, 15 February 2024

Preface

*Paul Preston**

As a historian much of whose work has taken the form of biography, I have long felt the need for psychological insight into the lives and characters that I have studied. At the same time, I have been deeply conscious of the need to avoid the simplistic conclusions that could be dismissed as *psychobabble*. Whenever relevant, I have sought professional commentary on issues regarding unresolved childhood trauma and adult perversions.

Chapter 6 of the present volume is a remarkable example of the profundity and sophistication that is brought by Arturo Ezquerro's application of John Bowlby's attachment theory, psychodynamic psychiatric formulations and group analysis to a historical figure. I cannot help wondering what perceptions would be uncovered if it were possible to inveigle him into making comparably thorough applications of his methodology to many other politicians whose lives I have scrutinised.

I am thinking principally of chronicled significant political figures such as the dictator General Francisco Franco, the disgraced King Juan Carlos and Communist leaders such as Santiago Carrillo and Dolores Ibárruri, *La Pasionaria*. The list is not exhaustive; a number of other, past and present, international political leaders also come to mind.

Anyhow, when I consider how Dr Ezquerro's deeply insightful, and *outsightful*, psychoanalytic and psychiatric commentary has enhanced understanding of a difficult-to-understand character such as the filicidal Captain Gonzalo de Aguilera, I cannot help wondering about what he would have brought to my research on other perverse *architects of terror* that I examined alongside Captain Aguilera; for example, purveyors of fake news, like the theologian Father Joan Tusquets and the poet and playwright José María Pemán, and mass murderers, like General Emilio Mola and General Gonzalo Queipo de Llano. This might be too much to ask for – but who knows?

Having said that, in this volume, *The Power of Group Attachment*, Arturo Ezquerro and María Cañete offer plenty of food for thought to people who, like myself, are not specialists in mental health. They are rendering attachment theory and group analysis accessible to anyone interested in understanding the consequences of unresolved personal and collective trauma, particularly regarding the damage caused to emotional development and interpersonal relationships, as well as the wider damage that manifests itself through sociopolitical violence, terror, military conflict and, in extreme situations, genocide and holocaust. Moreover, they show effective and compassionate therapeutic interventions to repair these ruptures.

Their fascinating and distinctly readable explanation of attachment theory, group dynamics and group attachment (both healthy and perverse) across the lifespan illuminates the psychological processes which, in my own work, I endeavour to understand. They provide a key to understanding how deeply flawed leaders are able to transpose their psychological disturbance onto their countries, in ways that both feed upon and inflame their own and their citizen's anxieties and flaws, contributing to generate the sort of disparate, rigid and frequently authoritarian *group think* they need to stay in power.

In magisterial terms, Dr Ezquerro and Dr Cañete provide a comprehensive, and decidedly comprehensible, manual for making sense of the intricate nature of the mind, the beauty and potential tragedy inherent in human relationships, as well as the highly complex, and often disturbing, group dynamics that operate in the increasingly frightening world in which we live.

London, January 2024

Note

* **Sir Paul Preston KBE**, Professor of International History, London School of Economics. Author of over thirty books, including *The Spanish Holocaust* (*The Sunday Times* History Book of the Year for 2012) and *Architects of Terror* (*The Times* History Book of the Year for 2023).

Foreword

Earl Hopper

Within the broad church of Group Analysis, which includes psychoanalytical group psychotherapy of various persuasions, or as some colleagues would argue vice versa, a small sub-group has extended and developed the work of Dr John Bowlby and his immediate successors concerning the basic theory of attachment and its clinical applications. Currently, Dr Arturo Ezquerro and Dr María Cañete are the leading spokespersons for this perspective, which I regard as a continuation of the project of psychoanalysis as a social psychology more generally. In *Group Analysis Throughout the Life Cycle*, the first volume of their significant contribution, they focus on clinical work; and in *The Power of Group Attachment,* they focus on theoretical issues, but always with clinical illustrations and empirical examples of their argument.

This change of focus allows the authors to become more imaginative and perhaps more assertive in their efforts to raise questions about the original attachment paradigm, using Group Analysis as both an implicit and explicit frame of reference. Whereas classically, attachment processes have been regarded as a manifestation of a biological system that drives and governs the infant's relationships to mother's body and mind in the service of survival and continuing maturation, in this somewhat revised or modified approach, the mother is a subject in relationship to her infant and inevitably to others as well, both actually, mentally and emotionally within an extended context of time and space. Mother is not merely a passive recipient of various kinds of object seeking processes, but also an active initiator of these processes. Thus, attachment can be considered in terms of traumatogenic processes stemming from failed dependency on the actual and potential objects of attachment, as can the nature of perverse attachments to social systems with particular parameters.

Dr Bowlby stressed that in the "beginning" the body of the mother was the baby's entire universe. Subsequent entities of attachment would, in effect, be based on apperception. However, if mother is located in a context of her own environment, then primary attachment to her body and mind are likely to include her own objects and various configurations of them. For example, although attachment to the "land" of one's people and one's nation may be a developmental displacement from mother's body and mind, such processes may also be primary, and of recursive importance.

It follows that social systems are not merely abstract constructions or models but entities or, at least, potential entities that possess socio-cultural-political facticity. Their matrices can and do become objects of attachment. However, social systems also initiate both projective and introjective processes. It can be argued that through the actions of the incumbents of their co-constructed roles, social systems have agency.

Taking the array of endorsements as the poetry of the group, or as what Foulkes would have called the music of the group, it is clear that a rather diverse collection of senior colleagues appreciates these further lines of enquiry. I am sure that readers will find these essays to be a fertile and fecund source of ideas and confirmation of the value of the study of attachment processes. I am very pleased to include this second volume of clinical essays in the New International Library of Group Analysis. They will be useful in teaching clinical Group Analysis in general. The bibliographical material is international in scope, and includes work from several related disciplines.

Earl Hopper
Series Editor
London, April 2024

Introduction

A radical group attachment viewpoint

Arturo Ezquerro and María Cañete

The main rationale of this book and the previous volume of this series, *Group Analysis Throughout the Life Cycle* (Ezquerro and Cañete, 2023a), is to fill a gap in the specialist group-analytic and attachment literature, principally on the fundamental role played by group attachment and open-ended development in our survival and evolution as individuals, as human group organisation, and as a species.

Indeed, these two volumes have been conceived, primarily, for the benefit of group analysis and attachment theory; but they also serve other forms of individual and group psychotherapy, psychoanalysis, the wider mental health field, and organisational life.

Certainly, in our work and research for this project, we have brought into play knowledge and findings from a number of disciplines and schools of thought: anthropology, sociology, philosophy, psychiatry, psychotherapy (individual and group), psychoanalysis, developmental psychology, neuroscience, literature and poetry, as well as group analysis and attachment theory.

Group Analysis is not only an effective and beneficial form of psychotherapy, but also a creative and democratic way of understanding our complex social nature, within which the integration of the stranger group is a cornerstone. On the other hand, attachment theory is probably the most well-known and influential theorical constellation in the field of psychosocial development throughout the lifespan.

Definitely, attachment theory and group analysis are not only compatible but have much to offer to each other. However, group analysis has largely shied away from attachment thinking and, until recently, the attachment literature has paid little attention to group lives in general and to group psychotherapy in particular.

Furthermore, research on group attachment pales into insignificance when compared with other group-analytic and attachment research. This lack of cross-fertilisation is paradoxical. It may have something to do with the politics of, both, attachment (Kraemer and Roberts, 1996) and group analysis (Ezquerro, 1996).

To quite a significant extent, group analysis inherited some prejudices and misconceptions about attachment. Indeed, when John Bowlby presented the blueprint of his attachment theory at a scientific meeting of the British Psychoanalytical Society, in June 1957, his work was massively criticised and, worse, he was subjected to

DOI: 10.4324/9781003271956-1

personal attacks by some of his colleagues, mainly those from the Kleinian group, who accused him of trying to destroy psychoanalysis (Ezquerro, 2017).

Even today, attachment is still perceived as a *foreign* concept within mainstream British psychoanalysis, and it is minimally studied within the foundation, diploma and qualifying courses at the Institute of Group Analysis, in the United Kingdom.

In the circumstances, this volume and its predecessor have been designed and structured with the core learning objective of bringing the fields of attachment and group analysis closer together, as well as endeavouring to integrate them coherently.

0.1 The interface between interpersonal and group attachment

Human attachment is an evolutionarily rooted, species-wide inbuilt system for meaningful social connection, which has the main function of maximising survival, for both the individual and the species; it is at the core of our sociability and *groupality*.

Attachment relationships are universal across and throughout the lifespan, although their characteristics and manifestations vary depending on cultural and sociopolitical context, as well as on developmental stage. Attachment has been present in all cultures since the cradle of humankind, and is not only applicable to the interpersonal domain but also pertinent to an array of group contexts.

Inevitably, attachment involves person-to-person and person-to-group relationships, and can be better understood when we incorporate anthropological and cross-cultural perspectives.

In one way or another, each and every person would inevitably bring their own attachment history to the groups *to* which, or *in* which, they belong. And they would form different types of attachment with people holding prominent positions in the group and, also, with other members and with the group-as-a-whole.

The genesis and early development of group analysis and of attachment theory took place in the context of conflict and world war, when there were massive threats to survival. In parallel ways, both bodies of knowledge and clinical practice have been creative responses to those threats – ultimately, with the aim of maximising survival and repairing the psychological damage inflicted upon individuals, families and society by huge losses, ruptures and devastation.

Early psychoanalysis had put an emphasis on unconscious and intrapsychic processes at the expense of external reality. In contrast to that, relational psychoanalysis, group analysis and attachment theory have emphasised the fact that the individual is a social and political animal. Consequently, these schools of thought have opened up a new dimension, in which relationships and real-life events could be ignored no longer, with regard to the shaping and re-shaping of mental processes, as well as personal and group development.

John Bowlby (1973, 1980, 1988a, 1988b) was keen on replacing traditional psychoanalytic jargon, such as *internal objects*, by a more dynamic and evolving conception of mental life. In fact, he coined the construct *internal working models* (rather than *internal objects*), in order to give a sense of ongoing developmental work as a life-long task. To a large extent, this construct consists of mental representations of attachment relationships.

Bowlby was influenced by and became closer to positions of contemporary relational and social psychoanalysis (Layton and Leavy-Sperounis, 2020), and he showed a clear appreciation of group-analytic thinking and practice.

As a matter of fact, in the mid-1980s, he ran seminars on attachment theory at the London Institute of Group Analysis, as reported by Marrone (1998). Previously, Bowlby (1991) had conducted a psychotherapy group for mothers and babies over three decades at the Tavistock Clinic.

A fundamental way in which Bowlby's theorising diverged from that of traditional psychoanalysis was that he listened to children and parents' actual experiences, and paid less attention to fantasy. His method differed from that used by Sigmund Freud, whose developmental theories were partly constructed from the clinical material obtained during the treatment of his adult patients, extrapolating backwards. Every now and then, this Freudian approach has led to a perception of ordinary child development through the eyes of adult psychopathology.

In contrast, Bowlby's approach looks at development from a *progressive* rather than *regressive* perspective; it is based on real-life events during childhood and other developmental stages throughout the life cycle. He perceived both interpersonal and group attachment as necessary and complementary for optimal development. These two attachment domains serve a biological and psychosocial function to maximise survival and growth.

During early life stages, attachment helps secure assistance at times of threat or danger, and encourages safe exploration and healthy development. An early attachment relationship contains elements of *asymmetrical reciprocity*, as the child is largely at the receiving end of care and protection. As the individual grows older, attachment bonds with peers, partners and groups involve greater levels of *symmetrical reciprocity* – a feature that becomes especially prominent in adulthood.

The needs for meaningful human connectedness, for environmental responsiveness and internal homeostasis, are deeply ingrained physiological and socioemotional requirements that are universal rather than age or phase specific (Ezquerro, 2017).

Bowlby challenged the position of classical psychoanalytic theory which viewed adult attachment needs as indicative of *regression* to immature behaviour, with its inherent pejorative connotation of psychopathology:

In sickness and calamity, adults often become demanding of others; in conditions of sudden danger or disaster, a person will almost certainly seek proximity to another known and trusted person. In such circumstances, an increase of attachment behaviour is recognised by all as natural.

It is therefore extremely misleading for the epithet 'regressive' to be applied to every manifestation of attachment behaviour in adult life, as . . . the term carries the connotation pathological or, at least, undesirable . . . To dub attachment behaviour in adult life regressive is indeed to overlook the vital role it plays in the life of man from the cradle to the grave.

(Bowlby, 1969: 208)

The very month prior to his death, aged 83, Bowlby (our teacher, mentor and friend, during the last six years of his life) was still actively working and exploring uncharted territory. He made a simple, yet far-reaching statement:

The potential of attachment theory is unknown.

(Bowlby, 1991, personal communication to Arturo Ezquerro)

Time has proved him right.

Attachment, like evolution, is no longer a theory but an existential reality that permeates every aspect of our personal, professional and group lives, in multiple contexts, from infancy all the way into old age.

Indeed, attachment theory has undergone its own evolution. We would high-point just a few publications:

- It started out, primarily, as a theory about child development (Bowlby, 1958, 1969, 1973; Ainsworth, Blehar, Waters and Wall, 1978; Sroufe, 1995; Cassidy and Shaver, 2008),
- its influence spread to the study of adolescent development (Crittenden, 2005; Sroufe, 2005; Atger, 2007; Yap, Allen and Ladouceur, 2008; Perry, 2009; Allen and Miga, 2010; Flaherty and Sadler, 2011),
- adult attachment (Sperling and Berman, 1994; Feeney and Noller, 1996; Bowlby, 1988a, 1991; Ainsworth, 1991; Sroufe, 2005; Cassidy and Shaver, 2008; Mikulincer and Shaver, 2014; Ezquerro and Cañete, 2023a),
- couple attachment (Simpson and Rholes, 1998; Clulow, 2001; Ludlam and Nyberg, 2007),
- older adults' attachment (Antonucci, Akiyama and Takahashi, 2004; Evans and Garner, 2004; Ezquerro, 2023; Ezquerro and Cañete, 2023b),
- society as a secure base or otherwise (Kraemer and Roberts, 1996; Marris, 1996; Duschinsky, Greco and Solomon, 2015; Ezquerro, 2023),
- psychosis (Cañete and Ezquerro, 2012, 2017; Danquah and Berry, 2014; Robbins, 2019; Berry, Bucci and Danquah, 2020; Summers and Adshead, 2020),
- psychoanalysis and psychotherapy (Marrone, 1998; Fonagy, 2001; Holmes, 2001, 2010, 2014; Wallin, 2007; Cortina and Liotti, 2010; Ezquerro 2017, 2023; Robbins, 2019; Bateman and Fonagy, 2019),
- and group psychotherapy (Ezquerro and Bajaj, 2007; Markin and Marmarosh, 2010; Ezquerro, 2010, 2017, 2023; Marmarosh, Markin and Spiegel, 2013; Marmarosh, 2014, 2017, 2020, 2021; Tasca, 2014; Flores, 2017; Mikulincer and Shaver, 2017; Fonagy, Campbell and Bateman, 2020; Bateman, Campbell and

Fonagy, 2021; Tasca and Maxwell, 2021; Ezquerro and Cañete, 2023a; Tasca and Marmarosh, 2023).

Survival, adaptation and healthy growth are enhanced by the ability of children, adolescents, adults and older adults to explore their environment with confidence, which is facilitated by the experience of having a secure base in their attachment figures from which to explore. These notions of secure base and exploration are fundamental to attachment theory, and their relevance extends to the whole life-course and to every aspect of human existence – including group lives.

Attachment (and more specifically *group attachment*) is highly relevant to group life in general and to group psychotherapy in particular. The group has played a critical survival role in the evolution of the human species (Caparrós, 2004; Cortina and Liotti, 2010). In view of this evidence, conceiving the group as an attachment figure and secure base is not as implausible as it perhaps initially sounds.

In the first volume of his trilogy on *Attachment and Loss*, Bowlby (1969) advanced the concept of *group attachment*. According to him, a group-as-a-whole can come to constitute an attachment figure:

> During adolescence and adult life, a measure of attachment behaviour is commonly directed not only towards persons outside the family but also towards groups and institutions other than the family. A school or college, a work group, a religious group or a political group can come to constitute for many people a subordinate attachment-figure, and for some people a principal attachment-figure. In such cases, it seems probable, the development of attachment to a group is mediated, at least initially, by attachment to a person holding a prominent position within that group.
>
> (Bowlby, 1969: 207)

Following on from Bowlby's group perspective, we may affirm that the internal world of a person is necessarily configured through mental representations of interactions and attachment relationships with significant others and groups, as well as with the places where the person was born and raised and where he or she established key connections through education, work and love (Ezquerro, 2021).

The current trend is that person-to-person attachment and person-to-group attachment represent two different but interrelated domains. In order to understand the core elements of group attachment, it is essential to identify what it is that people bond with when they relate with a group-as-a-whole (Sochos, 2014; Ezquerro, 2023).

In addition, studying the nature of group attachment as a distinct domain may enhance our insights into other important group phenomena, such as the desperate search for absolute protection or security and undisputable certainty – something that is so often evident in totalitarian political ideology and religious uncritical zeal (see Chapter 6). These phenomena can be conceptualised as *perverse group attachment* (Ezquerro, 2019, 2021).

0.2 Synopses of the book chapters

The themes outlined above will be further examined and elaborated upon in six chapters, as follows:

Chapter 1, entitled *Group attachment created humankind*, is structured in two distinct but interconnected sections:

- Drawing on updated findings from anthropology and cross-cultural attachment studies, the first takes the reader to the cradle of humankind, showing the struggle of our Pleistocene ancestors to survive, to explore and to grow. It provides a plausible narrative of the evolution of human attachment, and postulates a radical hypothesis that *group attachment created humankind*. Certainly, without the unprecedented and distinct collaborative nature of human group attachment, early hominins would not have evolved into modern humans.
- The second section digs into the evolution of the concept of group attachment and reviews relevant literature on *attachment and group psychotherapy*, an emerging field which has been growing steadily in the last two decades. It also explores how group attachment can apply to organisations (an evolved type of group life) and takes the view that any organisation can be usefully conceived of as a potential *group attachment space*.

Amalgamating insights and outsights from both sections, it concludes that *group attachment* is a useful construct for group analysis, group psychotherapy and other therapeutic disciplines, as well as for the understanding of human evolution and survival, organisations, intra-group and inter-group relations, and personal development.

Chapter 2, entitled *Bipolar disorder: ups and downs affecting interpersonal and group life*, examines the challenges that bipolar patients present in therapy group settings, and reviews relevant literature on the subject from the fields of psychiatry, psychoanalysis, attachment and group psychotherapy. It highlights two main findings:

- Homogeneous psychotherapy groups for bipolar affective disorders are beneficial, particularly those using psychoeducational and integrative approaches.
- Heterogeneous group-analytic psychotherapy with bipolar patients is highly beneficial in the long term.

As an illustration of the latter, a piece of group-analytic qualitative research is presented. This includes clinical material from a weekly outpatient heterogeneous group that was pushed to the limit by a bipolar patient, who also made the group conductor work harder than usual, requiring him to be especially vigilant on boundaries and limit setting. Transference interpretations often needed to aim at translating the difficult behaviour of this patient into a language of repairing ruptures in interpersonal and group attachment relationships.

In view of the positive outcome of this case study, for the patient and for the group, the chapter aims to encourage group analysts and other practitioners to include bipolar patients in their psychotherapy treatment programmes, as well as to offer a more hopeful and less discriminatory approach to this disabling condition.

Chapter 3, entitled *Fostering a group attachment culture in a day-unit for psychotic patients*, describes the flexible application of group analytic and attachment principles in a therapy group programme for patients with a longstanding history of psychosis, which ran weekly in the context of a day-psychotherapy project in an inner-London community setting. People referred to the project were isolated and found it really difficult to establish any secure interpersonal or group attachment.

The chapter reviews relevant research on group psychotherapy for psychotic patients, and also explores the influences that traditional psychoanalytic and attachment conceptions of psychosis have had on contemporary theoretical and clinical approaches to the subject. A piece of qualitative clinical-process research is presented to illustrate the steady development of a therapeutic group-analytic culture and group-attachment ethos, which enabled many of the patients to eventually perceive the therapists and the group as a secure-enough base. These patients achieved deeper levels of exploration, communication and understanding, which resulted in better and more autonomous functioning, more satisfactory relationships and a greater capacity to cope with everyday life.

This study aims to stimulate further qualitative research with this population, as well as to encourage group analysts and other mental health practitioners to increasingly use attachment-based psychodynamic therapy groups in the treatment of psychosis.

Chapter 4, entitled *Suicide risk: when group attachment is not enough, or is it?*, contains a case of qualitative clinical-process research, in which concurrent individual and group psychotherapy were combined in the treatment and management of a middle-aged man, who was a suicide risk. He had a history of major attachment ruptures and other traumatic experiences, which contributed to psychotic breakdowns, suicide attempts and in-patient psychiatric admissions. Whilst attending the group therapy programme, the patient stabbed himself and nearly died, which provoked much anxiety in the other patients and staff.

The chapter includes a thorough review of the literature on combined treatment and, also, an appraisal of relevant studies on the suicide question from the disciplines of sociology, anthropology, philosophy, psychoanalysis, attachment theory and wider mental health. Elaborating on from these studies, an exploration of interpersonal and group attachment processes is offered, as a theoretical and clinical aid for the understanding and management of suicidal crises. It concludes that suicide prevention is necessarily a collective task for which an attachment-based ethos can make a significant difference. Combining individual and group psychotherapy, coordinating healthcare systems, agreeing national and global strategies, and involving society by and large can definitely be of help. Indeed, suicidal patients often need more than one secure base.

Chapter 5, entitled *Group cohesion versus group coherency through an attachment lens*, shows how clinicians and researches have largely categorised *group cohesion* as a crucial therapeutic factor and precondition for effective group psychotherapy. It then offers a complementary view that, in the longer term, a group that only operates at the cohesion level may restrict significantly its own therapeutic potential. In contrast, the concept of *group coherency* is highlighted as an organising principle that promotes deeper understanding and more mature levels of functioning, which are key to healthy relationships, personal growth and group development.

To validate this working hypothesis, the chapter reviews the literature on *cohesion* and *coherency*, from the fields of psychoanalysis, group analysis, group psychotherapy, complexity and attachment theory, and also presents a piece of qualitative clinical-process research from a weekly outpatient group. The conductor made a mistake, but examined his countertransference and learned from it, which helped change the group's complex *modus operandi* from undifferentiated cohesion to coherency, as members worked through their conflicts and accepted and integrated their differences.

The chapter aims to contribute to the theoretical understanding and clinical applications of both *cohesion* and *coherency* from group-analytic and attachment standpoints, including insights from complexity theory, as well as recent developments on ruptures and repairs in group psychotherapy.

Chapter 6, entitled *A case of perverse group attachment*, examines a constellation of dyadic attachment, family attachment and group attachment experiences (as well as other psychosocial, cultural and political factors) which contributed to the dual filicide perpetrated by Captain Gonzalo de Aguilera (a count, landowner, cavalryman and propaganda press officer during the Spanish Civil War). After reviewing relevant literature on filicide, this study employs a combined methodology of historical investigation, in conjunction with psychiatric, attachment-based and group-analytic clinical formulations. In doing so, it takes into account a highly complex context of brutal group dynamics of national depression and exaltation, unresolved trauma, military rebellion, war, dictatorship, genocide and holocaust.

Following on from Bowlby's conception of group attachment, and from key findings provided within the growing discipline of forensic psychotherapy, the chapter scrutinises Captain Aguilera's life circumstances and whereabouts; his interpersonal and group attachment relationships; his world within and around him. This study specifically explores the influence that Aguilera's group attachment history (as well as the cruel ideology and violent group dynamics to which he was exposed) may have had on his personality development, his bizarre thinking and his murderous behaviour. Finally, a reasoned explanation of what the author has elsewhere described as *perverse group attachment* is offered.

0.3 Some learning points and concluding thoughts

As the book unfolds, different readers will choose different learning journeys. We would like to highlight some of our own learning points, as follows:

- Human attachment is an evolutionarily rooted, species-wide in-built system that serves survival and growth (both physical and emotional) for individuals, groups, and the species.
- The instinctual attachment substrate manifests itself through various types of behaviour (proximity-seeking, exploration, distance-regulation and so on). It optimally develops into meaningful and caring relationships with distinct people and with groups. Affectional bonds and affect regulation are an integral part of healthy attachment relationships.
- Although biologically based, attachment is culturally influenced. So, a more thorough study of the ways in which culture and evolution interact will enhance our understanding and appreciation of the plasticity of attachment processes.
- Indeed, since the cradle of humankind, attachment has involved a combination of person-to-person and person-to-group relationships, in various socio-cultural and environmental contexts. Thus, it can be better understood when we incorporate anthropological and cross-cultural perspectives.
- It is necessary to expand research studies into the factors that influence the attachment dynamic, such as household income, parental stress, racism, discrimination and other relevant environmental contributors. It makes little sense to consider attachment relationships in isolation, without their socio-political context.
- In fact, an exclusive focus on dyadic attachment may eclipse processes that emotionally connect people more broadly to others, to groups and to the wider community, which fosters optimal development.
- There are publications stating that the attachment system is *activated* by actual or perceived danger. This can be misleading. It would be better and more accurate to say that, under such circumstances, the proximity-seeking component of the attachment system is activated.
- Healthy attachment is about regulating the distance, rather than mere proximity, according to environmental conditions. Identifying attachment only with proximity-seeking overlooks the fact that attachment is also a relationship, in which attuned responsiveness and accessibility are key.
- When we explore, at a distance from our base, we do not disconnect from our attachment figures who constitute such a base; we can in fact be deeply connected with them when they are not physically present. Our attachment system stays activated.
- For Bowlby (1988b), the attachment system is homeostatic, and exploration is an integral component of a healthy attachment system. Like other homeostatic systems, attachment is always activated, as it is a *sine qua non* for survival. Attachment deactivation would eventually lead to death or suicide. As Bowlby put it: Ultimately, behind any suicide act, there is a crisis of attachment.

- Suicide should be taken as a public-health problem, which must be approached from a group perspective. Effective prevention can only improve as a collective enterprise that involves society-as-a-whole. And the problem of suicidality should be treated in line with other life-threatening conditions.

Since most of the chapters contain vivid examples of group-analytic psychotherapy, we would like to emphasise that a patient may have different attachment styles with the group conductor, with specific members, and with the group-as-a-whole. Undeniably, although members' dyadic attachment styles are important in the group therapy context, they are nonetheless an incomplete picture of the whole group experience.

Quite often, after a long and difficult working day, the patient may need care and protection from their attachment figures and, whilst *commuting* to a therapy group session, may not know exactly who is going to be there at that particular time, but can still feel reassured that he or she will receive the protection and care needed from the psychotherapy group itself, provided that their attachment with such a group is secure-enough.

In this context, group attachment is secure-enough when the group is available, sensitive and responsive, in such a way that members can protest, disagree with and challenge each other and the group therapist without fear of punishment, abandonment or rejection.

Taking into account clinical and non-clinical realities of interpersonal and group lives (as outlined earlier in the above learning points and in the book chapters' synopses), in the present volume, we shall explicitly employ a radical view that was implicitly stated in the previous volume:

> there is no such thing as individual or interpersonal attachment without group attachment.
>
> (see Chapter 1)

This idea is consistent with Earl Hopper's (2003) conception of the social unconscious:

> The unconscious mind of a person is always a socially unconscious mind in its origins, content, development and maintenance, and so there is no such thing as an individual without a social context and no such thing as a personal unconscious that does not include a social unconscious.
>
> (Hopper, in Einhorn, 2013: 239)

Social unconscious dynamics can manifest through social media in ways that are detrimental for our minds, relationships and group life. In *The Chaos Machine*, Fisher (2023, 2024) has investigated the inside story of how Facebook, Twitter, YouTube, and other social network prey on psychological frailties to create the algorithms that drive everyday users to extreme opinions and, increasingly, extreme actions. The result is a cultural shift towards a world in which people are polarised, not by beliefs based on facts, but by misinformation, outrage and fear.

We need an antidote to counteract this meteoric rise and troubled legacy of the *tech titans*, on our minds and on the world at large, before it is too late. In the following chapter, we will invite the reader to learn from our Pleistocene ancestors' natural survival strategies, within which group collaboration and group attachment were key. We would like to suggest that, in the digital revolution era, we need a benign group attachment *re(e)volution* . . .

Anyhow, throughout each and every chapter, we shall draw on our professional experience and skills in dealing with a broad range of problems, as well as on our limitations in understanding and managing complex situations, by which our ideas have changed and evolved over time. This book will provide the reader with good opportunities to learn, identify with and feel part of true, stirring stories and insights. We hope you enjoy it!

References

Ainsworth MDS (1991) Attachment and other affectional bonds across the life cycle. In: Parkes CM, Stevenson-Hinde J and Marris P (eds) *Attachment Across the Life Cycle*. London and New York: Routledge, pp. 33–51.

Ainsworth MDS, Blehar MC, Waters E and Wall S (1978) *Patterns of Attachment: A Psychological Study of the Strange Situation*. Hillsdale, NJ: Lawrence Erlbaum.

Allen JP and Miga EM (2010) Attachment in Adolescence: A move to the level of emotional regulation. *Journal of Social Personal Relationships* 27(2): 181–190.

Antonucci TC, Akiyama H and Takahashi K (2004) Attachment and close relationships across the life span. *Attachment and Human Development* 6(4): 353–370.

Atger F (2007) L'attachement à l'adolescence. *Dialogue* 175(1): 73–86.

Bateman A, Campbell C and Fonagy P (2021) Rupture and repair in mentalization-based group psychotherapy. *International Journal of Group Psychotherapy* 71(2): 371–392.

Bateman A and Fonagy P (2019) Mentalization-based treatment for borderline and antisocial personality disorder. In: Kealy D and Ogrodniczuk JS (eds) *Contemporary Psychodynamic Psychotherapy: Evolving Clinical Practice*. London: Elsevier Academic Press, pp. 133–148.

Berry K, Bucci S and Danquah AN (eds) (2020) *Attachment Theory and Psychosis: Current Perspectives and Future Directions*. New York: Routledge.

Bowlby J (1958) The nature of the child's tie to his mother. *International Journal of Psychoanalysis* 39: 350–373.

Bowlby J (1969) *Attachment and Loss. Vol 1: Attachment* (1991 edition). London: Penguin Books.

Bowlby J (1973) *Attachment and Loss. Vol 2: Separation, Anxiety and Anger* (1991 edition). London: Penguin Books.

Bowlby J (1980) *Attachment and Loss. Vol 3: Loss, Sadness and Depression* (1991 edition). London: Penguin Books.

Bowlby J (1988a) *A Secure Base: Clinical Applications of Attachment Theory.* London: Routledge.

Bowlby J (1988b) Developmental Psychiatry Comes of Age. *American Journal of Psychiatry* 145(1): 1–10.

Bowlby J (1991) The role of the psychotherapist's personal resources in the treatment situation. In: Duschinsky R and White K (eds) *Trauma and Loss: Key Texts from the John Bowlby Archive* (2020). Abingdon: Routledge, pp. 214–223.

Cañete M and Ezquerro A (2012) Bipolar Affective Disorders and Group Analysis. *Group Analysis* 45(2): 203–217.

Cañete M and Ezquerro A (2017) Developing a group-analytic culture in a day-project for psychotic patients. *Psychosis* 9(2): 149–156.

Caparrós N (ed) (2004) *Y el Grupo Creó al Hombre*. Madrid: Biblioteca Nueva.

Cassidy J and Shaver PR (eds) (2008) *Handbook of Attachment: Theory, Research, and Clinical Applications* (second edition). New York: The Guilford Press.

Clulow C (ed) (2001) *Adult Attachment and Couple Psychotherapy.* London: Brunner-Routledge.

Cortina M and Liotti G (2010) Attachment is about safety and protection, intersubjectivity is about sharing and social understanding. The relationships between attachment and intersubjectivity. *Psychoanalytic Psychology* 27(4): 410–441.

Crittenden PM (2005) Attachment Theory, Psychopathology, and Psychotherapy: The Dynamic-Maturational Approach. *Psicoterapia* 30: 171–182.

Danquah AN and Berry K (eds) *Attachment Theory in Adult Mental Health: A guide to clinical practice*. London and New York: Routledge.

Duschinsky R, Greco M and Solomon J (2015) The Politics of Attachment: Lines of Flight with Bowlby, Deleuze and Guattari. *Theory, Culture and Society* 32(7–8): 173–195.

Einhorn S (2013) Book Review. Hopper E and Weinberg H (eds) (2011) *The Social Unconscious in Persons, Groups, and Societies. Vol I: Mainly Theory*. London: Karnac Books. *Group Analysis* 46(2): 239–241.

Evans S and Garner J (eds) (2004) *Talking Over the Years: A Handbook of Dynamic Psychotherapy with Older Adults*. Hove: Brunner Routledge.

Ezquerro A (1996) The Tavistock and Group-Analytic Approaches to Group Psychotherapy: A Trainee's Perspective. *Psychoanalytic Psychotherapy* 10(2): 155–170.

Ezquerro A (2010) Cohesion and Coherency in Group Analysis. *Group Analysis* 43(4): 496–504.

Ezquerro A (2017) *Encounters with John Bowlby: Tales of Attachment*. London: Routledge.

Ezquerro A (2019) Sexual abuse: a perversion of attachment? *Group Analysis* 52(1): 100–113.

Ezquerro A (2021) Captain Aguilera and filicide: An attachment-based exploration. *Attachment: New Directions in Psychotherapy and Relational Psychoanalysis* 15(2): 279–297.

Ezquerro A (2023) *Apego y Desarrollo a lo largo de la vida: El poder del apego grupal.* Madrid: Editorial Sentir.

Ezquerro A and Bajaj P (2007) Combining individual and group-analytic psychotherapy: When the group is not enough, or is it? *Group: The Journal of the Eastern Group Psychotherapy Society* 31(1–2): 5–16.

Ezquerro A and Cañete M (2023a) *Group Analysis throughout the Life Cycle: Foulkes Revisited from a Group Attachment and Developmental Perspective*. London and New York: Routledge.

Ezquerro A and Cañete M (2023b) Older adults deserve better in society. *Attachment: New Directions in Psychotherapy and Relational Psychoanalysis* 17(2): 212–225.

Feeney J and Noller P (1996) *Adult Attachment.* London: Sage Publications.

Fisher M (2023) *The Chaos Machine: The Inside Story of How Social Media Rewired Our Minds and Our World*. London: Quercus Publishing.

Fisher M (2024) *Las redes del caos: La historia secreta de cómo las redes sociales empobrecen la mente y erosionan el mundo*. Barcelona: Península.

Flaherty SC and Sadler LS (2011) A review of attachment theory in the context of adolescent parenting. *Journal of Paediatric Health Care* 25(2): 114–121.

Flores PJ (2017) Theory and Practice of Group Therapy Attachment Theory and Group Psychotherapy. *International Journal of Group Psychotherapy* 67(sup1): S50–S59.

Fonagy P (2001) *Attachment Theory and Psychoanalysis*. New York: Other Press.

Fonagy P, Campbell C and Bateman A (2020) Mentalizing, attachment, and epistemic trust in group therapy. In: Marmarosh CL (ed) *Attachment in Group Psychotherapy*. London and New York: Routledge, pp. 20–45.

Holmes J (2001) *The Search for the Secure Base: Attachment Theory and Psychotherapy*. London: Routledge.

Holmes J (2010) *Exploring in Security: Towards an Attachment-Informed Psychoanalytic Psychotherapy*. New York: Routledge.

Holmes J (2014) Attachment theory in therapeutic practice. In: Berry K and Danquah AN (eds) *Attachment Theory in Adult Mental Health: A Guide to Clinical Practice*. London: Routledge, pp. 16–32.

Hopper E (2003) *The Social Unconscious: Selected Papers*. London: Jessica Kingsley Publishers.

Kraemer S and Roberts J (eds) (1996) *The Politics of Attachment: Towards a Secure Society*. London: Free Association Books.

Layton L and Leavy-Sperounis M (2020) *Toward a Social Psychoanalysis: Culture, Character, and Normative Unconscious Processes*. London and New York: Routledge.

Ludlam M and Nyberg V (eds) (2007) *Couple Attachments: Theoretical and Clinical Studies*. London: Karnac Books.

Markin RD and Marmarosh CL (2010) Application of adult attachment theory to group member transference and the group therapy process. *Psychotherapy Theory, Research, Practice and Training* 47(1): 111–121.

Marmarosh CL (2014) Empirical Research on Attachment in Group Psychotherapy: Moving the Field Forward. *Psychotherapy* 51(1): 88–92.

Marmarosh CL (2017) Attachment in Group Psychotherapy: Bridging Theories, Research and Clinical Technique. *International Journal of Group Psychotherapy* 67(2): 157–160.

Marmarosh CL (ed) (2020) *Attachment in Group Psychotherapy*. London and New York: Routledge.

Marmarosh CL (2021) Ruptures and repairs in group psychotherapy: From theory to practice. *International Journal of Group Psychotherapy* 71(2): 205–223.

Marmarosh CL, Markin R and Spiegel E (2013) *Attachment in Group Psychotherapy*. Washington, DC: The American Psychological Association.

Marris P (1996) The Management of Uncertainty. In Kraemer S and Roberts J (eds) *The Politics of Attachment: Towards a Secure Society*. London: Free Association Books, pp. 192–199.

Marrone M (1998) *Attachment and Interaction*. London: Jessica Kingsley Publishers.

Mikulincer M and Shaver PR (2014) *Attachment in Adulthood: Structure, Dynamics, and Change*. New York: The Guilford Press.

Mikulincer M and Shaver PR (2017) Augmenting the sense of attachment security in group contexts: The effects of a responsive leader and a cohesive group. *International Journal of Group Psychotherapy* 67(2): 161–175.

Perry A (ed) (2009) *Teenagers and Attachment: Helping Adolescents Engage with Life and Learning*. London: Worth Publishing.

Robbins M (2019) *Psychoanalysis meets Psychosis: Attachment, separation, and the undifferentiated unintegrated mind*. New York: Routledge.

Simpson JA and Rholes WS (eds) (1998) *Attachment Theory and Close Relationships*. New York: The Guilford Press.

Sochos A (2014) *Attachment Security and the Social World*. Basingstoke: Palgrave Macmillan.

Sperling MB and Berman WH (eds) (1994) *Attachment in Adults: Clinical and Developmental Perspectives.* New York: The Guilford Press.

Sroufe LA (1995) *Emotional Development: The organization of emotional life in the early years.* Cambridge: Cambridge University Press.

Sroufe LA (2005) Attachment and development: A prospective, longitudinal study from birth to adulthood. *Attachment and Human Development* 7(4): 349–367.

Summers A and Adshead G (2020) Bringing together psychodynamic and attachment perspectives on psychosis. In: Berry K, Bucci S and Danquah AN (eds) (2020) *Attachment Theory and Psychosis: Current Perspectives and Future Directions.* New York: Routledge, pp. 131–143.

Tasca GA (2014) Attachment and Group Psychotherapy: Introduction to a Special Section. *Psychotherapy* 51(1): 53–56.

Tasca GA and Marmarosh C (2023). Alliance rupture and repair in group psychotherapy. In: Eubanks CF, Samstag LW and Muran JC (eds) *Rupture and repair in psychotherapy: A critical process for change.* Washington, DC: American Psychological Association, pp. 53–71.

Tasca GA and Maxwell H (2021) Attachment and group psychotherapy: Applications to work groups and teams. In: Parks CD and Tasca GA (eds) *The Psychology of Groups: The Intersection of Social Psychology and Psychotherapy Research.* New York: American Psychological Association, pp. 149–167.

Wallin DJ (2007) *Attachment in Psychotherapy.* New York: The Guilford Press.

Yap MB, Allen NB, Ladouceur CD (2008) Maternal socialization of positive affect: the impact of invalidation on adolescent emotion regulation and depressive symptomatology. *Child Development* 79(5): 1415–1431.

Arturo Ezquerro: https://orcid.org/0000-0002-9910-4576
María Cañete: https://orcid.org/0000-0001-7967-1103

Chapter 1

Group attachment created humankind

Arturo Ezquerro and María Cañete

1.1 Introduction

The group represents a humanising space *par excellence*, an embodiment of the full dimension of real human life, with its internal, interpersonal and multipersonal experiences and dynamics; it can also be a therapeutic space (Cañete and Ezquerro, 2012; Ezquerro, 2023), as well as a socio-political context (Ettin, 2001).

Through evolution, the group became an adaptive social organisation that serves survival and promotes our development, as individuals, organisations, institutions and, ultimately, the human species (Caparrós, 2004).

In this chapter, we will research into attachment and group concepts, with a view to unravelling the nature and vicissitudes of *group attachment*, a concept originally formulated by John Bowlby (1969), in the first volume of his trilogy on *Attachment and Loss*.

In his ground-breaking formulation of attachment theory, Bowlby (1958) was overtly evolutionary in his approach. Overtime, and paradoxically, mainstream attachment literature has largely overlooked natural selection, adaptation and other core tenets of evolutionary theory.

In the above circumstances, in this chapter, we shall emphasise that key processes of person-to-group attachment are distinct from, but interrelated with, person-to-person attachment processes. Both manifestations of human attachment are deeply rooted in our evolution as a species.

Likewise, group attachment is related to and interconnected with, but clearly distinct from, other group concepts such as *group identification*, *group affiliation* and *group belonging*. We will elaborate on this, in various subsections of this chapter, from contemporary attachment research, as well as anthropological, psychoanalytic, sociological, cross-cultural and group-analytic standpoints.

Interestingly, Sigmund Freud, who was also keen on anthropological perspectives in his study of the mind, paid attention to group processes:

> We must conclude that the psychology of the group is the oldest human psychology [. . .] there was only a common will, there were no single ones.
>
> (Freud, 1922: 122)

DOI: 10.4324/9781003271956-2

Studying the nature of group attachment as a full-fledged domain can improve our understanding of other important group phenomena, both positive or reparative (see Chapters 2, 3, 4, 5) and negative or even perverse (see Chapter 6). In this latter sense, we would like to postulate that the desperate search for absolute protection and security, as well as the desire for undisputable certainty, are often evident in totalitarian political ideology and religious uncritical zeal – which may result in a dynamic of *perverse group attachment*.

Indeed, humans are highly vulnerable for many years after birth, for longer than the offspring of any other animal species. The need for group protection, nourishment and education that children and adolescents carry, over such a long period of time, has no equivalent in the animal kingdom.

It takes a group to raise a child. This characteristic feature of humankind has had a bearing on the development of, both, our extraordinary social capabilities and our unique social problems.

Attachment issues are universal but vary across different cultures. In any case, the mother-child dyad cannot exist in isolation. A mother, particularly a new mother, needs to be the recipient of caregiving and support by others.

Mothers and children are situated within larger family and social groups and cultural networks, and these networks affect the manifestations of person-to-person and person-to-group attachment relationships. Therefore, in order to see the whole picture, it is essential to examine the holistic nature of human attachment.

1.1(i) Contents and aims of the chapter

In order to disentangle the themes outlined above, this chapter is structured in two distinct but interconnected sections:

- Drawing on updated findings from anthropology and cross-cultural attachment studies, the first section takes the reader to the cradle of humankind, showing the struggle of our Pleistocene ancestors to survive, to explore and to grow. It provides a plausible narrative of the evolution of human attachment, and postulates a radical hypothesis that *group attachment created humankind*. Certainly, without the unprecedented and distinct collaborative nature of human group attachment, early hominins would not have evolved into modern humans.
- The second section digs into the evolution of the concept of group attachment and reviews relevant literature on *attachment and group psychotherapy*, an emerging field which has been growing steadily in the last two decades. It also explores how group attachment can apply to organisations (an evolved type of group life) and takes the view that any organisation can be usefully conceived of as a potential *group attachment space*.

Integrating insights and outsights from both sections, we can conclude that *group attachment* is a useful construct for group analysis, group psychotherapy and other therapeutic disciplines, as well as for the understanding of human evolution and survival, organisations, intra-group and inter-group relations, and personal development.

In the previous volume of this series, *Group Analysis throughout the Life Cycle*, we had suggested that group attachment has been largely treated as the *Cinderella* subject within the specialist attachment literature (Ezquerro and Cañete, 2023). However, there have been some notable exceptions; we will refer to them as this chapter unfolds. But let us start with a captivating journey to, and from, the cradle of humankind.

1.2 Section I: An exploration through human evolution

Since he presented the blueprint of his attachment theory, Bowlby (1958) was overtly evolutionary in his approach.

Despite this, as we pointed out earlier, a significantly large number of contemporary attachment researchers, scholars and clinicians have overlooked natural selection, adaptation and other core tenets of evolutionary theory.

Being part of a group of trainees who worked with John Bowlby during the last six years of his life (1984–1990), we think it is time to get back to him to re-examine some important aspects of human development, culture and group attachment.

Drawing meticulously on Darwinian natural selection, Bowlby viewed attachment through the lens of human evolution and delineated the pressures on our attachment system in what he called the *environment of evolutionary adaptedness* (Bowlby 1969). Indeed, pan-species attachment characteristics have been arrived at through processes of natural selection and adaptation (Chapin, 2013).

Furthermore, Bowlby (1988b) conceived human development as an ongoing interaction with an ever-evolving environment. Consequently, he was sceptical about traditional viewpoints that perceived development through the lenses of rather fixed phases or stages. Instead, he preferred to describe such an open-ended growth as taking place within an array of developmental pathways.

In this section, we invite the reader to embark with us on a passionate journey through the complexities and beauty of our evolutionary path. We shall emphasise Bowlby's claim that attachment is a species-wide developing system that is evolutionarily rooted and maximises survival, not only during infancy but throughout the entire life cycle (Ezquerro and Cañete, 2023).

1.2(i) The birth of humankind

Among contemporary anthropologists, there is widespread consensus that the genus *Homo* first evolved in East Africa some two and a half million years ago, from *Australopithecus*, an earlier genus of apes that had begun to develop an incipient form of bipedal locomotion.

In 1974, a group of archaeologists found unusual remains of the skeleton of a nonhuman primate. During the excavation work, a catchy Beatles song, 'Lucy in the Sky with Diamonds', could be heard blaring out over and over again. The bones found corresponded to a female who was immediately named *Lucy*; it could not have been otherwise!

Later studies showed that *Lucy* lived in what is now Ethiopia, approximately three million two hundred thousand years ago (Jungers, 1988). She had a small skull, but her skeleton was already built in such a way that it allowed her to walk in a half-upright posture.

This important discovery about *Australopithecus* indicates that bipedalism began before the massive increase in brain size in human primates.

Currently, it is largely accepted that the most primitive representative of the genus *Homo* was *Homo habilis*, which evolved more than two million, three hundred thousand years ago (Antón, 2012).

The reason for this conclusion lies in the fact that it is the oldest human ancestor for whom there is clear evidence of a rudimentary technology for the production and use of stone tools. Initially, the brains of these archaic humans were about the same size as that of a chimpanzee.

However, over the next million or so years, an unprecedented process of brain growth occurred. With the arrival of *Homo erectus* and *Homo ergaster*, the size of the brain had doubled. This remarkable growth of the brain coincided with the appearance of complex Acheulean stone tools, which were built with two symmetrical faces. But this was not a random coincidence: the areas of the brain that got expanded were those used for complex tasks, such as the manufacture of these types of tools (Cortés López, 2009; Zollikofer et al, 2022).

It has also been postulated that *Homo erectus* and *Homo ergaster* were the first to use fire. Since prehistoric times, in fact, there has been an intimate relationship between fire and the *cohesion* of the human group (see also Chapter 5).

The image of our ancestors (or our children at a summer camp) sitting in a circle around a bonfire, at night, after a long day, is a powerful symbol of group communication and harmony. Certainly, it is a decisive bonding experience which, in some circumstances, can have therapeutic value.

The group analyst Mark Ettin (1992) referred to the healing properties attributed to circular configurations in remote cultures. In some religious traditions, rotating circular motion has symbolised the process of creation. In many primitive clans, including pre-Columbian indigenous tribes, the ritual of dancing in a circle around a fire was thought to awaken the forces of nature; for instance, to attract rain and obtain a good harvest.

It is now clear that the development and internalisation of intragroup and intergroup relations, experiences and culture contributed to the growth of the human brain. Several studies on primates have shown that the larger prefrontal and temporoparietal areas of the neocortex, the larger the average size of the groups in which these primates live (Sallet et al, 2011; Gladwell, 2012).

The need to manage the complexities of increasingly larger, and more sophisticated, social groups came to be another vital evolutionary pressure that contributed to the growth of the human brain.

According to Tomasello (2014), the distinct hallmark of human evolution can be attributed to the development of three interrelated threads, for which the group was a *sine qua non*:

- the creation of complex tools and their application in increasingly sophisticated technology;
- the creation of complex and larger group structures, social systems and organisations to facilitate and expand social interaction;
- the creation of conventional symbols, which includes the use of spoken and written language and other forms of symbolisation, such as music. No doubt, symbols had a major impact on social group relations.

In contrast to nonhuman evolution, the weaving together of these threads gradually yielded the intergenerational transfer of knowledge and culture and, to a significant extent, replaced DNA as the trademark of human evolution (Wilson, 2013). The group was at the core of such a distinct evolutionary path.

Indeed, a crucial distinguishing feature of human adaptation was the acquisition of knowledge that is transmitted to us by our social group. As Gergely and Jacob (2012) suggested, this process became necessary partly because of the *learnability problem* created by the increasing use of sophisticated tools.

In order to produce progressively more complex tools, our Pleistocene human ancestors required increasingly wide-ranging and more ambitious levels of group collaboration and communication.

It has been suggested that the capacity for communication (both emitting and receiving) has provided an overwhelmingly selective advantage, in relation to the appropriate and fully functional use of instruments (Gergely and Jacob, 2012).

From a thought-provoking sociopolitical perspective, Friedrich Engels (1876) suggested that bipedal locomotion was a decisive step in the transition from ape to human.

In fact, all extant anthropoid apes can stand erect and move around on their feet alone, but only in case of urgent need and in a clumsy way. The majority rest the knuckles of the fist on the ground. In our Pleistocene ancestors, the hands were gradually *liberated* and greater dexterity acquired, which was inherited and perfected from generation to generation.

Engels (1876) further argued that the hand is not only the organ of labour, but also the *product* of labour. Only by cumulative labour, by adaptation to new operations through the inheritance of muscles, ligaments and the ever-renewed employment of this inherited finesse in increasingly sophisticated work, has the human hand achieved the high degree of perfection required to conjure into production or operation. Today, we can enjoy beautiful pieces of music, paintings and sculptures, as well as benefit from medical surgery.

But the hand did not exist alone, it was only one member of an integral, highly complex organism. And what benefited the hand, benefited also the whole body it served, including the brain. This evolution widened horizons at every new advance.

Humans were constantly discovering innovative, hitherto unknown properties in natural objects.

And, most importantly, the development of labour necessarily helped to bring members of primitive societies closer together by increasing mutual support and joint activity, and by making clear the advantages of collaboration to each individual and to the group-as-a-whole.

In turn, humans arrived at the point where they had something to say to each other. Necessity created the organ; the undeveloped larynx of the ape was progressively transformed by modulation to produce continually more complex sounds, and the organs of the mouth gradually learned to pronounce one articulate word after another. In short, according to Engels (1876), labour is the prime basic condition for all human existence and, in a metaphorical sense, *labour created humankind.*

1.2(ii) The growth of the human group

Human culture has the distinctive characteristic that it accumulates modifications over time. This process has been called the *ratchet effect* and has led to humans' unique form of *cumulative cultural evolution* (Tennie, Call and Tomasello, 2009).

Inevitably, the evolution of the human group was a crucial part of the process of survival and adaptation to a hostile environment. As a species, the group made us more intelligent, resilient and humorous!

Yes, laughter played a role in the development of the human group. Robin Dunbar (2012) investigated this. He described how primate societies are characterised by bonded social relationships of a kind that are rare in other mammal taxa. These bonded relationships, which provide the basis for coalitions, are sometimes underpinned by endorphin mechanisms mediated by social grooming.

However, bonded relationships of this kind impose constraints on group size, as the time available for social grooming is relatively short. When ecological pressures have demanded larger groups, primates have needed to evolve new bonding mechanisms.

Dunbar (2022) further argued that these pressures involved increasing the size of vocal and visual communication repertoires, in order to grow the group size beyond the limit that could be bonded by grooming.

These primates co-opted laughter as a form of group chorusing that would intensify the sense of bonding between those who laugh together. Thus, laughter became an early evolutionary innovation; the most likely time for the origin of human-like laughter was the appearance of the genus *Homo.*

Group analysis, in its own way, has paid significant attention to human laughter (see Chapter 3). In particular, Murray Cox (1995) explored the role of laughter as an aid towards structuring the group therapeutic process:

> The ability to laugh at himself is, paradoxically, an indication that a man is able to take himself seriously. Similarly, a group that dares to accept laughter, will also be able to tolerate tears.

> (Cox, in Cañete and Ezquerro, 1999: 508)

And, as further stated by Cox (1995), when laughter is not a psychological defence, it might come to be an enriching reinforcement of corporate solidarity.

Apart from laughter, other communication devices have played a role in the evolution of the human group.

In recent decades, a number of authors have studied the emergence of the ability to understand other people's dispositional and motivational states, which is largely acquired in the context of attachment relationships (Fonagy, Luyten and Allison, 2015).

This capability for social cognition, or *mentalising* (Fonagy and Bateman, 2008; Bateman and Fonagy, 2019), is now thought to underpin the remarkable human capacity to tolerate and benefit from meaningful interactions within very large social groups – something that is inconceivable in nonhuman primates.

As we mentioned earlier, the size of the social group clearly correlates with the size of the neocortex. There is a direct link between social group complexity and communicative complexity, which appeared to have given *Homo sapiens* a clear superiority and greater chances of survival over other hominins groups (Sallet et al, 2011).

Comparisons of the skulls of Neanderthals with those of *Homo sapiens* carbon dated to roughly the same historical epoch (when they coexisted in Europe) have shown that the Neanderthals had relatively larger eyes, which implies the possession of significantly larger visual processing areas, a likely adaptation to the long dark nights of European winters. In contrast, *Homo sapiens*, which evolved originally in Africa, specialised less on vision and body control and more on communication, problem solving and social networking (Pearce, Stringer and Dunbar, 2013).

The capacity to communicate is likely to have evolved more rapidly and effectively when less brain capacity was taken up with vision and body control and, ultimately, gave a massive evolutionary advantage to *Homo sapiens* in Europe and elsewhere. In particular, Neanderthals may have had less social networking over wide geographical terrains, which may have given *Homo sapiens* an essential advantage as the Ice Age descended on Europe (Fonagy, Luyten and Allison, 2015).

Alongside the above arguments, Smith et al (2010) proposed that the period of immaturity (requiring close protection, nurturing care and socioemotional investment) became more prolonged for *Homo sapiens*, as compared with Neanderthals, based at least on discoveries about the maturation of teeth (or later loss of milk teeth). These findings indicate the growing importance of the transgenerational transmission of knowledge within human culture (Wilson, 2013).

Whilst Neanderthals and *Homo sapiens* may have descended from a common ancestor (*Homo heidelbergensis*), *Homo sapiens* emerged out of Africa as a superior adaptation. This was not in terms of physical strength or visual acuity, but in terms of the capacity for symbolic thinking and the transmission of knowledge. These abilities enabled *Homo sapiens* to collaborate in larger numbers and more sophisticated group structures (Herrmann et al, 2007).

1.2(iii) Migratory processes: survival and exploration

Our far-distant hominin ancestors lived under conditions of high mortality. More than one and a half million years ago, some of the steadily evolving human groups started to migrate out of their African homeland.

It could have been due to local resources shrinking, with a concomitant bigger threat to survival. Bobe, Behrensmeyer and Chapman (2002) claimed that, during that time, environmental changes resulted in a reduction of woodlands and other resource availability.

In addition, humans concomitantly evolved an increasing urge for more adventurous explorations, since groups were becoming stronger and more capable of searching for new horizons and more propitious environmental resources. Initially, these groups of migrants established themselves in Asia and Europe; at later stages, in Oceania and America (Keller, 2013; Harari, 2014).

In our view, and from an attachment perspective, migration can be conceived as part of the process of building resilience in the human species:

> Migration is often a search for interaction with a new environment that may maximise survival; it can also be a form of exploration, a key tenet of attachment theory.
>
> (Ezquerro, 2019b)

At this point, we must say that mainstream attachment literature has put an overwhelming emphasis on proximity-seeking. This generalised bias can be explained because it is a type of behaviour that can be easily measured, and for which standard measurements have been established.

However, exploration is also a distinct type of attachment behaviour and deserves more space in attachment research. According to Gaskins (2013), exploration is in fact a universal, intrinsically-motivated activity in humans that might be organised by cultural values and practices. Exploration is inevitably linked to the experience of having a secure base, which may take different configurations (Ezquerro 2019c, 2020b, 2021b).

Anyhow, if we all were honest and consistent enough, in society, with the original survival meaning of migratory processes, we would have to rebel against the barriers and walls that are erected to keep migrants away, unless they bring with them one million dollars, euros or pounds – or something like that.

From an evolutionary perspective, human beings, regardless of where they are born should have a right to live in any country; this should be a universal right, in line with our ancestors' *freedom of movement* (Ezquerro, 2020a, 2021a).

1.2(iv) The need for group attachment

Indeed, bipedalism played a part in a nomadic way of living, as well as in migratory processes.

Nevertheless, in order to optimize the developing upright gait, modifications to the anatomical structure of the body were required. Consequently, our far-distant ancestors evolved narrower hips, which considerably constricted the birth canal in women. These anatomical changes took place whilst, in parallel, the brain was growing rather massively.

In short, early humans were faced with an apparently irresolvable conflict between these two *opposing* evolutionary pressures: bigger brains versus smaller hips.

Since the birth canal came to be disproportionately small, compared to that of other primates, the process of labour and delivery of a human baby became a major hazard in itself: maternal mortality related to childbirth increased (Ezquerro, 2022).

In the circumstances, the human species had to develop a new survival strategy: giving birth earlier. Those women who delivered a baby when the brain was less developed had a greater chance of surviving. Therefore, the process of natural selection favoured early births. But this phenomenon had its consequences.

The human infant had to be born prematurely and came into the world, not only with an immature brain, but also with many of the organism's vital systems underdeveloped and, hereafter, displayed an extraordinarily long and intense need for care and protection.

This reality directly impacted the human attachment system, which had to evolve and differentiate itself from the attachment system of other mammals and nonhuman primates.

Given the high level of maternal mortality, if the baby had invested its entire attachment repertoire exclusively in the biological mother, from day one, it would have put itself into a dangerous position, should the mother not have survived. The high-risk perinatal situation for the mother required a definite involvement of other group members for the care and protection of the offspring, particularly of orphaned infants, with a view to maximising survival for the individual and the species.

As a result, early human attachment was relatively undifferentiated for the first six or so months. Infants needed to keep their options open within the group into which they were born. As a consequence, *allomothering* and *group attachment* became essential components of human evolution and survival (Ezquerro, 2022).

For our Pleistocene ancestors raising children required substantial help from other members of the family group and the wider tribal group (Keller, 2013). The long period of sheer dependency on others and the mental plasticity of human infants are idiosyncratic features of our species.

In the African savannah, there were plenty of predators around. In order to survive, the baby needed to be protected by, and receive care from, the group.

Experiencing and internalising group attachment would certainly contribute to a growing feeling of inner security and would maximise survival, both physical and emotional, in the longer term. We shall elaborate on *alloparenting* and *group attachment* in a subsection further below.

A turning point in the development of the attachment system is the arrival of autonomous locomotion. From about six months onwards, at the point when archaic (and modern) human infants became able to move around on their own through crawling and walking, the risk of being hurt or coming to harm increased drastically. Consequently, a need for a more intense relationship with a clearly identified and accessible primary attachment figure developed. This was usually, although not necessarily, the biological mother if she had survived.

Quick decisions had to be made in the face of an external threat or danger and the infant or small child had to know, very rapidly, who to turn to; a fraction of a second could make a difference between life and death.

Furthermore, in order to minimise danger, human infants also needed to know from whom to keep a distance and, around the same age, they developed a *wariness of strangers*.

It should be noted that there are still many *predators* around in our societies of the 21st century, although these dangers are now of a different type: domestic or traffic accidents, drowning, kidnapping, physical or sexual abuse, or other forms of mistreatment or exploitation and so forth (Bowlby, 1984; Ezquerro, 1995, 2019a).

Once an infant begins to be mobile it is crucial to be mindful of the environmental risks, such as the presence of sharp objects, fires, places from which they might fall, water hazards, strangers and so on.

Even when willing to go quite a distance away from the caregiver, the infant likes to know that the caregiver is available and accessible. That explains the strength of both separation anxiety and stranger anxiety.

1.2(v) Does stranger mean danger?

There is a direct link between the increasing *awareness of strangers* (of who is a known interlocutor and who is not) and a strong preference for people who are familiar, which develops alongside this awareness.

Social referencing (checking with a familiar person before engaging with a non-familiar one) is an important part of the process and a good example of a heightened reliance on social partners, which emerges in conjunction with locomotion (Ezquerro and Cañete, 2023).

Stranger anxiety, which varies from mere wariness to full blown fear, is often described as one of the characteristic behaviours of attachment. Recognising people as familiar, and a comfortableness in interacting with them, is not unique to primary attachment figures, as it can also happen with other types of affiliative relationships. However, there are different types of culturally constructed social experience that might amplify or diminish stranger anxiety, based on the amount of exposure the infant has to strangers.

As happened in the Pleistocene, in modern infants, wariness of strangers and preference for a specific primary attachment figure also manifest with special intensity from six months onward. The anxiety that infants show towards any stranger is likely to be influenced by the nature of previous experiences with strangers, in their daily life. In the presence of an attachment figure, children are usually willing to engage with a friendly stranger.

Gaskins (2013) pointed out that an infant who is raised in a small community or kept at home most of the time is likely to have little exposure to strangers, let alone interact with them. On the other hand, if infants are taken along to places their caregivers need to go, they will have greater exposure to strangers and may even interact with them. Infants who are comfortable with many social partners might be more flexible in accepting new social interlocutors and find strangers less intimidating.

Benign attachment experiences enable the developing child to read, understand and remember other people's feelings, mental states and intentions. As mentioned earlier, this process of advanced social cognition, deeply rooted in our evolution, has been increasingly known as *mentalising* (Fonagy and Bateman, 2008).

1.2(vi) Alloparenting and group attachment

The care provided by group members other than the genetic mother or father has been described as *alloparenting* (Crittenden and Marlowe, 2013).

Contemporary hunter-gatherer populations, although often overlooked in mainstream attachment literature, are suitable for exploring models of multiple caregiving and group attachment. These populations constitute the closest approximation to Bowlby's (1969) *environment of evolutionary adaptedness.*

The nomadic foraging lifestyle characterised human evolution until the Neolithic or New Stone Age, so contemporary foragers can provide unique insights into our Pleistocene ancestors. In other words, by studying multiple child care and group care structures in nomadic hunters and gatherers in the present day, we are better able to situate attachment processes in the environment that gave rise to them (Chisholm, 1996).

In the first volume of his trilogy on *Attachment and Loss* Bowlby (1969) affirmed that the human infant can become attached to many people other than the mother. According to him, although attachment is universal, its manifestations vary cross-culturally depending upon the child's home and community environment.

In consonance with Bowlby, Susan Seymour (2013) highlighted that there are practical reasons to consider children as having a network of attachment figures, as this group care configuration ameliorates separation anxiety and other expressions of distress when one of the caregivers is absent. Children learn to trust and to be comforted by other carers outside the immediate family, within the wider tribal group.

From naturalistic observation data in modern forager groups, it is possible to conclude that, although mothers usually represent the primary caregiver, there is a basic pan-forager model of child care. This involves a wide array of caregivers who routinely provide high-quality investment to infants and children (Meehan and Hawks, 2013; Crittenden and Marlowe, 2013).

A good example of this pan-forager model can be observed in the Hadza of Tanzania: mothers are the primary caregivers and a wide range of group members, both related and unrelated, routinely contribute with high-investment care (nutritional, educational and socio-emotional) throughout infancy and childhood. These caregivers include fathers, siblings, grandparents, cousins, aunts, uncles, distant relatives and non-kin. In fact, unrelated individuals spend considerable time participating in child care (Wall-Scheffler and Myers, 2013).

Alloparental care is in fact a widespread phenomenon among social insects, birds and mammals; it varies greatly across and within different species, families, subfamilies and groups of primates (Burkart and Van Schaik, 2010). More specifically, allomothering comprises a wide variety of behaviours, including carrying, provisioning, grooming, touching, nursing and protecting infants from predators or conspecifics.

One of the evolutionary pressures on human infants has been a need to develop social skills that enable them to form strong bonds with multiple caregivers, with a view to maximising survival. Many studies have shown that cooperative breeding and alloparenting provide significant benefits for the development, learning and socialisation of offspring. The cooperative group protects offspring and may also lead to the enhancement of cognitive abilities, especially those that are related to social interactions (Burkart and Van Schaik, 2010).

Other studies have suggested that cooperative group breeding may have led to the evolution of greater cognitive flexibility and problem-solving abilities in infants (Burkart, Hrdy and Van Schaik, 2009).

This is because navigating complex social situations with multiple caregivers requires a high level of cognitive ability, including understanding and responding to social cues, communicating effectively and finding solutions to adapt to a changing environment. In addition, greater social tolerance and sensitivity to others' signals enhance social learning and alliance-making.

The above findings lend strong support to the notion that humans evolved as cooperative caregivers, so the child internalised a sense of *group attachment*, after feeling secure and responded to when needed within the tribal group. Among foragers, regular physical contact and affectionate responses in the group promote children's felt security, which gradually contributes to the development of an internal working model in which the individual perceives people and the wider environment as safe and caring (Ezquerro, 2004, 2015).

Aka children, who live in south-western Central African Republic and in northern Congo Republic, display attachment behaviours to an average of six individuals. Yet, findings like this on early social environment, and on the role of multiple attachment figures and of group attachment, have not been fully integrated into attachment theory (Meehan and Hawks, 2013).

A number of other authors have written about alloparenting and multiple caregiving, and have pointed out that this practice is very widespread cross-culturally and has persisted after the hunting-gathering era:

Multiple child care is a universal practice with a long history, not a dangerous innovation:

(Howes and Spieker, 2008: 317)

Alloparenting, or multiple child care, is associated with early hominins' increased capacities for "mindreading" – for improved decoding of the mental states of others, and figuring out who would help and who would hurt.

(Hrdy, 2009: 66)

Phenomenologically and psychologically, we can no longer believe, as many psychodynamic theorists did, that there is one basic relationship – that with the mother – from which all the others derive.

(Konner, 2010: 447)

Many foraging societies combine group attachment and interdependent orientations with a high tolerance for individual autonomy. It has been hypothesised that interdependence might be, in part, an outcome of shared caregiving practices (Hrdy, 2009). A pan-forager cognitive model of sharing, cooperation and trust, based on multiple secure attachments within the group, has been proposed as the product of a social environment that includes high rates of physical contact, many caregivers and the constant presence of significant others.

In this context, we can affirm that the group-as-a-whole becomes an attachment figure in its own right. As Bowlby (1969) put it: a group can come to constitute, for many, a subordinate attachment figure and, for some, a primary attachment figure.

Of course, alloparenting is not identical to group attachment, but having multiple and reliable attachment figures in the group will provide the child with an experience that help is available within that particular group, regardless of who might be accessible at any given time. An internal working model of the group has been internalised.

In most contemporary hunter-gatherer groups, exclusive primary attachment is lessened in favour of diffuse attachment to several caregivers from the mother's and father's side and from the wider community. Seniority connotes elements of giving, protecting and teaching; for each individual the community becomes encoded as a caregiving other, providing additional care, sustenance and protection.

By way of illustration, in the Murik society (Papua New Guinea), by the age of three years, children spend most of their time immersed in groups, circulating through households and the wider tribe, learning about the benefits of reciprocity in large social networks (Barlow, 2013). The Murik can be described as willing explorers who take initiatives and are confident in their abilities. They are also portrayed as highly social with a keen responsibility to others, loyal to kin and community, and reliant on group membership for help and protection.

In this culture, Barlow (2013) differentiated two forms of attachment: one is more focused and person-specific, whilst the other is more diffuse, role oriented and group-specific. According to her, each type of attachment provides a basis for models of cultural competence and personhood. Primary attachment underwrites strong paired relationships. Diffuse attachment provides multiple contexts in which security, recognition and validation can be found.

Noticeably, as children grow, they gradually take on the role of caregiver and can become attachment figures to others, like younger siblings and peers. In their extended family and peer group relationships, they receive and offer caregiving and contribute to the development of more diffuse group attachment bonds. Away from the immediate domestic household, peer groups often become a refuge of diffuse attachment.

Siblings are prominent figures in many children's early life and may come to constitute the first peer group experience. Sibling relationships in early development are commonly seen as preparations for the kind of relationships children will establish with peers and friends outside the family (Sanders, 2004; Hindle and Sherwin-White, 2014; Dunn, 2014; Parker, 2020). Initially, the sibling is not really an attachment figure. However,

> as parents are absent either emotionally or physically, the siblings may be forced to reach out for one another.
>
> (Bank and Kahn, 1997: 123)

Barlow (2013) further explained that the Murik eco-cultural adaptation requires highly flexible work regimes, in which household composition and caregiving personnel change constantly to accommodate weather conditions, sea tides, resource exploitation and trade in a precarious environment.

If we accept that attachment relationships are an adaptive system integral to the definition of self, other, and relatedness, it is then crucial that we understand it in terms of our most important adaptive structure: the group and its power to create culture. The Murik case demonstrates that personal and group developmental processes are thoroughly intertwined with a cultural system of meaning.

Jeannette Mageo (2013) studied the psychodynamics of attachment in Samoa. She observed that, when interpersonal security with primary attachment figures is at stake, the group helps direct children away from these problematical dyadic attachment relationships towards group attachment. Successful enculturation can help developing individuals to form secure attachment bonds to the group, and to establish an

> emotional connection to the group as a whole.
>
> (Morelli and Henry, 2013: 245)

1.2(vii) The cultural acquisition device

Earlier, we saw that human attachment is an evolutionarily rooted, species-wide in-built system that has the main purpose of maximising survival, for the individual and the species.

Inevitably, attachment involves person-to-person and person-to-group relationships, and can be better understood when we incorporate anthropological and cross-cultural perspectives.

Suzanne Gaskins (2013) suggested that, from the outset, attachment provides the infant with new capabilities for entering into social group engagement and cultural understanding. According to her, in order to disentangle this *puzzle*, it is necessary to take into account and integrate the following facts:

- the human attachment system is evolutionary, essential and universal;
- the system is shaped and reshaped by experiences through social interactions across the life cycle;
- there is significant variation in how these interactions manifest across cultures.

Elaborating on that, Gaskins proposed looking at the attachment system as having skeletal and flesh elements. The *skeleton* of attachment is a universal physical and emotional system that promotes survival, exploration and growth.

The *flesh* includes caregivers' integration of the developing child's capacities into their own cultural system of understanding and practices of social interaction. This process of integration leads to the expression of attachment behaviours that are quite varied:

each culture puts flesh on the bones of attachment in a distinct way.

(Gaskins, 2013: 59)

Along these lines, Melvin Konner (2010) coined the concept of the *cultural acquisition device*, meaning a capacity that is necessary for infants in all cultures to enter into the specific social practices that allow them to become legitimate participants in their particular culture, and effective group members – for which attachment is a critical component.

Cultures vary in how they respond to the acquisition, or otherwise, of these new abilities. Cultural differences in understandings and practices are likely to influence the course of child and adolescent development in ways that are not universal. In contrast to the dominant *western* perspective that multiple caregivers put infants at risk of not forming deep and healthy attachment, there are some advantages in having multiple attachment figures, as well as some possible disadvantages.

Sarah Hrdy (2009) showed ethnographic evidence that, in today's world, humans often distribute caregiving of infants and children across multiple members of the family, as well as members of wider social groups.

As stated by her, the primary advantage is that infants who are attached to multiple caregivers are less vulnerable to depression and anxiety if one caregiver (like the mother) dies or is separated from the infant. Mothers' death has always been a legitimate concern, especially given the risks of childbirth.

In addition, infants with positive experiences of multiple caregivers can place their trust in more people than just the mother and are more likely to perceive the world as a benign place for them to explore. These children have to develop a more complex working model of social relations, since people's interactions with them are quite different, based on personality, age, roles, status and so forth.

Thus, infants with multiple caregivers may be pushed to develop a more sophisticated theory about how other people think, which may accommodate a more complex set of experiences, to build an adequate working model of the world (Gaskins, 2013).

As a possible disadvantage, we need to be aware that the natural propensity is for infants, from about six months onward, to have a preferred primary attachment figure, and that being exposed to multiple uncoordinated, or conflicting, attachment figures can be confusing and difficult to integrate for the developing child (Ezquerro and Cañete, 2023).

In any case, children need to have confidence that their needs will be met by other people in a predictable way in order for trust to be established. However, it is not essential to have complete consistency across all caregivers. In fact, a variety of models of social interaction across caregivers may lead to a more sophisticated and robust working model of social interaction.

1.2(viii) Monotropic versus multiple caregiving

Morelli and Henry (2013) pointed out that, although the primacy of the mother in the life of her baby is undeniable, there is substantial evidence that mothers are not singular providers of care and they alone cannot meet all the demands inherent in raising a child.

Care sharing is likely a part of our human legacy. The expression of attachment in children and caregivers alike is culturally and ecologically situated. Several bases of security (similar though not identical) may coexist in time and place (see Chapter 4).

As advanced earlier, the human infant requires high levels of nutritional, cognitive, behavioural and socioemotional investment over a long period of time, which extends beyond childhood into the juvenile years. There is an increasing pressure of learning a wealth of information and culture prior to adulthood.

Following on from the old African adage *it takes a village to raise a child*, no doubt, it takes a group to grow an adult. And these processes are deeply rooted in the evolution of human group attachment (Ezquerro, 2023).

Raising children is, indeed, energetically expensive: it requires provisioning and other types of high-investment care for which mothers need to rely on other group members, in the family and the wider social group. It has been proposed that reliance on *allomaternal* support is a central characteristic of human life history, and that humans evolved as cooperative breeders (Hrdy 2009). This was key to the survival of the individual, the group and the human species.

The survival function of *alloparenting* was also highlighted by Aiello and Key (2002). According to them, during the Pleistocene, the availability of a wide range of helpers-at-the-nest from family and other members of the tribal group, offering support in the form of caregiving and provisioning, would have allowed populations of early hominins to survive and expand.

Furthermore, Crittenden and Marlowe (2013) suggested that allomothers can gain inclusive fitness benefits from helping their kin, and that unrelated individuals may likewise be motivated to invest in the young, thereby gaining potential benefits such as increased strength in social bonds or access to childcare support for their own offspring. This had been described a form of *mutualistic collaboration* (Tomasello et al, 2012).

We can find a plausible theoretical explanation of the workings and probabilities of allomaternal investment, in Hamilton's (1964) rule – which states that an individual might be expected to help another, whenever the benefit to the recipient is greater than the cost to the helper divided by the degree of relatedness between them.

Human attachment is flexible enough to allow for adaptation to local environmental conditions. This is supported by neuroscientific evidence of plasticity (Belsky and de Haan, 2011). This adaptive flexibility can help us revise the traditional pejorative connotation that attributes pathology to the patterns of *insecure* attachment.

We would like to stress that insecure patterns of attachment can also be considered adaptive under certain conditions, such as when parents are unable or unwilling to invest in their infants, often as a result of living in ecologically risky, highly stressful or dangerous environments.

In these instances, within a modern evolutionary framework, as outlined by Simpson and Belsky (2008), infants or young children may adapt by avoiding closeness to parents and could try to secure resources elsewhere. Alternatively, they may become anxiously demanding and overtly vigilant in order to secure resources from parents at the most opportune times.

Healthy development depends on how well an individual balances the need for protection and felt security with the need for exploration and mastery of the social world and the wider environment. Insecure attachment can sometimes be seen as a survival adaptive strategy in particular circumstances, in an attempt to make the best out of a bad situation. Adaptations to risky environments may come at a cost, such as inadequate growth, patchy development and less nimble learning (Simpson and Belsky, 2008).

Much of the research that has examined various correlates of attachment security has predominantly concentrated on parental sensitivity, particularly maternal sensitivity. According to Morelli and Henry (2013), it is necessary to expand research studies into the factors that influence this sensitivity, such as household income, parental stress, racism, discrimination and other relevant environmental contributors.

All in all, it makes little sense to consider close attachment relationships in isolation, without their sociopolitical context.

An exclusive focus on dyadic attachment relationships may eclipse processes that emotionally connect people more broadly to others and to groups. The connection of oneself to groups, organisations and the broader community encourages and facilitates the taking and sharing of perspectives, and fosters optimal development.

Qualities that promote social harmony, such as being collaborative and accommodating to others and to the wider group context, accepting and integrating differences, have crucial developmental value.

1.2(ix) Further thoughts on group attachment

We referred earlier to Kathleen Barlow (2013), who studied attachment and culture in a society (Papua New Guinea), in which children are raised in a group context that fosters collaboration, interdependence and identification with the group. These qualities promote the development of healthy group attachment, as an important personal and cultural value.

In the words of Heidi Keller (2013), attachment is unequivocally a universal human need, but it looks differently and has different developmental trajectories across different cultural environments. By looking at attachment cross-culturally, as Bambi Chapin put it:

> we can have a better understanding of how diversity comes about – diversity among individuals, and diversity across and within groups.
>
> (Chapin, 2013: 160)

These data add to the growing body of work that is viewing attachment as biologically based yet culturally influenced. A more thorough study of the ways in which culture and evolution interact, especially in systems of care and protection, will enhance our understanding and appreciation of the plasticity of attachment processes.

It has been suggested that the flexibility provided by models of cooperative childcare may have been one of the keys to the success of early members of the genus *Homo* (Crittenden and Marlowe, 2013). During the Pleistocene, shifting ecological conditions necessitated the exploitation of new resources for which group attachment and collaboration allowed populations to survive and expand.

If our species' typical ability to empathise and cooperate with others is developed early in life, based to a large extent on routine interaction with a constellation of caregivers, we must give serious credence to the importance of models of multipersonal or group attachment.

The cooperative nature of human child rearing is evident cross-culturally. Having said that, even among foragers for whom allomaternal care is often ubiquitous, infants still receive the majority of their care from their mothers.

However, as previously stated, concentrating only on the mother-child dyad reduces our ability to understand the multiplicity of factors that contribute to other person-to-person attachment relationships, as well as person-to-group attachment, in a cross-cultural perspective throughout the life cycle (Ezquerro and Cañete, 2023).

1.2(x) Group selection and natural selection

In their study of primitive human groups, Cortina and Liotti (2010) pointed out that, through our evolution as a species, group cooperation enabled our Pleistocene ancestors to survive hostile environments. Furthermore, based on ethnographic data from various contemporary forager groups, they indicated that intragroup norms are established to sanction *deviant behaviour* that may represent an internal threat to the survival of the group.

In order to make sense of these group dynamics, the concept of *group selection* has been proposed (Bowles, 2006, 2009). This can be considered the group equivalent to *natural selection*. Simply put, in intergroup competition, groups with more cooperative and altruistic members will outcompete groups that are less cooperative and contain more selfish members.

In parallel to that, Boyd (2006) indicated that group selection requires a system of sanctions and punishment, which can spread the high costs of the enforcement of prosocial values to the group-as-a-whole.

Contemporary hunter-gatherer groups perform this function efficiently by the use of *levelling* mechanisms, which operate as a *social tax* and permit that the high price of implementing altruistic norms (and punishments for violators of these norms) be shared by the entire group, rather than by a few individuals.

This levelling function is achieved through the process of sharing cultural norms or values, an egalitarian ethos that is reinforced by instituting a gradient of sanctions. These sanctions can progress from blaming and shaming offenders to ostracising them and, in extreme cases, subjecting them to capital punishment (Boehm, 1999, 2012).

According to Tomasello et al (2012), our species-unique forms of cooperation (as well as our idiosyncratic forms of cognition, communication, and social life) derive all primarily from what has been described as *mutualistic collaboration*, in which social or *group selection* dynamics against uncollaborative members operate:

- In a first step, by necessity, humans became collaborative foragers; individuals were interdependent with one another and so had a direct interest in the wellbeing of their partners and the group. Our Pleistocene ancestors evolved new skills and motivations for collaboration, such as *joint intentionality*, not possessed by other great apes.
- In a second step, these new collaborative skills and motivations were scaled up to group life in general, as evolving human groups had to face competition for limited resources from other groups. As part of this new group-mindedness, they created cultural conventions, norms, organisations and institutions, which are all characterised by *collective intentionality*. In turn, the knowledge and acceptance of these specific group elements were incorporated into individual members way of being, marking them as affiliates of a particular cultural group.

Consequently, human cognition and sociality gradually evolved. Our ancestors became ever more collaborative and altruistic, whilst also becoming ever more interdependent.

The concept of *mutual aid* was formulated by the Russian biologist, philosopher and sociologist Peter Kropotkin (1908). He argued that aiding and protecting others, and serving the needs of the group rather than the individual, has been essential to the survival of our species and evident in early human societies. He further argued that cooperation is as important as competition, and that the highest achievements of the human race have been the result of group collaboration and of group attachment. According to Kropotkin, there is in nature a law of mutual aid, which is far more important than mutual contest.

Common membership of a social group and a sense of belonging to a greater human whole have in fact provided the backbone of human evolution as a species (Cortina and Liotti, 2010). Group attachment is more obvious and straightforward in cooperative groups, particularly when members share goals and world views.

Other research has shown that people usually prefer the groups they belong in (or are familiar with) and within which they feel comfortable and safe. It is easier to seek comfort and support from these groups or from their members or leaders at times of need (Sochos, 2015).

However, humans have also developed a capacity to collaborate and, over time, form attachments with less familiar or even stranger groups (Mikulincer and Shaver, 2001; Haidt, 2013). This characteristic is idiosyncratic of the human species and has survival value.

Interestingly, group analysis is a form of psychotherapy in the context of a group of strangers; it is about making a home of the *stranger group* (Nitzgen, 2008, 2019; Schlapobersky, 2016; Ezquerro, 2023; Ezquerro and Cañete, 2023), as we shall explore further in the section that follows.

1.3 Section II: Group attachment as an evolving concept

In his early research, John Bowlby (1951, 1958, 1959) gave priority to the study of interpersonal attachment relationships within the family group, especially with primary attachment figures.

The need for person-to-group attachments had been implicit since our earliest ancestors evolved, as per the evidence shown in Section I of this chapter. However, it was not until 1969, in the first volume of his trilogy on *Attachment and Loss*, that Bowlby explicitly advanced the concept of group attachment.

He pointed out that, in addition to individual or interpersonal attachment, human beings also establish group attachment relationships with different groups *to* which or *in* which they belong or with which they identify.

In these groups, individuals can be looked after, cared for and protected, and they can also care for others, play, learn, work, collaborate, grow, and fulfil their potential as a person:

> During adolescence and adulthood, a significant portion of attachment behaviour is commonly directed not only toward people outside the family, but also toward groups and institutions other than the family.

A school or university, a work group, a religious group or a political group can become a secondary attachment figure for many people and, for some, a primary attachment figure. In such cases, it seems likely, the development of group attachment is usually mediated, at least initially, by attachment to a person who occupies a prominent position within that group.

(Bowlby, 1969: 207)

Undoubtedly, John Bowlby conceived the human mind as a social emergent and he collaborated with others throughout his life.

In fact, his attachment theory is very much the product of *collaborative thinking* (Fonagy, Luyten and Allison, 2015). From his perspective, in conjunction with interpersonal attachment, group attachment is fundamental for the integral and healthy development of the person (Bowlby, 1969, 1991a).

1.3(i) An implicit sense of group attachment

Although Bowlby did not formulate the concept of group attachment until 1969, his previous work indicated that he indeed considered benign group attachment processes as key to healthy personal development and wellbeing.

As a matter of fact, his dissertation for membership of the British Psychoanalytical Society, *The influence of early environment in the development of neurosis and neurotic character* (Bowlby, 1940), was devoted to the relevance of the social environment for the prevention of mental health problems.

Since his appointment as Director of the Children and Parents Department of the Tavistock Clinic in 1946, Bowlby carefully selected the composition of both his clinical and research teams.

One of his early recruitments, in 1948, was James Robertson who had worked at the Hampstead residential nursery that Anna Freud and Dorothy Burlingham opened for children evacuated from bombed areas of London, during the Second World War. This unit contained group care structures that mitigated the children's pain, after being separated from their families (Freud and Burlingham, 1944).

The good service provided at the Hampstead nursery contributed to the appointment of Anna Freud and her team to do an extraordinary piece of work. In 1945, they set up a therapeutic project for six children (three boys and three girls), survivors of the Holocaust. Their parents were murdered in the gas chambers at the time they were babies, which prevented the formation of parent-child attachments.

The children were put together as a group and moved from one concentration camp to another, for more than three years, until they were rescued by the Russians, kept together in a castle in today's Czech Republic, for several more months, and later sent to West Sussex in England for treatment.

Prior to their arrival, these orphans had been deprived of the possibility of forming interpersonal attachments with any adult. However, as a compensatory strategy, they established a primary attachment to the very group of which each of them was a part. This experience of group attachment was fundamental for their survival (Freud and Dann, 1951).

The interested reader can find links between Anna Freud's outstanding work on *group upbringing* and contemporary attachment theorising, including the role of group attachment in therapeutic settings and in the promotion of healthy social life (Ezquerro, 2017a, 2023; Ezquerro and Cañete, 2023).

No doubt, Bowlby chose Robertson for his experience as a valuable member of Anna Freud's team and, also, for his sensitivity to social injustice. Soon after his arrival at the Tavistock, as part of Bowlby's new research project, Robertson started to observe children who had been sent off to a ward at the Central Middlesex Hospital, in London. In terms of the institution as a potential attachment space, conditions were poor.

The Platt Report, formerly known as the Welfare of Sick Children in Hospital (Ministry of Health, 1959), found that inpatient medical institutions at the time were miserable places for children who, whilst in hospital, had to follow strict and rigid ward routines and were not allowed to play. Moreover, parents were under no circumstances allowed to visit their children outside a stringent and brief weekly visit (Ezquerro, 2017a).

From the outset, Robertson picked up the children's distress – something that staff did not seem able or willing to recognise. He became very concerned about the institution's caring deficits and thought about the possibility of making a film. No professional outside Bowlby's team seemed to take his concerns seriously enough.

Bowlby supported Robertson's idea about film-making, and refined it into a far-reaching document – which became a vital and now classic film: *A Two-Year-Old Goes to Hospital* (Bowlby and Robertson, 1952a, 1952b). It certainly stimulated a great deal of interest and came to be known to professionals, politicians and public across the world. Anna Freud and her team were great enthusiasts, in spite of the fact that she and Bowlby differed on theory.

The reviews of the film in the medical journals were quite unanimously encouraging. The idea that hospitals would need to do things differently was taking shape. The medical superintendent at the Central Middlesex Hospital honestly said:

> Well, I am sorry it is my hospital. But I accept that it is an objective record which should be shown widely.
>
> (Robertson and Robertson, 1989: 45)

In November 1952, Robertson and Bowlby presented the film at the Royal Society of Medicine in London to some three hundred professionals who were outside the field of mental health.

This audience included general practitioners, paediatricians, nurses, managers and administrators. Health economy policy-makers soon became aware of the message (Ezquerro, 2017a, 2017b).

The dissemination of the film marked the beginning of a major shift in professional and public opinion – leading to policy changes in hospitals and other child care institutions. It was a milestone, particularly regarding improvements in the institutional care of young people and in the understanding of the effects of separation. The film also played a role in the development of attachment theory.

Although the concept of group attachment had not been explicitly spelled out yet, the work of Anna Freud, John Bowlby and their teams contributed to the development of *group attachment spaces* in social services and healthcare institutions. Over the next few decades, the study of attachment flourished, with solid scientific and clinical grounds (Bowlby, 1969, 1973, 1980, 1988a). It became increasingly apparent that attachment theory would have to go beyond individual, couple, family and therapeutic entities to also encompass groups, organisations, institutions and other social systems (Marris, 1996).

Kraemer and Roberts (1996) edited a remarkable volume, *The Politics of Attachment: Towards a Secure Society*, which was the result of the combined work of a number of professionals with social consciousness. They shared a common conviction that we all have a powerful need to belong, to be attached to people, places and groups, and that social and political processes must reflect that – in such a way that, ultimately, citizens can perceive society as a secure base.

1.3(ii) Systematic research on group attachment

At the end of the 20th century, Smith, Murphy and Coats (1999) embarked on a landmark piece of research, which turned out to be the first systematic attempt to apply attachment theory to group processes. They examined the attachment bonds that a large number of college students established with various groups and societies, in the context of university life.

This study provided empirical evidence that human beings form attachment relationships not only with other individuals but also with social groups. The main findings can be summarised as follows:

- For optimal wellbeing, people need to remain emotionally close to social groups.
- Group attachment and group identification are different phenomena, although they interrelate.
- Students with lower scores on group attachment and group identification participate less frequently in group activities, make more negative evaluations of social groups, and tend not to perceive groups as sources of security and support.
- Overall, person-to-group attachment includes some of the functions that regulate person-to-person attachment.
- More specifically, both types of attachment bonds include a search for support and protection, as well as the development of mutual responsiveness and a degree of emotional intimacy, which are key relational processes.
- Finally, both interpersonal attachment and group attachment are affected by the early experiences that one has had in the family and other group spaces. These

experiences influence future interpersonal and group relations. However, new experiences can modify attachment styles internalised in the early stages of development.

The importance of integrating dyadic attachment and group attachment, in the overall adjustment to the transition to college life, was subsequently emphasised by Marmarosh and Markin (2007).

Rom and Mikulincer (2003) studied some attachment issues in a work context within various organisations. They compared people who had predominantly experienced secure attachment relationships with people who had not.

They found that the former showed a greater ability to cope with stressful challenges, to establish positive group interactions, to work collaboratively with colleagues and to hold pleasant memories of their group experiences. As a result, these people operated more effectively and harmoniously in teamwork situations, both at instrumental and socio-emotional levels.

Sochos (2015) proposed that, in addition to studying dyadic or interpersonal attachment relationships, it is necessary to develop an integrative framework that brings together different psychosocial and group domains. According to this author, and following Bowlby's teaching, social institutions can become attachment figures. And group attachment can be considered a significant bond in its own right, like interpersonal attachment, although with different characteristics.

Certainly, the functions of attachment can extend beyond the domains of dyadic relationships or individual self-regulation and, thus, contribute to our understanding of broader sociocultural and political phenomena. In this sense, Sochos posed a food-for-thought question:

> Do human beings need the protection and security offered by the social group in a way similar to the child needing the protection of the caregiver, and the human adult the commitment and recognition of intimate peers?.
>
> (Sochos, 2015: 986)

Other studies have likewise suggested that, in addition to the dyadic attachment system, there is a group attachment system that, based on evolution, predisposes humans to seek security and to form emotional bonds with social groups (Wajda and Makara-Studzińska, 2018a, 2018b). Although these two attachment systems (dyadic and group) are different, in many ways they overlap, influence each other, and have important similarities.

According to these authors, person-to-person attachment and person-to-group attachment represent two relatively independent but interconnected domains. In order to understand the nature of group attachment, it is essential to identify what exactly people attach themselves to when they relate, not only to individual members, therapists or leaders *of* (or *in*) the group but also to the group-as-a-whole.

1.3(iii) Attachment and group analysis

Attachment processes are of huge relevance for group analysis, but have been largely overlooked in the group-analytic literature (Ezquerro and Cañete, 2023). In this section, as in the book as a whole, we aim to make explicit what has always been implicit but not always acknowledged: the centrality of attachment in group analysis.

Indeed, our attachment histories are deeply embedded in and constitute an integral part of the social unconscious. This, as Earl Hopper pointed out,

is at the core of the group-analytic perspective.

(Hopper, 2023: xvii)

Yet, only a handful of group analysts have attempted to integrate John Bowlby's attachment theory with SH Foulkes' (the *father* of group analysis) theorising:

- In a pioneering article, Liza Glenn (1987) shared some of the ideas generated during her period of supervision with John Bowlby. She postulated that, under optimal conditions, the so-called **group matrix** can be perceived as an attachment figure and a secure base. Indeed, the group is a *matrix* of interpersonal relationships and the events which unfold in it are interpersonal phenomena (Foulkes, 1948, 1969, 1973). Further examples of how the group-analytic matrix operates can be seen in Chapters 2, 3, 4 and 5.
- In a dissertation for membership of the Institute of Group Analysis (*Attachment and its circumstances: does it relate to group analysis?*), it was stated that attachment theory gives primary status to socio-emotional and affective bonds, and provides a solid and empirical basis for group analysis, which has its roots in the premise that the essence of human beings is social (Ezquerro, 1991).
- Felicity de Zulueta (1993) investigated the traumatic roots of human destructiveness and concluded that serious alterations in the early attachment system, such as child abuse and maltreatment, are a fuel for future aggression and violence: *attachment gone wrong*.
- Jason Maratos (1996) highlighted the relevance of attachment relationships in the co-construction of our individual self and our group self.
- Mario Marrone (1998), who was also supervised by John Bowlby, explored similarities between attachment theory and the sociocultural school of psychoanalysis, which is linked to the group-analytic approach. Likewise, he advocated for the implementation of a type of group therapy that be based on attachment, as part of the training of psychotherapists, so that they improve their understanding of their patients and of themselves.
- In her work as a forensic psychiatrist, Gwen Adshead (1998) noted that mental health professionals must offer sufficient continuity and reliability to their patients and, at times, must become attachment figures, especially for the more

vulnerable patients (most of whom have not had sufficiently secure experiences of interpersonal and group attachment).

- In a comprehensive and personal biography of John Bowlby, Ezquerro (2017a, 2017b) looked at the genesis and development of attachment theory, largely from a group-analytic perspective.
- Finally, in *Group Analysis throughout the Life Cycle*, Ezquerro and Cañete (2023) worked together towards an integration of the fields of attachment and group analysis, and revisited the work of Foulkes from a group attachment and developmental perspective.

It is worth pointing out that, in his many publications, Foulkes barely referred to attachment or to human development, let alone a life-long group attachment and developmental perspective (Sroufe, 2005; Ezquerro and Cañete, 2023). In fact, the words development or attachment do not appear in any of the indexes of his books, despite being implicit in the nature of the clinical work.

These terms are also absent in the index of the book *The Practice of Group Analysis* (Roberts and Pines, 1991), with contributions from the first generations of group analysts. This text is still considered, to a large extent, a theoretical and clinical model to follow within this modality of group psychotherapy. This shying away from an evolutionary and attachment perspective, within mainstream group-analytic thinking and practice, is, to put it mildly, paradoxical.

In Section I of this chapter, we stressed the survival value of group collaboration and altruistic behaviour, something that is highly relevant to group analysis and other forms of group psychotherapy. Indeed, group cooperation enabled early humans to raise their children, survive hostile environments, hunt effectively and protect their settlements against external threats.

Anthropological research into the evolution of the human group, including *group selection* processes, confirmed that collaborative groups have greater chances of survival and growth (Cortina and Liotti, 2010). Furthermore, to ensure optimal group cooperation, intragroup norms were created to sanction *deviant behaviour* that may represent an internal threat to the survival of the group. In group therapy, psychic survival is often at stake.

Interestingly, thinking about deviant behaviour against the background of human evolution, and *mutatis mutandis*, Foulkes had posed a question about what, on the surface, could be perceived as one of the riddles of group-analytic psychotherapy: if all the patients deviate, one way or another, from what is in any given community considered healthy or normal, how can they possibly be of use to each other therapeutically?

Inspired by field theory, as formulated by Kurt Lewin (1939), the answer that Foulkes provided came to be one of the touchstones of group analysis. His statement has also been described as a *basic law* of therapeutic group dynamics:

collectively they constitute the very norm from which, individually, they deviate.

(Foulkes, 1964: 297)

As part of its own evolution, group analysis has been paying increasing attention to the impact of culture, oppression, racism and social injustice, as well as power, privilege and position in groups (Burman, 2021; Sunyer, 2021; Blackwell, 2023). In today's world, it is particularly important to explore minority statuses, discrimination and hatred of some members, as well as other cultural factors, as they become apparent during pre-group individual assessments and the ongoing therapeutic process (see Chapters 2, 3 and 4).

A number of other group researchers have demonstrated how discrimination, racism and oppression can be damaging to people at psychological, emotional, social and spiritual levels (Kirkinis et al, 2021). On the other hand, social psychologists have shown how satisfactory group attachment can buffer effects of discrimination and how fitting relationships, particularly with primary attachment figures, are associated with reduced prejudice and less discriminatory attitudes and behaviours toward people outside one's own social or racial group (Mikulincer and Shaver, 2007, 2022).

Indeed, attachment theory (including both interpersonal and group attachment) is a useful conceptual framework for understanding and fighting prejudice, discrimination, racism and inequality.

The recent COVID-19 pandemic was too tragic an example that exposed the devastating effects of racism, social marginality, ageism and other systems of inequality, as well as the ways in which race and class contribute in tandem to compound disadvantage in multiple and lethal forms (Ezquerro, 2020b; Marmarosh, Forsyth, Strauss and Burlingame, 2020; Marmarosh, 2022).

According to Godlee (2020), we cannot really tackle global crises unless we confront racism, which is a public health issue because it kills people and puts ethnic-minority groups at risk. Racism is all our responsibility. A review by Public Heath England (PHE), during the early stages of the pandemic found that people from ethnic minorities were disproportionately more likely to be infected and to die from COVID-19. Minority black-ethnic groups had 486 women and 649 men diagnosed for an average of 100,000 population across the country, whilst majority white-ethnic groups had 220 diagnoses for women and 224 for men for the same population (Iacobucci, 2020: 386).

Tedros Ghebreyesus, an Ethiopian public health researcher and the first African to become Director-General of the World Health Organization declared that no one should accept a world in which some people are protected whilst others are not. Is this statement a utopia of equality and secure-enough attachment for all?

Certainly, in the context of an emergency like COVID-19, it became obvious that interpersonal attachment relationships within the family, no matter how secure they might be, are not sufficient to protect everyone. A wider group level of relationships and interventions is required. Citizens need to know that they can count on the protection of healthcare organisations and institutions. And this can be seen as a form of group attachment.

Sadly, the pandemic visibly showed that, in virtually every country across the world, sociosanitary structures were grossly deficient. In particular, the most vulnerable members of society, migrants, ethnic minorities, the ill and old, were tragically let down. Group attachment was not secure enough for them.

In the above circumstances, group-analytic psychotherapists and other mental health professionals need to develop a genuine sense of social consciousness alongside their clinical work. This may imply having to go beyond the comfort zone of the consulting room, in order to address problems effectively in the social, cultural and political arenas.

In a global world, for societies to survive and to grow in the longer term, fostering large-group solidarity, inclusiveness and benign group attachment is probably the best way forward. It is our personal and collective responsibility to contribute to that. It is necessary to create and inhabit group attachment spaces where everyone can find shelter, care and protection: ultimately, society as a secure-enough base.

1.3(iv) Attachment and wider group psychotherapy

Since the turn into the 21st century, a number of attachment-related researchers, scholars and clinicians have increasingly included core tenets of attachment theory into the practice of group psychotherapy. Overall, this is considered the most effective form of treatment to address and resolve relationship problems, in interpersonal and group contexts, as shown by Burlingame and Jensen (2017), in their summary of major research findings of the previous twenty-five years (1992–2017).

These authors concluded that, in addition to helping with relationship difficulties, group psychotherapy is an empirically well-supported treatment for a large number of psychiatric-related diagnoses, including anxiety, depression, bipolar disorder, social phobia, obsessive compulsive disorder, substance abuse, eating disorders, trauma, HIV/AIDS, breast cancer, chronic pain, schizophrenia and borderline personality disorder (Burlingame and Strauss, 2021; Whittingham, Marmarosh, Mallow and Scherer, 2023). In Chapters 2, 3, 4 and 5, the reader will also find a number of cases of qualitative clinical-process research that corroborate the effectiveness of this type of treatment.

Unlike individual psychotherapy, in which the main emphasis is on the relationship between therapist and patient, group psychotherapy offers patients good opportunities for identifying with, differentiating from and belonging to something bigger than themselves. They can make therapeutic use of these processes, establishing a meaningful connection, and often attachment, to fellow members *in* the group as well as *to* the group itself (Ezquerro and Cañete, 2023; Ezquerro, 2023; Tasca and Marmarosh, 2023).

Furthermore, not only do patients co-construct relationships with other members, they also develop an overall experience of the group climate or culture. Under optimal circumstances, they can become attached to this therapeutic and enabling group matrix (Ezquerro, 2017a, 2023; Flores, 2017; Marmarosh 2020, 2021; Marmarosh et al, 2022; Ezquerro and Cañete, 2023; Tasca and Marmarosh, 2023).

Certainly, in the last two decades, the study of attachment processes has significantly penetrated the field of group psychotherapy (Whittingham, Lefforge and Marmarosh (2021). This very much welcomed development and extension of attachment theory is influencing research and practice within the group treatment modality, as well as facilitating a richer understanding of dynamics of group leadership, group cohesion and coherency (see Chapter 5), and of the change process that occurs through group exchange.

It has become increasingly acceptable to suggest (implicitly or explicitly) that, within an appropriate group climate and benign therapeutic culture, patients can perceive the psychotherapy group as an attachment figure in its own right (Glenn, 1987; Ezquerro, 1991, 1996, 2017a, 2017b, 2023; Cañete and Ezquerro, 1999, 2012, 2017; Markin and Marmarosh, 2010; Flores, 2010, 2017; Marmarosh, Markin and Spiegel, 2013; Marmarosh and Tasca, 2013; Marmarosh, 2017, 2020, 2021; Ezquerro and Cañete, 2023; Joyce and Marmarosh, 2023).

In addition, the neurosciences have provided us with insights that focus on the crucial importance that recurring authentic face-to-face social interactions have on neural processes. Attachment theory has incorporated neuroscientific evidence to promote the creation of an enriched group environment that enhances opportunities for reliable engagements among group members (Flores, 2010, 2017; Gantt and Agazarian, 2011; Ezquerro, 2023; Kivlighan and Tasca, 2023).

In particular, Gantt and Agazarian (2011) studied the group's ability to act as a security provider, and how this affects individuals at the very level of neural integration. They found that supportive group experiences improve the regulation of the limbic circuit by the middle prefrontal area and, also, enhance the capability of the left hemisphere to provide a new, more functional, narrative.

Indeed, caring does good things to the brain, whether the person is receiving it or providing it, as it happens in group-analytic psychotherapy and other psychodynamic modalities of group treatment, in which patients can give and receive care (either at the same time or in succession) and, eventually, become a group of co-therapists (Ezquerro, 1989, 1996; Pines, 1998). Moreover, collaboration with fellow members and other healthy group attachment processes, whether in a group psychotherapy setting or otherwise, activate some of the pleasure centres of the brain – the same parts that are stimulated by *rewards* like food (Knapp, 2002).

Some contemporary researchers (Wajda and Makara-Studzińska, 2018b; Tasca, Mikail and Hewitt, 2021; Kivlighan and Tasca, 2023) have reviewed the main studies that examine how members' attachment patterns influence group processes, and how psychological defences and attachment relationships can change, even after group treatment has ended.

Definitely, research on attachment style in mental health treatment has primarily concentrated on dyadic attachment in individual psychotherapy, followed by the study of the dyadic attachment histories of individual members and their dyadic attachment patterns towards the group conductor and fellow members, as they find expression in the therapy group. Research on group attachment *per se*, meaning here the attachment style that each person shows towards the group-as-a-whole, has been overlooked in the literature, to a large extent.

There is empirical evidence that members with anxious-avoidant or dismissing attachment patterns encounter difficulties with therapeutic group dynamics such as connecting with other people, participating in intimate exchange and self-disclosure, and showing empathy. For these patients the effects of therapy are weaker, even if they remain in the group (Rom and Mikulincer, 2003; Shechtman and Rybko, 2004; Shechtman and Dvir, 2006).

On the other hand, Holtz (2005) found that members with anxious-preoccupied or ambivalent attachment patterns are more vulnerable to low self-esteem and depression. However, they participate more readily in psychodynamic group therapy, and display a higher level of covenant with the group, than people with avoidant attachment styles. These effects were not so clearly noted in groups with a cognitive-behavioural approach (Tasca et al, 2006).

In connection with that, Tasca and Balfour (2014) and Tasca, Balfour, Ritchie and Bissada (2007) found that group psychotherapy was particularly beneficial for patients with significantly anxious-preoccupied attachment patterns, as they became able to gradually form more secure dyadic relationships in the group, resulting in better regulation of affect and improved interpersonal skills.

Other studies have revealed that, for a large number of patients with various psychiatric diagnoses, a benign group climate or culture promotes lower levels of attachment anxiety and maximises the effectiveness of group psychotherapy (Kirchmann et al, 2012). Certainly, the perception of the group as a secure base can result not only in secure group attachment during the therapy, but also in improved interpersonal attachment when the group has ended (Cañete and Ezquerro, 2012; Maxwell et al, 2014; Ezquerro and Cañete, 2023).

In addition, Keating et al (2014) and Maxwell et al (2014), in their studies on homogeneous groups for women with binge eating disorders, found that most members developed secure-enough group attachment, which was related to more secure attachment in dyadic relationships one year after group therapy had ended.

In an innovative study, Marmarosh et al (2006) examined therapists' ratings of their own internal working models of their previous group experiences, and how these had an impact on the therapeutic process. They found that therapists with more group attachment anxiety assumed that patients would hold more negative myths and misconceptions, about group treatment, than therapists with less group attachment anxiety. Indeed, in psychodynamic approaches (individual and group), the handling of countertransference is key to good therapeutic outcomes.

Undeniably, although members' dyadic attachment styles are important in the group therapy context, they are nonetheless an incomplete picture of the whole group experience. In a previous subsection of this chapter, we discussed in detail a pioneering study on group attachment in the context of university life, by Smith, Murphy and Coats (1999). These social psychology researchers found that it was possible to have more or less secure dyadic attachments, whilst having less or more secure attachments to the group itself.

Members internal working models of their group attachment experience may certainly include images of oneself as a valuable or, otherwise, unworthy member of the group. And the group-as-a-whole might be perceived as warm, caring, supportive and enabling or, otherwise, rejecting or even persecuting.

As explained earlier, Smith, Murphy and Coats (1999) demonstrated empirically that attachment in dyadic relationships is a different construct from that of group attachment; both are interconnected and yet distinct. This relates to the fact that some of the needs that are addressed in the intimacy of the relationship with a partner, or carer, are dissimilar from those addressed in a group context. But there are overlaps.

Holtz and Marmarosh (2003) were amongst the first in properly examining group attachment styles in a group therapy context. They found that members' positive dynamics of group attachment enhanced group cohesiveness and helped develop a sense of collective self-esteem, which had a beneficial influence on therapeutic outcome.

In another study, Marmarosh et al (2009) further emphasised the links between group attachment and some of the most commonly employed group therapy constructs, such as group climate or culture, generic group cohesion and member attitude towards the group-as-a-whole.

Elaborating on that, Markin and Marmarosh (2010) specifically differentiated dyadic from group attachment styles and established several possible combinations. Members can show predominantly secure attachments to other individuals and to the group itself (secure-secure), insecure attachment to both (insecure-insecure), secure dyadic attachment but insecure group attachment (secure-insecure) or the other way around (insecure-secure).

In their outstanding work, these practitioners found that members with reasonably secure dyadic attachment styles but insecure group attachment (who often fear rejection by the group) can be protected from having a negative group experience and from dropping out of treatment, as they are able to connect and establish secure-enough attachment relationships with the group therapist and with fellow members.

According to Markin and Marmarosh (2010), when members do not experience the group itself as a secure base, but can perceive some of the other individual members as more secure attachment figures, they are likely to try to *subgroup* and avoid wider group intimacy. From an attachment theory perspective, subgrouping can be interpreted as an attempt to meet attachment needs from the internalised expectations that dyadic relationships are safer and more manageable than dealing with the whole group.

On the other hand, for members with a history of insecure interpersonal attachments, as stated by Bowlby (1969), group attachment may compensate for earlier developmental deficits in their dyadic attachments, as the group itself becomes a primary attachment figure, usually from adolescence onward. In cases like this (insecure-secure), the group-as-a-whole can be perceived as a secure-enough base.

These people are likely to show robust loyalty to the group, identify with it and feel they belong *in* it, whilst they struggle to form dyadic attachments.

Ruptures and disruption in early attachment relationships usually hinder the development of a capacity for emotional regulation, empathy and intimacy. Patients with such a background might be perceived, on the surface, as an easy-going group member, a dynamic that they might bring from their previous peer group or cultural group experiences (Ezquerro and Cañete, 2023). However, it is more difficult to get to know them and reach them at a deeper personal level.

Finally, Markin and Marmarosh (2010) referred to insecure-insecure members, particularly those with avoidant attachment styles, and found that, more often than not, they terminate group treatment prematurely and abruptly. This finding is consistent with previous research (Tasca et al, 2006).

Without any relational buffer to help regulate their affects, these patients are likely to develop a rather negative (and sometimes unmanageable) transference, coming from internal working models of neglectful or abusive attachment relationships in both interpersonal and group contexts. They are prone to feel overwhelmed and full of rage, as they relive early traumatic experiences. And they often resort to disoriented or disorganised attachment patterns.

A large number of group practitioners are reluctant to include patients with such a profile in their therapy groups, at least initially. Markin and Marmarosh suggested that a period of individual therapy is highly recommended, prior to inviting people with insecure dyadic and group attachment styles to enter group treatment. That is advisable, particularly for patients who need the one-to-one nurturing that they had not experienced in their lives.

Having said that, some people who have been severely abused and traumatised by their early carers or attachment figures may feel intimidated by and fearful of a close one-to-one therapeutic encounter. For these people, a psychotherapy group, with its diluted, less intense and more diverse *transferences*, might well be more bearable a treatment situation to start with. And it can be followed by individual psychotherapy at a later stage.

In the following chapters we will present a number of qualitative clinical-process research cases, including bipolar disorder, psychosis and schizoaffective disorder, as well as deeply disorganising sexual abuse and suicide risk. Group-analytic psychotherapy proved to be effective and beneficial for most of the patients, although it was sometimes necessary to combine it with individual psychotherapy or family therapy concurrently, and with a wider institutional group therapeutic containment.

On balance, for the composition of psychotherapy groups, we are in favour of heterogeneity of personalities, mental health problems and attachment styles, in order to maximise the group's therapeutic potential. This is consistent with Markin and Marmarosh's (2010) advice that a mix of secure and insecure patterns of dyadic and group attachment works better, as members can learn from each other' strengths and weaknesses. Indeed, interpersonal and vicarious learning processes are important therapeutic factors in group therapy (Pines, 1998).

As a further development in the application of attachment theory to group psychotherapy, there is an ongoing trend that includes helpful mentalisation-based insights. In particular, Fonagy, Gergely and Jurist (2002) and Fonagy, Campbell and Bateman (2017) postulated that, in healthy development, two crucial skills emerge from secure attachment experiences. These skills are critical to successfully navigating the social world:

1) An ability to take another's perspective, which is now widely called *mentalisation* or *reflective functioning*.
2) A capacity for developing basic trust in others, which has been conceptualised under the term *epistemic trust*.

Both of these capacities are adaptive to human survival and relate to wellbeing, relationship satisfaction and symptom remission; they can be vital tools for the effectiveness of group psychotherapy. When the group is functioning as a secure base, it facilitates members' ability to tolerate painful feelings and explore other people's minds (Marmarosh et al, 2022).

Building on this, Tasca, Mikail and Hewitt (2021) explored how attachment and reflective functioning can be further addressed in group psychotherapy, and how a dynamic-interpersonal approach can greatly facilitate the growth of such an important skill.

In connection with that, Bateman, Campbell and Fonagy (2021), Rutan (2021) and Bateman et al (2023) delineated how the process of repairing ruptures in group psychotherapy can promote reflective functioning, as group members seek to understand diverse perspectives and develop a capacity for tolerating and working through their differences (see Chapter 5).

Fonagy, Campbell and Bateman (2017) further described how trauma can disrupt epistemic trust because caregivers are inconsistent and become unreliable as sources of care and information. Traumatised adults (and groups) learn to reject communications from others and from outside groups, when these are incongruent with their own beliefs and viewpoints.

Indeed, these people can sometimes respond in an adaptive way to the, often painful, social environment around them. However, at other times, they are not open to new experiences. This defensive strategy to *protect* themselves from further trauma can be counterproductive, as it prevents them from taking in important information that could ultimately be useful in relational terms.

The application of attachment thinking into the broad field of group psychotherapy is gaining momentum, which reminds us of Bowlby' statement that the potential of attachment theory is unknown (Kraemer, Steele and Holmes, 2007).

Of course, the potential of the group-as-a-whole as an attachment figure in its own right, and the deeper nature of group attachment in the wider organisational and life context, have not been sufficiently studied yet. However, the landscape has been gradually changing, as outlined above.

For the reader interested in the evolution of the group attachment construct and its applications into group psychotherapy, we would highlight the following, comprehensive but not exhaustive, bibliography:

Smith, Murphy and Coats (1999), Cañete and Ezquerro (1999, 2012, 2017), Mikulincer and Shaver (2001, 2017, 2022), McCluskey (2002, 2007), Shechtman and Rybko (2004), Marmarosh et al (2006), Ezquerro and Bajaj (2007), Marmarosh et al (2009), Ezquerro (2010, 2017a, 2017b, 2023), Flores (2010, 2017), Markin and Marmarosh (2010), Page (2010), Marmarosh, Markin and Spiegel (2013), Marmarosh and Tasca (2013), Tasca (2014), Marmarosh (2014, 2017, 2020, 2021), Sochos (2015), Fonagy, Luyten and Allison (2015), Wajda and Makara-Studzińska (2018a, 2018b), Marmarosh, Forsyth, Strauss and Burlingame (2020), Rutan (2021), Tasca and Maxwell (2021), Marmarosh et al (2022), Ezquerro and Cañete (2023), Tasca and Marmarosh (2023).

Overall, these authors show many instances in which well-functioning psychotherapy groups come to constitute secure attachment spaces, within which personal and interpersonal changes occur. Group therapeutic processes include how attachment failures or ruptures can be safely explored, made sense of and repaired; how attunement, empathy and resilience can develop in the group and, in turn, how internal working models and attachment patterns can be modified.

But let us now explore the vicissitudes of group attachment in the wider organisational context.

1.3(v) Organisations as a group attachment space

As described in Section I of this chapter, human groups evolved into organisations through processes of *group selection* – the group equivalent to *natural selection*. Organisations and social institutions are complex group structures and crucial elements in our evolution, and in the shaping of society and culture.

A social institution is a group or organisation that has specific systems of roles, traditions, norms and expectations; it bands individuals together in search of common purposes, and functions to meet a range of individual and group needs in society. The family, government, religion, education and media are all examples of social institutions. Their common purposes include granting members certain rights and privileges, as well as expecting from them the accomplishment of some commitments and obligations (Nickerson, 2023).

Social institutions work as the backbone of a society, make it function and influence how it is structured. Without social institutions a society cannot achieve fulfilment in terms of economy, knowledge, relationships and, ultimately, survival and wellbeing.

A social institution is organised around the preservation of basic societal values. Whilst laypersons are likely to use the term *institution* loosely, sociologists tend to describe social institutions in terms of their key characteristics, as outlined by Nickerson (2023):

1. They are meant to be enduring and stable.
2. They serve a common purpose, ideally providing better chances for human survival and flourishing.
3. They have roles that need to be filled.
4. They govern the behaviour and expectations of individuals within a given community.
5. The rules that govern them are usually ingrained in the basic cultural values of society.

The expression *organisational attachment* has been used to describe the level of attachment and security that individuals have in their organisations. It is essentially a form of group attachment that contains a set of psychological contracts (either explicit or implicit) between the organisation and its members or employees. According to Sung et al (2017), organisational group attachment consists of perceptions of:

a) The level of job security offered.
b) Job satisfaction.
c) Job continuity – whether their roles change or stay the same.
d) Distributive justice – how employees feel they and their department or team are treated compared to other groups.
e) Personal statuses – which include both social status and comparative status within the organisation.

At this point, we would like to share with the reader an idea that any organisation can be usefully conceived as a potential *group attachment space*. We are partly borrowing this idea from the late John Southgate, who proposed looking at organisations as an *attachment space* (Southgate, 1996). He was a symbolic *sibling* of ours, as we shared with him some of our supervision with John Bowlby – a powerful organisational experience in its own right.

There are several elements that have a significant impact on the nature and functioning of organisations; for instance, the fact that people often bring to the workplace and to other group configurations to which they belong, or to which they are connected, some aspects of their attachment histories (conscious and unconscious), including their unresolved or unprocessed trauma. The latter is particularly relevant to psychoanalysis, psychotherapy, psychology, psychiatry and other mental health institutions, as beautifully put across by Mark Linington (2012).

In a diversity of contexts, we establish interpersonal attachments *in* the organisation, as well as a distinct group attachment *to* the organisation as-a-whole. In training organisations, like the Institute of Psychoanalysis or the Institute of Group Analysis, it is possible to identify many significant attachment-related events; some of these can be particularly powerful.

We can recall the first session with our assessor or with our training analyst; the first evening with our training group; or the first meeting with our tutor, manager or supervisor. All these events can stay with us as nodal attachment experiences, and can evoke other events originally belonging to earlier stages in our lives.

The intimate diet we are exposed to during our training and our work, and the way in which it is linked to previous attachment relationships, will have an impact on the quality of our group attachment to the organisation, as well as on our perception of it as a group attachment space.

1.3(vi) Conceptualising group attachment

As originally stated by Smith, Murphy and Coats (1999), group attachment usually refers to internal working models of social, organisational or therapy groups. As studied in their social group attachment scales, these multiple models provide new insights into the nature of people's psychological ties to groups and can also be characterised as secure, insecure-preoccupied or insecure-avoidant. Group attachment predicts several important outcomes, including care, protection, support and other emotions concerning group life, as well as time and activities shared with group members, collective self-esteem and ways of resolving conflict.

Edward Lawler (2007) provided a definition of group attachments (in the plural) as the strength of the ties that individuals have to a social unit (e.g. local groups, larger organisations, communities and other institutions). Such attachments presuppose an existing group membership or group identity (e.g. definitions of self and others in terms of group connections and relationships).

Lawler further elaborated that group attachments can be construed as a mechanism through which large, impersonal organisations generate and sustain high levels of group-oriented behaviour, such as citizenship, commitments and obligations.

These attachments to the organisation may be even more important when members are physically separated and communicate from a distance, as it is more and more common in the workplaces of today.

Group attachments may also be important if the organisation moves managers or employees frequently to different locations, or if there are significant costs associated with turnover. Affective ties in which the organisational identity becomes self-defining for employees should have strong effects on their willingness to make personal sacrifices for the organisation.

According to Baldassarri and Grossman (2013), group attachment is a dispositional mechanism that transcends proximity to and knowledge of a specific member of the group, and that can be defined as the strength of one's identification with a given group, in which the stronger the identification, the more willing an individual member will be to share resources with other group members.

Group attachment can also be viewed as a generalisation from past experiences, extending them to a broader set of people. Exposure to a subset of in-group members fosters positive expectations about the group in general, leading one to perceive its members as more honest, friendly and trustworthy than members of out-groups.

Empirically, however, social identity theory studies are unable to isolate the effect of group attachment from that of social proximity: both mechanisms are simultaneously at work in most group experiences. Group identification often originates from interactions within the group: people are likely to be more familiar with in-group members, and have more information about their needs, deeds and priorities (Baldassarri and Grossman, 2013).

Adopting an identity-based conception of social proximity or distance, a few studies have demonstrated that individuals are more willing to make deeper connections with in-group than out-group members. In-group favouritism has been observed not only where group membership was based on ascribed categories, such as ethnicity, religion or political partisanship, but also in cases where it was randomly assigned, as well as in laboratory settings where scholars induced minimal or trivial group identities (Sochos, 2015).

No doubt, a person's sense of self is related to his or her experiences of social identity and group attachment. Once people identify themselves as part of a group, they are likely to behave in prescribed or expected ways towards other members, as well as to the group-as-a-whole.

As further stated by Baldassarri and Grossman (2013), personal and group identities result from processes of categorisation, identification and comparison, in which individuals (including oneself) are classified into groups by context-specific attributes. The ego's prosocial behaviour toward a person classified as an in-group member does not (necessarily) stem from their proximity; rather, it is (at least partially) derived from the ego's level of attachment to the shared group.

Attachment from person-to-group is embodied in individuals' beliefs about themselves as valuable or less valuable group members, along with their beliefs about the group's acceptance or rejection of them (Smith, Murphy and Coats, 1999; Smith, Coats and Murphy, 2001).

More specifically, when individuals have positive beliefs about themselves as worthy members of a group and view the group as accepting of them, they are referred to as having secure affectional bonds to this particular group, and they develop a secure-enough group attachment style. Just as children with secure affectional ties to their caregivers feel less threatened and more adventurous, group members whose affectional ties to groups are secure feel likewise safer to explore (Lee and Ling, 2007).

Edward Lawler (2007) studied the role of shared responsibility in the development of affective group attachments, interweaving ideas from social exchange and social identity theories. In summary, he presented three main arguments:

1) People engaged in task interaction would inevitably experience positive or negative emotions from those interactions.
2) Tasks that promote more sense of shared responsibility across members lead people to attribute their individual emotions to groups or organisations.
3) Group attributions of own emotions are the basis for stronger or weaker group attachments.

Lawler concluded that social categorisation and structural interdependence promote healthy group attachment, by producing task interactions that have positive emotional effects on those involved. Indeed, people have mental models of their own selves as group members, as well as of groups as sources of identity, esteem and attachment. These models affect thoughts, emotions and behaviours related to group membership.

Two of the common dimensions of attachment to groups, such as attachment preoccupation and avoidance, can be assessed with good reliability, validity and over-time stability. These group domains are distinct from (though related to) dyadic attachments and from other measures of group identification (Smith, Murphy and Coats, 1999). Further research from other social psychologists have linked group identities to self-esteem enhancement, self- protection during threat, and emotion regulation (Forsyth, 2014).

Moreover, as discussed earlier, group attachment predicts several important outcomes, including emotions concerning the group, time and activities shared with such a group, social support, collective self-esteem and ways of resolving conflict. This comprehensive conceptualisation provides new insights into the nature of people's psychological ties to groups.

In the context of our multidisciplinary (and interdisciplinary) study, it is important to delineate how attachment to groups departs from alternate constructs. For example, group attachment is interconnected with, yet distinct from, group identification (Tajfel and Turner, 1979). Whereas group identification is an individual's cognitive self-identity, based on an overlapping of personal attributes with those of the group (Turner et al, 1987; Dutton, Dukerich and Harquail, 1994; Smith and Henry, 1996), group attachment is a personalised affect-driven relationship tie to the group (Ezquerro and Cañete, 2023).

There are overlaps, since both group attachment and group identification can lead people to favour fellow members over non-members (Mullen, Brown and Smith, 1992), to describe themselves as prototypical group members (Spears, Doosje and Ellemers, 1997), and to cooperate with other members, even putting the interests of the group above personal interests (Turner et al, 1987; Karau and Williams, 1997).

We discussed earlier that, in the attachment and group psychotherapy literature, the term group attachment has been usually employed to describe the various attachment styles or patterns that members establish in their relationship with the group-as-a-whole. This makes sense, particularly in terms of facilitating quantitative research.

Having said that, *within* the group itself, relationships are complex, multilayered and multidirectional, involving interpersonal, multipersonal and even *transpersonal* connections, which play a significant part in the shaping of an overall sense of group attachment. There are many elements located in-between members, at conscious as well as unconscious levels, which contribute to the formation of what has been described as group mentality (Bion, 1961), group matrix (Foulkes, 1964), social unconscious (Hopper, 1996, 2023), group culture (Weinberg, 2003), group climate (Markin and Marmarosh, 2010) and group attachment (Ezquerro and Cañete, 2023).

In the group-analytic literature the *group matrix* construct is widely used to describe the common shared ground that ultimately determines meaning and significance, and upon which all communications and interpretations (verbal and non-verbal) resonate and rest (Foulkes, 1964, Glenn, 1987).

Foulkes (1973) further differentiated two core elements in this construct: a *foundation* group matrix that is constituted by past family, cultural and other social experiences, and a *dynamic* group matrix that emerges through the interactions and relationships, taking place as part of group processes, in the here-and-now.

It is obvious that, Foulkes' foundation group matrix contains previous experiences of dyadic and group attachment, since childhood, which will have an impact on the dynamic group matrix of the group's ongoing therapy sessions.

Consequently, we would prefer to put across a broader conception of *group attachment* as a useful construct for group analysis, group psychotherapy and other therapeutic disciplines, as well as for the understanding of human evolution and survival, organisations, intra-group and inter-group relations, and personal development.

In this sense, considering the evolutionary roots of attachment as an in-built system that serves survival, we would like to revisit a definition that one of us proposed elsewhere, amalgamating and integrating insights and outsights from the group-analytic and attachment schools of thought:

> Group attachment can be conceived as a construct that brings together a complex constellation of attachment relationships, *in* the group, *to* the group and *with* the group; that is, with its members, its leaders and the group-as-a-whole, with a view to maximising survival, growth and creativity as individuals, human organisation and species.
>
> (Ezquerro, 2019d, 2022)

This formulation is the result of what we have learned over time. Initially, from our work with John Bowlby during six years, followed by our study of the attachment and group psychotherapy literature and our practice as group analysts, for more than three decades.

Our conception of the group attachment construct is meant to stimulate further revision and discussion on the subject and, in light of future research and developments from the group-analytic and attachment fields, it is open to nuances, variations, evolution and refinement.

As an outstanding theory-builder, Bowlby (1974, 1991b) was precise and rigorous. He taught us that a good theory must not only make sense in terms of the validity of its formulations, but it should also be capable of guiding clinicians to improve their practice, as well as mapping new directions for future research and validation. He emphasised that such a theory should be open to revision, expansion and refinement, in order to accommodate itself to novel data obtained via new observations or explorations.

The group attachment construct that we propose is consistent with John Bowlby's (1969) formulation of some of the processes involved in the co-construction of attachment to the group itself, which is often mediated by and include attachment to leaders and to other people holding a prominent position within the group, as he put it. In this way, group attachment overlaps with and encompasses interpersonal and multipersonal attachment.

Indeed, in psychotherapy groups, the quintessential and life-long human need to give and receive care, support and protection is readily activated and, optimally, fosters healthy group attachment. Group exchange, with its giving and receiving ingredients, is at the core of attachment relationships and makes life more meaningful.

Furthermore, with our broad group-analytic and attachment perspective, and in line with Sochos' (2015) ideas, we would like to maximise the potential of attachment theory to include a larger organisational, sociocultural and political dimension, which can provide valuable links between not only personal and interpersonal domains, but also purposeful connections in small, large and global group contexts.

Of course, there are some dangers. Elaborating on from John Eipper's (president of the World Association of International Studies) contribution in the preliminary pages of this volume:

> the evolutionary and universal need for group belonging and group attachment can be exploited by nefarious leaders, pushing the collective to act in ways unthinkable to individuals, who in fact become attached to ideological (and often murderous) systems, when they feel their own and their country's survival is at stake (see Chapter 6).

We are aware that our approach might be perceived as a *huge leap*. Having said that, we are clear that humanity needs a fundamental shift, a radical change, a group attachment *re(e)volution* in the current context of dehumanising military conflict and cruelty towards the *other*, as well as the carelessness of neoliberal policies contributing to our planet's global warming and its concomitant threat to life itself.

During the Pleistocene, group attachment was a necessary base for our survival as a species. *Mutatis mutandis*, healthy group attachment has to be, once more, key to working through and surviving the unprecedented challenges we are facing in the 21st century.

1.4 Conclusion

Human attachment is an evolutionarily rooted, species-wide in-built system to connect meaningfully with a social environment in order to survive. The attachment system is flexible enough to allow for adaptation to local environmental conditions; neuroscientific evidence of plasticity supports this.

Attachment theory has, indeed, been grounded in the notion of humans' strong motivation to survive and, therefore, it might be employed to explain a wide range of behaviours, feelings, thoughts and relationships in multiple group contexts.

Moreover, the growing use of the group attachment construct is expanding the theory and influencing research and practice in the group psychotherapy field, as well as facilitating a richer understanding of group leadership, group cohesion and coherency, and the process of change that occurs through group exchange.

In order to ascertain the vicissitudes of interpersonal and group attachment, it is necessary to include the cultural, sociopolitical and other contextual aspects of people's diverse group lives that put flesh on the skeleton of the attachment system.

Healthy personal development depends on how well an individual balances the need for care, protection and felt security with the need for exploration and mastery of the social world and the wider environment. This requires an equilibrium between person-to-person attachment and person-to-group attachment, and involves a kind of autonomy that can recognise the functioning and principles of each particular group, in order to decide whether being a member is worthwhile.

Mainstream attachment theory needs to account more for the broad range of developmental pathways known to exist in human societies. Further input from evolutionary anthropologists as well as from cross-cultural and ethnographically-informed research would strengthen the theory. A more ecologically and culturally sophisticated attachment research agenda would provide more sensitive and appropriate intervention strategies for use in both clinical and community settings, as well as in society at large.

The premise that *group attachment created humankind* has been qualified empirically by the fact that, without the unprecedented and distinct collaborative nature of human group attachment, early hominins would not have evolved into modern humans and, as a species, we would not have come this far on our evolutionary path.

In the real world we live in, equal to how an individual cannot exist apart from and outside the social context, there is no such thing as an individual or dyadic attachment which does not include group attachment.

References

Adshead G (1998) Psychiatric staff as attachment figures. *British Journal of Psychiatry* 172(1): 64–69.

Aiello LC and Key C (2002) Energetic consequences of being a *Homo erectus* female. *American Journal of Human Biology* 14(5): 551–565.

Antón SC (2012) Early *Homo*: Who, When, and Where. *Current Anthropology* 53(6): 278–298.

Baldassarri D and Grossman G (2013) The effect of group attachment and social position on prosocial behavior. Evidence from lab-in-the-field experiments. *PLoS One* 8(3): e58750. Available at: https://journals.plos.org/plosone/article?id=10.1371/journal.pone.0058750.

Bank S and Kahn M (1997) *The Sibling Bond.* New York: Basic Books.

Barlow K (2013) Attachment and culture in Murik society: Learning autonomy and interdependence through kinship, food, and gender. In Quinn N and Mageo JM (eds) *Attachment Reconsidered: Cultural Perspectives on a Western Society*. New York: Palgrave Macmillan, pp. 165–188.

Bateman A, Campbell C and Fonagy P (2021) Rupture and repair in mentalization-based group psychotherapy. *International Journal of Group Psychotherapy* 71(2): 371–392.

Bateman A, Fonagy P, Campbell C, Luyten P and Debbané M (2023) *Cambridge Guide to Mentalization-Based Treatment (MBT)*. Cambridge Guides to the Psychological Therapies. Cambridge: Cambridge University Press.

Bateman A and Fonagy P (2019) Mentalization-based treatment for borderline and antisocial personality disorder. In: Kealy D and Ogrodniczuk JS (eds) *Contemporary Psychodynamic Psychotherapy: Evolving clinical practice*. London: Elsevier Academic Press, pp. 133–148.

Belsky J and de Haan M (2011) Annual research review. Parenting and children's brain development: the end of the beginning. *Journal of Child Psychology and Psychiatry* 52(4): 409–428.

Bion WR (1961) *Experiences in Groups and Other Papers*. London: Tavistock Publications.

Blackwell D (2023) The dialectics of Chat: Privilege, power and institutional racism. *Group Analysis* 56(4): 541–557.

Bobe R, Behrensmeyer AK and Chapman RE (2002) Faunal change, environmental variability, and late Pliocene hominin evolution. *Journal of Human Evolution* 42(4): 475–497.

Boehm C (1999) *Hierarchy in the Forest: The Evolution of Egalitarian Behavior*. Cambridge, MA: Harvard University Press.

Boehm C (2012) *Moral Origins*. New York: Basic Books.

Bowlby J (1940) The influence of early environment in the development of neurosis and neurotic character. *International Journal of Psychoanalysis* 21: 154–178.

Bowlby J (1951) *Maternal Care and Mental Health*. Geneva: World Health Organization.

Bowlby J (1958) The nature of the child's tie to his mother. *International Journal of Psychoanalysis* 39: 350–373.

Bowlby J (1959) The roots of human personality. In Halmos P and Iliffe A (eds) *Readings in General Psychology*. London: Routledge & Kegan Paul, pp. 108–129.

Bowlby J (1969) *Attachment and Loss. Vol 1: Attachment* (1991 edition). London: Penguin Books.

Bowlby J (1973) *Attachment and Loss. Vol 2: Separation, Anxiety and Anger* (1991 edition). London: Penguin Books.

Bowlby J (1974) Problems of marrying research with clinical and social needs. In Connolly K and Bruner J (eds) *The Growth of Competence*. London: Academic Press, pp. 303–307.

Bowlby J (1980) *Attachment and Loss. Vol 3: Loss, Sadness and Depression* (1991 edition). London: Penguin Books.

Bowlby J (1984) Violence in the family as a disorder of the attachment and care-giving systems. *The American Journal of Psychoanalysis*, 44(1): 9–27.

Bowlby J (1988a) *A Secure Base: Clinical Applications of Attachment Theory*. London: Routledge.

Bowlby J (1988b) Developmental Psychiatry Comes of Age. *American Journal of Psychiatry* 145(1): 1–10.

Bowlby J (1991a) The role of the psychotherapist's personal resources in the treatment situation. In: Duschinsky R and White K (eds) *Trauma and Loss: Key Texts from the John Bowlby Archive* (2020). Abingdon: Routledge, pp. 214–223.

Bowlby J (1991b) Postscript. In: Parkes CM, Stevenson-Hinde J and Marris P (eds) *Attachment Across the Life Cycle*. London and New York: Tavistock/Routledge, pp. 293–297.

Bowlby J and Robertson J (1952a) A two-year-old goes to hospital: A scientific film. *Proceedings of the Royal Society of Medicine* 46(6): 425–427.

Bowlby J and Robertson J (1952b). Recent trends in the care of deprived children in the UK. *Bulletin of the World Federation for Mental Health* 4(3): 131–139.

Bowles S (2006) Group competition, reproductive leveling, and the evolution of human altruism. *Science* 314(5805): 1569–1572.

Bowles S (2009) Did warfare among ancestral hunter-gatherers affect the evolution of human social behaviors? *Science* 324(5932): 1293–1298.

Boyd R (2006) The puzzle of human sociality. *Science* 314(5805): 1555–1556.

Burkart JM, Hrdy SB and Van Schaik CP (2009) Cooperative breeding and human cognitive evolution. *Evolutionary Anthropology: Issues, News, and Reviews* 18(5): 175–186.

Burkart, JM and Van Schaik CP (2010) Cognitive consequences of cooperative breeding in primates. *Animal Cognition* 13(1): 1–19.

Burlingame GM and Jensen J (2017) Small Group Process and Outcome Research Highlights: A 25-Year Perspective. *International Journal of Group Psychotherapy* 67(sup 1): S194–S218.

Burlingame GM and Strauss B (2021) Efficacy of small group treatments: Foundation for evidence-based practice. In: Barkham N, Lutz W and Castonguay LG (eds) *Bergin and Garfield's Handbook of Psychotherapy and Behavior Change: 50th anniversary edition*. Hoboken, NJ: John Wiley & Sons, pp. 583–624.

Burman E (2021) Frantz Fanon and revolutionary group praxis. *Group Analysis* 54(2): 169–188.

Cañete M and Ezquerro A (1999) Group-Analytic Psychotherapy of Psychosis. *Group Analysis* 32(4): 507–514.

Cañete M and Ezquerro A (2012) Bipolar Affective Disorders and Group Analysis. *Group Analysis* 45(2): 203–217.

Cañete M and Ezquerro A (2017) Developing a group-analytic culture in a day-project for psychotic patients. *Psychosis* 9(2): 149–156.

Caparrós N (ed) (2004) *Y el Grupo Creó al Hombre*. Madrid: Biblioteca Nueva.

Chapin BL (2013) Attachment in rural Sri Lanka: the shape of caregiver sensitivity, communication and autonomy. In Quinn N and Mageo JM (eds) *Attachment Reconsidered: Cultural Perspectives on a Western Society*. New York: Palgrave Macmillan, pp. 143–163.

Chisholm JS (1996) The evolutionary ecology of attachment organization. *Human Nature* 7(1): 1–37.

Cortés López, JL (2009) *Diccionario histórico-etnográfico de los pueblos de África*. Madrid: Mundo Negro.

Cortina M and Liotti G (2010) Attachment is about safety and protection, intersubjectivity is about sharing and social understanding. The relationships between attachment and intersubjectivity. *Psychoanalytic Psychology* 27(4): 410–441.

Cox M (1995) *Structuring the Therapeutic Process: Compromise with Chaos. The Therapist's Response to the Individual and the Group*. London: Jessica Kingsley Publishers.

Crittenden AN and Marlowe FW (2013) Cooperative child care among the Hadza: Situating multiple attachment in evolutionary context. In Quinn N and Mageo JM (eds) *Attachment Reconsidered: Cultural Perspectives on a Western Society*. New York: Palgrave Macmillan, pp. 67–83.

Dunbar RIM (2012) Bridging the bonding gap: the transition from primates to humans. *Philosophical Transactions of the Royal Society of London, Series B: Biological Sciences* 367(1597): 1837–1846.

Dunbar RIM (2022) Laughter and its role in the evolution of human social bonding. *Philosophical Transactions of the Royal Society of London, Series B: Biological Sciences* 377(1863): 20210176.

Dunn J (2014) Sibling relationships across the life-span. In: Hindle D and Sherwin-White S (eds) *Sibling Matters: A Psychoanalytic, Developmental and Systemic Approach*. London: Karnac Books, pp. 69–81.

Dutton JE, Dukerich JM and Harquail CV (1994) Organizational images and member identification. *Administrative Science Quarterly* 39(2): 239–263.

Engels F (1876) The part played by labour in the transition from ape to man. In Engels F (ed) *Dialectics of Nature (1883)*. London: Wellred (2012).

Ettin M (1992) *Foundations and Applications of Group Psychotherapy: A Sphere of Influence*. Boston, MA: Allyn and Bacon.

Ettin M (2001) A psychotherapy group as a sociopolitical context: The case of the 'silent majority'. *Group Analysis* 34(1): 39–54.

Ezquerro A (1989) Group psychotherapy with the pre-elderly. *Group Analysis* 22(3): 299–308.

Ezquerro A (1991) *Attachment and its Circumstances: Does it Relate to Group Analysis?* Theoretical dissertation for membership of the Institute of Group Analysis (IGA). Archives IGA Library, London.

Ezquerro A (1995) Group Therapy within the NHS III: Should we invest in Group Psychotherapy? A Personal Account. *Group Analysis* 28(4): 453–457.

Ezquerro A (1996) The Tavistock and Group-Analytic Approaches to Group Psychotherapy: A Trainee's Perspective. *Psychoanalytic Psychotherapy* 10(2): 155–170.

Ezquerro A (2004) El grupo en la clínica. Segunda parte: Enfoques grupo-analíticos. En Caparrós N (ed) *Y el Grupo Creó al Hombre*. Madrid: Biblioteca Nueva, pp. 212–227.

Ezquerro A (2010) Cohesion and Coherency in Group Analysis. *Group Analysis* 43(4): 496–504.

Ezquerro A (2015) John Bowlby: The Timeless Supervisor. *Attachment: New Directions in Psychotherapy and Relational Psychoanalysis* 9(2): 165–175.

Ezquerro A (2017a) *Encounters with John Bowlby: Tales of Attachment*. London: Routledge.

Ezquerro A (2017b) *Relatos de apego: Encuentros con John Bowlby*. Madrid: Psimática.

Ezquerro A (2019a) Sexual abuse: a perversion of attachment? *Group Analysis* 52(1): 100–113.

Ezquerro A (2019b) Europe: What Europe? Paper presented at The Brexit Conference. Institute of Group Analysis, London (26 January).

Ezquerro A (2019c) The power of group work: Personal recollections on Peter Bruggen. *Group Analysis* 52(3): 362–374.

Ezquerro A (2019d) The Power of Group Attachment. Paper presented at Group Analysis North Open Seminar. University of Manchester, UK (8 November).

Ezquerro A (2020a) Brexit: Who is afraid of group attachment? Part I. Europe: what Europe? *Group Analysis* 53(2): 234–254.

Ezquerro A (2020b) Attachment and survival in the face of Covid-19. *Attachment: New Directions in Psychotherapy and Relational Psychoanalysis* 14: 171–187.

Ezquerro A (2021a) Brexit: Who is afraid of group attachment? Part II. Democracy: what democracy? *Group Analysis* 54(2): 265–283.

Ezquerro A (2021b) Captain Aguilera and filicide: An attachment-based exploration. *Attachment: New Directions in Psychotherapy and Relational Psychoanalysis* 15: 279–297.

Ezquerro A (2022) El Poder del Apego Grupal. Paper presented at The Power of Group Attachment Conference. International Attachment Network, Quito, Ecuador (15 January).

Ezquerro A (2023) *Apego y Desarrollo a lo largo de la vida: El poder del apego grupal*. Madrid: Editorial Sentir.

Ezquerro A and Bajaj P (2007) Combining individual and group-analytic psychotherapy: When the group is not enough, or is it? *Group: The Journal of the Eastern Group Psychotherapy Society* 31(1–2): 5–16.

Ezquerro A and Cañete M (2023) *Group Analysis throughout the Life Cycle: Foulkes Revisited from a Group Attachment and Developmental Perspective*. London and New York: Routledge.

Flores PJ (2010) Group psychotherapy and neuro-plasticity: an attachment theory perspective. *International Journal of Group Psychotherapy* 60(4): 546–70.

Flores PJ (2017) Attachment Theory and Group Psychotherapy. *International Journal of Group Psychotherapy* 67(sup1): S50–S59.

Fonagy P and Bateman A (2008) The development of borderline personality disorder: A mentalizing model. *Journal of Personality Disorders* 22: 4–21.

Fonagy P, Campbell C and Bateman A (2017) Mentalizing, Attachment, and Epistemic Trust in Group Therapy. *International Journal of Group Psychotherapy* 67(2): 176–201.

Fonagy P, Gergely G and Jurist EL (2002) *Affect Regulation, Mentalization and the Development of the Self.* London: Routledge.

Fonagy P, Luyten P and Allison E (2015) Epistemic petrification and the restoration of epistemic trust: A new conceptualization of borderline personality disorder and its psychosocial treatment. *Journal of Personality Disorders* 29(5): 575–609.

Forsyth DR (2014) *Group Dynamics.* Belmont, CA: Wadsworth Cengage Learning.

Foulkes SH (1948) *Introduction to Group Analytic Psychotherapy.* London: Heinemann.

Foulkes SH (1964) *Therapeutic Group Analysis.* London: George Allen & Unwin.

Foulkes SH (1969) *Psychothérapie et Analyse de Groupe* [Psychotherapy and Group Analysis]. Paris: Payot.

Foulkes SH (1973) The Group as Matrix of the Individual's Mental Life. In: Foulkes E (ed) (1990) *SH Foulkes Selected Papers: Psychoanalysis and Group Analysis.* London: Karnac Books, pp. 223–234.

Freud A and Burlingham D (1944) *Infants without Families.* London: Allen & Unwin.

Freud A and Dann S (1951) An experiment in group upbringing. *Psychoanalytic Study of the Child* 6: 127–168.

Freud S (1922) Group Psychology and the Analysis of the Ego. In: Strachey (ed) *The Standard Edition of the Complete Psychological Works of Sigmund Freud* (Vol. 18). London: The Hogarth Press, pp. 64–143.

Gantt SP and Agazarian YM (2011) The group mind, systems-centred functional subgrouping, and interpersonal neurobiology. In Hopper E and Weinberg H (eds) *The Social Unconscious in Persons, Groups, and Societies.* London: Karnac Books, pp. 99–123.

Gaskins S (2013) The puzzle of attachment: Unscrambling maturational and cultural contributions to the development of early emotional bonds. In Quinn N and Mageo JM (eds) *Attachment Reconsidered: Cultural Perspectives on a Western Society.* New York: Palgrave Macmillan, pp. 33–64.

Gergely G and Jacob P (2012) Reasoning about instrumental and communicative agency in human infancy. In Benson JB, Xu F and Kushnir T (eds) *Advances in Child Development and Behavior Vol 43: Rational Constructivism in Cognitive Development.* Waltham, MA: Academic Press/Elsevier, pp. 59–94.

Gladwell M (2012) *The Tipping Point: How Little Things Make a Big Difference.* London: Abacus.

Glenn L (1987) The group matrix as a secure base. *Group Analysis* 20(2): 109–126.

Godlee F (2020) Racism: The other pandemic. *British Medical Journal* 8249: 378.

Haidt J (2013) *The Righteous Mind: Why Good People are Divided by Politics and Religion.* London: Penguin.

Hamilton WD (1964) The genetical evolution of social behaviour. I. *Journal of Theoretical Biology* 7(1): 1–16.

Harari YN (2014) *Sapiens: A Brief History of Humankind.* London: Vintage Books.

Herrmann E, Call J, Hernández-Lloreda MV, Hare B and Tomasello M (2007) Humans have evolved specialized skills of social cognition: The cultural intelligence hypothesis. *Science* 317(5843): 1360–1366.

Hindle D and Sherwin-White S (eds) (2014) *Sibling Matters: A Psychoanalytic, Developmental and Systemic Approach*. London: Karnac Books.

Holtz A (2005) Measuring the therapy group attachment in group psychotherapy: A validation of the social group attachment scale. *Dissertation Abstracts International: Section B. Sciences and Engineering* 65(9): 4832.

Holtz A and Marmarosh C (2003) Cohesiveness or the collective identity: Predicting well-being in therapy group members. Poster presented at the Annual Meeting of the American Psychological Association, Toronto, Canada (7–10 August).

Hopper E (1996) The Social Unconscious in Clinical Work. *Group* 20(1): 7–42.

Hopper E (2003) *The Social Unconscious: Selected Papers*. London: Jessica Kingsley Publishers.

Hopper E (2023) Foreword. In: Ezquerro A and Cañete M *Group Analysis throughout the Life Cycle: Foulkes Revisited from a Group Attachment and Developmental Perspective*. London and New York: Routledge, pp. xvii–xix.

Howes C and Spieker S (2008) Attachment relationships in the context of multiple caregivers. In: Cassidy J and Shaver PR (eds) *Handbook of Attachment: Theory, Research, and Clinical Applications*. New York: The Guilford Press, pp. 317–332.

Hrdy SB (2009) *Mothers and Others: The Evolutionary Origins of Human Understanding*. Cambridge, MA: The Belknap Press of Harvard University Press.

Iacobucci G (2020) PHE review has failed ethnic minorities. *British Medical Journal* 8249: 386–387.

Joyce AS and Marmarosh C (2023) Group Selection, Group Composition and Pre-Group Preparation. In: MacNair-Semands R and Whittingham M (eds) *Group Psychotherapy Assessment and Practice: A Measurement-Based Care Approach*. London: Routledge.

Jungers WL (1988) Lucy's length: Stature reconstruction in *Australopithecus afarensis* (A.L.288–1) with implications for other small-bodied hominids. *American Journal of Physical Anthropology* 76(2): 227–231.

Karau, SJ and Williams KD (1997) The effects of group cohesiveness on social loafing and social compensation. *Group Dynamics Theory Research and Practice* 1(2): 156–168.

Keating L, Tasca GA, Gick M, Ritchie K, Balfour L and Bissada H (2014) Change in attachment to the therapy group generalizes to change in individual attachment among women with binge eating disorder. *Psychotherapy* 51(1): 78–87.

Keller H (2013) Attachment and Culture. *Journal of Cross-Cultural Psychology* 44(2): 175–194.

Kirchmann H, Steyer R, Mayer A, Joraschky P, Schreiber-Willnow K and Strauss B (2012) Effects of adult inpatient group psychotherapy on attachment characteristics: An observational study comparing routine care to an untreated comparison group. *Psychotherapy Research* 22(1): 95–114.

Kirkinis K, Pieterse AL, Martin C, Agiliga A, Brownell A (2021) Racism, racial discrimination, and trauma: a systematic review of the social science literature. *Ethnicity and Health* 26(3): 392–412.

Kivlighan M and Tasca GA (2023) Assessing Outcomes in Group Psychotherapy. In: MacNair-Semands R and Whittingham M (eds) *Group Psychotherapy Assessment and Practice: A Measurement-Based Care Approach*. London: Routledge.

Knapp L (2002) Brains Want to Cooperate. *Science* (24 July). Available at www.wired.com/2002/07/study-brains-want-to-cooperate/

Konner M (2010) *The Evolution of Childhood: Relationships, Emotion, Mind*. Cambridge, MA: Harvard University Press.

Kraemer S and Roberts J (eds) (1996) *The Politics of Attachment: Towards a Secure Society*. London: Free Association Books.

Kraemer S, Steele H and Holmes J (2007) A tribute to the legacy of John Bowlby at the centenary of his birth. *Attachment and Human Development* 9(4): 303–306.

Kropotkin PA (1908) *Mutual Aid: A Factor of Evolution*. London: Heinemann.

Lawler EJ (2007) Affect and Group Attachments: The Role of Shared Responsibility. In: Mannix E, Neale MA and Cameron PA (eds) *Research on Managing Groups and Teams, Vol. 10: Affect and Groups*. Leeds: Emerald Publishing Ltd, pp. 185–216.

Lee S and Ling S (2007) Understanding Affectional Ties to Groups from the Perspective of Attachment Theory. In: Mannix E, Neale MA and Cameron PA (eds) *Research on Managing Groups and Teams, Vol. 10: Affect and Groups*. Leeds: Emerald Publishing Ltd, pp. 217–248.

Lewin K (1939) Field Theory and Experiment in Social Psychology. *American Journal of Sociology* 44(6): 868–896.

Linington M (2012) Attachment, Trauma, and Organisations. *Attachment: New Directions in Psychotherapy and Relational Psychoanalysis* 6: 232–248.

McCluskey U (2002) The Dynamics of Attachment and Systems-Centred Group Psychotherapy. *Group Dynamics: Theory, Research, and Practice*, 6(2): 131–142.

McCluskey U (2007) A Model of Group Psychotherapy Based on Extended Attachment Theory: A Preliminary Report. *Irish Association of Humanistic and Integrative Psychotherapy*, 52: 71–81.

Mageo JM (2013) Towards a Cultural Psychodynamics of Attachment: Samoa and US Comparison. In Quin N and Mageo JM (eds) *Attachment Reconsidered: Cultural Perspectives on a Western Society*. New York: Palgrave Macmillan, pp. 191–214.

Maratos J (1996) Self through attachment and attachment through self in group therapy. *Group Analysis* 29(2): 191–198.

Markin RD and Marmarosh CL (2010) Application of adult attachment theory to group member transference and the group therapy process. *Psychotherapy Theory, Research, Practice and Training* 47(1): 111–121.

Marmarosh CL (2014) Empirical Research on Attachment in Group Psychotherapy: Moving the Field Forward. *Psychotherapy* 51(1): 88–92.

Marmarosh CL (2017) Attachment in Group Psychotherapy: Bridging Theories, Research and Clinical Technique. *International Journal of Group Psychotherapy* 67(2): 157–160.

Marmarosh CL (ed) (2020) *Attachment in Group Psychotherapy*. London and New York: Routledge.

Marmarosh CL (2021) Ruptures and repairs in group psychotherapy: From theory to practice. *International Journal of Group Psychotherapy* 71(2): 205–223.

Marmarosh CL (2022) Attachments, trauma, and COVID-19: Implications for leaders, groups, and social justice. *Group Dynamics: Theory, Research, and Practice* 26(2): 85–102.

Marmarosh CL, Forsyth DR, Strauss B and Burlingame GM (2020) The psychology of the COVID-19 pandemic: A group-level perspective. *Group Dynamics: Theory, Research, and Practice* 24(3): 122–138.

Marmarosh CL, Franz VA, Koloi M, Majoes RC, Rahimi AM, Ronquillo JG, Somberg R, Swope JS and Zimmer K (2006) Therapists' group attachments and their expectations of patients' attitudes about group therapy. *International Journal of Group Psychotherapy* 56(3): 325–338.

Marmarosh CL and Markin RD (2007) Group and personal attachments: Two is better than one when predicting college adjustment. *Group Dynamics: Theory, Research, and Practice* 11(3): 153–164.

Marmarosh CL, Markin RD and Spiegel E (2013) *Attachment in Group Psychotherapy*. Washington, DC: American Psychological Association.

Marmarosh CL, Sandage S, Wade N, Captari LE and Crabtree S (2022) New horizons in group psychotherapy research and practice from third wave positive psychology: a practice-friendly review. *Research in Psychotherapy* 25(3): 643.

Marmarosh CL and Tasca GA (2013) Adult attachment anxiety: Using group therapy to promote change. *Journal of Clinical Psychology* 69(11): 1172–1182.

Marmarosh CL, Whipple R, Schettler M, Pinhas S, Wolf J and Sayit S (2009) Adult attachment styles and group psychotherapy attitudes. *Group Dynamics: Theory, Research, and Practice* 13(4): 255–264.

Marris P (1996) The Management of Uncertainty. In Kraemer S and Roberts J (eds) *The Politics of Attachment: Towards a Secure Society*. London: Free Association Books, pp. 192–199.

Marrone M (1998) *Attachment and Interaction*. London: Jessica Kingsley Publishers.

Maxwell H, Tasca GA, Ritchie K, Balfour L and Bissada H (2014) Change in attachment insecurity is related to improved outcomes one year post group therapy in women with binge eating disorder. *Psychotherapy* 51(1): 57–65.

Meehan CL and Hawks S (2013) Cooperative breeding and attachment among the Aka forages. In Quinn N and Mageo JM (eds) *Attachment Reconsidered: Cultural Perspectives on a Western Society*. New York: Palgrave Macmillan, pp. 85–113.

Mikulincer M and Shaver PR (2001) Attachment theory and intergroup bias. *Journal of Personality and Social Psychology* 81(1): 97–115.

Mikulincer M and Shaver PR (2007). Boosting attachment security to promote mental health, prosocial values, and inter-group tolerance. *Psychological Inquiry* 18(3): 139–156.

Mikulincer M and Shaver PR (2017) Augmenting the Sense of Attachment Security in Group Contexts: The Effects of a Responsive Leader and a Cohesive Group. *International Journal of Group Psychotherapy* 67(2): 161–175.

Mikulincer M and Shaver PR (2022) Enhancing the "broaden-and-build" cycle of attachment security as a means of overcoming prejudice, discrimination, and racism. *Attachment and Human Development* 24(3): 260–273.

Morelli GA and Henry PI (2013) Afterword: Cross-cultural challenges and attachment theory. In Quinn N and Mageo JM (eds) *Attachment Reconsidered: Cultural Perspectives on a Western Society*. New York: Palgrave Macmillan, pp. 241–249.

Mullen B, Brown R and Smith C (1992) Ingroup bias as a function of salience, relevance, and status: An integration. *European Journal of Social Psychology* 22(2): 103–122.

Nickerson C (2023) Social Institutions in Sociology: Definition and Examples. *Simply Sociology*. Available at www.simplypsychology.org/social-institution.html

Nitzgen D (2008) Development by adaptation: Notes on applied group analysis. *Group Analysis* 41(3): 240–251.

Nitzgen D (2019) Comment on Vollon, Gimenez and Bonnet: The psychotic transference in groups. *Group Analysis* 52(4): 561–570.

Page TF (2010) Applications of Attachment Theory to Group Interventions: A Secure Base in Adulthood. In Bennett S and Nelson JK (eds) *Adult Attachment in Clinical Social Work*. New York: Springer, pp. 173–191.

Parker V (2020) *A Group-Analytic Exploration of the Sibling Matrix*. London: Routledge.

Pearce E, Stringer C and Dunbar RIM (2013) New insights into differences in brain organization between Neanderthals and anatomically modern humans. *Proceedings of the Royal Society, Series B: Biological Sciences* 280(1758): 20130168.

Pines M (1998) *Circular Reflections: Selected Papers on Group Analysis and Psychoanalysis*. London: Jessica Kingsley Publishers.

Roberts J and Pines M (eds) (1991) *The Practice of Group Analysis*. London: Routledge.

Robertson J and Robertson J (1989) *Separation and the very young*. London: Free Association Books.

Rom E and Mikulincer M (2003) Attachment theory and group processes: The association between attachment style and group-related representations, goals, memories and functioning. *Journal of Personality and Social Psychology* 84(6): 1220–1235.

Rutan JS (2021) Rupture and repair: Using leader errors in psychodynamic group psychotherapy. *International Journal of Group Psychotherapy* 71(2): 310–331.

Sallet J, Mars RB, Noonan MP, Andersson JL, O'Reilly JX, Jbabdi S, Croxson PL, Jenkinson M, Miller KL, Rushworth MF (2011) Social network size affects neural circuits in macaques. *Science* 334(6056): 697–700.

Sanders R (2004) *Sibling Relationships: Theory and Issues for Practice.* New York: Palgrave Macmillan.

Schlapobersky JR (2016) *From the Couch to the Circle: Group-Analytic Psychotherapy in Practice.* New York: Routledge.

Seymour SC (2013) It takes a village to raise a child: Attachment theory and multiple child care in Alor, Indonesia, and in North India. In Quinn N and Mageo JM (eds) *Attachment reconsidered: Cultural perspectives on a Western theory.* New York: Palgrave Macmillan, pp. 115–139.

Shechtman Z and Dvir V (2006) Attachment style as a predictor of behavior in group counseling with preadolescents. *Group Dynamics: Theory, Research, and Practice* 10(1): 29–42.

Shechtman Z and Rybko J (2004) Attachment style and observed initial self-disclosure as explanatory variables of group functioning. *Group Dynamics: Theory, Research, and Practice* 8(3): 207–220.

Simpson JA and Belsky J (2008) Attachment theory within a modern evolutionary framework. In Cassidy J and Shaver (eds) *Handbook of Attachment: Theory, Research, and Clinical Applications.* New York: The Guilford Press, pp. 131–157.

Smith E and Henry S (1996) An in-group becomes part of the self: Response time evidence. *Personality and Social Psychology Bulletin* 22(6): 635–642.

Smith E, Murphy J and Coats S (1999) Attachment to groups: Theory and management. *Journal of Personality and Social Psychology* 77(1): 94–110.

Smith E, Coats S and Murphy J (2001) The self and attachment to relationship partners and groups: Theoretical parallels and new insights. In: Sedikides C and Brewer MB (eds) *Individual Self, Relational Self, Collective Self.* London: Psychology Press, pp. 109–122.

Smith TM, Tafforeau P, Reid DJ, Pouech J, Lazzari, JP, Guatelli-Steinberg D et al (2010) Dental evidence for ontogenic differences between modern humans and Neanderthals. *Proceedings of the National Academy of Sciences of the United States of America* 107(49): 20923–20928.

Sochos A (2015) Attachment – beyond interpersonal relationships. *The Psychologist* 28(12): 986–981.

Southgate J (1996) An Attachment Perspective on Dissociation and Multiplicity. Paper presented at The Third Annual John Bowlby Memorial Conference. Centre for Attachment-based Psychoanalytic Psychotherapy, London (23–24 February).

Sroufe LA (2005) Attachment and development: A prospective, longitudinal study from birth to adulthood. *Attachment and Human Development* 7(4): 349–367.

Sung W, Woehler ML, Fagan JM, Grosser TJ, Floyd TM, Labianca GJ (2017) Employees' responses to an organizational merger: Intraindividual change in organizational identification, attachment, and turnover. *Journal of Applied Psychology* 102(6): 910–934.

Sunyer KM (2021) The psychotherapy group, immigrants' camp. *Group Analysis* 54(2): 199–208.

Spears R, Doosje EJ and Ellemers N (1997) Self-Stereotyping in the Face of Threats to Group Status and Distinctiveness: The Role of Group Identification. *Personality and Social Psychology Bulletin* 23(5): 538–553.

Tajfel H and Turner JC (1979) An integrative theory of inter-group conflict. In: Austin WG and Worchel S (eds) *The Social Psychology of Inter-Group Relations.* Monterey, CA: Brooks/Cole, pp. 33–47.

Tasca GA (2014) Attachment and Group Psychotherapy: Introduction to a Special Section. *Psychotherapy* 51(1): 53–56.

Tasca GA and Balfour L (2014) Attachment and eating disorders: a review of current research. *International Journal of Eating Disorders* 47(7): 710–717.

Tasca GA, Balfour L, Ritchie K, Bissada H (2006) Developmental changes in group climate in two types of group therapy for binge-eating disorder: a growth curve analysis. *Psychotherapy Research* 16(4): 499–514.

Tasca GA, Balfour L, Ritchie K and Bissada H (2007) Change in attachment anxiety is associated with improved depression among women with binge eating disorder. *Psychotherapy: Theory, Research, Practice, Training* 44(4): 423–433.

Tasca GA and Marmarosh C (2023). Alliance rupture and repair in group psychotherapy. In: Eubanks CF, Samstag LW and Muran JC (eds) *Rupture and repair in psychotherapy: A critical process for change*. Washington, DC: American Psychological Association, pp. 53–71.

Tasca GA and Maxwell H (2021) Attachment and group psychotherapy: Applications to work groups and teams. In: Parks CD and Tasca GA (eds) *The Psychology of Groups: The Intersection of Social Psychology and Psychotherapy Research*. New York: American Psychological Association, pp. 149–167.

Tasca GA, Mikail SF and Hewitt PL (2021) *Group Psychodynamic-Interpersonal Psychotherapy*. Washington, DC: American Psychological Association.

Tasca GA, Ritchie K, Conrad G, Balfour L, Gayton J, Daigle V and Bissada H (2006) Attachment scales predict outcome in a randomized controlled trial of two group therapies for Binge Eating Disorder: an aptitude by treatment interaction. *Psychotherapy Research* 16(4): 106–121.

Tennie C, Call J and Tomasello M (2009) Ratcheting up the ratchet: on the evolution of cumulative culture. *Philosophical Transactions of the Royal Society Biological Sciences* 364(1528): 2405–2415.

Tomasello M, Melis AP, Tennie C, Wyman E and Herrmann E (2012) Two Key Steps in the Evolution of Human Cooperation. The Interdependence Hypothesis. *Current Anthropology* 53(6): 673–692.

Tomasello M (2014) *A natural history of human thinking*. Cambridge, MA: Harvard University Press.

Turner JC, Hogg MA, Oakes PJ, Reicher SD and Wetherell MS (1987) *Rediscovering the social group: A self-categorization theory*. Oxford: Basil Blackwell.

Wajda Z and Makara-Studzińska M (2018a) Attachment in group psychotherapy. Part 1: Theoretical aspects. *Psychoterapia* 186(3): 7–17.

Wajda Z and Makara-Studzińska M (2018b) Attachment in group psychotherapy. Part 2: Empirical research. *Psychoterapia* 187(4): 57–67.

Wall-Scheffler CM and Myers MJ (2013) Reproductive costs for everyone: How female loads impact human mobility strategies. *Journal of Human Evolution* 64(5): 448–456.

Weinberg H (2003) The culture of the group and groups from different cultures. *Group Analysis* 36(2): 253–268.

Wilson DS (2013) Human cultures are primarily adaptive at the group level. *Cliodynamics: The Journal of Theoretical and Mathematical History* 4: 102–138.

Whittingham M, Lefforge NL and Marmarosh C (2021) Group psychotherapy as a specialty: An inconvenient truth. *American Journal of Psychotherapy* 74(2): 60–66.

Whittingham M, Marmarosh CL, Mallow P and Scherer M (2023) Mental health care equity and access: A group therapy solution. *American Psychologist* 78(2): 119–125.

Zollikofer CPE, Bienvenu T, Beyene Y, Suwa G, Asfaw B, White TD and Ponce de Leon MS (2022) Endocranial ontogeny and evolution in early *Homo sapiens*: The evidence from Herto, Ethiopia. *Evolution Anthropology* 119(32): 1–7.

Zulueta F de (1993) *From Pain to Violence: The Traumatic Roots of Destructiveness*. London: Whurr.

Arturo Ezquerro: https://orcid.org/0000-0002-9910-4576
María Cañete: https://orcid.org/0000-0001-7967-1103

Chapter 2

Bipolar disorder
Ups and downs affecting interpersonal and group life

Arturo Ezquerro and María Cañete

2.1 Introduction: The worst disaster that can befall a group?

People suffering from bipolar affective disorder have a high morbidity and suicidality. They also experience significant difficulties in mood and affect regulation. In addition, they struggle to form and sustain satisfactory relationships and to establish secure group attachment.

In the circumstances, we need to ask ourselves if these patients are suitable for group-analytic treatment or other forms of group psychotherapy. Certainly, group analysis includes a multi-personal or social dimension, which can be crucial in the understanding and management of patients suffering from this condition.

Within psychiatry, bipolar affective disorders are considered a complex constellation of severe and chronic mental illness. They include at least three main subcategories, as outlined by Grigolon et al (2019):

- bipolar disorder type I, defined by the presence of a manic episode;
- bipolar disorder type II, defined by the presence of a hypomanic episode and a major depressive episode;
- bipolar disorder type III, defined by a bipolarity that has been induced by the use of antidepressants or other drugs.

Mania is usually characterised by an exalted mood (often irritable and irritating), brisker physical and mental activity levels, rapid thought, increased and faster speech, quickened perceptions, suspiciousness, impulsiveness and a marked tendency to inappropriately seek out other people, resulting in serious interpersonal and group difficulties.

In *hypomania*, these changes are less intense but may also profoundly disrupt the lives of these patients, their families and acquaintances, and the communities in which they live and work. The range of symptoms in the manic phase (from those found in mild or moderate hypomania to florid psychosis in acute mania) is as wide as that found in the depressive phase (Jamison, 1993).

Virginia Woolf, an acclaimed English modernist writer, whose work has been translated into more than 50 languages, struggled with the two poles of the illness

DOI: 10.4324/9781003271956-3

and eventually killed herself. In *A Room of One's Own*, she reflected on her fight to reconcile such opposite states:

> The beauty of the world . . . has two edges, one of laughter, one of anguish, cutting the heart asunder.
>
> (Woolf, in Jamison, 1993: 128)

Throughout her life, Virginia Woolf was troubled by intermittent periods of psychotic depression and mania, for which there was no effective intervention during her lifetime. She attempted suicide several times and had to be institutionalised on a number of occasions.

In the circumstances, it was remarkable that she managed to keep her creativity alive, right until her *surrender* in 1941, aged 59, when she committed suicide by drowning herself in a river. Prior to this, she wrote a heart-breaking note to her husband:

> Dearest, I feel certain I am going mad again. I feel we can't go through another of those terrible times. And I shan't recover this time. I begin to hear voices, and I can't concentrate. So, I am doing what seems the best thing to do. You have given me the greatest possible happiness. You have been in every way all that everyone could be. I don't think two people could have been happier until this terrible disease came.
>
> I can't fight any longer . . . I can't go on spoiling your life any longer.
>
> (Woolf, in Bell, 1972: 226)

Suicide is indeed a major hazard, but not the only risk, of not treating manic-depressive illness. In addition to the suffering caused by individual attacks of mania and depression, for the majority of patients the natural course of the disease, when left untreated, is to worsen over time: the attacks become more frequent and more severe (Arieti and Bemporad, 1980; Varma, 1997; Greenwood, 2020).

Moreover, full recovery without further episodes is rare and the outcome into old age poor. Bipolar patients who have been hospitalised spend about 20 per cent of their lifetime (from the onset of their disorder) in one episode of the illness or another, and 50 per cent of bipolar episodes last between two and seven months (Angst and Sellaro, 2000).

Bipolar disorders substantially reduce psychosocial functioning and are associated with a loss of between 10 and 20 potential years of life (Müller-Oerlinghausen, Berghofer and Bauer, 2002). The mortality gap between populations with bipolar disorders and the general population is principally a result of excess deaths from cardiovascular disease and suicide.

Chen and Dilsaver (1996) reported a lifetime rate of suicide attempts in those with bipolar disorder of 30 to 40 per cent, compared with 4 per cent in those with other psychiatric disorders. Müller-Oerlinghausen, Berghofer and Bauer (2002) reported that between 10 and 20 per cent of people with bipolar illness end up taking their own life. From a slightly different angle, at least two-thirds of those people who commit suicide have been found to have suffered from depression or from manic-depressive illness.

In this high-risk context, it is understandable that psychotherapists (including group analysts) tend to feel reluctant or uneasy about accepting bipolar patients in their clinics. Dealing with these patients' unpredictable behaviour and mood swings is difficult enough, and having to contain suicide risk is undeniably anxiety-provoking for family and mental health professionals. The suicide of a person always has a strong impact on relatives and caring professionals (see Chapter 4).

According to McIntyre et al (2020), bipolar disorder has a heritable predisposition of almost 70 per cent. Bipolar type I has a close genetic association with schizophrenia, whilst bipolar type II has a close genetic association with major depressive disorder.

Although the pathogenesis of bipolar disorders is not clearly determined, implicated processes include disturbances in neuronal-glial plasticity, monoaminergic signalling, inflammatory homoeostasis, cellular metabolic pathways and mitochondrial function.

Furthermore, the high prevalence of childhood maltreatment in bipolar patients and the association between childhood maltreatment and suicidality underscore the important role of adverse environmental exposures on the presentation of manic-depressive illness.

In spite of the fact that bipolar illness has high rates of morbidity and early death (or maybe because of it), it is striking that the journal *Group Analysis* has scarcely published clinical papers on the treatment and management of bipolar patients. A few exceptions include: Powles (1989), Winther and Sorensen (1989), Hallensleben (1994), Lefevre (1994), Cañete and Ezquerro (1999, 2004, 2012).

Irwin Yalom (1970), one of the most well-known gurus in the fields of existential and group psychotherapy, described bipolar patients as the worst *disaster* that can befall a group. According to him, patients going through a manic episode can be so actively involved that they may try to dominate the group, with little or no capacity to reflect. This might leave other members bemused, depleted and bruised.

On the other hand, bipolar patients can be negatively affected by the stimulation of multiple interpersonal inputs in the group, which may escalate their symptoms and lead to further decompensation.

The late Lionel Kreeger, a founding member of the Institute of Group Analysis, stated that the manic patient is a trial and might at times be uncontainable in the group setting. After more than 40 years of clinical experience as a psychiatrist and group analyst, he confessed:

The few times in my professional life when I have had to take action and remove a patient from the group . . . have been because of a florid manic episode.

(Kreeger, 1991: 124)

Having said that, in Kreeger's view, despite the fact that manic-depressive patients create concern and anxiety in the group, particularly due to their reckless behaviour and the suicide risk, they can be mostly containable in a therapeutic group setting – provided that the group is settled and functioning well-enough. Yet, the conductor is often pushed to work really hard.

2.1(i) Contents and aims of the chapter

This chapter examines the challenges that bipolar patients present in therapy group settings, and reviews relevant literature on the subject from the fields of psychiatry, psychoanalysis, attachment and group psychotherapy. It highlights two main findings:

- Homogeneous psychotherapy groups for bipolar affective disorders are beneficial, particularly those using psychoeducational and integrative approaches.
- Heterogeneous group-analytic psychotherapy with bipolar patients is highly beneficial in the long term.

As an illustration of the latter, a piece of group-analytic qualitative research is presented. This includes clinical material from a weekly outpatient heterogeneous group that was pushed to the limit by a bipolar patient, who also made the group conductor work harder than usual, requiring him to be especially vigilant on boundaries and limit setting. Transference interpretations often needed to aim at translating the difficult behaviour of this patient into a language of repairing ruptures in interpersonal and group attachment relationships.

In view of the positive outcome of this case study, for the patient and for the group, the chapter aims to encourage group analysts and other practitioners to include bipolar patients in their psychotherapy treatment programmes, as well as to offer a more hopeful and less discriminatory approach to this disabling condition.

2.2 Historical context: From the Old Testament through the Classics to the Mystics

Mood fluctuations appear to have been as olden as the dawn of humankind, or at least as ancient as the Old Testament. In religious terminology, Psalm 30 contains a description of two abrupt changes of mental states, which resembled the mood switches of bipolar affective disorder:

> O Lord, you brought up my soul from Sheol, restored me to life from among those gone down to the Pit . . . Weeping may linger for the night, but joy comes with the morning . . .

> O Lord, be my helper! You have turned my mourning into dancing: you have taken off my sackcloth and cloth me with joy, so that my soul may praise you and not be silent.

(in Stein, 2009: 550)

Recurrent affective disorders, characterised by sharp cyclical variations in moods and energy levels have been described in medical terms at least since the time of Hippocrates of Kos, in the 5th century BCE. A number of Greek physicians wrote recognisable profiles of mania and melancholia, predominantly conceptualised as caused by unbalanced humours.

However, the fullest early clinical descriptions of the two conditions are attributed to Aretaeus in the 2nd century CE (Porter, 1995). Born in Asia Minor, Aretaeus studied medicine in Alexandria and moved to Rome, where he wrote his observations:

> The patients are dull or stern, dejected or unreasonably torpid, without any manifest cause . . . And they also become peevish, dispirited, sleepless . . . They are prone to change their mind readily, to become base, mean-spirited, illiberal, and in a little time perhaps simple, extravagant, munificent not from any virtue of the soul but from the changeableness of the disease.
>
> (Porter, 1995: 409)

The terms *mania* and *melancholia* were widely used, although mainly as separate entities. Interestingly, the Greeks and the Romans used baths with various types of salts (including lithium) to calm down agitated or euphoric patients and, sometimes, to stimulate those with profound depression (Legg and Krans, 2019).

Poetry was indeed a creative way of trying to find meaning in dramatic mood changes, and of working towards healing. In *The Dark Night of the Soul*, the 16th century Spanish mystic and poet Saint John of the Cross (1578) associated depression with a descent into a dark and featureless shadow realm, where what had once provided pleasure became now meaningless. He wrote of a *spiritual winter* where the agony is immensely severe:

> the soul feels itself to be perishing and melting away.
>
> (Saint John of the Cross, in Taransaud, 2020: 110)

However, John of the Cross found a purpose in the night of the senses: a stimulus for change, temporarily slowing us down, rendering us less receptive to the external world, so that we can direct our attention to what is going on within. For him, moments of hopeless despair can be a pathway to emotional growth and intrapersonal intimacy, granting us access to uncharted territories within the self.

By forcing the spirits downwards, depression compels us to confront what hides in the dark corridors of the psyche, bringing to conscious awareness that which needs healing.

2.2(i) Melancholia and mania in the Early Modern period and Industrial Age

In the 17th century, in his book *The Anatomy of Melancholy*, the English writer Robert Burton (1621) advocated treating the condition with music and dance.

This creative piece of work primarily served as a literary collection of commentary on melancholy and a vantage point of the full effects that it has on society at large. In addition, the volume expanded deeply into the symptoms of what is now known as major depressive disorder.

Legg and Krans (2019) reported that, towards the end of the 17th century, the Swiss physician Theophilus Bonet published *Sepuchretum*. In this volume, Bonet linked mania and melancholy in a condition that he called *manico-melancholicus*. This was a substantial step in putting together the two poles and advancing towards diagnosing the disorder as a single entity.

However, according to Pichot (1995), the modern era of bipolar disorder did not really begin until the mid-19th century when two French psychiatrists, Jean-Pierre Falret and Jules Baillarger, studied the condition more deeply.

On 31 January 1854, Baillarger presented to the French Imperial Academy of Medicine a *biphasic* mental illness causing recurrent oscillations between mania and depression, which he termed *la folie à double forme* (dual-form insanity).

Two weeks later, on 14 February, Falret presented a similar description to the Academy on what was essentially the same disorder, for which he coined the term *la folie circulaire* (circular insanity).

Both Baillarger and Falret gave clinical descriptions of patients switching through severe depression and manic excitement. These accounts can be deemed as the first accurate and proper medical diagnoses of manic-depressive illness.

Both clinicians bitterly disputed as to who had been the first one to conceptualise the condition. It was Falret who, additionally, referred to a genetic connection in this *circular insanity* – something that has been supported by subsequent medical research to this day (Pichot, 1995; Harrison, Geddes and Tunbridge, 2018; Walss-Bass and Fries, 2019; McIntyre et al, 2020).

It should also be noted that both Falret and Baillarger attempted to separate this specific and distinct type of circular or dual-form madness from what appeared to have been described as mania and depression in other conditions, particularly psychotic disorders. And, in different ways, they also tried to point out that anyone could become loud, agitated, restless, hyperactive, and even dangerous, given the right (or the wrong) conditions (Leader, 2013).

Prior to Baillarger and Falret, the (also French) psychiatrist Jean-Étienne Esquirol (1838) had observed that the progressive abandonment of physical restraints in asylums coincided with a decrease in the use of the term *mania*. According to him, the less the patient was stopped from moving, the less he would be described as manic, suggesting that the term often had a reactive sense, because the patient was being restrained or obstructed in one way or another.

A more derogatory view of manic-depressive psychosis is attributed to the Swiss psychiatrist and eugenicist Eugen Bleuler (1911, 1924). He considered that psychosis (more or less synonymous then with either schizophrenia or manic-depressive illness) should be treated as a form of organic degeneracy.

At one point, Bleuler seemed to have come to the conclusion that such persons are racially inferior and should be sterilised to prevent contamination of the human species!

2.3 Contemporary psychiatric perspectives

The understanding of manic-depressive illness changed with Emil Kraepelin, a German psychiatrist who broke away from Sigmund Freud's theory that the *repression* of desires played a large role in mental illness. In his ground-breaking work, *Manic Depressive Insanity and Paranoia*, Kraepelin (1921) divided psychotic disorders into the organic and the functional; the latter being *dementia praecox* (schizophrenia) and manic-depressive psychosis.

Kraepelin considered bipolar psychosis to have a biological origin, though accepting that psychological factors act as precipitants. He postulated that the main basis for the *malady* must be sought in permanent changes which are frequently innate – perhaps always, as he put it. However, Kraepelin conceded that affective disorders lie along a multidimensional continuum without clear natural divisions.

According to Berrios and Porter (1995), Kraepelin's synthesis contributed to a commonality of views on affective disorders amongst European psychiatrists. However, there were some idiosyncratic differences. The British worried about clinical description, severity and classification; the French about inheritance and environmental triggers; the Germans debated a great deal the question of constitution and personality factors.

Kraepelin's classification of mental disorders remains the basis used by most mental health professional associations today. The term *bipolar* referring to the polar opposites of mania and depression first appeared in the American Psychiatric Association's Diagnostic and Statistical Manual of Mental Disorders (DSM) in its third revision, in 1980. It was part of an attempt to use a more benign diagnostic language, and stop calling these patients *maniacs* – something that was not unusual amongst professionals and public at the time.

The original observations that Kraepelin made are consistent with contemporary psychiatric research, which strongly suggests the existence of biological pathology in manic-depressive illness; for example, recent genetic studies (McGuffin et al, 2003; McIntyre et al, 2020) show heritability of up to 70 per cent in bipolar affective disorders.

Significantly also, in a way similar to Kraepelin's insights, Farmer, Eley and McGuffin (2005), Levandowski and Grassi-Oliveira (2018), and Grigolon et al (2019) showed that what is inherited is a genetic vulnerability, which then necessitates environmental and psychosocial triggering factors (such as early attachment disruptions and other traumatic experiences) that translate such vulnerability into bipolar illness.

These authors pointed out that individuals with a predisposition to bipolar disorder are highly sensitive to environmental stressors, particularly to experiences of childhood maltreatment such as neglect and abuse perpetrated by their attachment figures. These traumatic experiences significantly increase the risk of developing the illness. In fact, childhood maltreatment not only influences the development of bipolar disorder but may likewise modulate the phenotypic expression of the illness.

According to former professor of psychiatry at Johns Hopkins University Medical School, Kay Jamison (1993), the rhythms and cycles of manic-depressive illness are strikingly similar to those of the natural world, as well as to the death-and-regeneration and dark-and-light cycles that have so often been captured in poetry, music, theatre and painting over the centuries.

Psychotherapy was frequently offered to patients suffering from bipolar disorder during the first half of the 20th century, as psychoanalysis was the prevailing psychotherapeutic paradigm of that era. It relied on transference and development of insight to bring about change.

However, in view of the fact that many *manic* patients had marked impairments in their capacity for introspection, some practitioners felt that psychotherapy was not generally successful with manic-depressive patients and that the disorder was best treated primarily by other means.

2.3(i)   The impact of lithium on the management of manic-depressive psychosis

In the late 1940s, with the formal introduction of lithium as a mood stabiliser in the treatment of bipolar illness, with better responses than previous therapeutic interventions, researchers and clinicians tended to view the condition as a biologic illness amenable to biochemical management.

The focus shifted towards optimising pharmacologic treatments and, for the next 30 or so years, less attention was paid to psychoanalysis, psychotherapy and psychosocial interventions. However, after three decades of pharmacotherapy as the mainstay of treatment for bipolar illness, it became clear that medication offered only partial relief for patients.

The current view is that pharmacological interventions alone are associated with low rates of remission, high rates of recurrence, residual symptoms and psychosocial impairment (Cotrena, Branco, Shansis and Fonseca, 2020). According to these authors, the combination of psychotherapy (particularly group psychosocial interventions) and medication became increasingly recommended for the overall management of bipolar illness.

Gradually, the field moved from conceptualising bipolar disorder as a disorder requiring only medication to an illness that, like many chronic disorders, is best treated using a combination of pharmacotherapy and psychotherapy.

Indeed, at face value, psychotherapy for bipolar disorder makes a lot of sense: the illness is characterised by a high degree of psychosocial impairment, interpersonal dysfunction, low rates of medication adherence and diminished cognitive performance.

Each of these domains is reasonably addressed by psychotherapeutic interventions, especially when delivered in combination with pharmacotherapy, as recent research has shown (Serravalle, Iacono, Hodgins and Ellenbogen, 2020; Levandowski and Grassi-Oliveira, 2018; Picardi et al, 2019; Cotrena, Branco, Shansis and Fonseca, 2020; Greenwood, 2020).

In fact, these exhaustive clinical trials have demonstrated the effectiveness and efficacy of bipolar-specific psychotherapies for the treatment of bipolar disorder.

Unlike the psychodynamic therapies of earlier periods in the 20th century, which focused on intrapsychic conflicts and acquisition of insight, contemporary bipolar-specific psychotherapies tend to employ more directive and symptom-focused strategies. McIntyre et al (2020) highlighted the following:

- encouragement of medication adherence,
- provision of psychoeducation,
- involvement of family members,
- development of strategies for relapse prevention,
- exploration of the reciprocal relationship between mood and either cognitions or interpersonal relationships or both, and
- establishment of regular sleep-wake cycles.

The above study reinforced the findings of a previous review of psychotherapy for adults with bipolar disorder, by Swartz and Swanson (2014).

These authors conducted a search of the literature for outcome studies published between 1995 and 2013; they identified 35 reports of 28 randomised controlled trials testing individual or group psychosocial interventions for adults with bipolar disorder. These reports include systematic trials investigating the efficacy and effectiveness of individual psychoeducation, group psychoeducation, individual and group psychotherapy, family therapy and integrated care management.

In particular, Swartz and Swanson (2014) found plenty of evidence that the combination of medication and psychosocial interventions reliably show advantages over medication alone, on measures of symptom burden and risk of relapse. Overall, the findings of the above studies were consistently clear: those bipolar patients who receive psychotherapy, whether delivered in a group or an individual format, fare better than those who do not.

2.3(ii) Early 21st century: Bipolar times

We should also be aware of the fact that, the beginning of the 21st century has seen an exponential upsurge in the diagnosis of bipolar disorder. Whereas the period that followed the Second World War was called the *age of anxiety*, and the 1980s and 1990s the *antidepressant era*, it seems that we are now going through *bipolar times*, as described by Darian Leader (2013).

In the post-war years, a diagnosis of manic-depressive disorder applied to about one per cent of the population. This has increased so dramatically that some five per cent of adults in the USA have now a psychiatric diagnosis of bipolar disorder, and nearly 25 per cent are *suffering* from some form of bipolarity, according to The

National Institute of Mental Health (Legg and Krans, 2019). This is consistent with the findings of most contemporary textbooks of psychiatry:

> The conventional figure of one per cent for bipolar disorders in the general population is being challenged, and there are now convincing data that this group of disorders may account for five per cent of the population and up to 50 per cent of all depressions.
>
> (Sadock, Sadock and Ruiz, 2009: 1629)

Unfortunately, due to social stigma, funding issues and lack of education, less than 40 per cent of people with bipolar disorder receive what this Institute calls minimally adequate treatment (particularly regarding psychotherapy). Mood stabilisers are routinely prescribed to adults and children alike. In the period from the mid-1990s to the mid-2010s, prescriptions increased by 400 per cent (Leader, 2013).

We do believe that our predominant neoliberal culture is playing a part in the *promotion* of bipolarity. Celebrities like Catherine Zeta-Jones, Jean-Claude Van Damme, Mike Tyson and Stephen Fry, as well as CIA agent Carrie Mathison (a fictional character in a television series), have spoken openly about their bipolar conditions.

Business manuals advocate the cultivation of a certain degree of *mania* in order to play the markets, and executives are actually told to ride a *manic* high to increase sales and productivity. Furthermore, the exhilaration, energy and inflated confidence that characterises hypomania, or the early phases of mania, seem well suited to the exhortations to achievement, productivity and intensity that today's businesses demand (Leader, 2013).

In a fiercely competitive world, in which job stability and security are increasingly eroded, employees (and the self-employed) have to prove their worth by working longer and longer hours, in order to sell their products and make their projects successful. Self-help books tend to promote the idea that nothing is impossible and that people must follow their dreams.

Bipolarity might seem to fit the turbulent and roller-coaster rhythms of the early 21st century. However, there are many psychiatric casualties, and most people suffering from manic-depressive illness can vividly describe awful ups and downs – which often become a nightmarish part of their lives.

Bipolar disorder can be a severe and very disabling illness. It is often associated with poor social functioning, reduced rates of employment, high levels of substance misuse and elevated risk of suicide.

Mainstream psychiatry has substantially improved the management of bipolar disorder. When combined with psychotherapy, medication has produced significant benefits in both the management of acute episodes and relapse prevention. Evidence for this can be found in the guidelines of the British Association of Psychopharmacology for treating bipolar disorder (Goodwin, 2003).

Compared with placebo, mood stabilisers have been shown to be more effective at preventing relapse of any mood episode. They also reduce the severity of any relapses that occur and increase the time in between episodes (Smith et al, 2007).

However, the risk for non-first-episode patients has been calculated to be around 50 per cent during the 12 months following a manic episode, despite adherence to mood-stabilising medication (Tohen, Waternaux and Tsuang, 1990). These findings highlight the fact that compliance to medication is necessary but not sufficient for a large proportion of bipolar patients. Consequently, psychotherapy must be a substantial part of the equation.

On the one hand, many patients with bipolar disorder are hardly amenable to psychotherapy without the back-up of psychiatric medication. On the other hand, pharmacotherapy alone does not address the developmental failures and internal conflicts of bipolar patients.

Additionally, during manic and major depressive periods, it is often difficult to relate to others, which may lead to isolation (Lucas, 1998, 2004). Human beings are social animals by nature – that is to say, animals whose fulfilment can only approach completeness in psychosocial context, in a group.

2.4 Psychoanalytic and attachment contributions

From its inception, classical psychoanalysis contributed to the understanding and psychodynamic formulations of bipolar affective disorders. Karl Abraham (1911) postulated that, in those patients with a diagnosis of *manic-depressive insanity*, hatred paralyses love. According to him, this hatred has its origins in infancy and is largely unconscious. It indicates a developmental failure in the individuation process. The natural course of forming an emotionally close and reciprocal attachment is feared because of a heightened sensitivity to loss.

Although primitive identification processes are normally left behind in healthy development, in manic-depressive conditions, immature identification tends to persist and is reactivated under external stress or internal fears of loss of the *loved object* (usually the mother or primary attachment figure). In the circumstances, in adolescent and adult stages, other attachment figures are invested with maternal significance to compensate for that, creating situations of longstanding emotional *dependency* or anxious attachment.

Sigmund Freud (1917) took the issue of identity formation further and described a form of identification in *melancholia*, in which unconscious aggression towards the *bad object* is redirected inwardly into the self. According to him, this process also plays an important part in ordinary mourning. Introjections of blame, treating the self as a devalued and despised entity, can be seen as a temporary diversion from experiencing powerful feelings of rage towards a lost or rejecting other.

In severe depression, however, the extreme protestations of self-blame and self-hatred can be understood as a pathological defence that aims to protect the *loved object*. At the same time, this might be a way of trying to avoid facing the full impact of loss, which prevents the self from dealing with it effectively.

It should be noted that Freud also described the *switch* from depression to mania and recognised its defensiveness, which is habitually expressed in massive *denial*.

Melanie Klein (1935) had a special interest in the study of manic-depressive states. She paid specific attention to what she described as the attitude of superiority and control in the mind of the manic patient. She also emphasised that unconscious *envy* and *jealousy* can be present in a highly destructive form.

As reported by her, the *manic-self* is omnipotently full of triumph, grandeur and contempt, and attacks its *dependence* on the object. There is no guilt or remorse, and reparation is not real but *magical*, as the self does not acknowledge the damage. Concern for the fate of the object is absent.

However, most early psychoanalysts tended to agree that, in broad terms, the degree of developmental failure in manic-depressive psychosis is not as severe as the fragmentation characteristic of schizophrenia. The fact that, apart from the manic episodes, the self wants to spare and preserve the object attests to a level of development that is comparatively more advanced than that of schizophrenic illness.

Therefore, in consonance with classical psychoanalytic theory, given the right therapeutic conditions, analytic approaches can achieve good results with bipolar patients.

In the Kleinian tradition, Bion (1957, 1970) investigated further the underlying developmental failure in patients with manic-depressive illness. His concept of maternal *containment* was a breakthrough in terms of understanding early human development and, also, the shaping of the inner world of psychotic and non-psychotic patients alike.

Bion's holistic formulation of the psychotic and non-psychotic parts of the personality became a good theoretical aid for the therapeutic management of people with bipolar affective disorders.

The understanding of manic-depressive psychosis was likewise enhanced by the introduction of attachment theory to the British Psychoanalytical Society (Bowlby, 1958), as well as by subsequent attachment research that provided evidence for the links between early childhood relationships and the development of a capacity for the regulation of emotions and affects (Schore, 1994; Sroufe, 2005; Wagner-Skacel et al, 2020; Morán-Kneer et al, 2022; Craba et al, 2023).

In his recent book *Psychoanalysis meets Psychosis*, Michael Robbins (2019), an American psychoanalyst and former professor of psychiatry at Harvard University, suggested that attachment theory provides a useful framework for the understanding of emotional regulation difficulties in people suffering from schizophrenia and manic-depressive psychosis.

According to Robbins, neurotic individuals are able to negotiate major transitions of separation and individuation with reasonable success and, as a result, are capable of recognising and experiencing intrapsychic conflict. However, he further argued:

> Psychosis, by contrast, arises from failure of attachment and consequent inability to separate from the mothering person and integrate a mind of one's own. The result is inability to live independently and experience and resolve internal conflict.

(Robbins, 2019: 12)

Attachment in early childhood is crucial for the formation of personality structure. In response to an inconsistent caregiver, individual children become naturally anxious and may develop hyperactivating strategies. This can often amplify distress and contribute to a failure in emotional regulation.

On the other hand, secure attachment contributes to the creation of a physiological reactivity buffer that helps the child to deal with stress more effectively.

In addition, early attachment history and other social relationships have a distinct impact on epigenetic modification of gene expression, which consequently influences behavioural patterns. Furthermore, the quality of attachment and social support in subsequent developmental stages is highly relevant for a patient's course of illness and life trajectory (Greenwood, 2020).

Morriss, van der Gucht, Lancaster and Bentall (2009) reported on a piece of research from the universities of Nottingham, Liverpool, Lancaster and Bangor, which looked into attachment style in patients with bipolar disorder. They studied 148 people, 107 of whom had a diagnosis of bipolar illness. They found that 78 per cent of the bipolar patients had an insecure attachment style compared to only 30 per cent of those unaffected by the disease.

In its origins, an attachment style or pattern can be defined as the way in which we carry our relationship with our closest childhood caregivers (usually our mother and other primary attachment figures) into our own adult relationships (Sroufe, 2005).

Roughly speaking, attachment styles can be described as *secure* or *insecure.* Secure attachment is characterised by comfort with intimacy and autonomy, and with a positive model of oneself and others. Insecure attachment can be further divided into four types, which provide a reasonable frame but should not be taken rigidly:

- *anxious-avoidant,* in which people are fearful of intimacy and socially distant;
- *anxious-preoccupied,* in which people are ambivalent about relationships, having a negative model of the self and an idealised model of the other;
- *dismissing*, in which people have an inflated model of the self, but denigrate the other and are dismissive of the value of intimacy; and
- *disorganised*, in which people habitually have a history of abusive experiences perpetrated by early attachment figures.

The above patterns are particularly useful for research and for the understanding of mental states, emotions and behaviour. However, quite often, life is not that crystal clear; attachment styles can intermingle, depending on circumstances, and can be modified with new experiences in our interactions with an ever-evolving social environment. Indeed, Bowlby (1988) emphasised attachment plasticity across the life cycle. Having said that, he likewise stated that we usually have a predominant attachment style; once this is established, it tends to persist.

In accordance with Bowlby (1980), we may say that attachment and other social relationships are core developmental elements of human existence. Shaped by the early family environment, our attachment system and processes have a lifelong impact on wellbeing or otherwise. For optimal development, interpersonal and group attachment need to complement each other and have to be integrated (see Chapter 1).

We would also like to emphasise that attachment theory highpoints the way through which development can be supported or hindered by attachment experiences, leading either to mental health or to psychopathology.

For the latter, Bowlby (1988) advocated psychotherapeutic interventions in which therapists can show that they believe in their patients, so the patient can trust the therapeutic process and perceive the therapist as a secure-enough base.

A number of clinicians (Taylor-Thomas and Lucas, 2006; Miklowitz et al, 2007; Wagner-Skacel et al, 2020) have studied some important aspects of attachment-based psychotherapy with bipolar patients. These practitioners paid especial attention to the role played by the development of *epistemic trust* in the therapeutic process.

As stated by Fonagy and Allison (2014), *epistemic trust* is a belief in the authenticity and relevance of interpersonally transmitted information.

Following on from this theoretical and practical construction, the above clinicians employed epistemic trust as a key therapeutic factor in their groups, which helped bipolar patients perceive the therapist and the group as a secure-enough base.

In their clinical experience, the provision of such a secure base created the conditions that assisted their patients with the task of changing the rigidity that characterised their enduring personality difficulties. The re-learning of flexibility allowed them to understand better their attachment difficulties, to gain self-control and to repair some of the ruptures in their relationships.

As stated earlier, for optimal development, we need both healthy person-to-person and person-to-group attachment. Some people who have experienced disruptions in their early individual attachments might be lucky enough to have positive group attachment experiences, which may partly compensate for the early deficits.

This compensatory process is typically more complicated for people suffering from bipolar disorders. These people have a strong propensity for *falling out* in group situations and, more often than not, groups perceive them as a *threat* and may marginalise or even expel them. Establishing a satisfactory level of group attachment is crucial, but it can be particularly difficult and challenging for the bipolar patient.

2.5 Review of the literature on group psychotherapy with bipolar patients

This review is comprehensive enough. However, it mainly focuses on the literature that we consider more relevant to integrative, psychodynamic and group-analytic approaches, which certainly constitute a broad church. It is beyond the scope of this chapter to review all the group techniques and interventions.

A large part of the research on group psychotherapy for patients with a diagnosis of bipolar disorder has concentrated on the more severe end of the bipolar spectrum, particularly on those who are concurrently treated with lithium or other mood stabilisers. We would highlight the following contributions:

Van Gent and Zwart (1994), Cerbone, Mayo, Cuthbertson and O'Connell (1992), Peet and Harvey (1991), Wulsin, Bachop and Hoffman (1988), Kripke and Robinson (1985), Jamison and Akiskal (1983), Kanas (1993, 1999, 2021), Kanas and Cox (1998), Hallensleben (1994), Castle et al (2010), Henken et al (2020), Janis et al (2021) and Goldbach et al (2023).

The therapy groups in the above case studies were homogeneous (for bipolar patients only). This format has the advantage of focusing specifically on bipolar symptoms and problems.

Moreover, the majority of the above patients had been unwell for a number of years; they usually required antipsychotic medication on top of the mood stabilisers, and went through frequent relapses that necessitated hospital inpatient admissions. The results showed a significant decrease of relapse rates and hospitalisations, better psychosocial functioning, an increase in euthymic states and enhanced self-reported wellbeing, for those patients who attended regularly.

However, in some of the groups, attrition was high with a significant number of patients dropping out of treatment. For those who persevered, compliance with medication improved during the period of group therapy, which contributed to a better use of the group and more positive outcomes.

Another important finding in the treatment of the more severe cases, as reported by the patients themselves, was that they benefited from the opportunity to discuss with fellow sufferers their difficulties in coming to terms with a chronic and disabling illness.

The main approaches employed by the group therapists were quite structured, directive, psychoeducational and integrative. The predominant culture in these groups was one based on mutual support, information-giving and the sharing of similar experiences.

Indeed, the need for cohesion and common ground in the management of bipolar disorders has influenced the direction of case studies and process research. This was thoroughly reviewed by Kanas (1993, 1999, 2021), Kanas and Cox (1998) and Hallensleben (1994). These and other clinicians gradually developed an integrative approach; which tries to put together theories and techniques from psychoanalytic, psychoeducational and interpersonal models.

The integrative approach has incorporated a number of treatment goals for bipolar patients:

- A first goal involves learning more about their illness, either from the group therapists or from other patients.
- A second goal involves learning to cope with the vicissitudes and sequelae of their illness.
- A third goal relates to gaining insight and improving relationships through group-analytic discussions. At this level, transference interpretations are more likely to occur.

In a focused piece of process research, Kanas and Cox (1998) analysed the first 31 weekly sessions of an outpatient group with bipolar patients, in which 81 per cent of the discussion topics were related to one of the above goals. Compared with a normative sample of general psychotherapy groups with neurotic and characterological problems, the bipolar group scored significantly higher on a measure of cohesion (see Chapter 5) and significantly lower on measures of avoidance and conflict.

Additionally, the goals of sharing information about the disease, talking about ways of coping with its symptoms and sequelae, as well as gaining insight and improving relationships, were often attained.

The specialist group-analytic literature has also paid attention to homogeneous groups for bipolar affective disorders (Winther and Sorensen, 1989; Powles, 1989; Lefevre and Morrison, 1997; Mace and Margison, 1997; Schermer and Pines, 1999).

These clinicians highlighted the role of introjection of blame in the depressive phase of the disorder and concluded that, in contrast to normal grief, bipolar patients tend to experience a pathological sense of loss located within a self, which is perceived as incomplete, decayed, helpless and despicable.

These practitioners also emphasised that manic patients are prone to being stuck in powerful defence mechanisms, such as splitting, denial and omnipotence.

Winther and Sorensen (1989) found one of Foulkes' (1964) core ideas particularly relevant to their bipolar patients: in a therapy group, members collectively constitute the very norm from which they deviate. These authors stated that, although all their group patients came across as being exceedingly unstable and unpredictable, on the whole, they were able to persevere and to reality-correct each other.

Despite the general trend to predominantly conduct homogeneous groups for this population, a number of group-analytic psychotherapists have written about working with bipolar patients in their heterogeneous groups (Kreeger, 1991; Greenberg, 1997; Kapur, 1999; Chazan, 1999; Urlic, 1999; Cañete and Ezquerro, 2012).

These clinicians took up the challenge of working through the impact of the bipolar patient on the group, and of bridging the considerable gap between their patients' differing needs, with a view to maximising therapeutic potential. Heterogeneous groups have the additional advantage of being inclusive, so bipolar patients in these groups can experience a sense of belonging in an ordinary community, without being segregated as a *deviant* population.

This is consistent with one of the key principles of group analysis, as advanced by Foulkes (1975): the wider the range of experience that a therapy group contains, the greater the opportunity for therapeutic learning and change. Some of the above group-analytic authors described in detail the clinical advantages and disadvantages of introducing bipolar patients to their existing heterogeneous groups:

Kreeger (1991) specifically outlined the challenges presented by patients going through a manic phase, which sometimes required temporary cessation of group membership. But he concluded that, when the existing heterogeneous group was solid-enough and working reasonably well, most of his bipolar patients benefited from group-analytic psychotherapy.

Cañete and Ezquerro (2012) reported on the successful outcome for a bipolar patient, a middle-aged man who disturbed the equilibrium of a previously well-functioning group, and who at times required specific interventions from the conductor on boundaries and limit setting. These interventions made him more aware of the impact of his behaviour on the group. In turn, he became able to reflect and change both in the group and in his own life outside the group, as well as to contribute to the wellbeing of his fellow group members.

Greenberg (1997) reported that some of his bipolar patients had a psychiatric breakdown, whilst in the group, and necessitated hospitalisation. After this crisis, it was difficult for them to return to the group because they felt ashamed and vulnerable. In fact, they required additional individual support during the process of re-entering the group. He also referred to feelings of guilt expressed by other members and to specific group difficulties in recovering the capacity to handle conflictive issues with care.

Greenberg concluded that, before introducing a bipolar patient to an existing group, the therapist must not only assess the patient carefully, but also evaluate the group's capacity to navigate through the complicated issues that will likely arise.

2.6 A clinical case study by Arturo Ezquerro

During the mid- and late 2000s and early 2010s, I conducted a weekly, slow-open, heterogeneous outpatient group, in an NHS specialist psychotherapy service, within a multi-ethnic inner London district.

When **Bob** (a 40-year-old special needs teacher with a longstanding history of bipolar disorder) joined this group, right from the outset, he had a significant impact on each of the other eight members.

2.6(i) The referral and assessment process

Bob had been referred to me, as the consultant-in-charge and clinical governance lead for the service, by his community mental health team, following a suicide attempt (an overdose of sleeping tablets) during an episode of severe depression after being made redundant.

At the initial psychotherapy assessment, he was initially quiet, unresponsive and showed motor retardation. His wife Jennifer, a 35-year-old psychiatric nurse, accompanied him and did most of the talking.

Bob's presentation reminded me of Charles Darwin's description of melancholia in his 1872 book, *The Expression of Emotions in Man and Animals*:

After the mind has suffered from an acute paroxysm of grief, and the cause still continues, we fall into a state of low spirits; or we may be utterly cast down and dejected . . . no longer wish for action, but remain motionless and flaccid; the eyelids droop . . .

The corners of the mouth are drawn downwards, which is so universally recognised as a sign of being out of spirits. . . .

(Darwin, 1872, in Shorter, 2009: 473)

Darwin was not a clinician but, nonetheless, he realised there was some special feature in the physiognomy of melancholic individuals that was diagnostic of their underlying mental state.

As I was observing Bob closely, Jennifer said she was feeling guilty about not having pushed hard enough for a psychotherapy referral for her husband in the past. His GP and his psychiatrist saw no point in referring Bob, as he was reluctant to accept such a referral, and she gave in to him.

This time, Jennifer had strongly and unequivocally demanded the referral, whilst giving him an ultimatum:

If you don't have psychotherapy, I will leave you!

Since Bob was anxious about losing his wife, he accepted being referred for psychotherapy.

In the past, he had gone through a number of episodes of clinical depression; he was treated with antidepressant medication. On each occasion he recovered promptly from his depressive symptoms and, straightaway, became elated, uninhibited, hyperactive, highly irritable and irritating. This put an increasing strain on the marriage.

His psychiatrist described this reaction as hypomania, made a diagnosis of bipolar disorder type II and prescribed mood stabilisers. But Bob stopped taking them as, he said, they prevented him from being his real self.

Despite being aware of the fact that his mother had a diagnosis of bipolar disorder type I, and of being conversant with the heritability of the condition, Bob did not accept his psychiatric diagnosis.

Over the years, his mother had needed a number of inpatient hospital admissions due to both florid episodes of mania and psychotic depression. The maternal illness significantly disrupted Bob's development. He could not form a secure attachment with her. And his father, who looked after him when his mother was unwell, died of a heart attack when he was six.

A few weeks after his father's death, Bob was sent to a boarding school for children with emotional and behavioural difficulties, in which he was bullied and did not have any positive peer-group experience.

Following the death of her husband, Bob's mother had a number of casual sexual relationships during her elation period, but she never remarried or settled in a stable relationship. Bob was received into care several times, for short periods, in connection with his mother's hospital admissions.

Interestingly, he became a teacher at another special-needs boarding school, where he seemed to be a protective and caring person for the children. However, he experienced significant difficulties in the daily interactions with his colleagues, which eventually contributed to his redundancy. He had met his wife, who was the sister of one of the school's teachers, at one of the half-term parties.

My assessment of Bob was a twofold process. On the one hand, I assessed his suicide risk and his capacity to relate to me and, potentially, to people in the group. I saw him several times individually and, despite a history of being highly defended and not showing much insight, he was able to engage with me.

He disclosed that, with his overdose, he did not really want to kill himself but was only trying to mitigate his overwhelming psychic pain. However, it could have been lethal if his wife had not been at home, and so I took the suicide risk very seriously.

When we discussed the prospect of group therapy for him, Bob expressed a wish for stability in his life and his marriage, as his wife was at the end of her tether, whilst he kept falling out with friends and acquaintances. He also told me that he wanted to be more curious about people, to understand what makes them *tick*, and to improve his capacity to form and sustain satisfactory relationships.

On the other hand, keeping Bob in mind, I reassessed the current functioning of the psychotherapy therapy group that I had been conducting for the previous five years:

Most members had a range of neurotic and personality problems, including various forms of anxiety and depression; some had been severely traumatised in their childhood, including sexual abuse; one had a history of psychosis with two inpatient admissions in the past but he was reasonably stable at the moment. The group was solid-enough and functioning well in analytic terms.

Taking into account all the pros and cons, I considered that Bob could make a good use of group psychotherapy and that this particular group could accommodate him.

In addition, some of my junior doctors in training sat with me (one at a time) in the group circle during their placement; they played a mixed role of being observers and, at times, co-therapists. This dual function helped me with the therapeutic task and provided an extra layer of reflection and containment in the group.

2.6(ii) A newcomer in an ongoing psychotherapy group

Of the eight existing groups patients, when Bob joined, only two were founder members.

As a *slow-open* group, it was an integral part of the therapeutic frame that, when people made sufficient progress, they left in a planned fashion and newcomers were invited to join. For the majority of patients, average stay in the group was about two and a half to three years.

In the initial stages, **Bob** felt wooden and shut off from everyone. He said that he had no brains (something that his mother had often told him as a child, after he was diagnosed with dyspraxia) and that he would never be able to get a job again.

He added that he could not concentrate on any task and that he had fleeting ideas about the possibility of taking another overdose, which generated significant apprehension in the group. Despite this and other anxieties, he was received with both sympathy and empathy by his fellow group members.

Claire, a 35-year-old business woman, commented that, during a period of post-natal depression, she had also had suicidal ideation but the group helped her understand that she was trying to get away from unbearable feelings about her belief that she was not a good-enough mother.

Listening to that was a relief for Bob, who felt understood and gradually became able to engage with the group in the following weeks and months, without experiencing further suicidal thoughts.

I was proactive and, before the summer holiday, I requested a review for Bob with his psychiatrist and suggested that it should take place during the forthcoming group break, as a safety net. The timing was important to help Bob experience a sense of continuity of care, something that his mother had been unable to provide for him.

However, before the weekly group sessions resumed, I received a message from his psychiatrist letting me know that Bob did not turn up for his review appointment. I was concerned.

In the first group session after the break, **Bob** reported that, unilaterally, he had decided to double the dose of his antidepressant medication because, he said, he wanted to be on top of things as quickly as possible.

He showed pressure of speech and disclosed that, during the break, he went through a period of overactivity and great productivity; he denied missing the group at all. In fact, he said that he did not feel any *attachment* to the group and only attended the sessions to please his wife. He smiled mischievously and, after a brief pause, added with some derision:

Nevertheless, the group is a good intellectual exercise for me, sometimes; aha!

Some members commented that he appeared to be a completely different person. In the group, he now was pedantic and overcorrected everyone. When confronted, he became effervescent and aggressive. Group members started to look quite alarmed by this sudden change.

2.6(iii) Protecting personal and group boundaries

I became particularly concerned because of Bob's complete lack of awareness about the impact of his behaviour on other people. I was especially alert since one of my professional responsibilities, as a group therapist, was to ensure that no-one would be damaged by another member's psychopathology. I decided to ask an open question in the group about how everyone was feeling in respect of Bob's new image.

However, before anybody was able to respond, **Bob** commented with excitement that he had got a new job as a salesman and that, in just one week, he had made a huge profit – something, he said, other people would have been unable to make in many months. He added that he had completely recovered from his depression and that he no longer needed therapy.

Mood in hypomania is usually ebullient, self-confident and often transcendent; but it almost always exists with an irritable underpinning. In addition, although elevated, hypomanic mood is generally both fluctuating and volatile.

The perceptual changes that are present in hypomanic and manic patients reflect the close and subtle links that exist between elevated mood, a distorted sense of wellbeing, and expansive and grandiose thought. Quite often, behaviour of these patients also comes across as unstoppable.

Bob was all over the place and group members were looking at me enquiringly, with an expression of dismay on their faces.

Bearing in mind Bob's mental state, and the needs of the group as a whole, I realised that I had to choose my intervention, very carefully. With some anxiety about not causing any harm, I talked in a calmed fashion:

Bob, I appreciate you are less depressed than how you were before the break. But I wonder if, here and now, you are also trying to sell a grandiose image of someone who can magically get better in one week whilst other people in the group would need many months. In denying your need for the therapy group, are you devaluing other members and inflating your own value?

During my intervention, Bob was giggling noticeably, but he replied quickly:

Your interpretation is too Freudian and laughable; I don't buy it!

Kay, a 42-year-old unemployed woman with a history of paternal sexual abuse, commented that she was feeling irritated by Bob, particularly as he seemed to be dominating the group at a time when she was feeling vulnerable and had important things to talk about, because she had experienced a difficult break.

People in the room unanimously said that they wanted to listen to Kay. She then explained that, with the help of a relative, she had arranged to see her mother after 15 years without any contact. She said she had high expectations, but the meeting went badly.

After a pause, Kay added that, following this eventful encounter, she felt overwhelmed by her unresolved anger towards her mother for not protecting her from the paternal sexual abuse. She could not understand why her mother was so dismissive and pretended the abuse had not happened.

In a rather humorous and opinionated fashion, **Bob** interrupted Kay to say that, in the specialist psychoanalytic literature, incest is considered not real but a product of the child's fantasies. **Kay** became agitated and shouted:

What? . . . I've had enough!

She then stood up abruptly and walked towards the door. I asked her to stay but she left.

Claire exclaimed that she was furious with **Bob,** because he had been brutal to **Kay**, and added that she was also going to leave. I then said that it was my job to protect her and other people in the group.

Looking at Bob, I added that, in the circumstances, his comment had been highly insensitive to Kay's feelings and completely out of order. He tried to justify it but, whilst making a calming gesture with my hands, I invited him to wait and reflect on his actions.

As Bob did not look convinced at all, but indicated that he wanted to carry on arguing with me and with everyone, I slowly stated that I may need to ask him to leave the group temporarily to protect other members. I added that I would then see him separately to review his treatment.

I was pleasantly surprised that, after this boundary intervention, Bob was able to stay in the room listening to people without interrupting or correcting them, although he sometimes gesticulated in disagreement with some of what was said.

After the session, I liaised with his psychiatrist who asked him to stop taking his antidepressant medication and replace it with mood stabilisers. However, Bob refused to take the mood stabilisers and I must confess that I failed to persuade him to follow this piece of sensible medical advice.

It is not unusual for bipolar patients in a manic phase to refuse taking medication, as they enjoy the highs and emotional intensity of the moment. They often say, as **Bob** was now saying, that mood stabilisers interfere with the clarity and rapidity of their thought and, also, diminish their levels of enthusiasm and energy.

After coming off his antidepressants, Bob's hypomanic elation was rapidly replaced by depression, just in a matter of a few weeks. Only then, he became able to express some guilt over Kay's departure and asked me to give his apologies to her.

I had to see **Kay** for three individual sessions. She was reluctant to return to the group whilst Bob remained a member; but I managed to persuade her to do so, as I explained that **Bob** was now more respectful and, at the same time, people in the group were able to get on with him better.

Kay returned to the group two months after the painful incident, and it was possible to work analytically with her and with Bob.

2.6(iv) Group cohesion versus group coherency

During the first session after Kay's return, Bob recognised that he had displaced and projected onto her much of the repressed hostility towards his own mother for rejecting him and sending him to a boarding special school, when he was only six – the very year his father had died.

Bob had disturbed the equilibrium of the group. The conflict that he generated pushed members to retreat to a more primitive form of group cohesion, where the emphasis was on asserting their common ground at the expense of not dealing with differences – in contrast with a more sophisticated and higher-functioning level of coherency, in which differences can be worked through and integrated in the group culture (see Chapter 5).

This defensive group mechanism was a legitimate strategy in the face of a threat to the group's survival, represented by Bob's out-of-control hypomanic (or manic) behaviour. Boundary work became crucial to restore a sense of group safety and to contain Bob's disturbance. As members gradually regained a feeling of emotional security, they became more able to deal with his unpredictability, and to tolerate and integrate other differences.

The need for cohesion and sameness was gradually replaced by more advanced levels of communication and coherency. These two positions were not static. In fact, the visible group fluctuations between cohesion and coherency enabled Bob to reflect on his own mood fluctuations, to accept other members' weaknesses and to grow in reasonable harmony with them. But it was hard work . . .

Bob stayed in the group for nearly five years. During this time, he developed a better capacity for insight and for the regulation of his difficult emotions; his interactions with other members changed towards more mature levels of reciprocity.

Eventually, he was able to go back into teaching. His mood gradually became more stable within his ups and downs, which became significantly less intense and more manageable. The ending of his therapy was carefully prepared and supplemented with some joint sessions for him and his wife.

Two years after his group therapy had ended, Bob sent me a letter with a brief update and asked me to read it out in the group:

> I didn't know until I entered group psychotherapy how seven or eight people would have such a strong impact on me. You listened to me, fought with me, supported me and challenged me.

> I look back on how you managed my insensitivity to Kay with gratitude, because it made me more compassionate in thinking of others before I speak . . .

> You respected the boundaries to maintain the integrity of the group, which is why it worked so well for me. Thank you!

2.7 Discussion

Groups constitute a humanising space *par excellence* – an expression of real human life, including internal and interpersonal experience. We are born into a group and, right from the beginning, we carry the raw material for our *groupishness*. Groups are at the core of human existence and can also be a therapeutic space,

> that of human beings who are trying to understand and to help themselves and each other.
>
> (Pines, 1996: 189)

From a radical perspective, the individual self is not only a part of the group but it also *is* a group (Caparrós et al, 2004). We are a group even without knowing it. Being in an analytic therapy group affords opportunities for realising it, by placing us in a position where we have no option but to give up the illusion of existing in an isolated (and *manic*) autoerotic omnipotence (Freud, 1917).

After this painful discovery, it is necessary to face reality and to work through the demand of achieving a more mature personal identity: a *group-self* that would no longer be split off from the *individual self.*

The group-analytic situation allows for an exploration of the inner world through an intimate dialogue, usually, between seven to nine people who are otherwise strangers to one another. According to Foulkes, the *father* of group analysis,

> this group situation highlights internal interaction, transgresses the boundaries of the individual, of what is usually considered internal, intrapsychic, and shows it to be shared by all.
>
> (Foulkes, 1973: 230)

As well as problems, each group patient brings a different wealth of experience and wisdom, which can be pooled in dealing with change. That is a true interface between the inner and outer world.

Bipolar patients are highly vulnerable to mood fluctuations; on the other hand, an analytic group can offer them plenty of opportunities to search for and find their middle ground. However, the shifting and destructive unpredictability of people with such a disorder poses a major risk to the stability required for satisfactory therapeutic relationships.

Some groups can be polarised, in their own right, which may seriously disturb the precarious equilibrium of bipolar patients. Therefore, group-analytic psycho-therapy can be both a remedy for and a challenge to the bipolar mind.

> This dilemma places us before an intriguing paradox in the use of group analysis: when more means less. A large number of studies indicate that when members of a pathological or deviant population are aggregated, their pathological or deviant characteristics are aggravated. The old asylums were an example of this. Another instance can be seen in the dissemination and consolidation of criminality within the sub-culture of most prisons.

Thus, how can therapeutic groups work in the opposite direction? How is it possible that exposure to one's own problems, as they are experienced in the life of other people, may bring about change?

During the Second World War, at Northfield Military Hospital, Foulkes had to provide therapy for those servicemen who were trapped in a subculture of what was then described as combat shell shock or w*ar neurosis*.

Within that context, he was very much aware that the group's pooling of experience at the extremities of human problems might be expected to aggravate their aberrant features. For a while, he hesitated: if they all deviate from what is in any given community considered healthy or normal, how can they possibly be of any use to each other therapeutically? But his answer was this:

> Collectively they constitute the very norm from which, individually, they deviate.
>
> (Foulkes, 1964: 297–298)

This principle is a cornerstone for group analysis, which implies that we all deviate from the norm but to different degrees (see Chapter 1). Schlapobersky (1996) suggested that conductors need to compose a therapy group selectively and to foster a therapeutic culture that is drawn, in a balanced way, from the personalities and personal resources of its members.

Foulkes (1964) postulated that deviants agree collectively between them upon the very same basic values held by their own community. And it is this underlying humanity (or health) in any deviant (or pathological) subgroup that becomes its most potent therapeutic resource. In due course, this leads to a group culture that is normative, normalising and healing, as it happened in Bob's case.

Analytic observations in groups allow us to see healthy and pathological processes in a unique way, as they unfold within the patient's inner world in a relational context. Yet, despite this therapeutic potential, there is often uneasiness about applying group-analytic therapy to people with bipolar disorders.

As outlined earlier, this clinical reservation was influenced by Yalom (1970)'s powerful statement that a bipolar patient is the worst disaster that can befall the group! Or is it?

It is generally agreed (Kreeger, 1991) that outpatient group-analytic therapy is not indicated for patients who are in the middle of an acute manic phase. However, patients who are in a hypomanic or depressive phase are usually able to tolerate the group experience. And the group can tolerate them.

Well-functioning psychotherapy groups are good vehicles for exposing and correcting the self-care problems of deeply depressed patients. Likewise, such groups can be instrumental in confronting denial as a manic psychological defence, as well as examining maladaptive patterns of relating. All these therapeutic functions can be observed and implemented by every group member (including the therapists) in the here-and-now of the sessions (Foulkes, 1964; Pines, 1986; Ezquerro and Bajaj, 2007; Ezquerro, 2010; Ezquerro and Cañete, 2023).

The therapeutic process is enhanced by the co-construction of a benign group-analytic *matrix* (see Chapters 1, 3 and 5). This was conceptualised by the *father* of group analysis, SH Foulkes (1964, 1973), as the common shared ground which ultimately determines meaning and significance of all events and upon which all communications and interpretations, verbal and non-verbal, rest (Glenn, 1987).

The initial reservations expressed by Yalom can indeed help group therapists be sufficiently cautious but also encourage them to modify their interventions in order to accommodate bipolar patients.

In fact, in a later development, Yalom (1983) suggested that those patients who correct unadjusted interpersonal behaviour, and take the risk of new behaviour in the here-and-now group situation, will become able to transfer the acquired knowledge to real-life situations outside the group – as it happened with Bob. For him, the correcting group experience was a turning point in the therapeutic process.

Of course, there is no guarantee that Bob's treatment success equates to a permanent life insurance policy. When his therapy ended, he was aware that he would need to keep an eye on himself in order to identify future life stressors at an early stage, with a view to managing them successfully, prevent a crisis and stay at the coping level.

Bob acknowledged that he was in a better position to get on with such an open-ended task because, he said, he had gradually incorporated (over five years of therapy) something that could make an important difference to his future wellbeing: the internalisation of the new experience acquired in the group. Thus, the self-reflected or internal benign group became a regulatory and integral part of his (no longer) bipolar mind.

2.8 Conclusion

Bipolar affective disorders constitute a group of severe and long-lasting mental illness, with high morbidity and suicidality, as well as major difficulties in mood and affect regulation, and significant problems in making and maintaining satisfactory relationships and in establishing secure group attachment.

Therefore, accepting people suffering from bipolar disorders for group-analytic therapy is challenging and carries certain risk for the bipolar patient, for the group and, also, for the therapist. Having said that, the risk can be managed, paying special attention to boundaries and limit setting, so these patients can benefit from the reflective and diverse psychosocial dimension of well-functioning, heterogeneous psychotherapy groups. A twofold assessment of patient and group is a crucial part of the process.

Groups differ considerably depending on the characteristics and personalities of their members, as well as the style of the group conductor and the nature of the clinical setting. Likewise, patients with bipolar illness vary in their presentation, according to the phase of the disorder, its severity, and their individual and social needs. The permutations created by these and other variables are huge and highlight the complexity of clinical decisions.

The piece of group-analytic quality research and specialist literature review presented in this chapter support the conclusion that bipolar patients can be suitable for psychodynamic group therapy. In this respect, several findings can be highlighted:

- First, homogeneous therapy groups for bipolar disorders, particularly those using psychoeducational and integrative approaches, are decidedly effective in the management of this condition.
- Second, heterogeneous group-analytic therapy with bipolar patients is highly beneficial in the long term, especially when combined with mood-stabilisers, whilst medication alone is not an effective-enough way to treat this illness.
- Third, a group attachment process that is based only on cohesion, rather than coherency, resembles internalised patterns of an anxious attachment style.
- Fourth, the experience of surviving the differences and challenges presented by bipolar patients can lead to the establishment of a more secure and healthier interpersonal and group attachment experience, which in turn promotes healing, tolerance and better-adjusted personal growth.

Finally, thinking about society at large, tolerance of (as well as quality of life for) bipolar patients can be enhanced by an increased awareness that the cycles and rhythms experienced by these people are not so different from those of the natural world. In fact, dark-and-light cycles, as well as death-and-regeneration sequences, have so often been captured in painting, theatre, music and poetry since ancient times.

Note: The clinical material presented in this chapter has followed strict guidelines from the General Medical Council to protect the confidentiality due to patients.

References

Abraham K (1911) Manic-depressive insanity. In: *Selected Papers of Karl Abraham* (1953 edition). New York: Basic Books, pp. 137–157.

Angst J and Sellaro R (2000) Historical perspectives and natural history of bipolar disorder. *Society for Biological Psychiatry* 48(6): 445–457.

Arieti S and Bemporad J (1980) *Severe and Mild Depression: The Psychotherapeutic Approach*. London: Tavistock Publications.

Bell Q (1972) *Virginia Woolf: A Biography*. London: The Hogarth Press.

Berrios G and Porter R (eds) (1995) *A History of Clinical Psychiatry: The Origin and History of Psychiatric Disorders*. London: The Athlone Press.

Bion WR (1957) Differentiation of the Psychotic from the Non-psychotic Personalities. *International Journal of Psychoanalysis* 38: 266–275.

Bion WR (1970) Container and Contained Transformed. In: *Attention and Interpretation*. London: Tavistock Publications, pp. 106–124.

Bleuler E (1911) Dementia Praecox oder die Gruppe der Schizophrenien. In: Aschaffenburg G (ed) *Handbuch der Psychiatrie*. Leipzig: Deuticke.

Bleuler E (1924) *Textbook of Psychiatry*. New York: The Macmillan Company.

Bowlby J (1958) The nature of the child's tie to his mother. *International Journal of Psychoanalysis* 39: 350–373.

Bowlby J (1980) *Attachment and Loss: Vol. 3. Loss, Sadness and Depression* (1991 edition). London: Penguin Books.

Bowlby J (1988) *A Secure Base: Clinical Applications of Attachment Theory.* London: Routledge.

Burton R (1621) *The Anatomy of Melancholy: What it Is, with All the Kinds, Causes, Symptomes, Prognostickes, and Several Cures of it. In Three Maine Partitions with their several Sections, Members, and Subsections. Philosophically, Medicinally, Historically, Opened and Cut Up.* Google books. Available at https://en.wikipedia.org/wiki/The_Anatomy_of_Melancholy

Cañete M and Ezquerro A (1999) Group-Analytic Psychotherapy of Psychosis. *Group Analysis* 32(4): 507–514.

Cañete M and Ezquerro A (2004) Gruppenanalytishe Psychotherapie der Pychose. In: Hayne M and Kunzke D (eds) *Moderne Gruppenanalyse.* Giessen, Germany: Psychosozial-Verlag, pp. 253–261.

Cañete M and Ezquerro A (2012) Bipolar Affective Disorders and Group Analysis. *Group Analysis* 45(2): 203–217.

Caparrós N, Ezquerro A, Kaes R, Neri C, Rodrigué E and Sanfeliu I (2004) *Y el Grupo Creó al Hombre.* Madrid: Biblioteca Nueva.

Castle D, White C, Chamberlain J, Berk M, Berk L, Lauder S, Murray G, Schweitzer I, Piterman L and Gilbert M (2010) Group-based psychosocial intervention for bipolar disorder: randomised controlled trial. *British Journal of Psychiatry* 196(5): 383–388.

Cerbone M, Mayo J, Cuthbertson B and O'Connell R (1992) Group therapy as an adjunct to medication in the management of affective disorder. *Group: The Journal of the Eastern Group Psychotherapy Society* 16(3): 174–187.

Chazan R (1999) The Group as Therapist for Psychotic and Borderline Personalities. In Schermer VL and Pines M (eds) *Group Psychotherapy of the Psychoses: Concepts, Interventions and Contexts.* London: Jessica Kingsley Publishers, pp. 200–220.

Chen YW and Dilsaver SC (1996) Lifetime rates of suicide attempts among subjects with bipolar and unipolar disorders relative to subjects with other Axis I disorders. *Biological Psychiatry* 39(10): 896–899.

Cotrena C, Branco LD, Shansis FM and Fonseca RP (2020) Predictors of quality of life in bipolar disorder: A path analytical study. *Psychiatry Research* 285: 112846. Available at https://doi.org/10.1016/j.psychres.2020.112846

Craba A, Marano G, Kotzalidis GD, Avallone C, Lisci FM, Crosta ML, Callea A, Monti L, De Berardis D, Lai C, Balocchi M, Sessa I, Harnic D, Sani G and Mazza M (2023) Resilience and Attachment in Patients with Major Depressive Disorder and Bipolar Disorder. *Journal of Personalized Medicine* 13(6)10.3390/jpm13060969. Available at https://doi.org/10.3390/jpm13060969

Darwin C (1872) *The Expression of the Emotions in Man and Animals.* London: John Murray.

Esquirol JE (1838) *Les maladies mentales considérées sous les rapports médical, hygiénique et médico-légal.* Paris: Baillière.

Ezquerro A (2010) Cohesion and Coherency in Group Analysis. *Group Analysis* 43(4): 496–504.

Ezquerro A and Bajaj P (2007) Combining individual and group-analytic psychotherapy: When the group is not enough, or is it? *Group: The Journal of the Eastern Group Psychotherapy Society* 31(1–2): 5–16.

Ezquerro A and Cañete M (2023). *Group Analysis throughout the Life Cycle: Foulks Revisited from a Group Attachment and Developmental Perspective.* London and New York: Routledge.

Farmer A, Eley TC and McGuffin P (2005) Current strategies for investigating the genetic and environmental risk factors for affective disorders. *British Journal of Psychiatry* 186(3): 179–181.

Fonagy P and Allison E (2014) The role of mentalizing and epistemic trust in the therapeutic relationship. *Psychotherapy* 51(3): 372–380.

Foulkes SH (1964) *Therapeutic Group Analysis*. London: George Allen and Unwin Ltd.

Foulkes SH (1973) The Group as Matrix of the Individual's Mental Life. In: Foulkes E (ed) (1990) *SH Foulkes Selected Papers: Psychoanalysis and Group Analysis*. London: Karnac Books, pp. 223–234.

Foulkes SH (1975) *Group Analytic Psychotherapy*. London: Gordon and Breach.

Freud S (1917) Mourning and Melancholia. In: Strachey (ed) *The Standard Edition of the Complete Psychological Works of Sigmund Freud* (Vol. 12). London: The Hogarth Press, pp. 243–258.

Glenn L (1987) The group matrix as a secure base. *Group Analysis* 20(2): 109–126.

Goldbach N, Reif A, Preuss H, Erhart M, Zabel K, Windmann S and Oertel V (2023). A randomized trial of group therapy for resource activation for patients with affective disorder. *Journal of Psychotherapy Integration* 33(1): 1–19.

Goodwin GM (2003) For the Consensus Group of the British Association for Psychopharmacology: Evidence-based guidelines for treating bipolar disorder. *Journal of Psychopharmacology* 17(2): 149–173.

Greenberg M (1997) What can group therapy do to help? In: Varma V (ed) *Managing Manic Depressive Disorders*. London: Jessica Kingsley Publishers, pp. 141–152.

Greenwood TA (2020) Creativity and bipolar disorder: A shared genetic vulnerability. *Annual Review of Clinical Psychology* 16: 239–264.

Grigolon RB, Trevizol AP, Cerqueira RO, Lee Y, Mansur RB, McIntyre RS and Brietzke E (2019) Hypersomnia and bipolar disorder: A systematic review and meta-analysis of proportion. *Journal of Affective Disorders* 246(1): 659–666.

Hallensleben A (1994) Group psychotherapy with manic-depressive patients on lithium: ten years' experience. *Group Analysis* 27(4): 475–482.

Harrison PJ, Geddes JR and Tunbridge EM (2018) The emerging neurobiology of bipolar disorder. *Trends in Neurosciences* 41(1): 18–30.

Henken HT, Kupka RW, Draisma S, Lobbestael J, van den Berg K, Demacker SMA and Regeer EJ (2020) A cognitive behavioural group therapy for bipolar disorder using daily mood monitoring. *Behavioural and Cognitive Psychotherapy* 48(5): 515–529.

Jamison K (1993) *Touched with Fire: Manic-Depressive Illness and the Artistic Temperament*. New York: The Free Press.

Jamison K and Akiskal H (1983) Medication compliance in patients with bipolar disorder. *Psychiatric Clinics of North America* 6(1): 175–192.

Janis RA, Burlingame GM, Svien H, Jensen J and Lundgreen R (2021) Group therapy for mood disorders: A meta-analysis. *Psychotherapy Research* 31(3): 342–358.

Kanas N (1993) Group psychotherapy with bipolar patients: a review and synthesis. *International Journal of Group Psychotherapy* 43(3): 321–333.

Kanas N (1999) Group Therapy with Schizophrenic and Bipolar Patients: Integrative Approaches. In: Schermer VL and Pines M (eds) *Group Psychotherapy of the Psychoses: Concepts, Interventions and Contexts*. London: Jessica Kingsley Publishers, pp. 129–147.

Kanas N (2021) *Integrative Group Therapy for Psychosis: An Evidence-Based Approach*. New York: Routledge.

Kanas N and Cox P (1998) Process and content in a therapy group for bipolar outpatients. *Group: The Journal of the Eastern Group Psychotherapy Society* 22(1): 37–42.

Kapur R (1999) Clinical Interventions in Group Psychotherapy. In: Schermer VL and Pines M (eds) *Group Psychotherapy of the Psychoses: Concepts, Interventions and Contexts*. London: Jessica Kingsley Publishers, pp. 280–298.

Klein M (1935) A contribution to the psychogenesis of manic-depressive states. In: *Writings of Melanie Klein, 1*. London: The Hogarth Press, pp. 262–289.

Kraepelin E (1921) *Manic-Depressive Illness and Paranoia*. Edinburgh: E & S Livingstone.

Kreeger L (1991) The psychotic patient. In: Roberts J and Pines M (eds) *The Practice of Group Analysis*. London: Routledge, pp. 123–127.

Kripke D and Robinson D (1985) Ten years with a lithium group. *McLean Hospital Journal* 10: 1–11.

Leader D (2013) *Strictly Bipolar*. London: Penguin Books.

Lefevre D (1994) The power of countertransference in groups for the severely mentally ill. *Group Analysis* 27: 441–447.

Lefevre D and Morrison F (1997) The Hawthorn project: A group psychotherapy project with chronically psychotic inpatients. In Mace C and Margison F (eds) *Psychotherapy of Psychosis*. London: Gaskell.

Legg TJ and Krans B (2019) The History of Bipolar Disorder. *Healthline*. Available at https://www.healthline.com/health/bipolar-disorder/history-bipolar

Levandowski ML and Grassi-Oliveira R (2018) Influence of early childhood trauma on risk for bipolar disorder. In: Soares JC, Walss-Bass C and Brambilla P (eds) *Bipolar disorder vulnerability: perspectives from pediatric and high-risk populations*. London: Elsevier.

Lucas RN (1998) Why the cycle in a cyclical psychosis? An analytic contribution to the understanding of recurrent manic-depressive psychosis. *Psychoanalytic Psychotherapy* 12(3): 193–212.

Lucas RN (2004) The management of depression – analytic, antidepressants or both? *Psychoanalytic Psychotherapy* 18(3): 268–284.

Mace C and Margison F (eds) (1997) *Psychotherapy of Psychosis*. London: Gaskell Publishers.

McGuffin P, Rijdsdijk F, Andrew M, Sharm P, Katz R and Cardro A (2003) The heritability of bipolar affective disorder and the genetic relationship to unipolar depression. *Archives of General Psychiatry* 60(5): 497–502.

McIntyre RS, Berk M, Brietzke E, Goldstein BI et al (2020) Bipolar Disorders. *The Lancet* 396(10265): 1841–1856.

Miklowitz DJ, Otto MW, Frank E, Reilly-Harrington NA, Kogan JN, Sachs GS, Thase ME, Calabrese JR, Marangell LB, Ostacher MJ, Patel J, Thomas MR, Araga M, Gonzalez JM and Wisniewski SR (2007) Intensive psychosocial intervention enhances functioning in patients with bipolar depression: Results from a 9-month randomized controlled trial. *American Journal of Psychiatry*, 164(9): 1340–1347.

Morán-Kneer J, Ríos U, Costa-Cordella S, Barría C, Carvajal V, Valenzuela K and Wasserman D (2022) Childhood trauma and social cognition in participants with bipolar disorder: The moderating role of attachment. *Journal of Affective Disorders Report* 9: 1–8 100359. Available at https://doi.org/10.1016/j.jadr.2022.100359

Morriss RK, van der Gucht E, Lancaster G and Bentall RP (2009) Adult attachment in bipolar 1 disorder. *Psychology and Psychotherapy: theory, research and practice* 82(3): 267–277.

Müller-Oerlinghausen B, Berghofer A and Bauer M (2002) Bipolar Disorder. *The Lancet* 359 (9302): 241–247.

Peet M and Harvey N (1991) Lithium maintenance: one. A standard education programme for patients. *British Journal of Psychiatry* 158(2): 197–200.

Picardi A, Pallagrosi M, Fonzi L et al (2019) Attachment in Patients with Bipolar and Unipolar Depression: A Comparison with Clinical and Non-clinical Controls. *Clinical Practice and Epidemiology in Mental Health* 15(1): 143–152.

Pichot P (1995) The birth of the bipolar disorder. *European Psychiatry* 10(1): 1–10.

Pines M (1986) Coherency and its Disruption in the Development of the Self. *British Journal of Psychotherapy* 2(3): 180–185.

Pines M (1996) The self as a group: the group as a self. *Group Analysis* 29(2): 183–190.

Porter R (1995) Mood Disorders: Social Section. In: Berrios G and Porter R (eds) *A History of Clinical Psychiatry: The Origin and History of Psychiatric Disorders*. London: The Athlon Press, pp. 409–420.

Powles WE (1989) Group Psychotherapy with Affective Disorders: Critical Impressions of Trends and Strategies. *Group Analysis* 22(1): 7–17.

Robbins M (2019) *Psychoanalysis meets psychosis: Attachment, separation, and the undifferentiated unintegrated mind.* New York: Routledge.

Sadock BJ, Sadock VA and Ruiz P (eds) (2009) *Kaplan & Sadock's Comprehensive Textbook of Psychiatry.* Philadelphia, PA: Wolters Kulzwer, Lippincott Williams & Wilkins.

Saint John of the Cross (1578) *The Dark Night of the Soul* (1959 edition). New York: Image Books.

Serravalle L, Iacono V, Hodgins S and Ellenbogen MA (2020) A comprehensive assessment of personality traits and psychosocial functioning in parents with bipolar disorder and their intimate partners. *International Journal of Bipolar Disorders* 8(1): 8.

Schermer VL and Pines M (eds) (1999) *Group Psychotherapy of the Psychoses: Concepts, Interventions and Contexts.* London: Jessica Kingsley Publishers.

Schlapobersky J (1996) A Group-Analytic Perspective: From the Speech of Hands to the Language of Words In: Cordess C and Cox M (eds) *Forensic Psychotherapy: Crime, Psychodynamics and the Offender Patient. Vol. 1.* London: Jessica Kingsley Publishers, pp. 227–243.

Schore AN (1994) *Affect Regulation and the Origin of the Self.* Hillsdale, NJ: Erlbaum.

Shorter E (2009) Darwin's contribution to psychiatry. *The British Journal of Psychiatry* 195(6): 473–474.

Smith LA, Cornelius V, Warnock A, Bell A and Young AH (2007) Effectiveness of mood stabilisers and antipsychotics in the maintenance phase of bipolar disorder: a systematic review of randomized controlled trials. *Bipolar Disorders* 9(4): 394–412.

Sroufe LA (2005) Attachment and development: A prospective, longitudinal study from birth to adulthood. *Attachment and Human Development* 7(4): 349–367.

Stein G (2009) Did the author of Psalm 30 have cyclothymia or bipolar disorder? *The British Journal of Psychiatry* 195(6): 550.

Swartz HA and Swanson J (2014) Psychotherapy for Bipolar Disorder in Adults: A Review of the Evidence. *Focus* 12(3): 251–266.

Taransaud D (2020) Depression is a thirty-ton whale . . . and it sings in the wrong key. *Attachment: New Directions in Psychotherapy and Relational Psychoanalysis* 14(1): 107–114.

Taylor-Thomas C and Lucas RN (2006) Consideration of the role of psychotherapy in reducing the risk of suicide in affective disorders: A case study. *Psychoanalytic Psychotherapy* 20(3): 218–234.

Tohen M, Waternaux GM and Tsuang MT (1990) Outcome in mania: a four-year prospective follow-up of 75 patients utilizing survival analysis. *Archives of General Psychiatry* 47(12): 1106–1111.

Urlic I (1999) The Therapist's Role in the Group Treatment of Psychotic Patients and Outpatients: A Foulkesian Perspective. In: Schermer VL and Pines M (eds) *Group Psychotherapy of the Psychoses: Concepts, Interventions and Contexts.* London: Jessica Kingsley Publishers, pp. 148–180.

Van Gent EM and Zwart FM (1994) A long follow-up after group therapy in conjunction with lithium prophylaxis. *Nordic Journal of Psychiatry* 48(1): 9–12.

Varma V (ed) (1997) *Managing Manic Depressive Disorders.* London: Jessica Kingsley Publishers.

Walss-Bass C and Fries GR (2019) The Methylome of Bipolar Disorder: Evidence from Human and Animal Studies. In: Jurga S and Barciszewski J (eds) *The DNA, RNA, and Histone Methylomes. RNA Technologies.* New York: Springer.

Wagner-Skacel J, Bengesser S, Dalkner N, Mörkl S, Painold A, Hamm C, Pilz R, Rieger A, Kapfhammer H-P, Hiebler-Ragger M, Jauk E, Butler MI and Reininghaus EZ (2020) Personality Structure and Attachment in Bipolar Disorder. *Frontiers in Psychiatry* 11: 410. Available at https://doi.org/10.3389/fpsyt.2020.00410

Winther G and Sorensen T (1989) Group therapy with manic-depressives: dynamic and therapeutic aspects. *Group Analysis* 22(1): 19–30.

Wulsin L, Bachop N and Hoffman D (1988) Group therapy in manic depressive illness. *American Journal of Psychotherapy* 42(2): 263–271.

Yalom ID (1970) *The Theory and Practice of Group Psychotherapy*. New York: Basic Books.

Yalom ID (1983) *Inpatient Group Psychotherapy*. New York: Basic Books.

Arturo Ezquerro: https://orcid.org/0000-0002-9910-4576

María Cañete: https://orcid.org/0000-0001-7967-1103

Chapter 3

Fostering a group attachment culture in a day-unit for psychotic patients

Arturo Ezquerro and María Cañete

3.1 Introduction

A 28-year-old man with a diagnosis of *paranoid schizophrenia* introduced himself to a therapy group saying that he was a "psychotic patient". A fellow group member asked him:

"What is psychosis for you?"

The new patient looked surprised but responded without hesitation:

"Psychosis is an overwhelming inability to cope with everyday life".

The idea behind this powerful communication had been advanced by the Swiss psychiatrist and psychoanalyst Gustav Bally, in a paper presented at the Second International Symposium for the Psychotherapy of Schizophrenia, in 1959. Bally provided a psychosocial perspective on psychosis and encouraged professionals to look at the psychotic patient, above all, as:

an adult who throughout his life had constantly been confronted with situations with which he could not cope.

(Bally 1964, quoted in Benedetti, 2006: 35)

The above was part of a set of three symposia, organised by Christian Müller and Gaetano Benedetti, two young and enthusiastic psychoanalysts who were dissatisfied that psychosis was predominantly treated with sleeping cures, insulin-shock and electroshock (known, euphemistically, as ECT or electro convulsive therapy). At the time, antipsychotic medication was just starting to be used. Müller and Benedetti advocated the development of a more humane and participative approach to the treatment of psychosis.

Further international symposia on the psychotherapy of psychosis have taken place regularly to the present. In the early days, participating professionals were

DOI: 10.4324/9781003271956-4

psychoanalytically orientated. In the 1980s, there was a shift to encompass a plurality of approaches, making a significant contribution to a broader and more integrated orientation. A new organisation with its own constitution was created at the London Symposium, in 1997: The International Association for Psychosocial Approaches to Psychosis (ISPS). We both attended this scientific meeting and joined the new organisation.

ISPS aims, and actively works, to promote greater knowledge of the different psychosocial treatment modalities for psychosis and their better integration with each other, and with other psychiatric and pharmacological approaches. Under the ISPS umbrella, there are psychoanalytic, psychodynamic, humanistic, cognitive-behavioural (CBT), art-based, attachment-based, systemic and holistic approaches, delivered to individuals, groups and families. Group-analytic methods have been increasingly used by ISPS members.

This organisation also provides networks where professionals, patients and carers can share their ideas, hopes and struggles, and in which they can also examine their differences through constructive dialogue.

Moreover, ISPS stimulates professionals, patients and carers to publish their experiences and findings in a number of platforms, including books, the media and the journal *Psychosis* that was created in 2009.

Through our work as psychiatrists and psychotherapists for over four decades, we have come to the view that, in addition to some genetic vulnerability, psychosis is closely related to severe disruptions in early attachment relationships and other traumatic experiences, seriously affecting a person's capacity to relate to other people and to cope with ordinary life.

We have also seen many patients using their resources, in individual, family and group psychotherapy, to work through and recover from their psychotic experiences.

Under certain conditions, any person can potentially have psychotic symptoms. External stressors (such as life-threatening events or long sleep deprivation) and physiological factors (such as high fever, some medical illnesses and prescribed medication or illicit drugs) may precipitate psychotic episodes.

Nick Kanas (2021), a world-renowned expert on group therapy for psychosis, reported on his own transient experience of psychotic symptoms. When he was a young medical student, and after being on-call with no sleep for 36 hours, he heard voices calling him whilst walking down a long corridor. He looked around and did not see anyone . . .

He then laughed at himself and thought that he badly needed some rest. His sense of reality was temporarily impaired, but his ability for reality-testing was intact and he was able to dismiss the voices. In contrast to that, psychotic patients may believe that their hallucinations are real and might even produce a delusional belief as an explanation.

This chapter navigates through an attachment-based psychotherapeutic philosophy to working with people suffering from psychosis, in terms of both person-to-person and person-to-group attachment. It shows that it is possible to work analytically with psychotic patients in groups, despite the traditional psychoanalytic prejudice that it is not feasible for them to form a therapeutic relationship with, or transference to, the analyst.

The American psychoanalyst, and former professor of psychiatry at Harvard University, Michael Robbins (2019) stated that the basic problem of psychosis has more to do with the nature and quality of the attachment relationships such persons establish than whether they can form relationships to begin with. We certainly agree with Robbins' statement.

As mental health professionals we are responsible for trying our best to provide the conditions within which our patients can develop their resources to understand their difficulties, manage and overcome their symptoms, learn coping strategies and relate meaningfully with other people (Ezquerro and Cañete, 2023).

In particular, attachment-based group interventions foster a culture in which psychotic patients can perceive the therapy as a secure-base environment, from which to explore how to relinquish their psychological defences and become active collaborators in their own therapeutic process. Those patients who persevere have a greater chance to succeed, as the reader will find in the qualitative case study research that is presented further on.

3.1(i) Contents and aims of the chapter

This chapter describes the flexible application of group analytic and attachment principles in a therapy group programme for patients with a longstanding history of psychosis, which ran weekly in the wider context of a day-psychotherapy project in an inner-London community setting. People referred to the project were isolated and found it really difficult to establish any secure interpersonal or group attachment. The chapter reviews relevant research on group psychotherapy for psychotic patients, and also explores the influences that traditional psychoanalytic and attachment conceptions of psychosis have had on contemporary theoretical and clinical approaches to the subject.

A piece of qualitative clinical-process research is presented to illustrate the steady development of a therapeutic group-analytic culture and group-attachment ethos, which enabled many of the patients to eventually perceive the therapists and the group as a secure-enough base. This long-term therapeutic process helped these patients achieve deeper levels of exploration, communication and understanding. In turn, this resulted in better and more autonomous functioning, more satisfactory relationships and a greater capacity to cope with everyday life.

The chapter aims to stimulate further qualitative group case studies and process research with this population, as well as to encourage group analysts and other mental health practitioners to increasingly use attachment-based psychodynamic therapy groups in the treatment of psychosis.

3.2 Traditional psychoanalytic perspectives on psychosis

A full review of the psychoanalytic and attachment literature on psychosis is beyond the scope of this chapter, which mainly focusses on a clinical case study in which it was possible to effectively develop a therapeutic group-analytic and group-attachment culture, in a long-term day-project for psychotic patients. The current section primarily outlines some of the significant differences in the conception of psychosis between traditional psychoanalytic and attachment theories, as per the teachings of Sigmund Freud and John Bowlby.

In *Psychoanalysis Meets Psychosis*, Robbins (2019) suggested that our understanding of psychosis has been distorted by the age-old belief that the illness is the result of a hereditary neuro-degenerative defect. According to him, the idea that afflicted individuals have lost all or parts of their mind evolved over centuries of alienation, marginalisation, discrimination and other forms of rejection of people with psychosis.

The basic assumption of a brain defect has also permeated psychoanalytic efforts into the understanding and treatment of psychosis. Sigmund Freud seemed to have come to the conclusion that psychotic patients are unable to form a therapeutic relationship with, or transference to, the analyst and, hence, are beyond the scope of psychoanalysis. He also assumed that psychotic people are incapable of developing and sustaining an ordinary *neurotic* mental structure. How did Freud come to develop these ideas?

In 19th-century Continental Europe, there were two main traditions of psychiatry: the Germanic, which paid special attention to the study of the *psychoses*, and the French, which was more interested in examining the *psychoneuroses*. In 1885, Freud, a German-speaking Austrian, went to Paris to train with Charcot and was influenced by the French school of psychiatry more than by any other. Partly because of this, Freud was originally predisposed to see the psychoses as having identical origins, functions and mechanisms to those of the psychoneuroses.

According to Freud's (1911a) early thinking, both neurotic and psychotic patients turn away from reality because they find it unbearable. This estrangement can be expressed in many different ways, including that of hallucinations. The *ego* tries to reject unacceptable aspects of reality but its attempt is not fully successful.

The intolerable ideas that were meant to be discarded may come back as a hallucinatory wish-fulfilment, a paranoid delusion, a dissociative disorder, a conversion paralysis, a phobia or other pathological (psychotic or neurotic) manifestations.

Freud (1911a) believed that mental life is governed by two principles: pleasure and reality. As claimed by him, the *pleasure principle* leads the psyche to avoid the pain or unpleasure aroused by increases in instinctual tension. This might be done by fantasising or *hallucinating* the satisfaction necessary to reduce such tension. His early description did not imply that pleasure is positively pursued but that unpleasure is avoided.

Furthermore, he postulated that there is a universal aim to achieve homeostasis, conceived as a built-in tendency to keep instinctual tension at an *optimal* level. For him, optimal meant *minimal* – an economic principle to save energy.

To be more precise, from Freud's early perspective, the mind is originally operated by the tension between pleasure and unpleasure. As the *ego* develops, this is modified and gradually replaced by the *reality principle*. The latter leads the individual to put hallucinatory wish-fulfilment behind him and build reality-based adaptive behaviour. In this new phase of development, satisfaction is not obtained by relieving instinctual tension, but by accommodating facts and becoming attached to *objects* (usually other persons) in the external world.

Freud's original formulations indicate that, whilst the pleasure principle is innate and primitive, the reality principle is acquired and mastered during development. However, the supersession of the pleasure principle by the reality principle is not accomplished all at once. In fact, the pleasure principle is never completely conquered and has to be repressed; for example, by sublimation or other psychological defence mechanisms.

Following on from the formulation of the two mental-life principles, Freud also postulated the existence of *primary processes* which, according to him, belong to the first stage of development and are more primitive and rudimentary than *secondary processes*. Primary processes are mainly characterised by unconscious mental activity; secondary processes by conscious thinking, which includes memories of additional sensory qualities that go beyond the pleasure principle (Freud, 1920).

Primary-process activities display condensation (as images fuse) and displacement (as images swap). These processes are mainly governed by the pleasure principle, use mobile or *de-cathected* (disinvested) energy, and ignore the categories of space and time. Literally, a baby cannot wait and may want the breast here and now. In *topographical* terms, primary processes are the mode of operating of the *id* – for short, Freud's description of instincts and impulses. On the other hand, secondary-process thinking obeys the laws of grammar and formal logic, uses bound or *cathected* energy, and is governed by the adaptive behaviour of the reality principle.

Freud (1920) affirmed that primary processes are ontogenetically and phylogenetically more ancient than secondary processes. In his view, the latter develop in parallel with the ego and serve adaptation to the external world. In his opinion, dreaming and hallucinating are prominent expressions of primary processes, whereas secondary processes manifest themselves in abstract and verbal thinking.

In the first instance, Freud believed that phenomena such as emotions, daydreaming, children's play and imaginative fantasy (as well as some artistic and creative activities) are split off and kept free from reality-testing. Over time, he partly modified his view and accepted that these activities contain in fact a mixture of the two processes.

In the end, he was able to reconcile the two principles that he had previously assumed to be antagonistic and incompatible opposites (Freud, 1920).

In spite of this evolution of Freudian theorising, there is still a misconception amongst some psychoanalytic practitioners that primary processes are pathological *per se*. Literally, it would imply that ordinary child development is pathological; in fact, it is not. The true reality is that a combination of primary and secondary processes persists throughout life.

In terms of Freud's (1911a) early thinking, most psychotic symptoms (including thought disorders) tend to be interpreted as an impairment of ego functions, a rupture in the connection between the ego and external reality, and a return to primary processes (*regression*).

Later, Freud (1924) hypothesised that, following this breakdown in the relationship between the ego and the external world, there might be an attempt at restitution in the psychotic person; that is, an effort to re-invest (re-cathect or re-attach) with newly found energy the *objects* (persons) that had been de-cathected.

From this last perspective, the psychotic formation can be interpreted as a process of reconstruction and recovery, inasmuch as it might be an attempt (though a counterproductive one) that patients use to recapture a relationship with the external world.

Freud gave great importance to the concept of *regression* in the understanding of psychosis, and believed that regressed patients return to infantile or archaic levels of integration because they are unable to function at a higher level. His emphasis on regression distracted him from paying sufficiently adequate attention to the patients' wider context of attachment relationships and group life.

Freud worked individually with adult patients and not with children. His main therapeutic method was reconstructive. He tried to explain child development retrospectively, from his findings in the consulting room. His theoretical and clinical formulations were revolutionary at the time. However, in light of empirical studies based on systematic observations of infants in real-life situations, his libido theory was found to be inaccurate and not particularly useful for the understanding of psychosis (Bowlby, 1969; Stern, 1985; Berry, Bucci and Danquah, 2020).

In a few words, based on Freud's (1924) later theorising, neurosis is the result of a conflict between the *ego* and its *id*, whereas psychosis is a conflict between the *ego* and the *outer world* or environment. According to Bowlby (1969), the most important part of a person's early environment is constituted by their attachment figures – something that Freud appeared not to have taken fully into account or, perhaps, understood.

Indeed, Freud explored the nature of human attachment. In his *Three Essays on the Theory of Sexuality*, he mentioned the presence of a *grasping instinct* or extension of the grasp reflex, linked to catching hold of some part of another person. And he noted that an infant of eighteen months *disliked* being left alone (Freud, 1905).

Originally, he postulated that attachment was a secondary consequence of the mother providing satisfaction of physiological or sensual needs, and that fear of losing her was a growing tension of non-satisfaction which needed to be discharged.

Part of the problem was methodological. Freud appeared to put his theory of infantile sexuality first and, then, tried to conciliate his observations of attachment behaviour and attachment relationships with his sexual theory. In 1922, he wrote:

In the first instance the oral component instinct finds satisfaction by attaching itself to the sating of the desire for nourishment; and its object is the mother's breast. It then detaches itself, becomes independent and at the same time auto-erotic, that is, it finds an object in the child's own body.

(Freud, quoted in Klein, 1952: 435)

Over time, Freud gradually realised that his own theorising alone was insufficient to explain the nature of attachment and the wider meaning of our instinctual life. In 1925, he stated:

There is no more urgent need in psychology than for a securely founded theory of the instincts on which it might then be possible to build further. Nothing of the sort exists.

(Freud, quoted in Bowlby, 1969: 37)

In the last stage of his life, Freud seemed to concede that understanding the true nature of the powerful attachment bond was beyond his grasp. In 1931, he confessed:

Everything in the sphere of this first attachment to the mother seemed to me so difficult to grasp in analysis.

(Freud, quoted in Bowlby, 1969: 177)

And, in 1938, the year before his death, Freud made a passionate statement about the power of the early mother-child attachment and defined it as:

unique, without parallel, laid down unalterably for a whole lifetime, as the first and strongest love-object and as the prototype of all later love relations – for both sexes.

(Freud, quoted in Bowlby, 1958: 369)

3.3 Bowlby's attachment response to Freudian formulations

Bowlby challenged the view that attachment is a *secondary drive* to satisfy primary libidinal and physiological needs. He considered, unequivocally, that our hunger for attachment is as basic as the desire for food and sex. When he presented the blueprint of his attachment theory to the British Psychological Society, at a scientific meeting on 19 June 1957, he was subjected to personal attacks for stating the following:

> Psychological attachment and detachment are to be regarded as functions in their own right apart altogether from the extent to which the child happens at any moment to be dependent on the object for his physiological needs being met. These [attachment functions] were independent of the need to be fed and the satisfaction of sensuous need.
>
> (Bowlby, 1958: 371)

The ad hominem critical reaction of his psychoanalytic colleagues, particularly those from the Kleinian group, was so hostile and highly emotional that even one of them exclaimed:

> "Bowlby? Give me Barabbas".
>
> (in Ezquerro, 2017: 90)

In fact, in response to witnessing the Kleinian hostility towards John Bowlby, Anna Freud commented: "Dr Bowlby is too valuable a person to get lost to psychoanalysis" (Freud A, quoted in Ezquerro, 2017: 81). However, Anna Freud banned Bowlby's paper on attachment (Karen, 1998). She was probably anxious to *protect*, above all, her father's legacy.

Bowlby confronted drive theory and the death instinct, and underplayed the role of the *Oedipus complex*! The emotional reaction that many colleagues had to his *re-evolutionary* theory prevented them from realising that attachment was of huge consequence.

Mario Marrone (1998) reported that the Australian journalist Peter Ellingsen came to London to interview British psychoanalysts, in 1997. Ellingsen was struck by the fact that a large number of them made dismissive comments about Bowlby's work, whilst admitting that they had not read it!

Sadly enough, forty years after the initial blueprint of his attachment theory, leading Kleinian analysts like Hanna Segal believed that Bowlby "was attacking psychoanalysis and that his goal was to destroy it" (Karen, 1998: 112). That was far from the truth; Bowlby was in fact trying to provide a scientific basis for psychoanalytic theory (Ezquerro, 2017).

In the first volume of his trilogy on *Attachment and Loss*, Bowlby provided an evolutionary perspective that was lacking in earlier psychoanalytic formulations:

> Attachment behaviour is regarded as a class of social behaviour of an importance equivalent to that of mating behaviour . . .

It is held to have a biological function specific to itself . . . believed to develop within the infant as a result of his interaction with his environment of evolution- ary adaptedness, and especially of his interaction with the principal figure in that environment, namely his mother. Food and eating are held to play no more than a minor part in their development.

(Bowlby, 1969: 179–180)

Bowlby further elaborated on the crucial role that satisfactory attachment relation- ships play on the growth of a balanced personality, on the construction of a healthy social life and on the development of resilience:

In conclusion, let me outline the picture of personality development proposed. A young child's experience of an encouraging, supportive and co-operative mother, and . . . father, gives him a sense of worth, a belief in the helpfulness of others, and a favourable model on which to build future relationships.

Furthermore, by enabling him to explore his environment with confidence and to deal with it effectively, such experience also promotes his sense of compe- tence . . . personality becomes increasingly structured to operate in moderately controlled and resilient ways, and increasingly capable of continuing so despite adverse circumstances.

(Bowlby, 1969: 378)

One way in which attachment theory differs from traditional types of psychoana- lytic theory is its rejection of a model of development consisting of a series of stages, in any one of which an individual may become *fixated* or to which he may *regress*. Bowlby replaced it with a model in which an individual can be perceived as progressing along one or another of an array of potential *developmental path- ways* (Ezquerro, 2017).

Some of these pathways are compatible with healthy development; others devi- ate, in one or another direction, in ways that are incompatible with mental health, rendering the individual vulnerable to psychotic breakdown should he had met with seriously adverse events (Bowlby, 1973, 1988b).

According to Bowlby (1988a), traditional psychoanalytic models invoking phases of development were inaccurately based on the assumption that, at some phase of normal development, a child shows psychological features that, in another individual, would be regarded as signs of psychopathology:

Thus, a chronically anxious and clinging adult might be regarded as being fix- ated in or having regressed to a postulated phase of orality or of symbiosis; whilst a deeply withdrawn individual might be regarded as having regressed to a postulated phase of autism or of narcissism.

(Bowlby, 1988a: 135–136)

The regression hypothesis was deeply rooted in traditional psychoanalysis and Bowlby could not agree with it. In this respect, Anna Freud drew an unfortunate parallel between ordinary infant development and psychosis:

> In the young infant – as in the schizophrenic patient – we find egocentric, autistic behaviour, together with confusion between himself and the environment.
>
> (Freud A, 2001: viii)

As specified by Bowlby (1988a), regression is not suitable as a concept for the understanding of psychopathology and psychotic processes. In his view, however, severe disruptions of early attachment relationships, including abuse perpetrated by attachment figures, can lead to severe psychopathology such as psychosis.

John Bowlby had trained as a child psychiatrist in the mid-1930s before qualifying as an adult psychoanalyst in 1939. He later became Director of the Children and Parents Department at the Tavistock Clinic, in 1946. In *A Secure Base: Clinical Applications of Attachment Theory*, Bowlby (1988a) wrote about his reflections on several children whose pronouncedly paranoid ideas and behaviour made them appear either nearly or frankly psychotic.

Such children were often charming and endearing one moment and savagely hostile the next, the change occurring suddenly and for no apparent reason:

> Not infrequently these children are tormented by intense fear that some monster will attack them and they spend their time trying to escape the expected attack. In at least some of these cases there is cogent evidence that what is feared is an attack by one or other parent but, that expectation being unbearably frightening, the expected attack is attributed to an imaginary monster.
>
> (Bowlby, 1988a: 116)

Bowlby also referred to the case of six-year-old Sylvia as reported by Hopkins (1984). One of Sylvia's principal symptoms was a terror that chairs and other items of furniture, which she called Daleks, would fly across the room to strike her:

> Her terror was intense and, when she kept cowering and ducking as though about to receive a blow from a Dalek or some other monster, I thought she was hallucinating.
>
> (Hopkins, quoted in Bowlby 1988a: 116)

From the beginning, Sylvia also expressed the fear that her therapist would hit her like her mother did. In the therapy sessions, she regularly attacked her therapist and sometimes threatened to kill her.

Sylvia's referral had been made two years after her father died in a car crash. Following many interviews with a social worker, the mother confessed her massive rejection of Sylvia from the time of her birth, and the murderous feelings both she and the father had held for her.

The father had a violent temper and, in his not infrequent rages, had broken the furniture and thrown it across the room. He had recurrently beaten Sylvia up and had thrown her across the room as well.

Bowlby hypothesised that, behind the paranoid fear of a Dalek attack, there was a serious reality-based expectation of an attack by father or mother. The psychotic-like experiences of Sylvia and other children, as reported by Bowlby, had similar characteristics to those of adult patients suffering from dissociative disorder and other psychotic conditions, as a result of child abuse.

Bowlby's perspective on psychosis is significantly different from Freud's, as illustrated in the case of Paul Schreber, a German judge who suffered from paranoid schizophrenia and wrote about his experience in an autobiographical book: *Memoirs of my nervous illness*.

Freud did not treat Schreber but read his *Memoirs* and drew his own conclusions from it, in an essay entitled *Psychoanalytic notes on an autobiographical account of a case of paranoia* (Freud, 1911b). He thought that Schreber's disturbances resulted from repressed homosexual desires, and that these repressed inner drives were projected onto the outside world, leading to intense hallucinations, which were first centred on his psychiatrist and then around God.

From Freud's viewpoint, these hallucinations were projections of Schreber's feelings towards his brother and his father, respectively. Schreber strongly believed that his psychiatrist was persecuting him and making direct attempts to murder his soul and to change him into a woman, something that Freud thought to be *emasculation hallucinations*. Bowlby investigated the case of judge Schreber, on which Freud based his theory of paranoia, and supported the hypothesis advanced by other authors that his paranoid delusions

> were distorted versions of the extraordinary pedagogic regime to which the patient's father had subjected him from the early months of life.
>
> (Bowlby 1988a: 117)

3.4 Other psychoanalytic contributions

Indeed, psychoanalysis evolved beyond Freud. Melanie Klein (1946) postulated a complex mental life from the very moment of birth. She believed that psychotic mechanisms are produced by the infant's mind as part of ordinary development, as a result of the existence of a *death instinct*:

> The first form of anxiety is of a persecutory nature. The working of the death instinct within –which according to Freud is directed against the organism – gives rise to the fear of annihilation, and this is the primordial cause of persecutory anxiety . . . from inner sources.
>
> (Klein, 1952: 433)

Bowlby could not find scientific evidence for a death instinct, nor could he think of a research method to investigate it either. According to him, if we had been born with such an instinct, we would not have come this far on our evolutionary path. His disagreement with Klein's views further stimulated his determination to search deeply into the nature of attachment: truly, a life instinct (Bowlby, 1958; Ezquerro, 2017).

Within the Kleinian tradition, Wilfred Bion (1957) offered an idiosyncratic perspective. He suggested that, in an attempt to free themselves from a reality that cannot be tolerated, psychotic patients would attack the parts of their mind that are concerned with the perception of reality.

Bion saw this as an attempt to encapsulate the mad elements within a part of the personality, which he called *psychotic*, whilst trying to maintain sanity in another part of the personality, which he called *non-psychotic*.

According to Bion, the non-psychotic component of the personality aims to achieve a balance, between projection and introjection, to think differently about reality and to cope with it, rather than to evade it.

John Steiner (1991) elaborated on Bion's ideas and suggested that, sometimes, the division of the personality into psychotic and non-psychotic parts might be artificial as both elements can be seen to overlap:

> Like other defensive manoeuvres based on splitting it tends to break down under stress, and a frank psychosis may result if psychotic elements can no longer be segregated off and threaten to invade the whole personality.
>
> (Steiner, 1991: 201)

Further insights from the psychoanalytic treatment and management of psychotic patients can be appreciated in Fromm-Reichmann (1952), Sullivan (1953, 1962), Bally (1964), Searles (1965), Volkan (1990, 1995), Steiner (1991), Rosenfeld (1992), Lucas (1992, 1993), Arieti (1994), Jackson and Williams (1994), Rey (1994), Pines (1995), Schermer and Pines (1999), Caparrós (1999, 2004), Jackson (2001), Freeman, Cameron and McGhie (2001), Amador and David (2004), Benedetti (2006), Cullberg (2006), Müller (2006), Alanen, González de Chávez, Silver and Martindale (2009), Robbins (2019), Davoine (2021), Gaudillière (2021), Hamm et al (2022), Urlić et al (2022), Bateman et al (2023), Ridenour et al (2023) and Ruffalo (2023).

On the whole, these authors worked with psychotic patients individually. In different ways, they concur in the search for meaning beyond the psychotic symptom, put an emphasis on the relational side of the treatment, and endeavour to keep the communication going between patient and therapist.

The traditional psychoanalytic idea that psychotic patients are fundamentally *regressed* is still present but increasingly challenged. In fact, Robbins (2019) considered that regression is a *misnomer*. In this respect, Bally had pointed out:

> . . . too little consideration is paid to the fact that the patient is not just, nor even first and foremost, a little child or an infant, but rather at the same time an adult. . . .
>
> (Bally, 1964, quoted in Benedetti, 2006: 35)

Within the tradition of Spanish psychoanalysis, Nicolás Caparrós (1999) postulated that, for healthy personality growth, the infant needs a non-possessive primary attachment figure who provides him with consistent *asymmetric mirroring* (self-other), which gradually helps him develop a distinct sense of *oneness* and *otherness*. In contrast to that, there is a type of unhealthy, *undifferentiated mirroring* (self-self) that may generate a delusional fantasy or pseudo-separation:

> There is an outside that is myself.
>
> (Caparrós, 1999: 86)

According to Caparrós, there can be subtle forms of child abuse contributing to psychosis; to give an example, when a mother *disavows* the responsibility of encouraging her child to explore the environment, treating him as her *property* or an extension of her body.

This pathological mirroring severely disrupts the process of boundary formation that is required for the development of a distinct personal identity; it may eventually lead to psychotic breakdown.

As opposed to that, the harmonious recurrence of the sequence *in-sight* and *out-sight* contributes to the formation and maintenance of meaningful attachment relationships, and to the development of a fulfilling social life – something that is lacking in psychosis.

From the perspective of the French psychoanalytic tradition (Gaudillière, 2021), it was thought that psychosis emerges out of the destruction of otherness and so, for a long time, transference was considered impossible in psychotic patients, barring them from psychoanalytic treatment. But, in truth, transference takes a different form, in which the place of the other has to be *re-created* (Davoine, 2021).

3.5 Contemporary attachment standpoints on psychosis

Since Bowlby's death in 1990, the growth of attachment research and clinical applications of attachment theory has been exponential, including the study of psychosis (Cañete and Ezquerro, 2017; Lavin, Bucci, Varese and Berry, 2019; Berry, Bucci and Danquah, 2020; Ezquerro, 2021).

On the other hand, mainstream psychoanalysis has become more open to explore the role that early attachment disruptions might have in the aetiology of psychotic illness. In a recent innovative book, Robbins (2019) reflected on the rising interest of American psychoanalysis on attachment theory, and suggested that attachment-based thinking can provide a useful framework for the understanding of emotional regulation difficulties in people suffering from psychosis. He further argued:

> Psychosis . . . arises from failure of attachment and consequent inability to separate from the mothering person and integrate a mind of one's own. The result is inability to live independently and . . . resolve internal conflict.
>
> (Robbins, 2019: 12)

Jeremy Holmes (2014), one of the leading figures in the attachment field in the UK, has also used attachment theory as a framework for conceptualising psychosis. He suggested that different types of insecure attachments, such as avoidant, preoccupied and disorganised, can respectively tip into paranoia, confusion and fragmentation.

There is substantial evidence that insecure attachment increases the risk of developing psychotic illness. In particular, avoidant or dismissive and disorganised attachment styles are over-represented in people with a diagnosis of psychosis (Bucci, Emsley and Berry, 2017; Carr, Hardy and Fornells-Ambrojo 2017; Castilho et al, 2017; Lavin, Bucci, Varese and Berry, 2019; Berry, Bucci and Danquah, 2020; Pollard, Bucci, MacBeth and Berry, 2020).

In the first study (and the largest to date) that employed a validated self-report measure of attachment in psychosis, Bucci, Emsley and Berry (2017) found that a disorganised attachment pattern is significantly linked with a higher proportion of childhood physical and sexual abuse by attachment figures, and with more positive symptoms of psychosis (such as delusions and hallucination), in comparison with other attachment patterns.

This type of childhood trauma can lead to an irresolvable state of affairs. Abuse perpetrated by an attachment figure activates concurrent and contradictory impulses both to withdraw and to approach.

The situation becomes a self-perpetuating catch-22: abuse heightens alarm, which in turn intensifies attachment behaviour towards the source of abuse. The abusive attachment figure simultaneously rejects and attracts the child. This generates a highly anxious, disoriented and disorganised attachment pattern, rendering it difficult for the victim to develop an organised self-protective and self-regulatory personality structure (Ezquerro, 2017).

Along these lines, the disorganisation of the attachment system has also been conceptualised as the outcome of repeated interactions in which the infant experiences primary attachment figures as frightening or dissociated in times of stress (Berry, Bucci and Danquah, 2020). And the traumatic experiences leading to disorganised attachment have correspondingly been termed as *fright without solution* (Liotti, 2004).

In adulthood, the continuity of the disorganised attachment pattern of childhood has been named as unresolved or fearful attachment style. In relational terms, this is characterised by a confused push-and-pull style of relating to others, contributing to enormous relationship difficulties and increasing the risk of dissociation and other psychotic phenomena (Berry, Bucci and Danquah, 2020).

Pollard, Bucci, MacBeth and Berry (2020) utilised an expanded psychosis attachment measure, covering the widest possible spectrum of attachment styles. These authors confirmed that the vulnerability to the development and maintenance of psychosis is stronger in disorganised attachment than in other attachment patterns.

On the other hand, significant associations between avoidant or dismissing attachment patterns and psychosis, particularly paranoia, have been reported in a number of studies that investigated this relationship (Berry, Barrowclough and

Wearden 2008; Harder, 2014; Korver-Nieberg et al, 2015; Wickham, Sitko and Bentall, 2015; Fett et al, 2016; Lavin, Bucci, Varese and Berry, 2019; Ruffalo, 2023; Tiller, 2023).

Paranoia is one of the thought processes that is most commonly present in psychosis, particularly schizophrenia. It consists of an unfounded or exaggerated belief, characterised by themes of persecution, conspiracy and interpersonal threat, ranging from suspiciousness to highly distressing delusions.

Lavin, Bucci, Varese and Berry (2019) found consistent evidence of a significantly strong correlation between insecure attachment style and paranoia. These authors concluded that it is necessary to address mental representations of insecure attachment in the treatment of paranoia. According to them, therapeutic interventions that address insecure attachment working models and promote a more secure attachment are likely to help reduce paranoia.

Avoidant attachment is often associated with a more negative view of others, downregulation of affect and social withdrawal. These defensive strategies contribute to feelings of suspiciousness and of not being connected with other people. In the circumstances, the capacity to form any satisfactory group attachment is grossly impaired. This lack of social contact reduces opportunities for reality-testing, something that can be restored in the context of attachment-based group psychotherapy programmes.

According to Freeman, Cameron and McGhie (2001), the therapeutic staff of healthcare institutions must provide enough stability and reliability for the psychotic patient to perceive them as attachment figures.

In recent years, there has been an increasing interest in the application of attachment principles in the management and treatment of psychosis, including the shaping of effective group therapy and prevention programmes.

Indeed, attachment-based thinking has much to offer to the complex field of psychosis and group psychotherapy (Adshead and Aiyegbusi, 2014; Seager, 2014; Berry and Bucci, 2016; Berry, Varese and Bucci 2017; Cañete and Ezquerro, 2017; Summers and Adshead, 2020; Longden and Corstens, 2020; Weijers et al, 2020).

3.6 An outline of the literature on group psychotherapy for psychosis

By the very nature of their problems and symptoms, psychotic patients often mistrust people deeply and may attempt to ignore the very existence of the group. Yet, group methods in the treatment of schizophrenia have been used for over a century. One of the early therapeutic approaches, as reported by Lazell (1921), was based on psycho-educational techniques that were delivered in a lecture format followed by group discussion.

In the following decades, some psychoanalytic group approaches were tried – although with caution. We would highlight a few: Semrad (1948), Standish and Semrad (1951) and Spotnitz (1957). These authors acknowledged that purely insight-oriented work was too stressful for psychotic patients, as they require significant support and structure in the group.

Sullivan (1953) advocated an interpersonal model, which emphasised the relational nature of the typical problems presented in psychosis. For him, psychopathology is ultimately the result of difficulties in interpersonal relations. He suggested that psychotic patients have distorted perceptions of others and, in his approach, encouraged them to change by interacting in the here-and-now of the group sessions.

In the 1970s and 1980s, the stress was gradually put on eclectic approaches combining flexibly the psycho-educational, psychodynamic and interpersonal models. Kanas (1986, 1996, 2021) is one of the main exponents of this *integrative* approach. He analysed 43 research studies from 1950 onwards; these showed that group psychotherapy with psychotic patients is 67 per cent more effective than non-therapy in inpatient settings, and significantly more effective in outpatient settings (Kanas, 1986). He concluded that the therapeutic modalities that encourage interaction are more successful than those based on the use of interpretations.

Other authors supporting interactive approaches (Parloff and Dies, 1977; Melzer, 1979) reported that improvement in social functioning is the main beneficial effect of group therapy, as psychotic patients learn to overcome some of their mistrust in other people while in the safe atmosphere of a therapy group. This is encouraging for group psychotherapists considering the difficulties these patients have in establishing and sustaining relationships.

Remarkably, in the early days, group analysis paid little attention to psychosis. In his written work, SH Foulkes did not provide any systematic account of psychosis and psychotic transferences, but only scattered remarks and reflections on the subject (Nitzgen, 2019). However, in his first group-analytic publication (Foulkes and Lewis, 1944), the treatment of people suffering from psychosis in heterogeneous groups was encouraged in principle, with the warning that groups should not contain a majority of psychotic patients.

In his later writings, Foulkes made some more categorical statements on the subject. As a way of illustration, he stated that "groups with psychotics only were a different matter" (Foulkes, 1964: 35). Towards the end of his career, he added:

> undoubtedly, the person who later develops a psychosis, is also conditioned by his early group, and vice versa.
>
> (Foulkes, 1974: 276)

Overall, Foulkes thought of psychosis as a continuum and, like Bion (1957), affirmed:

> psychotic mechanisms are operative in all of us, and . . . psychotic-like mechanisms and defences are produced very early.
>
> (Foulkes, 1974: 276)

Resonating with Bowlby's (1988a) formulations on psychotic processes, Foulkes (1974) considered that psychosis is not a regression to early developmental stages, but a long-term by-product of primitive interactions and complicated emotions within the whole family environment.

The predominant clinical views of the early generation of group analysts can be found in a revealing book, *The Practice of Group Analysis*, which gives some clues about the reasons behind the shying away of group-analytic practitioners with regard to the treatment of psychosis:

> Two particular problems of working with psychotic patients are the potential disruption not only within the group, but also outside it, and the potential risk of suicide.
>
> (Kreeger, 1991: 126)

At the time the above book was written, just a handful of patients with a history of psychosis had been accepted at the Group Analytic Practice (a private out-patient clinic created by Foulkes and his early followers in London). These patients were only offered a place in a therapy group after an extended assessment, in which the clinician had to be reassured that the patient was sufficiently improved and stable.

Interestingly, there were some discussions at the Practice about creating a programme combining individual and group psychotherapy for psychotic patients; but the plan did not materialise. Most group-analytic practitioners at the time recommended that psychotherapeutic interventions with psychotic patients should take place in hospital settings.

Despite the precautions of the first generations of group analysts, since the early 1990s, there has been a significant growth in group-analytic clinical work with psychotic patients (Sandison, 1991, 1994; Chazan, 1993, 1999; Hummelen, 1994; Milders, 1994; Lefevre, 1994, 1999; Kapur, 1999; Smith, 1999; Correale, 1999; Resnik, 1999, 2005; Prior, 2007; Koukis, 2009; Urlić, 1999, 2010, 2012; Cañete and Ezquerro, 1999, 2012, 2017; Vollon, Gimenez and Bonnet, 2018; Urlić and González de Chávez, 2019; Branitsky, 2023; Kilpatrick and Kanas, 2023).

All these authors have consistently agreed with the view that, in order to engage patients and make the treatment effective, it is necessary to help them make sense of the psychotic experience and to apply group-analytic principles flexibly, according to the patients' circumstances and the characteristics of the particular therapeutic setting.

Vollon, Gimenez and Bonnet (2018) put forward a hypothesis that, in the early stages of a therapy group, psychotic transferences oscillate between restrictive and expansive movements. This can be expressed by a tendency, in these patients, either to withdraw (excluding themselves) or to engage in an undifferentiated way. These dynamics require from the conductors flexible and empathic interventions that promote the development of therapeutic group attachment.

In the past, most therapy groups were predominantly homogeneous, segregating patients either with a diagnosis of schizophrenia or of manic-depressive psychosis.

However, there is a growing trend to conduct groups that include a wider mix of psychotic problems (Cañete and Ezquerro, 1999, 2017; Martindale, Bateman, Crowe and Margison 2000; Urlić and González de Chávez, 2019).

A number of recent research studies have added to our understanding of the therapeutic factors contributing to the effectiveness of therapeutic group work for psychosis, and have concluded that group psychotherapy with psychotic patients can be as effective as individual psychotherapy. We would like to direct the interested reader to the following:

González de Chávez, Gutiérrez, Ducajú and Fraile (2000), Martindale, Bateman, Crowe and Margison (2000), Rico and Sunyer (2001), González de Chávez (2009), García-Cabeza and González de Chávez (2009), García-Cabeza, Ducajú, Chapela and González de Chávez (2011), Restek-Petrović et al (2014), Štrkalj Ivezić and Urlić (2015), Cañete and Ezquerro (2017), Blink Pesec et al (2019), Urlić and González de Chávez (2019), Kennard (2019), García-Cabeza (2019), Ruffalo (2023), Kilpatrick and Kanas (2023) and Branitsky (2023).

These authors' main findings include reports from patients affirming that they became more hopeful, overcame their isolation, improved self-knowledge and achieved greater personal autonomy, as a result of the group interventions. These clinicians also reported a decrease in the rates of in-patient admissions, as well as successful trials of reduced medication or no medication in their group patients.

Finally, many of the above practitioners reported on the wider therapeutic potential of group sessions, which enabled them to see their patients expressing a greater variety of aspects than they do in individual sessions.

3.7 A case study by María Cañete: Group-analytic therapy with psychotic patients

In the mid-1990s, a steering group was formed and joint funding from Health and Social Services was agreed, to create a weekly psychotherapy day project for adult patients with a longstanding history of psychosis. It was located in a community centre within a deprived inner-London district. I was appointed as consultant psychotherapist and group analyst to the project. The wider team consisted of clinical psychologists, social workers, junior doctors, community psychiatric nurses and occupational therapists.

The project offered a multi-layered and democratic group therapy programme, within the framework of the Care Programme Approach (CPA). It was based on a group-analytic premise that, despite their severe problems, psychotic patients have a potential capacity to be therapeutic to each other. They can develop this potential through building a genuine relationship between equals in the group, as well as between themselves and staff.

The group therapy programme was combined with a range of individual and family-based psychological interventions, including psychodynamic, systemic and cognitive-behavioural approaches. Patients had an extended assessment of their attachment history and difficulties. We provided them with information about the project, and realistic therapeutic goals were agreed with them. We also gave them a copy of our assessment report for their comments and changes before sending it to their referrers.

On reading the reports, most of the patients told us that they felt understood and rarely made any objections. This open communication helped patients and staff build a basis for a therapeutic alliance. Following the initial assessment, they were invited to a drop-in gathering and a community meeting, where they met other patients and staff in order to become familiar with the project.

As a day service, attendance was voluntary. After a minimum of four weeks, new patients could join the formal therapy programme. All patients had a key-worker with whom they held regular individual meetings to discuss treatment goals and progress, as well as any worries or concerns. Staff and patients had lunch together. Everyone was encouraged to help with preparing food, moving furniture and cleaning up. The overall timetable was as follows:

- 09.30 am: Staff meeting
- 10.30 am: Individual, family or small group therapy.
- 11.30 am: Drop-in session.
- 12.00 pm: News and views community group.
- 12.45 pm: Community lunch
- 01.30 pm: Individual, family or small group therapy. Psycho-educational groups.
- 02.30 pm: Staff supervision
- 04.00 pm: Staff reflective practice meeting or consultation with an external consultant.

Patients and staff participated in a community-style large group, called *news and views*: a forum in which people talked about local, national or world events, shared personal news, delivered messages from other people, welcome new members, and made democratic and consensual decisions affecting the project as a whole. For example, the name *Discovery Project* was chosen by the patients themselves.

In addition, they gave consent for outside professionals to visit the project. This community group also provided opportunities to talk about how people were getting on with each other.

All new patients were invited to join an introductory psycho-educational group for six to eight weeks, in which they could share their experiences and ask any questions. This group was very popular; staff and patients learned from each other.

Whenever possible, we invited professionals with expertise on particular themes to give a talk. Guest speakers included pharmacists, nutritionists, social workers and lawyers from advocacy services, as well as ex-service users. Topics discussed included:

- Information about psychotic experiences and their possible causes.
- Information about medication, how it works, its benefits and side effects.
- Training in stress management techniques and in relapse prevention strategies.
- Training in problem solving and active symptom management.
- Healthy living, including a balanced diet, budgeting and activity planning.

- Support in the community, welfare and legal matters.
- Engaging further with the project: from discovery to recovery, themes and stories of what helps people rebuild their lives.

At the end of each meeting, patients were asked to evaluate the session and to state how relevant it was for them. Sessions on medication, welfare and recovery scored particularly high.

3.7(i) The small therapy group: early stages

After the psycho-educational sessions, patients were invited to join one of the small psychotherapy groups available in the project. Each group had up to eight members, a conductor and a co-therapist. Everyone sat on equal chairs in a circle. Although the usual length of group-analytic psychotherapy sessions is 90 minutes, for practical reasons, it was agreed that our group sessions would run for one hour.

Following consultations with the patients, it was decided to have an observer in the room, who sat outside the group circle. We included this role primarily to help the therapists monitor group boundaries and communication. The observer provided live supervision for the conductors, in a way similar to the format used by systemic family therapists. Support systems outside the group were an important part of the care programme.

I shall now concentrate on a group that I co-conducted continuously for over sixteen years. On average, the co-therapist (usually a trainee) changed every one or two years. The group was *slow-open*: people joined and left when ready, after which they were replaced by newcomers.

The first couple of months were characterised by little spontaneous participation, despite our efforts to involve everyone. Some patients were restless and found it difficult to stay in their chair for one hour.

When a patient stood up, we invited him or her to talk about the reasons for doing so. Some blamed the medication; others just felt uncomfortable and tense.

Patrick, a 45-year-old writer with a diagnosis of paranoid schizophrenia, said that he needed to be "vigilant about some noises and voices in the surroundings". I asked him to elaborate on that and he then *confessed* that the voices were telling him that the CIA was after him, and that staff and patients were also conspiring against him. In the group, so far, he hardly talked to anybody apart from myself. After a pause, he whispered to me:

"You should go back to your country because, if you stay here, the CIA will kill you".

I was aware of my strong foreign accent and a number of questions came to mind, as he had now *included* me as a benign member within his paranoid system. I wondered about a conceivable conflict in Patrick's mind between wanting to protect me and wishing, unconsciously perhaps, to kill me off by sending me back to my country. As I had been inviting him to relate to other people (the conspirators) in the group, did I represent a disguised threat for him? I did not verbalise any of my mental speculations but decided to ask him:

"Patrick, would you really like me to go back to my country?"

He immediately responded:

"No, I don't want you to go because you are a good person and you are kind to me".

Other group members seemed to listen with curiosity, but did not join in the conversation. Communications during the rest of the meeting came across as rather disorganised and disjointed; they did not relate to one another.

At the beginning of the next session, **Harold**, a 39-year-old unemployed carpenter with a diagnosis of paranoid schizophrenia, commented that he was expecting some directives from the therapists. He added that his psychiatrist had always told him what to do. I acknowledged his expectations and said that, perhaps, this was an opportunity for him to learn how to make his own decisions.

Neither Harold nor other members responded to my comment. For the rest of the session, Harold was silent. Just a few minutes before the end, he suddenly stood up and walked towards the door. I asked him to stay but he left.

As an additional layer of containment there was a staff member in the common room (next to the therapy room) doing admin work. This colleague was available to talk to patients who might feel distressed or unable to complete a therapy session. The additional safety arrangement enabled us, the therapists, to stay with the group. Harold said to our *gatekeeper* colleague that there was a plot to make him believe that all other group members were patients, but he knew that everybody was a therapist pretending to be a patient. He was adamant that he did not want to return to the group.

Following this, Harold had a review meeting with his keyworker at the project, in which he said that he wanted a more directive approach. Following a discussion in the team, individual CBT sessions were offered to him. He agreed to participate in all the other activities of the day-programme, except the small therapy group.

In fact, **Harold** attended the project regularly for three and a half years and made steady progress. He was pleased to be offered a protected job in a picture-framing workshop and felt confident enough to move on. Our small therapy group did not contain his initial anxieties. However, the wider multidisciplinary structure of our community day-setting provided enough therapeutic containment to help him achieve the positive outcome he was looking for.

At the time of Harold's abrupt departure from the therapy group, we said to members that we had agreed with him a different therapeutic programme in the project. His leaving did not seem to have an impact on the functioning of the group; members did not comment on it.

After half a year in the life of the group, patients became gradually able to disclose some of their personal experiences. However, at these *early* stages, the group did not show enough cohesion (see Chapter 5); they felt fragile and shared their stories without personally relating to one another. There was not much eye contact between them, and they often appeared to engage in a sort of collective monologue, with little interaction. Their communications were mainly addressed to the therapists, who had to provide the glue that would keep the group together by making links between their stories.

The most common themes the patients brought to the group in this period were as follows:

- the difficult and angry relationships with fathers or absent fathers;
- their experience of having psychotic breakdowns;
- the lack of motivation in their lives;
- their isolation;
- their ambivalent relationships with siblings;
- their problematic experiences at school and with friends.

Remarkably, in the early group, members expressed angry feelings at many people but there was relatively little talk about their mothers. At a less conscious level, I wondered if they needed to protect their mothers from the expression of any hostile thoughts or feelings. They sometimes described situations of neglect, abuse or abandonment, in which the mother was unable to look after them. But they did not associate any of these difficulties with their anger.

Most of them tended to refer to their mothers as victims who had to survive under very difficult circumstances, whilst trying to keep the family together. They defended their mothers from criticism, often justifying the maternal behaviour unconditionally. As a woman, I considered the transference implications of this material. They hardly expressed any anger or criticism against me either (apart from the possible double meaning of Patrick advising me to go back to my country of birth to *protect* me from the CIA).

It could be argued that, symbolically, I was working with them (like their mothers) under the difficult circumstances of having to sustain the non-cohesive group together. However, at that point in the early development of the group, I was cautious and decided not to make transference interpretations in respect of the material about mothers or mother-figures.

I considered that, in the first instance, they needed to feel safe enough to form some sort of emotional *attachment* with me, with my co-therapist and, in turn, with one another and with the group-as-a-whole.

All of them had experienced significant disruptions in the early relationship with their parents, which prevented them from forming a secure attachment.

Many of our patients had been received into care, but the relationship with their carers was unsatisfactory and, in some cases, abusive. There were many changes of placements, foster families and children's homes. Exploring these issues openly was still too frightening for them; I thought it would have generated unbearable levels of anxiety. Our priority at the time was to create a benign, secure enough and supportive environment, in which they felt protected and cared for.

The psychoanalytic literature has often pointed out that the main anxiety against which psychotic patients defend themselves is *annihilation anxiety* (Klein, 1952; Cohn, 1988; Caparrós, 1999, 2004).

This kind of anxiety is a dreadful fear not to survive. No doubt, in psychotic anxieties, more often than not, psychic survival is at stake. Attachment serves protection and survival; hence, psychotic anxiety can be better understood from an attachment perspective than from an Oedipus complex viewpoint. Indeed, I wanted to protect the group from the risk of what has been described, in the work with psychotic patients, as:

an atmosphere of emptiness and desolation.

(Resnik, 1999: 122)

Given the fact that our group members presented themselves with disorganised, avoidant or dismissive attachment styles of relating, it was difficult for them to become securely attached to us (the therapists) or to the group, during the initial phase of treatment. For most of them, attachment bonds remained fragile for a long time. Although they were gradually getting closer to us, they still perceived other people in the group as if they were strangers to one another.

Patients' disclosures did not necessarily mean that they had developed a significant attachment to the group or a sound capacity to trust others. At this point in time, I thought they were highly defended and incapable of regulating the emotional distance; they seemed unable to build relationships based on mutuality and reciprocity.

Jerry, a 27-year-old student with a diagnosis of schizo-affective disorder, joined the group a few months after Harold had left. He attended regularly but talked little. In one session, some ten months after his arrival, he disclosed that he had recently offered shelter in his flat to a homeless stranger he met in the street. The following morning, he was shocked to find out that the stranger had stolen his most valuable and cherished possessions, before leaving.

Jerry felt devastated by the experience and decided to carry a kitchen knife when he was at home. Some members said that they were sorry about the robbery. Others commented that they would have felt too scared to invite a complete stranger to stay in their flats. Jerry remained withdrawn for the rest of the session and left the group a few weeks later.

Between six and nine months, babies who are securely attached begin to experience a wariness of strangers (see Chapter 1). This is a two-way process through which the child learns to regulate the distance: trusting and becoming close to people who are familiar and reliable, whilst being cautious about strangers who might be potentially dangerous (Ezquerro, 2017).

The capacity to regulate the distance can be impaired, as in Jerry's case, when the early attachment figures are abusive (Bowlby, 1988a; Ezquerro, 2010; Yakeley and Burbridge-James, 2018).

In these harmful circumstances, the child's unmet attachment needs could lead to seeking inappropriate or unsafe contacts, whilst still being unable to form close and satisfactory relationships. This may result in further harm.

A few months after Jerry's departure, my co-therapist and I said to the group that we would be soon attending a conference to give a talk about our work in the project. Initially, nobody seemed to pay attention to our announcement.

However, about one minute later, **Neil**, a 26-year-old barman with a diagnosis of schizophrenia, commented that he had met somebody who was called "doctor-doctor" and wondered if this person had two university degrees. **Helen**, a 42-year-old unemployed librarian with a diagnosis of paranoid schizophrenia, responded saying that she had also heard of someone who was called "sir-sir". After these comments, there was a sense of puzzlement in the group.

At this point, **Frank**, a 41-year-old musician with a diagnosis of manic-depressive psychosis, asked:

"What about parents? I haven't heard of anybody being called 'father-father' for having two children".

I then stated that they were communicating something important and asked them about the possible meaning. **Neil** responded promptly:

"It is all about recognition, isn't it?"

Looking around the circle, I further enquired:

"I wonder if our earlier announcement could be making people question who would get recognition, for the work we are doing together here at the project".

Neil looked at me and said:

"Yes, I agree with you. We are contributing by sharing with you our experience of being psychotic, because we know what it is like, and we deserved some recognition for that, not just a diagnostic label".

After a pause, **Neil** added:

"Psychiatrists don't really listen to us, because after a few minutes they just put on us the label of being psychotic".

Several group members nodded in agreement. Then, looking at Neil, I commented:

"I wonder if part of you may also feel that, here in the project, the professionals get the recognition for the work, whilst you get a diagnostic label".

Grace, a 32-year-old secretary with a diagnosis of schizophrenia, reacted quickly and said:

"I disagree with you! We are here as respected human beings. We feel that you listen to us and treat us as equals. And we go home feeling recharged".

It was rather pleasant to hear that, but I wondered about some possible *splitting* in some of the patients' minds between psychiatrists (who may not listen) and psychotherapists (who may listen). I was aware of the classical psychoanalytic interpretation of primitive splitting between *good objects* and *bad objects*.

However, I decided not to make any analytic interpretation at this stage. Instead, I commented that it was important for psychiatrists and psychotherapists to work together as a team to support them.

3.7(ii) Laughter: defence or enriching reinforcement?

One of the most remarkable aspects of psychosis is the way in which life changes are experienced and interpreted. Change can be resisted fiercely by powerful defences, as it is often associated with breakdown and deterioration. Normal mood fluctuations and other emotional responses are interpreted as presaging catastrophe. Fears of rejection and abandonment are manifested by being at odds with others, which can lead to extreme isolation.

We, the therapists, had learned something from the difficulties in holding the patients together, during the early stages of the group. We were now trying to foster an environment where our patients would feel progressively able to overcome their sealing-over strategies and to add a relational quality to their narratives, with a view to helping them make sense of and integrate their psychotic experience.

The perception of the group as a benign space where members can communicate safely, without feeling persecuted, is particularly important for psychotic patients.

At the beginning of its second year, the group was involved in a discussion about the stigma associated with having to depend on benefits, because it was a reminder of their vulnerability and their psychotic diagnosis. Several patients said that they were reluctant to give up their fatalistic view of life, because they thought it was more realistic than hanging on to a futile sense of hope.

Since he talked about his fear of the CIA, **Patrick** had sometimes been suspicious but was now participating actively in the stigma conversation; he stated:

"Being schizophrenic has become my profession and, through the social security benefits, the state is paying me a salary to do my job: that of being a schizophrenic citizen".

For many psychotic patients, paradoxically, chronicity represents stability. This may result in a group process that appears to be stagnated. One of the paramount tasks of the therapist is to modify the culture of the group, from one of stagnation into one of development. In the group-analytic model, the conductor, who progressively becomes a member, may need to join with the psychotic resistance and articulate it for the group.

This time, rather than talking to Patrick directly, I decided to bring other members in, whilst keeping the focus on the interesting material he had brought to the group. I asked:

"What do other people in the group think of what Patrick has just said about being a schizophrenic citizen?"

Grace responded that she felt reassured by the thought that she was not alone in the jobless situation. She added that Prince Charles had been waiting for so long to have a proper job, as King of the United Kingdom, that he could be considered unemployed as well. Then, **Jacob**, a 40-year-old unemployed teacher with a diagnosis of paranoid schizophrenia, commented:

"With the kind of benefits that Prince Charles receives, I would not mind being unemployed".

All in the group, including **Patrick**, shared a good laugh.

The use of humour seemed to allow members to feel more at ease and to partly come to terms with painful realities. This atmosphere of playfulness in the group brought to mind an old analytical joke, which I had learned during the years of my psychiatric training in Paraguay:

"A patient was in analysis, five times a week, and started each session telling his analyst that there was a crocodile under his bed. The analyst repeatedly interpreted this material as an expression of the patient's unsatisfied oral-aggressive needs and his hostility towards the analyst. However, these interpretations did not appear to have any significant impact on the patient.

Suddenly, the patient stopped coming to his therapy. The analyst became concerned and, unlike his usual practice, decided to telephone him at home. The patient's wife picked up the phone and told the analyst that her husband had been killed by a crocodile".

Of course, this is only a joke. However, it could be seen as a powerful reminder of the problems that some psychotic patients have with the task of discerning between internal and external realities. In contrast to other patients with whom the analysis tends to emphasise the internal world, external reality should not be neglected with psychotic patients.

In fact, sometime previously, a young man with a diagnosis of schizophrenia became front-page news in the British press when he was nearly killed after throwing himself into the lions' den at London Zoo!

The relevance of external reality has implications for the therapeutic technique. Whereas with non-psychotic patients it might be appropriate to interpret the symbolic meaning of their fantasies, with psychotic patients the analyst has to be prepared to take action sometimes to protect the patient from harm, as a reliable attachment figure would do.

Some psychotic patients in groups start a therapy session talking about real-life events that make them feel very anxious, to the point of not being able to concentrate on other things during the day or to sleep at night. They often become depressed, paranoid and withdrawn.

These reactions might be triggered by objectively simple matters; for example, a phone call from a relative, a door-to-door salesman trying to persuade them to change their gas supplier, or an application form from the department of social security to renew their disability living allowance. However, these patients subjectively experience such events as an intrusive and real attack on them by the external world.

Frank started a session feeling quite energetic. He reported that, during one of his recent breakdowns, he took his clothes off in the park. He then walked naked until he was stopped by the police in front of the local library. As he wanted to avoid going back to prison, he told the police that he was a mentally ill patient. Then, the officers took him to a psychiatric hospital.

I listened to Frank carefully but could think of nothing to say. **Roger,** a 42-year-old painter and decorator with a diagnosis of schizo-affective psychosis, who had also had the experience of serving a prison sentence, said:

"You could have told the police that you were going to return the books to the library".

There was unanimous laughter in the group, which lasted several minutes. This was followed by a deeper level of communication and disclosure. Members shared their experiences of getting into trouble with the law and, sometimes, being put in prison.

These unprecedented communications had a light touch that appeared to change the atmosphere in the group. After the session, we were reassured by reading:

The ability to laugh at himself is, paradoxically, an indication that a man is able to take himself seriously. Similarly, a group that dares to accept laughter will also be able to tolerate tears.

(Cox, 1995: 61)

In the next few weeks, members seemed to participate with new enthusiasm and a basic sense of trust developed. For some of them, this was a new experience. Being able to share a good laugh played an important part in the therapeutic group process (see Chapter 1).

At one point, **Patrick** commented that seeing the funny side of his illness was helping him to cope. His comment was well received in the group. Members started to show an increasing curiosity about other people's stories, and became more interested in getting to know one another at a deeper level.

At the beginning of a session, **Roger** (who had previously brought to the group an engaging sense of humour) said that he had had a horrible dream the previous night. He added that he was still feeling very upset and frightened. I invited him to talk about his dream.

Roger then said that the dream started with a visit he paid to his ex-girlfriend. It was chilly and raining. As he approached her house, he was surprised to see her with a new boyfriend in the garden. When she realised that he was walking towards the house, she closed the gate and went indoors, leaving him cold and wet.

After a pause, **Roger** reported that the dream had a second part in which his mother was going on holiday, leaving him alone once more. I asked him to elaborate on that.

He then explained that, in fact, his mother had left for the Continent the day before he had this dream. He added that he woke up in a state of panic and felt overwhelmed by memories of the last time he was admitted to a psychiatric hospital. At the time, he was convinced that he was the devil, but nobody believed him. The more nurses and doctors tried to reassure him that he was not the devil, the more guilty and isolated he felt.

My male co-therapist had the previous week announced that he would be leaving the group soon. He commented that Roger appeared to be a very guilty devil who could not enjoy being a real devil. He added that, in contrast to Roger, the real devil enjoys doing *devilish* things.

Roger looked surprised, whilst some of the other group members smiled mischievously. Eventually, he said that he was feeling so guilty in the dream that he was very anxious about having another breakdown. He then looked down and seemed disconnected.

I was aware of my co-therapist's imminent departure. After a brief pause, I told Roger that his guilt seemed to relate to the departures of significant people, both in the group and in his own life, like his mother's and his girlfriend's, perhaps wrongly believing that it was all his fault. **Roger** slowly looked up and said:

"Yes, it happened to me when I was nine. My parents separated and I thought it was my fault".

Looking at him, I responded:

"Carrying guilty feelings on behalf of other people must be a heavy burden, which can make you feel on the verge of a breakdown".

Roger was silent for a few moments and looked close to tears. He then talked about the day when his mother left home. He said he became anxious when he saw the luggage by the door; he felt his mother was going to leave but nobody said anything to him.

He remembered going to school on that very day with the conviction that he would never see his mother again, because he had been a bad boy. He sighed and added:

> "I can now see that I have always taken responsibility for what happened to my parents and to other people".

He also recalled that, during his psychotic breakdowns, he had an overwhelming feeling of guilt and responsibility for everything that was going wrong in the world. After the session, my co-therapist and I felt more optimistic about Roger's capacity for building a new bridge to connect meaningfully with the world around him.

According to Françoise Davoine (2021), laughter may work on the edge of tears, when silenced stories are expressed. It can also work through delusions, as one of her patients said: "at the crossroads of personal history and world History" (Davoine, 2021: 2).

In addition, Murray Cox (1995) taught us that the use of humour, playfulness and well-intentioned irony can help detoxify primitive affects and promote healthier levels of communication. According to him, when laughter is not a defence it may be an enriching reinforcement of corporate solidarity (see Chapter 1).

We had our laughter: defence or enriching reinforcement? How we long to know!

3.7(iii) Developing a therapeutic culture within the group matrix

In our group, humour helped members to gradually learn to relate to one another more directly, without having to rely on the therapists to connect them up.

We tried to identify and develop a common language with them, for which the use of metaphors proved crucial. This was a steady process which unfolded over the next couple of years in the life of the group.

A metaphor resembles reality from a safe distance. We found that metaphors could be an effective and valuable way of communicating thoughts and feelings, without generating unbearable levels of anxiety.

The use of metaphors enabled our patients to make links and, in turn, understand their traumatic past and difficult realities, without feeling too intimidated or exposed. In addition, metaphors helped some of them develop a capacity to regulate the distance.

Cox and Theilgaard (1987) described their experience of using *mutative* metaphors in group psychotherapy with mentally ill forensic patients. They explained how a metaphor can help touch the depths before it stirs the surface, in contrast to sharper or more direct interpretations.

Indeed, metaphors facilitate working towards understanding, but without threatening the defences that psychotic patients may have against the intolerable meaning of their experiences.

The therapeutic culture in our group progressively became more trusting and reflective, as illustrated in the following clinical material.

In the middle of the group room, we had two small tables that were placed together. On top of the tables there was a pot with a spider plant.

At the beginning of a session, **Greg**, a 36-year-old accountant with a diagnosis of schizo-affective disorder, and **Liza**, a 50-year-old retired hairdresser with a diagnosis of schizophrenia, engaged in a conversation, whilst they were trying to close the gap between the tables and to align them perfectly. I commented that they seemed to want to arrange the tables on behalf of the whole group. **Liza** replied:

"Well . . ., I am a perfectionist and I am disturbed by the gap".

Then, **Greg** said that he also was a perfectionist and felt concerned that, if the gap increased, the pot would fall and would be smashed. **Frank**, became interested in the conversation and said:

"If the pot breaks it would be a mess; the soil would spread all over the carpet. Who would then clean up the mess?"

At that point, everybody was participating in the discussion. **Jacob** said that he was not so concerned about the mess; his main worry was about what would happen to the plant if it lost the soil that was feeding it. **Sophie,** a 37-year-old artist with a diagnosis of manic-depressive psychosis, looked anxious and said:

"Without the container and the soil, the plant will die".

Then, **Greg** commented that the spider plant was very resilient and could survive with little care. **Sophie** responded:

"If the container is broken, the plant will need a new container".

Jacob intervened again and said:

"Containers can be replaced but life cannot".

Following these powerful reflections about containers and life, there was a brief pause. After this, I said that their thinking around the plant could be used as a metaphor for their own experiences of breaking down and surviving. To my pleasant surprise, the metaphor of the tables and the spider plant enabled members to explore more openly the factors that had contributed to their illness.

For a number of sessions, this was the main theme of our group discussions. All members had strong feelings of loss; some felt that their lives had been broken in two parts with a big gap in the middle, like our two tables in the room. For the majority, the gap consisted of those years when they were just drifting through life, unable to align their thoughts and acts together.

Nearly all of them had the first breakdown during the formative years of adolescence or early adulthood. They believed that, no matter how much they could achieve now, they would always feel short-changed for what they could have achieved if they had not had a psychotic breakdown. Their expectation of an ordinary life (career, marriage or partnership, children, long-term projects, etc.) was smashed by their illness and the *empty* years that followed. This overwhelming feeling of loss was particularly strong in the older members.

Despite their pessimism, most of them appreciated the opportunity to gain a deeper understanding and a stronger sense of group belonging. Showing empathy and supporting one another helped them feel they had something useful to give to others.

Their self-esteem improved and they felt more hopeful about having meaningful relationships with other people.

A number of them said that they would have liked to have had a therapy like this many years earlier, as it might have protected them from breaking down and being derailed from their expectations. We thought that this comment also reflected a wish they had for a protective attachment relationship, which could have helped them build a better organised, self-protective and self-regulatory personality structure.

In our own reflections in between sessions, it was helpful to read our group-analytic colleague Andrew Powell's view that metaphors facilitate understanding without threatening the patients' equilibrium:

Metaphor is often paradoxically primitive and concrete in its imagery and abstract in its implications . . . when a metaphor is assimilated and understood, reflective self-awareness is enhanced, the capacity for abstract discrimination widens and . . . the need for defensive operations to come into play is reduced.

(Powell, 1982: 130–131)

The lower level of defensiveness in the group enabled us, the therapists, to be more open about the use of transference interpretations.

Jacob had attended every single group meeting for over three years and participated quite actively. He started a group session talking about his anxieties when, on his way to the project that day, he saw some workers removing asbestos from a crack in the wall in his block of flats. The workers were wearing special protective clothes and masks, but there was no warning for the tenants or the public.

At this point, **Jacob** said he was worried about contamination. Other group members discussed some actions Jacob could take, like contacting the local Council to make a complaint or writing to the department of environmental affairs for advice. I thought that these practical suggestions were a good way of offering support to him, as his fears were based on a real threat. In fact, these comments from other group members helped him manage his anxiety better.

As Jacob's anxiety was contained, I thought it would be safe enough to explore the transference. I said to him:

"Jacob, maybe you are also expressing a fear about being contaminated in the group – something about which we, the therapists (like the workers), had not given you any warning".

Most members said that they could recognise their fear of being contaminated by other people's problems in the group. **Frank**, intervened to say that, after the sessions, he often found himself ruminating on some of what people had said. Sometimes, he felt suspicious and this made it difficult for him to come to some group sessions, although he persevered.

Then, **Jacob** said that he was also ruminating over thoughts, after some of the sessions. He added that being in touch with other people's problems was difficult for him and contributed to his wish to withdraw. However, the understanding and support received in the group was helping him carry on and overcome his isolation.

This is a good example of something that is experienced by many psychotic patients, who tend to deactivate attachment-related affect in order to manage the over-arousal that is often triggered by deep social interaction. As therapists, we have to be particularly sensitive when our patients show this dilemma between withdrawal and engagement. It is important not to put pressure on them in the context of high-arousal emotional material.

In connection with this, we must be prepared to face uncertainty about the appropriateness, timing and pace of interpretations. Stone (1996) suggested that some of the most difficult feelings that psychotic patients experience in therapy groups are triggered by the multiple transferences that emerge, as a result of the complex interactions between the *here and now* and the *then and there*.

Interpretations in such groups may have to be delivered gradually over weeks, months or even years. It is usually more effective to start with a description of what is easily observable and accessible, until it becomes safer to dig into less obvious meaning, step by step – something that can be described as *cumulative interpretation*, which resonates with the concept of *cumulative trauma*.

The following clinical material corresponds to the tenth year in the life of the group:

I usually announced the dates of my holiday breaks two months in advance. The co-therapist and I coordinated our holidays in such a way that one of us did always stay running the group to provide continuity of care. Over the years, possibly in connection with the seniority of my role, some members had reactions of anxiety after my announcements.

Ron, a 33-year-old unemployed plumber with a diagnosis of schizophrenia, and the youngest of three children, developed a pattern after such notices in which he repeatedly talked about his fear of being assaulted by his neighbours. He also showed increased generalised anxiety and paranoid ideation; on one occasion, he needed an inpatient hospital admission coinciding with my annual leave.

In the group, he recalled some of the traumatic events he had experienced in his family. His mother had a psychotic illness that necessitated a number of inpatient psychiatric admissions, when he was a child, and his father was frequently absent from home. This meant that Ron was often left alone with his older brothers who bullied him.

On one occasion before a holiday break, I tentatively suggested to Ron that, perhaps, my absences, as it had happened with his parents' absences, could be contributing to his feeling of being in danger. He responded promptly:

"I admire your extraordinary imagination. My fears have nothing to do with your being away".

The turning point for him came four years after he had joined the group, when some other members suggested that there might be a link between my absences and his own heightened anxieties.

Ron took on board what his fellow patients said, and commented that he now realised my absences reactivated the fears he had experienced as a child during his mother's absences. He added that, on those occasions, his brothers were cruel to him and made him feel unprotected and frightened.

Ron became emotional when he disclosed an incident in which his eldest brother took his pet fish from its bowl and put it in a pan of boiling water. The little fish popped and exploded like a balloon.

People in the group were shocked and supported Ron movingly. The experience strongly resonated with Jacob who had been a victim of bullying.

At the following session, **Jacob** said that the image of a fish exploding had haunted him during the whole week. He added that he was particularly disturbed by the thought that the environment you depend on, like the water for the fish, could turn against you.

In contrast to the disclosures in the early stages of the group, when people hardly engaged with one another, Ron's communication had a deeper and more meaningful impact and led to powerful resonances in other members. Some talked about depending on their parents who, by becoming ill or abusive, turned against them. In many ways, their life experiences were constantly corroborating their belief that they were alone, could not trust anybody or find someone to turn to and, as a result, had to fend for themselves. This painful realisation helped some of them feel stronger and more determined to survive.

Two years later, Ron completed his 'A' levels and went to university to study sociology – something he had wanted to do for a long time. He then felt confident enough to end his therapy, some six years after he had joined the group.

In the project, we thought that a group-analytic and group-attachment culture had gradually developed. Patients had become able to perceive that they were included in a wider *group matrix*, a useful concept advanced by Foulkes (1964, 1973), who described as the common shared ground which ultimately determines meaning and significance of all events and upon which all communications and interpretations, verbal and non-verbal, rest.

A benign group-analytic matrix fosters healthy group attachment, as implicitly stated in Liza Glenn's (1987) landmark article, *The group matrix as a secure base*, the first publication in which the fields of attachment theory and group analysis were linked, following her supervision with John Bowlby (see Chapters 1, 2 and 5).

3.7(iv) Endings and new beginnings

Over the 16 years I co-conducted this group, there were many departures and arrivals. For our members, saying hello to newcomers was not too difficult but saying goodbye was not an easy task. Certainly, it was easier to observe clear reactions to arrivals than to departures. We thought this could relate to the difficulties they had in exploring the impact that departures had on them, in their own lives outside the group. In the early stages of the therapy, they tended to defensively turn a blind eye to any form of separation, perhaps as an out-of-sight, out-of-mind strategy.

During that early period, one of the most striking features had been a general lack of acknowledgement of other group members. When someone did not attend a session, nobody else referred to or asked anything about the absent member.

We, the therapists, had to name in the group those patients who were unexpectedly absent and said that we would contact them. When we asked them why they had not left a message to let the group know, some said that it had not occurred to them to contact us because they thought their absence would not be noticed. They had not experienced attachment figures holding them in mind.

As the group matured over the years, members became more capable of acknowledging and working through separations than what they had been able to in the initial stages.

Martin, a 34-year-old drop-out student of architecture with a diagnosis of manic-depressive psychosis, had been a member of the group for five years.

Initially, his interaction with other people was characterised by his expectations of high intellectual standards, and his intolerance of what he considered futile discussions. His behaviour appeared to be a re-enactment of difficult relationships in his own life: he often fell out with relatives and friends, and had angry outbursts when dealing with public services.

It took Martin a long time to recognise that his intolerance of other people was a reflection of his struggle to keep out of mind his own sense of stagnation and disappointment.

This problem had become apparent after he failed his last exam at university, which also marked the beginning of his *career* as a mentally ill patient. In the last two years of his therapy with us, he worked particularly hard to refocus his efforts, and he became able to resume his studies nearly a decade after his psychotic breakdown.

Martin's relationship with the group and with the external world improved. He completed his degree as an architect and also felt confident to end his therapy at the project. His departure was acknowledged in the group. Members were pleased for him to move on up and wished him well.

At his last session, some were able to honestly express feelings of *healthy* envy and, also, of hope that they may become ready to move on in the not-so-distant future.

In contrast to how the group had function in the past, the session that followed Martin's leaving was devoted to him. **Frank** said that he had enjoyed the analytic comments that Martin usually made about movies.

Jim, a 31-year-old security guard with a diagnosis of schizophrenia, added that these insights stimulated him so much that, the previous weekend, he went back to the cinema – something he had not done for the previous ten years.

Sophie said that she admired Martin because he was a very intelligent and straightforward person; she added that she was missing him and feeling sad. Other members commented that they also felt sad and depressed when they talked about separations.

Bearing this in mind and in view of my senior role, when I decided to leave the project, I thought it would be especially important to give plenty of notice of my departure to patients and colleagues.

The service director and I were the only staff who had worked in the project from the outset. She and I had provided continuity for patients and colleagues alike, and we were perceived by many of them as reliable attachment figures who maximised survival for the project.

During the time I worked at the project, 132 patients (89 men and 43 women) attended our long-term therapeutic programme, of whom 64 people (44 men and 20 women) participated in the small psychotherapy group reported in this clinical case study.

For a therapy group with psychotic patients, the rate of attendance was significantly regular and consistent, above 75 per cent. Average group membership was five years. One member attended the group for 14 years.

We employed a modified version of CORE (clinical outcomes in routine evaluation) as a tool to monitor progress on a broad range of items, including anxiety, depression, traumatic experiences, physical problems, overall functioning, and risk to self and others. We also used an updated version of Larsen, Attkisson, Hargreaves and Nguyen's (1979) patient satisfaction questionnaire to measure the benefits of the therapy for them. The mean satisfaction score fell within the high-range level. As reported by our patients, the most helpful aspects of their treatment were:

- First, the opportunity of communicating and relating with other people who had similar problems.
- Second, keeping in touch with reality.
- Third, learning coping strategies.

- Fourth, overcoming their isolation.
- Fifth, developing autonomy and dealing effectively with everyday life.

I did not know what impact my departure could have on the psychotherapy group I was co-conducting, and on the project as a whole.

In the circumstances, I gave patients and colleagues more than one-year's notice with a view to having as much time as possible to work on separation and loss and on any unfinished business, as well as on reviewing the therapy and preparing for new beginnings.

In discussion with the staff, it was decided that Madeleine (a senior member of the team) would join me, as the co-therapist, some 18 months prior to my departure, so she would continue running the group afterwards.

Our strategy was for her to become increasingly more active in the sessions, so patients could perceive her as the future main therapist of the group and a reliable attachment figure.

Previous co-therapists had all been trainees. That had never been an issue because members perceived me as a reliable leader to whom they could become attached. This time, we considered the handover required to be organised with as much care as possible. In group-analytic terms, this process is also known as *dynamic administration.*

From an attachment perspective, reliability and continuity of care in the therapy group, as well as accessibility to the wider service as a whole, are crucial principles for the treatment and management of psychotic patients. Optimally, this can lead to a deep therapeutic experience of group attachment.

Interestingly, in the twelve months before I left the project, communications in the group increasingly focused on the patients' relationship with their mother or mother figures, particularly the difficulties they had in forming a secure attachment with them. For most members, these early attachment disruptions had resulted in an inability to establish satisfactory intimate relationships.

Gradually, they started to review the work done in the small therapy group and in the project by and large, as well as to explore more openly their relationship with me, with Madeleine, the wider team and other people in their own lives.

Nine months prior to my departure, at the beginning of a session, **Jim** started a conversation about his past difficulties with intimacy. It happened that all the patients in that particular meeting were men; in contrast, the two co-therapists and the observer outside the group circle were women.

He said that, during his adolescence, he was popular amongst his peers and girls showed an interest in him; but he felt too shy to invite any girl out. Since then, every time he found a girl attractive, he avoided her but became obsessed imagining the conversations they could be having. So, instead of a real relationship, it was all in his mind.

Jim attributed his shyness to the insecurity he felt following the experience he had, as a ten-year-old boy, of being sexually abused by a teacher. This trauma took much of his confidence away. In the group, he was now beginning to come to terms with it and wondered if he would be ready to move on.

He added that being able to put into perspective his traumatic experiences, and realising that they were similar to those of other group members, had helped him.

Other patients talked about their difficulties in exploring their sexuality. Some commented that they could not understand why they had been raised in a children's home, whilst their mothers were still alive. They grew up feeling that their mothers had rejected them; nobody took the trouble to explain to them the reasons why they were separated from their parents. They said that this experience affected their confidence and the way they related to other people, especially women.

At this point, Madeleine commented that they, the men, were talking about their intimate feelings in the presence of three women in the group room. She added that their exchanges and insights indicated that they were more prepared to explore intimacy.

Four weeks before my departure, **Jim** started the session saying that he had had a strange dream the previous night, in which Sandy (a tall and slim patient who was attending another small therapy group in the project) came from another planet, the planet of tall people. He realised it was weird but it felt very real, and he woke up feeling anxious and disturbed. Madeleine asked him to try to make sense of his dream.

Jim responded saying that, every so often, he thought that he was merely passing through this planet, like a bystander, not feeling really involved. However, at other times, he felt a strong sense of commitment and belonging. During these times, he frequently had a feeling of being very patriotic, very British.

After a pause, Jim added that he had reflected on his feelings about nationalism. He had a dilemma. On the one hand, when he was emotionally involved, his nationalistic feelings brought about a sense of connection, identity and belonging. On the other hand, he realised that nationalism may bring about hatred and xenophobia, something he did not want to be associated with. On balance, he was in favour of universalism and spirituality; which for him were connected to mutual understanding and reconciliation.

In response to Jim, **Jacob** said that he was sceptical about spirituality and the after-life. In his opinion, all emotions are produced in the brain and so disappear when we die. **Jim** replied that, for him, spirituality was linked to the possibility of being deeply connected to the meaning of things.

I commented that Jim and Jacob were reflecting on important existential questions, about which we all need to reflect from time to time. Apart from this sense of universality, I was also wondering about to what extent these themes might have been partly triggered by the fact that my departure was quite imminent. But I decided not to comment on that, at this point, as I thought it would be more valuable to wait and see how things developed.

Ron then commented that saying goodbye could mean that one may not see the leaving person again, as it occurs when someone dies. He added that it is impossible to know what happens after we die, since nobody has ever returned to planet Earth to let us know.

Richard joined the conversation at this point. He was a 32-year-old unemployed electrician with a diagnosis of schizophrenia, who had joined the group the previous year. With some sadness on his face, he commented:

"We probably just rot away in the ground".

Looking at Richard, Madeleine said:

"I would like to believe that we don't just disappear, but that our legacy stays after we have gone".

Greg, who had followed the conversation intently, responded:

"I agree with you. I think we leave behind a sense of how we have lived our life".

Richard, who appeared to be finding the conversation difficult, whispered:

"I do not believe I will go to heaven when I die".

Madeleine asked him:

"What do you mean Richard?"

To which he replied:

"All my close relatives have died: my mother, my father, my aunt and my uncle. I try to remember the good times".

Richard had been in the group for only ten months and he was coming across as being particularly vulnerable at this point. I was very much aware of his traumatic past.

When he was a small child, his father suddenly died and his mother committed suicide soon afterwards. He was looked after by his mother's sister. She and her husband died in a road accident when he was 17, which triggered his psychotic breakdown a few months later.

In the circumstances, I commented that some of the themes in the conversation appeared to also relate to the fact that my passage through the life of the project was coming to an end. I then reminded Richard that the group would continue after my departure, and that a new co-therapist would join the group to co-run it with Madeleine. He replied that he felt reassured by that.

At this point, I had to keep a sort of binocular vision: preparing members to face the forthcoming loss of their weekly therapeutic relationship with me, whilst reminding them about the fact that the group would continue running, after my departure.

For them, separation from me as a significant attachment figure was triggering memories about other separations, including death. Members became emotionally involved, whilst exploring their emotions.

Jim in fact became quite emotional. He said that, as a child, he was told that *boys don't cry*. Then, he recalled that, soon after his 19th birthday, his maternal grandmother (with whom he lived) died. She was the only reliable attachment figure in his life.

At first, he felt he was strong because he didn't cry; but, a few weeks after her death, he started to have panic attacks. One day, he felt he was dying and went to the Accident and Emergency Department of his local hospital:

"There, I started crying non-stop, like a baby. I needed to get it all out of my system".

At this point, Jim shed a few tears. This was followed by a holding, and containing, two-minute silence.

Then, **Jacob** said he could not remember the last time he cried. He added that he had not learned to handle farewells, particularly since he was prevented from saying goodbye to his mother because she suddenly had a stroke, went into deep coma and did not regain consciousness before she died.

Her death, when he was 18, came as a shock for him. As an adult, he managed to have a girlfriend for several years; however, she left him for his best friend, about which Jacob was devastated and utterly confused. It was after the break-up of the relationship with his girlfriend that he had a psychotic breakdown.

Before the end of that session, Jacob announced that he had decided not to come to the group for my last session, three weeks later, because he would feel too emotional and exposed in front of other people. He asked me to see him individually to say goodbye. I invited him to come to the group and then have an individual session. He accepted the latter but declined to come to the group.

Other members said they understood Jacob's feelings and appreciated his need for an individual session, as he had been my patient for 14 years.

All members, apart from Jacob, came to the final group session I conducted. It was a powerful experience for them, for Madeleine, for the observer and for me. Each member brought a goodbye card to express their gratitude. Sadness was the predominant feeling in all of us. And there were *sad but happy tears*, as some of them put it.

I was touched. This group made a lasting impression on me.

3.8 Discussion

This is a qualitative piece of research and, as such, has an important limitation that we should be cautious about extrapolation. However, the present study supports the ample evidence provided by the specialist literature that psychodynamic group therapy can be highly beneficial for psychotic patients. In this context, an effective group therapy programme is best approached as the undertaking of a team comprising complementary and coordinated abilities and experiences.

In our study, positive outcomes were enhanced by the development of an encompassing and accepting group-attachment culture, in which patients could form person-to-person and person-to-group attachments. The long-term continuity and stability of the day service, with a consistent multi-layered containment structure for the patients (as well as the regular supervision and support for the staff team), played an important part in making the overall therapeutic process successful.

Benedetti (2006) suggested that, for a therapy to be successful, the patient must acquire a feeling of reliance and trust. In healthy development, the mother-child attachment engenders a sense of *basic trust*. This is a complex interpersonal feeling which consists of an expectation, on the part of the child, that the mother will be there to love him and care for him; and, on the part of the mother, an expectation that the child will grow up to be a worthy and loving person (Arieti, 1994). Furthermore:

> In the therapeutic situation, the patient must experience something reminiscent of this basic trust, as perhaps he never experienced.
>
> (Arieti, 1994, quoted in Benedetti, 2006: 34)

This has also been conceptualised as *epistemic trust* (Fonagy and Allison, 2014): a belief in the authenticity and relevance of interpersonally transmitted information, which gives added value to the therapeutic process.

In our attempt to build a secure base for the patients of this study, who struggled to relate and to trust, we tried to foster honest and meaningful communication with them, as a two-way process that required consistency, reliability and mutual trust. In order to achieve this, we were inspired by Bally's attitude:

> For the psychotic patient, the analyst must present a pattern of behaviour; that is with his behaviour show real possibilities of association. But he can only do this by means of a steady steadfast constancy.
>
> (Bally, 1964, quoted in Benedetti, 2006: 35)

Alongside these parameters, Müller (2006) also wrote about his experience working with psychotic patients:

> I think that what is essential in the process of a therapy . . . is the unconditional personal commitment of a therapist who, starting from that which he has understood about his patient, attempts to deal with him in a different manner than he has experienced up to that point. It can be called 'correcting' experience.
>
> (Müller, 2006: 28)

Group affiliation and belonging require from members a basic capacity to relate meaningfully to others, as well as some degree of autonomy. Indeed, autonomy and relatedness can be threatening experiences for psychotic patients who struggle to function in the outside world. By its very nature, a therapy group may disturb the core around which some psychotic defences are built in order to avoid new experiences representing the challenge of life.

Within this frame of reference, repetitive and stereotyped psychotic behaviour might be understood as a defensive attempt to have a sense of familiarity and stability. This may result in a group process that appears to be stagnated, particularly in the early stages.

The group-analytic approach is broad enough (and flexible enough) to allow psychotic patients to participate to the degree with which they feel comfortable. They may be relatively silent for weeks or months and, only after this holding time, feel safe enough to join the group verbally.

In a context of real or imagined threats to survival, the maintenance of group life and the promotion of a constructive group-attachment culture are crucial for the emotional security and wellbeing of psychotic patients. One of the paramount tasks of the therapist is to modify the culture of the group, from one of stagnation into one of development, and to be particularly proactive in situations that potentially threaten the life of the group.

Boundaries have to be negotiated carefully in order to foster a therapeutic group culture that encourages members to interact with each other, which in turn promotes healthy group attachment.

The perception of the group as a caring, attachment space where members can communicate safely and support one another is vital. Group therapists have to persevere in the task of connecting up apparently disorganised and disjointed communications, until patients gradually learn to do so.

In a therapy group there are multiple transferences, which for psychotic patients can be more difficult to process than for non-psychotic patients. However, as the group matures, it is possible to make use of transference interpretations to link the *here and now* with past experiences. The conductor has to decide when the transference is *workable* in psychodynamic terms and when other types of intervention are safer and more effective.

The group-analytic process of *translation* is the group equivalent to making the unconscious conscious in the individual psychoanalytic situation.

Translation offers a wider range of responses: the conductor may choose to link, highlight, challenge, explain, confront or clarify the clinical material presented, depending on the patient's capacity to process it.

In this case study, we also found that metaphors can be an effective and helpful way of communicating thoughts and feelings in a non-threatening way. Metaphors are an important part of the group-analytic currency and facilitate a deeper understanding of the psychotic experience from a safe emotional distance.

In attachment terms, metaphors co-constructed with therapists as attachment figures can help psychotic patients regulate both emotion and distance.

3.9 Conclusion

Patients suffering from psychosis commonly have a background of traumatic disruptions in their early attachments. These experiences affect their capacity to trust people, to form secure attachments and satisfactory relationships, and to develop skills to look after themselves. Their capacity for communication, intimacy and participation in groups is usually impaired. But these ruptures can be repaired when new attachment spaces are created, in which patients become able to trust the therapists and themselves, and to perceive the therapy group as a secure-enough base.

In contrast to individual therapy, where the patient is supposed to be only at the receiving end, a group also provides opportunities to help fellow members. This promotes a sense of confidence and wellbeing when they realise that, besides their problems, they have something to give to others. An approach based on group-attachment thinking has the additional advantage of mitigating more visibly the stigma historically associated with psychosis.

The development of a benign group-attachment culture (including the long-term continuity and stability of the wider day-psychotherapy project) helped the majority of patients, in this case study, to engage with the therapeutic process. In turn, this reduced their isolation and promoted the development of their potential. Most of the patients became able to progress towards a better relationship with the outside world and a more autonomous life.

The task was challenging and daunting at times – but the overall experience was fulfilling and rewarding for patients and staff.

Note: The clinical material presented in this chapter has followed strict guidelines from the General Medical Council to protect the confidentiality due to patients.

References

Adshead G and Aiyegbusi A (2014) Four pillars of security: attachment theory and practice in forensic mental health care. In: Berry K and Danquah AN (eds) *Attachment Theory in Adult Mental Health: A Guide to Clinical Practice*. London: Routledge, pp. 199–212.
Alanen YO, González de Chávez M, Silver ALS and Martindale B (2009) *Psychotherapeutic Approaches to Schizophrenic Psychosis: Past, Present and Future*. London: Routledge.
Amador X and David A (2004) *Insight and Psychosis*. New York: Oxford University Press.
Arieti S (1994) *Interpretation of Schizophrenia*. London: Jason Aronson.
Bally G (1964) Psychoanalysis and social change. *American Journal of Psychoanalysis* 24(2): 145–152.
Bateman AW, Fonagy P, Campbell C, Luyten P and Debbané M (2023) Psychosis. In: Bateman AW, Fonagy P, Campbell C, Luyten P and Debbané M (eds) *Cambridge Guide to Mentalization-Based Treatment (MBT)*. Cambridge: Cambridge University Press, pp. 253–277.
Benedetti G (2006) The first three ISPS Symposia on the Psychotherapy of Schizophrenia in Cery (Lausanne) and Brestenberg (Zurich), 1956, 1959 and 1964. In: Alanen YO, Silver ALS and González de Chávez M (eds) *Fifty Years of Humanistic Treatment of Psychoses*.

Madrid: ISPS & Fundación para la Investigación y el Tratamiento de la Esquizofrenia y otras Psicosis, pp. 31–48.

Berry K, Barrowclough C and Wearden A (2008). Attachment theory: A framework for understanding symptoms and interpersonal relationships in psychosis. *Behaviour Research and Therapy* 46(12): 1275–1282.

Berry K and Bucci S (2016) What does attachment theory tell us about working with distressing voices? *Psychosis* 8(1): 60–71.

Berry K, Bucci S and Danquah AN (eds) (2020) *Attachment Theory and Psychosis: Current Perspectives and Future Directions*. New York: Routledge.

Berry K, Varese F and Bucci S (2017) Cognitive attachment model of voices: Evidence base and future implications. *Frontiers in Psychiatry* 8: 111. Available at www.frontiersin.org/journals/psychiatry/articles/10.3389/fpsyt.2017.00111/full

Bion WR (1957) Differentiation of the Psychotic from the non-Psychotic Personalities. *International Journal of Psychoanalysis* 38: 266–275.

Blink Pesec M, Avguštin Avčin B, Perovsek Šolinc N and Medved K (2019) Short- and long-term group psychotherapy for outpatients suffering from psychosis. In: Urlić I and González de Chávez M (eds) *Group Therapy for Psychosis*. London: Routledge, pp. 73–82.

Bowlby J (1958). The nature of the child's tie to his mother. *International Journal of Psychoanalysis* 39: 350–373.

Bowlby J (1969) *Attachment and Loss: Vol. 1. Attachment* (1991 edition). London: Penguin Books.

Bowlby J (1973) *Attachment and Loss: Vol. 2. Separation, Anxiety and Anger* (1991 edition). London: Penguin Books.

Bowlby J (1988a) *A Secure Base: Clinical Applications of Attachment Theory*. London: Routledge.

Bowlby J (1988b) Developmental Psychiatry Comes of Age. *American Journal of Psychiatry*. 145(1): 1–10.

Branitsky A (2023) Yalom's therapeutic factors in hearing voices groups: A facilitator's perspective. *Psychosis: Psychological, Social and Integrative Approaches*. Available at https://doi.org/10.1080/17522439.2023.2258594

Bucci S, Emsley R and Berry K (2017) Attachment in psychosis: A latent profile analysis of attachment styles and association with symptoms in a large psychosis cohort. *Psychiatry Research* 247: 243–249.

Cañete M and Ezquerro A (1999) Group-Analytic Psychotherapy of Psychosis. *Group Analysis* 32(4): 507–514.

Cañete M and Ezquerro A (2012) Bipolar Affective Disorders and Group Analysis. *Group Analysis* 45(2): 203–217.

Cañete M and Ezquerro A (2017) Developing a group-analytic culture in a day-project for psychotic patients. *Psychosis* 9(2): 149–156.

Caparrós N (1999) Splitting and Disavowal in Group Psychotherapy of for Psychosis. In: Schermer VL and Pines M (eds) *Group Psychotherapy of the Psychoses*. London: Jessica Kingsley Publishers, pp. 83–96.

Caparrós N (2004) *Ser Psicótico: Las Psicosis*. Madrid: Biblioteca Nueva.

Carr SC, Hardy A and Fornells-Ambrojo M (2017) Relationship between attachment style and symptom severity across the psychosis spectrum: A meta-analysis. *Clinical Psychology Review* 59: 145–158.

Castilho P, Martins MJ, Pinto AM, Viegas R, Carvalho S and Madeira N (2017) Understanding the effect of attachment styles in paranoid ideation: The mediator role of experiential avoidance. *Journal of Contextual Behaviour Science* 6(1): 42–46.

Chazan R (1993) Group Analytic Therapy with Schizophrenic Outpatients. *Group* 17(3): 164–178.

Chazan R (1999) The Group as Therapist for Psychotic and Borderline Personalities. In: Schermer VL and Pines M (eds) *Group Psychotherapy of the Psychoses*. London: Jessica Kingsley Publishers, pp. 200–220.

Cohn BR (1988) Keeping the Group Alive: Dealing with Resistance in a Long-Term Group of Psychotic Patients. *International Journal Group Psychotherapy* 38(3): 319–335.

Correale A (1999) Empathy with Psychotic States in the Institutional Group. *Group Analysis* 32(4): 525–534.

Cox M (1995) *Structuring the Therapeutic Process: Compromise with Chaos. The Therapist's Response to the Individual and the Group*. London: Jessica Kingsley Publishers.

Cox M and Theilgaard A (1987) *Mutative Metaphors in Psychotherapy*. London: Tavistock Publications.

Cullberg J (2006) *Psychosis: An Integrative Perspective*. New York: Routledge.

Davoine F (2021) Prologue. In: Gaudillière JM, *Madness and the Social Link*. New York: Routledge, pp. 1–4.

Ezquerro A (2010) Cohesion and coherency in group analysis. *Group Analysis* 43(4): 496–504.

Ezquerro A (2017) *Encounters with John Bowlby: Tales of Attachment*. London and New York: Routledge.

Ezquerro A (2021) Captain Aguilera and filicide: An attachment-based exploration. *Attachment: New Directions in Psychotherapy and Relational Psychoanalysis* 15(2): 279–297(19).

Ezquerro A and Cañete M (2023) *Group Analysis throughout the Life Cycle: Foulkes Revisited from a Group Attachment and Developmental Perspective*. London: Routledge.

Fett AK, Shergill SS, Korver-Nieberg N, Yakub F, Gromann PM and Krabbendam L (2016) Learning to trust: Trust and attachment in early psychosis. *Psychological Medicine* 46(7): 1437–1447.

Foulkes SH (1964) *Therapeutic Group Analysis*. London: George Allen & Unwin.

Foulkes SH (1973) The Group as Matrix of the Individual's Mental Life. In: Foulkes E (ed) (1990) *SH Foulkes Selected Papers: Psychoanalysis and Group Analysis*. London: Karnac Books, pp. 223–234.

Foulkes SH (1974) My philosophy in psychotherapy. In: Foulkes E (ed) (1990) *SH Foulkes Selected Papers: Psychoanalysis and Group Analysis*. London: Karnac Books, pp. 271–280.

Foulkes SH and Lewis E (1944) Group Analysis: Studies of the treatment of groups on psychoanalytic lines. *British Journal of Medical Psychology* 20: 175–184.

Freeman T, Cameron JL and McGhie A (2001) *Chronic Schizophrenia*. London: Routledge.

Freud A (2001) Preface. In: Freeman T, Cameron JL and McGhie A (eds) *Chronic Schizophrenia*. London: Routledge, pp. vii–viii.

Freud S (1905) Three Essays on the Theory of Sexuality. In: *Standard Edition Vol. 7. The Complete Works of Sigmund Freud* (1953 edition). London: The Hogarth Press, pp. 125–243.

Freud S (1911a) Formulations on the Two Principles of Mental Functioning. In: *Standard Edition Vol. 12. The Complete Works of Sigmund Freud* (1953 edition). London: The Hogarth Press, pp. 215–226.

Freud S (1911b) Psychoanalytic notes on an autobiographical account of a case of paranoia (*dementia paranoides*). In: *Standard Edition Vol. 12 The Complete Works of Sigmund Freud* (1953 edition). London: The Hogarth Press, pp. 9–82.

Freud S (1920) Beyond the Pleasure Principle In: *Standard Edition Vol. 18. The Complete Works of Sigmund Freud* (1953 edition). London: The Hogarth Press, pp. 3–64.

Freud S (1924) The Loss of Reality in Neurosis and Psychosis. In: *Standard Edition Vol. 19. The Complete Works of Sigmund Freud* (1953 edition). London: The Hogarth Press, pp. 183–190.

Fromm-Reichmann F (1952) Some aspects of psychoanalytic psychotherapy with schizo-phrenics. In: Brody E and Redlich F (eds) *Psychotherapy with Schizophrenia.* New York: International Universities Press, pp. 89–111.

García-Cabeza I (2019) Therapeutic factors in group psychotherapy for patients diagnosed with psychosis. In: Urlić I and González de Chávez M (eds) *Group Therapy for Psychosis.* London: Routledge, pp. 20–31.

García-Cabeza I, Ducajú M, Chapela E and González de Chávez M (2011) Therapeutic Factors and in Patients Groups with Psychosis. *Group Analysis* 44(4): 421–438.

García-Cabeza I and González de Chávez M (2009) Therapeutic Factors and Insight in Group Therapy for Outpatients Diagnosed with Schizophrenia *Psychosis* 1(2): 134–144.

Gaudillière JM (2021) *Madness and the Social Link.* New York: Routledge.

Glenn L (1987) The group matrix as a secure base. *Group Analysis* 20(2): 109–126.

González de Chávez M (2009) Group Psychotherapy and Schizophrenia. In: Alanen YO, González de Chávez M, Silver ALS and Martindale B (eds) *Psychotherapeutic Approaches to Schizophrenic Psychosis: Past, Present and Future.* New York: Routledge, pp. 251–266.

González de Chávez M, Gutiérrez M, Ducajú M and Fraile JC (2000) Comparative Study of Therapeutic Factors of Group Therapy in Schizophrenic Inpatients and Outpatients. *Group Analysis* 33: 241–264.

Hamm JA, Ridenour JM, Hillis JD, Neal DW and Lysaker PH (2022) Fostering intersub-jectivity in the psychotherapy of psychosis: Accepting and challenging fragmentation. *Journal of Psychotherapy Integration* 32(4): 377–389.

Harder S (2014) Attachment in schizophrenia: Implications for research, prevention and treatment. *Schizophrenia Bulletin* 40(6): 1189–1193.

Holmes J (2014) Attachment theory in therapeutic practice. In: Berry K and Danquah AN (eds) *Attachment Theory in Adult Mental Health: A Guide to Clinical Practice.* London: Routledge, pp. 16–32.

Hopkins J (1984) The probable role of trauma in a case of foot and shoe fetishism: aspects of the psychotherapy of a six-year-old girl. *International Review of Psychoanalysis* 4(1): 16–29.

Hummelen JW (1994) Group Analysis and the Psychoses. *Group Analysis* 27(4): 389–391.

Jackson M (2001) *Weathering the Storms: Psychotherapy for Psychosis.* London: Karnac Books.

Jackson M and Williams P (1994) *Unimaginable Storms: A Search for Meaning in Psycho-sis.* London: Karnac Books.

Klein M (1946) Notes on some Schizoid Mechanisms. *International Journal of Psychoa-nalysis* 27: 99–110.

Klein M (1952) The origins of transference. *International Journal of Psychoanalysis 33*(4): 433–438.

Kanas N (1986) Group Therapy with Schizophrenics: A Review of Controlled Studies. *International Journal of Group Psychotherapy* 36(3): 339–351.

Kanas N (1996) *Group Therapy for Schizophrenic Patients.* Washington, DC: American Psychiatric Press.

Kanas N (2021) *Integrative Group Therapy for Psychosis: An Evidence-Based Approach.* New York: Routledge.

Kapur R (1999) Clinical Interventions in Group Psychotherapy. In: Schermer VL and Pines M (eds) *Group Psychotherapy of the Psychoses.* London: Jessica Kingsley Publishers, pp. 280–300.

Karen R (1998) *Becoming attached: First relationships and how they shape our capacity to love.* New York: Oxford University Press.

Kennard D (2019) Groups in therapeutic communities for people suffering from psychosis. In: Urlić I and González de Chávez M (eds) *Group Therapy for Psychosis*. London: Routledge, pp. 108–118.

Kilpatrick C and Kanas N (2023) Is Virtual Group Therapy an Effective Alternative to In-Person Group Therapy for Patients with Early Psychosis? *International Journal of Group Psychotherapy* 73(3): 239–248.

Korver-Nieberg N, Berry K, Meijer C, de Haan L and Ponizovsky AM (2015) Associations between attachment and psychopathology dimensions in a large sample of patients with psychosis. *Psychiatry Research* 228(1): 83–88.

Koukis AE (2009) Depression in Psychosis and the Therapeutic Impact of the Group-Analytic Group. *Psychosis* 1(2): 167–177.

Kreeger L (1991) The Psychotic Patient. In: Roberts J and Pines M (eds) *The Practice of Group Analysis*. London: Routledge, pp. 123–127.

Larsen DL, Attkisson CC, Hargreaves WA and Nguyen TD (1979) Assessment of client/patient satisfaction: development of a general scale. *Evaluation Program Planning* 2(3):197–207.

Lavin R, Bucci S, Varese F and Berry K (2019) The relationship between insecure attachment and paranoia in psychosis: A systematic literature review. *British Journal of Clinical Psychology* 59(1): 39–65.

Lazell EW (1921) The Group Treatment of Dementia Praecox. *Psychoanalytic Review* 8: 168–179.

Lefevre DC (1994) The power of counter-transference in groups for the severely mentally ill. *Group Analysis* 27(4): 441–447.

Lefevre DC (1999) Psychotherapy Training for Nurses as Part of a Group Psychotherapy Project: The Pivotal Role of Counter-transference. In: Schermer VL and Pines M (eds) *Group Psychotherapy of the Psychoses*. London: Jessica Kingsley Publishers, pp. 324–346.

Liotti G (2004) Trauma, dissociation and disorganized attachment: Three strands of a single braid. *Psychotherapy: Theory, Research, Practice and Training* 41(4): 472.

Longden E and Corstens D (2020) Making sense of voices: perspectives from the hearing voices movement. In: Berry K, Bucci S and Danquah AN (eds) (2020) *Attachment Theory and Psychosis: Current Perspectives and Future Directions*. New York: Routledge, pp. 223–236.

Lucas RN (1992) The psychotic personality: A psychoanalytic theory and its application in clinical practice. *Psychoanalytic Psychotherapy* 6(1): 73–79.

Lucas RN (1993) The psychotic wavelength. *Psychoanalytic Psychotherapy* 7(1): 15–24.

Marrone M (1998) *Attachment and Interaction*. London: Jessica Kingsley Publishers.

Martindale B, Bateman A, Crowe M and Margison, F (2000) *Psychosis: Psychological Approaches and their Effectiveness*. London: Gaskell.

Melzer M (1979) Group Treatment to Combat Loneliness and Mistrust in Chronic Schizophrenics. *Hospital Community Psychiatry* 30(1): 18–20.

Milders C (1994) Kernberg's Object Relations Theory and the Group Psychotherapy of Psychosis. *Group Analysis* 27(4): 419–432.

Müller C (2006) Beginnings of the International Symposia for the Psychotherapy of Schizophrenia. In: Alanen YO, Silver ALS and González de Chávez M (eds) *Fifty Years of Humanistic Treatment of Psychoses*. Madrid: ISPS & Fundación para la Investigación y el Tratamiento de la Esquizofrenia y otras Psicosis, pp. 23–30.

Nitzgen D (2019) Comment of Vollon, Gimenez and Bonnet: The psychotic transference in groups. *Group Analysis* 52(4): 561–570.

Parloff MB and Dies RR (1977) Group Psychotherapy Outcome Research. *International Journal Group Psychotherapy* 27(3): 281.

Pines M (1995) Intimacy and Spontaneity in Group and Family Therapy: A Symposium. *12th International Congress of Group Psychotherapy*, Buenos Aires, Argentina.

Pollard C, Bucci S, MacBeth A and Berry K (2020) The revised Psychosis Attachment Measure: Measuring disorganized attachment. *British Journal of Clinical Psychology* 59(3): 335–353.

Powell A (1982) Metaphor in Group Analysis. *Group Analysis* 15(2): 127–135.

Prior J (2007) Psychosis and the Therapeutic Potential of Group Analytic Psychotherapy. *Advancing Practice in Bedfordshire* 4(1): 6–14.

Resnik S (1999) A Biography of Psychosis: Individuals, Groups and Institutions. In: Schermer VL and Pines M (eds) *Group Psychotherapy of the Psychoses*. London: Jessica Kingsley Publishers, pp. 97–128.

Resnik S (2005) *Glacial Times: A Journey through the World of Madness*. New York: Routledge.

Restek-Petrović B, Bogović A, Oresković-Krezler N, Grah M, Mihanović M and Ivezić E (2014) The perceived importance of Yalom's therapeutic factors in psychodynamic group psychotherapy for patients with psychosis. *Group Analysis* 47(4): 456–471.

Rey H (1994) *Universals of psychoanalysis in the treatment of psychotic and borderline states: Factors of space-time and language* (ed) Magagna J. London: Free Association Books.

Rico L and Sunyer M (2001) Análisis Comparativo de los Factores Terapéuticos Grupales en la Esquizofrenia II: Resultados y Discusión. *Psiquis* 22: 57–72.

Ridenour JM, Hamm JA, Neal DW, Hillis JD, Gagen EC, Zalzala AB and Lysaker PH (2023) Navigating an impasse in the psychotherapy for psychosis. *Journal of Contemporary Psychotherapy* 53: 235–243.

Robbins M (2019) *Psychoanalysis meets Psychosis: Attachment, separation, and the undifferentiated unintegrated mind*. New York: Routledge.

Rosenfeld H (1992) *The Psychotic: Aspects of the Personality*. London: Karnac Books.

Ruffalo ML (2023) The Psychotherapy of Schizophrenia: A Review of the Evidence for Psychodynamic and Non-Psychodynamic Treatments. *Psychiatry and Clinical Psychopharmacology* 33(3): 222–228.

Sandison R (1991) The Psychotic Patient and Psychotic Conflicts in Group Analysis. *Group Analysis* 24(1): 73–83.

Sandison R (1994) Working with Schizophrenics Individually and in a Group: Understanding the Psychotic Process. *Group Analysis* 27(4): 73–83.

Schermer VL and Pines M (eds) (1999) *Group Psychotherapy of the Psychoses*. London: Jessica Kingsley Publishers.

Seager M (2014) Using attachment theory to inform psychologically-minded care services, systems and environments. In: Berry K and Danquah AN (eds) *Attachment Theory in Adult Mental Health: A Guide to Clinical Practice*. London: Routledge, pp. 213–224.

Searles HF (1965) *Collective Papers on Schizophrenia*. London: The Hogarth Press.

Semrad EV (1948) Psychotherapy of the Psychosis in a State Hospital. *Diseases of the Nervous System* 9: 105–111.

Smith J (1999) Five questions about Group Therapy in Long-Term Schizophrenia. *Group Analysis* 32(4): 515–524.

Spotnitz H (1957) The Borderline Schizophrenic in Group Psychotherapy: The Importance of Individuation. *International Journal of Group Psychotherapy* 7: 155–174.

Standish CT and Semrad EV (1951) Group Psychotherapy with Psychotics. *Journal of Psychiatric Social Work* 20: 143–150.

Steiner J (1991) A Psychotic Organization of the Personality. *International Journal of Psychoanalysis* 72(2): 201–207.

Stern D (1985) *A View from Psychoanalysis and Developmental Psychology.* New York: Basic Books.

Stone WN (1996) *Group Psychotherapy for People with Chronic Mental Illness.* New York: The Guilford Press.

Štrkalj Ivezić S and Urlić I (2015) The capacity to use the group as a corrective symbiotic object in group analytic psychotherapy for patients with psychosis. *Group Analysis* 48(3): 315–331.

Sullivan HS (1953) *The Psychiatric Interview.* New York: Norton & Co.

Sullivan HS (1962) *Schizophrenia as a Human Process.* New York: Norton & Co.

Summers A and Adshead G (2020) Bringing together psychodynamic and attachment perspectives on psychosis. In: Berry K, Bucci S and Danquah AN (eds) (2020) *Attachment Theory and Psychosis: Current Perspectives and Future Directions.* New York: Routledge, pp. 131–143.

Tiller JL (2023) Attachment in psychosis. PhD Dissertation, University of Southampton. Available at https://eprints.soton.ac.uk/484118/1/AttachmentInPsychosisThesis_Submission_pdfa.pdf

Urlić I (1999) The Therapist's Role in the Group Treatment of Psychotic Patients and Outpatients: A Foulkesian Perspective. In: Schermer VL and Pines M (eds) *Group Psychotherapy of the Psychoses.* London: Jessica Kingsley Publishers, pp. 148–180.

Urlić I (2010) The Group Psychodynamic Psychotherapy Approach to patients with Psychosis. *Psychiatria Danubina* 22(1): 10–14.

Urlić I (2012) Group Psychotherapy for Patients with Psychosis: A Psychodynamic (Group-Analytic) Approach. In: Kleinberg JL (ed) *The Wiley-Blackwell Handbook of Group Psychotherapy of the Psychoses.* Chichester: John Wiley and Sons, pp. 547–570.

Urlić I and González de Chávez M (eds) (2019) *Group Therapy for Psychosis.* London: Routledge.

Urlić I, Klain E, Ivezić S, Restek-Petrović B and Grah M (2022) Croatia: The development of a psychodynamic approach to the comprehensive treatment of persons with psychic disorders. *Psychoanalytic Psychotherapy* 36(4): 347–362.

Volkan VD (1990) The Psychoanalytic Psychotherapy of Schizophrenia. In: Boyer LB and Giovacchini P (eds) *Master Clinicians on Treating the Regressed Patient.* Northvale, NJ: Jason Aronson.

Volkan VD (1995) *The Infantile Psychotic Self and Its Fates: Understanding and Treating Schizophrenics and other Difficult Patients.* Northvale, NJ: Jason Aronson.

Vollon C, Gimenez G and Bonnet C. (2018) The psychotic transference in groups. *Group Analysis* 52(4): 491–502.

Weijers JG, ten Kate C, Debbané M, Bateman AW, de Jong S, Selten JPCJ and Eurelings-Bontekoe EHM (2020) Mentalization and Psychosis: A Rationale for the Use of Mentalization Theory to Understand and Treat Non-Affective Psychotic Disorder. *Journal of Contemporary Psychotherapy* 50(3): 223–232.

Wickham S, Sitko K and Bentall RP (2015) Insecure attachment is associated with paranoia but not hallucinations in psychotic patients: The mediating role of negative self-esteem. *Psychological Medicine* 45(7): 1495–1507.

Yakeley J and Burbridge-James W (2018) Psychodynamic approaches to suicide and self-harm. *British Journal of Psychiatry Advances* 24(1): 37–45.

Arturo Ezquerro: https://orcid.org/0000-0002-9910-4576

María Cañete: https://orcid.org/0000-0001-7967-1103

Chapter 4

Suicide risk

When group attachment is not enough, or is it?

Arturo Ezquerro

4.1 Introduction: Individual or group psychotherapy for suicidal patients?

I was a student at the London Institute of Group Analysis, when the late Dennis Brown delivered a lecture, on psychosomatic disorders and the group, for the Foundation Course. It was the academic year 1987–1988. Brown played with an idea on the complementary nature of individual and group psychotherapies:

> After a period of successful individual psychotherapy, a patient becomes less neurotic but not necessarily more mature. And after a period of successful group psychotherapy a patient becomes more mature but not necessarily less neurotic.
> (Brown, 1988)

I later learned that this idea had been originally formulated by Michael Balint (1961). It made a lot of sense to me. Indeed, Dennis Brown was a coherent and experienced psychiatrist who had trained as a psychoanalyst and then as a group analyst; he had the best of both worlds.

At the time, I was co-conducting a weekly out-patient group at the Tavistock Clinic. The co-therapist and I struggled to contain emotionally a single, childless, deeply depressed and isolated late-middle-aged woman in the group. This patient was a Jewish survivor of the Holocaust and assessed as a suicide risk.

She brought horrific memories of the brutal social pathology of Nazism and of her time at Auschwitz, where all members of her family were exterminated in the gas chambers. Members were very sympathetic and supportive and, yet, she was feeling utterly helpless and often talked about an oppressive sense of guilt as a survivor. This often led her to experiencing disturbing suicidal ideation.

Our supervisor, Caroline Garland (1980, 1982), advised us to see this patient for additional individual sessions, as and when required, alongside the group sessions. That intervention proved highly beneficial for the patient, for group members and for the therapists, as it enabled us to be more efficient with our therapeutic task. Individual and group anxieties diminished considerably and, to our great relief, the patient survived (Ezquerro, 1989).

DOI: 10.4324/9781003271956-5

Suicide is one of the main causes of death in some age and gender groups; it is difficult to predict and prevent. Having said that, in a ground-breaking piece of work, *Le Suicide: Étude de sociologie* [Suicide: A Study in Sociology], Émile Durkheim (1897) showed that it is possible to make some accurate predictions about differing suicide rates by gathering comparative data from a large population. He discovered that men died by suicide more than women, childless persons more than parents, single more than married, Protestants more than Catholics or Jews, and the well-educated more than the poorly educated.

Durkheim was a French sociologist who pioneered the establishment of sociology as an academic discipline and is considered one of the architects of modern social science. Regrettably, the obvious practical implications of his findings on suicide (which are still relevant today) have received insufficient attention in prevention programmes (Frances, 2021).

Indeed, today, there is still permanency of suicide rates on a high or low level depending on the degree of industrialisation, religious affiliation and, interestingly, climate (with special significance in and around Europe). Northern countries with a high degree of industrialisation, Protestant religious affiliation and rather few sunny days have considerably higher suicide rates than southern countries with a low degree of industrialisation, Catholic or Jewish religious affiliation and larger numbers of sunny days (WHO, 2023; Samaritans, 2024).

The above differences could best be explained by the nature of interpersonal and group attachment bonding as a protective factor; whereas climate could influence biological rhythms and mental states, hence, triggering suicidal behaviour or otherwise.

At this point, I would like to suggest that we should not underestimate the protective role that religion has in terms of suicide prevention, under ordinary circumstances. Having said that, I would also like to point out that, under other circumstances, religious fanaticism and despair can lead to immolation, as in the case of suicide bombing.

Sigmund Freud appeared to have suggested that believing in God is basically a form of *collective neurosis*. This statement possibly underlies a death anxiety and a fear of oblivion, as well as a wish for being immortal. In contrast, the French psychoanalyst, and Holocaust survivor, Boris Cyrulnik (2017, 2018), in his book *Psychothérapie de Dieu* [Psychotherapy from God] referred to the fact that many people seem to develop a type of attachment relationship with God, which protects them from suicide and helps them construct resilience.

I must confess that the concept of *attachment with God* is not part of my theoretical thinking or clinical practice. Having said that, I do respect people's spirituality and their belief in the postulated existence of a superior being. When some of my patients have referred to a dyadic attachment with God, I have also appreciated a form of *group attachment*, as it involves a sense of group belonging and a connection with others who share such a belief.

Regarding gender, in the 21st century, there are substantial differences in suicidal behaviour that are similar to Durkheim's findings of the 19th century, with male huge preponderance in consummated suicide (four times as many men than women) and female vast preponderance in suicide attempts (WHO, 2023; Samaritans, 2024). The reasons for these sex differences in suicidality, which are consistently stable across countries, cultures and times, have not been well investigated and need further empirical research.

There is no doubt that psychosocial motives play not only an important role as triggers for suicidal acts but also are important determinants for the development of suicidal behaviour. The most important motive for suicidality is certainly the impending loss or rupture (real or perceived as such) of attachment relationships (Ezquerro, 2023).

As suicide requires a wilful attempt to die, it is generally accepted that it cannot occur in non-human animals. However, there have been anecdotal reports of domesticated animals unintentionally *killing* themselves by inanition, especially dogs. The main reason for this behaviour is the break-up of a long-held social tie with the people with whom the animal had maintained a sort of *attachment* relationship. Sometimes, dogs die after not accepting any food from another individual, following the death of their emotionally closest owner.

From a biopsychosocial perspective, in certain families, a *genetic* or *phenotypical* burden of suicidal behaviour could be confirmed by twin and adoption studies (McLaughlin, McGowan, O'Neill and Kernohan, 2014). This burden is often connected to psychiatric illnesses such as severe depression and bipolar affective disorder (see Chapter 2), as well as schizophrenia and borderline personality disorder.

Postmortem brain and peripheral biochemical studies have shown a dysfunction of the serotonergic system in suicide victims and suicide attempters (Mann, 2013; Turecki and Brent, 2016; Navarro et al, 2023). In psychopathological terms, this is correlated to a loss of impulse control, aggressiveness, affective instability and violent methods in the suicidal act.

Other empirical studies (Timmerman and Cholbi, 2020) have confirmed that, suicidal behaviour is linked to psychosocial factors and existential issues. However, empirical data about successful suicide prevention is still lacking and successful therapeutic interventions only exist for subgroups of suicide attempters and other high suicide-risk patients.

In addition, other researchers (O'Connor and Nock, 2014) have considered that, by and large, suicide has been regarded as a psychological problem within the individual. According to them, this incomplete comprehension of the problem might explain why, despite the increasing availability of psychological treatments during the 20th century, there has been little impact on overall suicide rates.

This fact had been vividly illustrated by Hillman and Ventura (1992) in their book *We've had a hundred years of psychotherapy and the world's getting worse*. In the circumstances, it is important to consider suicide as a public-health issue (Jenkins, 2022). Effective prevention can only improve as a collective enterprise that involves society-as-a-whole. And the problem of suicidality should be treated in line with other life-threatening conditions.

Although individual suicides are sporadic and unpredictable, aggregated group rates continue to be remarkably constant over time in any given place. However, this can change under particular circumstances; for example, suicide rates significantly drop during war time, which triggers a collective feeling of solidarity, and considerably rise during major financial crises. It is important to approach this problem from a group perspective. Ultimately, when a person dies by suicide, there is a societal failure.

According to Frances (2021), effective prevention requires reducing social disorganisation and correcting societal pathologies, not just treating mental disorder. This is consistent with previously held views on suicide prevention and the management of suicide risk (Shneidman, 1985; Van Orden et al, 2010; O'Connor and Nock, 2014; Bedi, Muller and Classen, 2014; Ford and Gomez, 2015; Adams, Balbuena, Meng and Asmundson 2016).

From a clinical practice standpoint, I discussed the management of suicide risk with my mentor John Bowlby (the *father* of attachment theory) in one of our regular supervision sessions, in 1990. He made a distinct observation in which he brought an attachment dimension to the problem, which made an awful lot of sense:

Ultimately, behind any suicide act, there is a crisis of attachment.
(John Bowlby, personal communication to Arturo Ezquerro, 1990)

I also discussed suicide risk with Malcolm Pines, my training analyst. Being a psychiatrist who had trained in psychoanalysis and in group psychotherapy with SH Foulkes (the *father* of group analysis), Pines considered well-functioning therapy groups optimal for the containment of suicide risk, as they often represent a microcosm of society, afford a deep exploration of the impact of societal pathologies and protect patients from excessive isolation.

Having said that, a particular group at a given time might not be containing enough and, regarding the more vulnerable group members, he stated:

It is sometimes necessary to give patients a session on their own.
(Pines, 1980: 174)

Earl Hopper, a sociologist, psychoanalyst and group analyst, initially advocated combined treatment for the most traumatised, vulnerable or difficult patients. Nevertheless, through his own experience as a clinician, he changed his mind:

I do not think in terms of individual versus group modalities of treatment for any patient. What I used to recommend only for my most difficult patients, I now recommend for them all.

(Hopper, 2001: 143)

4.1(i) Contents and aims of the chapter

This chapter has come to be a hybrid piece of work on both suicidality and combined psychotherapy treatment. Originally, it was conceived as a qualitative clinical-process study, in which concurrent individual and group psychotherapy were combined in the treatment and management of a middle-aged man, who was a suicide risk. He had a history of major disruptions and ruptures in his early attachment relationships, as well as other traumatic experiences, which contributed to psychotic breakdowns, suicide attempts and in-patient psychiatric admissions.

The patient joined a weekly outpatient psychotherapy group that I conducted in an NHS community hospital; he became strongly, though anxiously, attached to the group and made steady progress. However, following an unfortunate combination of adverse factors, including the break-up of the relationship with his girl-friend and the news of his father's impending death, the patient stabbed himself and nearly died.

On his return to the therapy group, several weeks later, members talked about feeling unable to cope with their increasing anxiety that, at the next attempt, their fellow member might *succeed* in killing himself. In the circumstances, I took the group's anxiety seriously and asked a colleague to offer weekly individual psycho-therapy for this patient, concurrently with the group sessions. In order to empiri-cally validate this clinical decision, I will include a thorough review of the literature on combined treatment.

Since the patient was so close to killing himself, which would have been a trau-matic experience for his family and for the professionals caring for him, I decided to expand the chapter and also include a thorough piece of research on suicidality. In doing so, I drew on relevant studies on the suicide question from the disciplines of sociology, anthropology, philosophy, psychoanalysis, attachment theory and wider mental health. Elaborating on from these studies, an exploration of interper-sonal and group attachment processes will be offered, as a theoretical and clinical aid for the understanding and management of suicidal crises.

From the specialist literature review and the qualitative clinical-process research presented, I shall conclude that suicide can be prevented in clinical settings and in society, although this is indeed a long shot. An increasing awareness and enhanced understanding of suicide-risk factors can help reduce suicide rates. This would have to be, necessarily, a collective task for which an attachment-based ethos can make a significant difference, within the wider context of comprehensive and mul-tisectoral plans and strategies, which are very much needed. In terms of clinical work, I will also conclude that people who seriously contemplate or attempt taking their life need to have several layers of containment, as well as access to more than one secure base.

With this chapter, I aim to contribute to suicide prevention and to the efficient management of suicide risk, both in clinical settings and in the wider context of society. Combining individual and group psychotherapy, coordinating healthcare systems, agreeing national and global strategies, and involving society by and large can definitely be of help.

As such, the theme of euthanasia and assisted suicide in terminally ill patients is beyond the scope of this chapter.

4.2 Combining individual and group psychotherapy with highly vulnerable patients

Before exploring suicidality further, let me review the literature on combined individual and group treatment. The first known clinical publication on the subject is attributed to Louis Wender and Aaron Stein, two of the pioneers of group therapy in the USA (Wender and Stein, 1949). However, a form of combined treatment had de facto been practised earlier during the origins of group analysis, both in the USA and in Europe.

The term *group analysis* was first coined by the American psychoanalyst Trigant Burrow (1927). He developed an interest in the individual's relationship to the social forces of which each person is a part, and used group sessions as a vehicle to complement his individual patients' psychoanalytic treatment. Burrow never obtained Freud's approval of his work and later replaced the term group analysis by *phylo-analysis* (Burrow, 1958).

SH Foulkes, a German-born psychoanalyst, was the founder of European group analysis. He was inspired by Burrow's early work and put the group at the centre of his therapeutic orientation. After being asked to surrender his passport, he had to flee Germany to the relative safety of England to escape the Nazi threat, in 1933.

At the outbreak of the Second World War, in 1939, Foulkes was seeing a number of patients individually for psychoanalytic treatment. That happened at his private practice in Exeter, a small city in the West of England. During the previous twelve or so years:

> He had often speculated how interesting it would be if his patients, lying on the couch one after another, could be brought together to meet, react and interact with each other.
>
> (Foulkes E, 1990: 13)

And, in 1940, he decided to put some of his individual patients together in a group, whilst he continued seeing them on a one-to-one basis, although less frequently. Thus, Foulkes' first experience of conducting a psychotherapy group was a way of combining individual and group-analytic treatment.

His first article on group analysis was written in 1942, whilst he was awaiting his call-up for the army as a medical officer; it was published two years later (Foulkes and Lewis, 1944). His co-author, Eve Lewis, was a co-therapist in some of the groups presented in the article. Altogether, a total of fifty patients were treated during the period 1940–1942.

In their original publications, Foulkes and Lewis (1944) and Burrow (1927) referred openly to the combination of group-analytic and individual psychotherapy. However, they did not expand on the advantages and disadvantages of this treatment modality.

In terms of his actual practice, Foulkes was initially enthusiastic and considered his method of combining both therapies concurrently to be, in most cases, the treatment of choice.

Yet, in his early writings, he did not seem to have developed a clear standpoint with regard to the implications of such a therapeutic combination. On balance, he saw both therapies as complementary and emphasised the need to combine them, particularly when in the group

> deeper, earlier, regressive levels are too active. This, significantly, coincides with the need for individual interview.
>
> (Foulkes, 1948: 31)

Having said that, he did not elaborate theoretically on his early experimentation and later appeared to change his mind:

> Further experience has made still clearer the merits and demerits of combined treatment or group analysis by itself and our bias has on the whole been to leave the group situation uncomplicated while the patient participates in a group .
>
> (Foulkes, 1964: 37)

He continued developing group analysis, which included the introduction of twice-weekly groups, and became passionate about the power of group treatment. In his last book, he eventually wrote:

> With more experience it becomes more and more likely that most problems can be solved in intensive group-analytic groups.
>
> (Foulkes, 1975: 67)

He became even more radical and stated that, if individual therapy had any place, it would be after group analysis and then only

> if it proves at all necessary.
>
> (Foulkes, 1975: 67)

Looking at the whole of his career as a group analyst, Foulkes seemed to have adopted a number of different positions (Ezquerro and Bajaj, 2007):

- First, he advocated what appeared to be a more developmentally natural (or orthodox?) order of individual therapy followed by group therapy. This could be seen as a replication of a normal sequence in ordinary child development, which usually starts with a one-to-one relationship with the mother (or mother figure) followed by increasing exposure to group situations: the family group, the peer group and so on.

- Second, he placed individual and group therapy sessions concurrently as the treatment of choice (a compromise?). I speculate that this could be a symbolic way of acknowledging that early human development happens in multiple contexts, simultaneously: the relationship with the mother, the father, the family group and wider social groups.

- Third, he advanced a powerful statement about the primacy of the group as a sole form of treatment (a radical view?). This is consistent with the views of a number of contemporary group-analytic theorists and practitioners (Hobdell, 1991; Pines, 1996; Maratos, 1996; Blackwell, 2021; Caparrós et al, 2004). According to these authors, the individual is always born out of a group, and the individual mind is necessarily a group mind.

- Fourth, later in his career, Foulkes developed an interest in a (pragmatic?) variant of the combined approach, in which group members were seen individually in turn, one per week, so that each member would be seen approximately once every two months (Hobdell, 1991). He never explained what led him to such a combination, although we may argue that this was a way of creating additional space for a more distinct review of his patients' progress on a regular basis.

According to Hobdell (1991), Foulkes' position on combined treatment fluctuated so much because he was, above all, an exploratory thinker whom we should not burden with a definite and unequivocal statement.

Having said that, Foulkes' basic trend or goal was to make the group experience complete in itself and, with increasing knowledge and ability, this was largely achieved in classical group-analytic practice.

Within this, a considerable large number of contemporary group analysts have suggested that only occasionally may members of the group need to be seen individually, to work on something for which there is insufficient time or space in the group.

Most of Foulkes' statements throughout his career followed the direction of the completeness of the therapeutic group experience. As he matured, he also tended to suggest time and again that, if someone needed individual analysis, this should preferably take place after the group treatment and, in that case, individual therapy should not be too long (Hobdell, 1991).

The late Foulkes' tradition had a powerful influence on a post-Foulkesian generation of group analysts, who developed a sort of pan-group therapeutic belief that there are no fundamental limitations to group therapy, even with the most complex cases.

And, when individual sessions are needed in addition to the therapy group, most group analysts tend to work from the major premise that the group is primary and comes before everything else:

The welfare and integrity of the group has to be maintained at all times.

(Hobdell, 1991: 141)

During my training as a group analyst, in the late 1980s and early 1990s, I was educated on the premise that the group must remain a format of foremost therapeutic significance, and should not be experienced as a mere adjunct to individual therapy. However, everyday clinical reality says that a significant proportion of patients experience individual sessions as more intense and valuable than group sessions.

In recent decades, mainstream group-analytic training in the UK has paid increasing attention to the needs that some patients have for individual therapy (Hopper, 2001; Behr and Hearst, 2005; Schlapobersky, 2016). This has resulted on a common attitude amongst contemporary group analysts to be more open-minded to flexibly giving group patients additional individual sessions in times of crisis.

When, as part of the assessment process, the indication at the outset is to combine both therapies, the tendency is to offer one after the other rather than concurrently. The usual pattern is to start with individual therapy for variable lengths of time, followed by group therapy; but it can be the other way around, depending on the specific needs of each patient.

In contrast to mainstream group analysis, most of the wider specialist group literature has concentrated on concurrent combined therapy. In the European context, I would highpoint Kulawik (1982), Filippi (1983), Battegay (1986), Cohn (1986), Ezquerro (1996), Hobdell (1991), Van Montfoort and Thelosen (1994), Zulueta and Mark (2000), Hopper (2001), Karterud, Johansen and Wilberg (2007), Ezquerro and Bajaj (2007) and Kegerreis (2007).

And in the American context, I would highlight Sager (1960), Aronson (1964), Porter (1980), Durkin (1983), Slavinska-Holy (1983), Lofton, Daugherty and Mayerson (1983), Wong (1988), Lipsius (1991), Rutan and Stone (1993), Ulman (2002), Dluhy (2007), Segalla (1996, 2007) and Schermer (2009).

Overall, these authors, emphasise the complementary nature of both therapies; for their clinical experience, the benefits of combined treatment outweigh the possible difficulties associated to a likely split transference. Optimally, patients would have the best of both worlds:

- On the one hand, the mirroring capacity of a therapy group can help patients to see aspects of themselves that an individual analyst may not supply.
- On the other hand, individual therapy can provide patients with a more intimate level of exploration that may not be available in the group.

The main reasons given by these clinicians for recommending concurrent combined treatment for group patients can be summarised as follows:

- First, in generic terms, when patients cannot achieve enough individuation in the group.

- Second, when the group's containing capacity is insufficient for the level of anxiety presented by the individual patient.
- Third, when the group cannot provide enough space for the patient's early or difficult material to be sufficiently explored.
- Fourth, and most importantly, when there is a major upheaval (such as a suicidal crisis) that needs unravelling, without compromising the safety of the patient or the overall balance of the group.

As one can expect, the above practitioners predominantly concentrated on patients who were highly vulnerable, from the outset or after a crisis. A large proportion of these patients had a diagnosis of *borderline personality disorder*, a condition associated with an increase in suicidality and self-injurious behaviour.

4.3 Suicide from an attachment perspective

In addition to the psychotherapy literature on combined treatment, with an emphasis on the management of major crises, including suicide risk and self-harm, there has been an increasing interest in the understanding of suicide from an attachment perspective. I have found especially helpful reading and learning from the following studies:

Bowlby (1973, 1979, 1980, 1984, 1988), Kaplan and Worth (1993), Ledgerwood (1999), Stepp et al (2008), Lizardi et al (2011), Levi-Belz, Gvion, Horesh and Apter (2013), Palitsky et al (2013), Berry, Roberts, Danquah and Davies (2014), Özer, Yildirim and Erkoç (2015), Kharsati and Bhola (2016), Miniati, Callari and Pini (2017), Wrath and Adams (2018), Yakeley and Burbridge-James (2018), Green, Berry, Danquah and Pratt (2021).

These works outline recurrent themes expressed by patients who show serious suicidal ideation, including attachment disruptions, depression, profound isolation, utter hopelessness, undigested anger, guilt and self-hatred.

There is also a consensus amongst the above authors that attachment theory is critical to the study and prevention of suicide. In particular, real abandonment or a persistent fear of abandonment (which is a form of abandonment in its own right) by a primary attachment figure leads to tremendous psychic pain and unbearable anxiety, increasing suicide risk in the long term.

In his revolutionary work, *On knowing what you are not supposed to know and feeling what you are not supposed to feel*, Bowlby (1979) outlined the emotional damage caused to children who misbehave when their parents threaten not to love them or even to leave them – sometimes using the threat of their own suicide!

In his clinical experience, these threats of tragic desertion were not uncommon and, frequently, created a state of overwhelming anxiety in the child, even more so than actual abandonment (Bowlby, 1973).

When parents use threats of abandonment to discipline their children, the message sent to the child is that he or she is expendable. When the threats of desertion are persistent over time, they lead to greatly increased suicidality later in life (Bowlby, 1980).

Green, Berry, Danquah and Pratt (2021) pointed out that, very often, suicidal behaviour is an expression of major problems in attachment relationships, signalling distress and anger towards an inconsistent or unavailable attachment figure.

According to these clinicians, individuals with anxious or avoidant attachment patterns, who experience a current threat, find it more difficult to draw on resources from interpersonal relationships as efficiently as their securely attached peers and, instead, may resort to suicidal thinking or para-suicidal behaviour as the crisis escalates.

In addition, Miniati, Callari and Pini (2017) stated that insecurely attached individuals usually have greater sensitivity to interpersonal threats such as separation, loss and rejection. The fear generated by these threats will inevitably activate the proximity-seeking component of their attachment system, unless it had been profoundly damaged by severe trauma resulting in massive disorganisation.

For avoidant individuals, in extreme cases, suicide might be the eventual outcome of a poorly activated attachment system. These people can be socially isolated, often feeling *rejected* and eventually becoming *rejecting* themselves. On the other hand, anxiously attached individuals, who crave for closeness but fear abandonment, may resort to suicidal gestures and behaviours to elicit care and support from others in the absence of more adaptive strategies.

Along these lines, Ledgerwood (1999) identified a number of commonalities among suicidal people from an attachment perspective, including the following:

- First, a child-parent relationship characterised by an underlying threat of desertion or taking away love.
- Second, an underlying ambivalence towards the parent reflecting simultaneous feelings of love and hate, with an inability to reconcile the two and a resulting feeling of guilt.
- Third, the family of the suicidal person is often characterised by a profound symbiotic relationship in which he or she must remain faithful only to the family, and normal striving for autonomy and relationships outside the family are seen as disloyal.
- Fourth, in this family environment, the suicidal individual fails to pass through the natural stages of psychological development, and becomes trapped in a struggle between detachment and enmeshment, leading to suicidal disintegration.

Interestingly, one of Franz Kafka (1983)'s short stories, *The Judgement*, vividly illustrates how attachment conflicts can reach levels so pathological that they may make some people become suicidal.

The story begins with the protagonist, Georg Bendemann, writing to an old friend in Russia about his engagement and impending marriage – something that his father strongly disapproves of. In Kafka's story, Georg's feelings of anger and resentment toward his father becomes evident (as do his feelings of love). The resentment comes in the form of an expressed wish that his father will fall from his bed and perhaps hurt or kill himself. Yet, rather than attacking his father, Georg throws himself over the bridge.

Along the same lines as Kafka's tragic story, Sigmund Freud paid attention to suicide and proposed a theory in which, at its heart, suicidal thinking and acting have to be preceded by an unconscious wish to kill an attachment figure or *object*:

> Probably no one finds the mental energy required to kill himself unless, in the first place, in doing so he is at the same time killing an object with whom he has identified himself, and, in the second place, is turning against himself a death-wish which had been directed against someone else.
>
> (Freud, 1920: 162)

Elaborating on this, and according to Leenaars (1988, 2001), the relationship between the suicidal person and the object of their intense attachment is characterised by enmeshment, which generates a great deal of ambivalence: the suicidal person both loves and hates their primary attachment figure.

Although suicide may be triggered by an immediate frustration or painful event, taking into account the person's whole attachment history, the suicidal act often indicates an increasing inability to cope with rage directed towards the primary attachment figures. This rage, in turn, is redirected towards the self (Hendin, 1991).

According to Ledgerwood (1999), these two processes happen simultaneously at an unconscious level; both contribute to the suicidal act:

- First, and paradoxically, the suicidal person seeks to be rid of the attachment figure (suicide is one method for doing this).
- Second, the suicidal person feels an intense guilt or self-blame over their hatred toward someone they very much care for and need.

The *solution* chosen to this catch-22 situation is suicide. The suicidal person, by their own death, permanently destroys the affectional bond with their attachment figures and, at the same time, is punished for his or her transgression against them.

Yakeley and Burbridge-James (2018) suggested that suicide and self-harm can be seen as acts with unconscious meanings, communications that may convey in action repressed thoughts, feelings and fantasies that cannot be allowed into consciousness or put into words.

Indeed, attachment thinking evolved from psychoanalysis; yet, psychoanalysis has not always used attachment concepts or insights as such. Having said that, a number of psychoanalytic practitioners have implicitly referred to the relevance of ruptures and disruptions in attachment relationships as key factors in the violence inherent in suicidal acts (Bell, 2008; Briggs, Lemma and Crouch, 2008; Hale 2008; Minne, 2008; Campbell and Hale, 2017).

It has also been suggested that previous traumas, involving neglect or abuse of the person's body in infancy or childhood, cannot be mentalised and remain trapped in the body (Fonagy and Target, 2007; Bateman and Fonagy, 2019; Bateman, Campbell and Fonagy, 2021). And the body may then become a medium of communication through which difficult internal dynamics of attachment relationships are expressed, including suicidal behaviour.

4.4 Further thoughts on suicidality

Earlier in this chapter we saw that there is a considerable increase of suicide rates in societies with a high degree of secularisation, industrialisation and individualisation.

In the USA, someone dies by suicide every 12 minutes (every 40 seconds worldwide), and it is particularly concerning that, in the era of digital revolution and social media, among today's high school American students, 60 per cent have at one point considered taking their lives, and 14 per cent have thought about it seriously in the past year (Fazel and Runeson, 2020).

However, suicide does not just occur in high-income countries; it is a global phenomenon in all known periods and all regions of the world (WHO, 2023). Although it was already found in Neolithic societies as well as in the old Greek and Latin societies, precise empirical data about suicide in different countries and cultures had been lacking up to the 19th century (Durkheim, 1897).

Thus, a description of the development of suicide from prehistoric times, through antiquity and the middle ages to modern times does not seem feasible.

4.4(i) An evolutionary perspective

At some stage in human evolution, our Pleistocene ancestors must have realised that the death of the body brings with it the death of the mind. The idea that death means mental oblivion is a sophisticated one that can be reached only by inference, not by mere contemplation. According to Humphrey (2017), this idea of death must have originated alongside language and symbolism about 100,000 years ago, spreading rapidly across human culture (see Chapter 1).

The consequences of becoming aware of one's own mortality for our ancestors' hold on life must have been significant. For those who would fear oblivion, it may have given them an additional reason to stay alive. But for others so unfortunate that they would welcome oblivion, it could have provided a reason to die. Consequently, a major advance in human sophistication and knowledge may lead to a dangerous outcome for human fitness and survival, by making *egotistic* (individual or group) suicide a potentially *attractive* option.

Moreover, from the viewpoint of evolutionary biology, egotistic suicide (simply to stop the self from hurting or suffering), whether committed individually or in groups, can only be severely disadvantageous. According to Bowlby (1988), and in contrast to the view of Sigmund Freud, Melanie Klein and many of their followers, if we had been born with a suicide or *death instinct*, we would not have survived as a species.

Certainly, in our evolution, we developed ambitions that are so much higher than *those* of other animals. Every human being has moments of despair; the equation hurting and being hurt is bound to be a part of life.

In today's world, many of those who kill themselves are young. Suicide is now the second most common cause of death in teenagers, the fourth leading cause of death among 15 to 29-year-olds, and the main cause of death in men under 50 years of age (WHO, 2023). Factors contributing to this high vulnerability to suicide that middle-aged men present were explored in the previous volume of this series *Group Analysis throughout the Life Cycle* (Ezquerro and Cañete, 2023).

If young people from the above age groups had not died by their own hand, with adequate help and secure-enough attachment around them, they would likely have repaired the ruptures, got over the hurt, and would have potentially made a success of their lives, contributing to improve their communities. Those who kill themselves ruin, at a stroke, their life potential for ever and cause long-term pain to related individuals and communities too. Thus, suicide contains aggression to others as well as self-aggression (Campbell and Hale, 2017).

Humphrey (2017) further argued that, at the level of evolutionary biology, egoistic suicide is clearly a mistake, a definite path to genetic extinction. But it is precisely because humans, alone amongst animals, rise above biology that they can make this mistake. Humans produce *reasons* to believe that by ending their live they can escape from pain. In other words, suicide might be wrongly taken as a rational solution to an immediate problem.

A sense of immediacy is often an integral component of many suicidal acts. There is empirical evidence that suicidal behaviour is frequently unplanned and impulsive, which makes prevention even more difficulty. A survey of 306 Chinese patients who had been hospitalised following a suicide attempt, found that 35 per cent had contemplated suicide for less than ten minutes, and 54 per cent for less than two hours (Humphrey, 2018).

Having said that, this clear sense of suicidal immediacy or impulsiveness does not contradict the view that there are pre-suicidal states of mind, which are often unconscious (Campbell and Hale, 2017).

An additional difficulty is that suicide can be exceedingly *infectious*. It can jump all too easily from one mind to the next. Humphrey (2017) provided some examples of suicide *contagion*:

- In Goethe's 18th-century novel, *The Sorrows of Young Werther*, a young man kills himself after falling hopelessly in love with a married woman. Following its publication in 1774, there were hundreds of copycat deaths in Germany.
- When Marilyn Monroe killed herself in August 1962, there were more than 200 extra suicides within a month.
- And after a popular South Korean actress hung herself in 2008, suicides jumped 66 per cent that month, with young hanging victims accounting for most of the increase.

4.4(ii) Approaching suicide risk with an ethos of "we are all in the same boat"

There is a growing body of evidence about the profound impact that the death of a person by suicide can have on families, friends, carers and clinicians. The feeling that one should have done better, in order to prevent the suicide, tends to persist; in some cases, it never goes away (Usborne, 2021).

Yet, there is little systemic recognition of this trauma which can lead to a range of negative outcomes for individuals, families and organisations, including professional burnout, mental health problems, career change or early retirement. And many families do not survive this kind of trauma.

In my clinical experience, when patients tell me that they want to kill themselves, deeply inside them, what they want is to end a state of psychic or physical pain – usually both, as mental distress affects the body and physical illness has an impact on mental states. Some patients feel unable to change things and simply wish to go. The prospective victim *wants* to stop suffering by any means, including suicide.

Both as a psychiatrist and a citizen, I have strong feelings in favour of the prevention of suicide. It has probably been the most important duty that I have needed to accomplish, and to which I have been existentially committed for more than 40 years, as a mental health professional. I have been immensely fortunate that, so far, none of my patients has died by suicide. But I keep my fingers crossed.

At one point, the suicide risk that I will present in the next section pushed me to the limit. I was privileged to have a good team working with me, so we could contain together the suicidal crisis of a middle-aged man.

Two factors were particularly important to promote the healing process. First, conducting a psychotherapy group in which (beside their own difficulties) patients were humane and sensitive to other members' problems. Second, collaborating with an enthusiastic junior colleague, who saw the patient alongside the group and was determined to keep him alive.

At this point, I think it might be useful for the reader to know that, in my work with suicidal patients, I have been aware of my own countertransference: personal experiences that at times resonated with those of the patient. Reflecting on this helped me understand and protect suicide-risk patients under my care.

As a late adolescent, I experienced a long crisis and became deeply depressed; I felt disconnected from everyone. I kept this to myself and did not seek help. My depression coloured and distorted reality; I felt no one, not even my attachment figures, could possibly understand me or be available for help . . . I struggled with suicidal thoughts and feelings for a while; eventually, I designed a plan to kill myself.

On the day I had intended to carry it out, providentially, Vicente, someone who knew me well, called me apart and said that I looked very depressed. He added he was worried that I might be planning to commit suicide. I was shocked by how perceptive his comments were, and felt reconnected with a fellow human being who also helped me reconnect with the wider group, with the world. Without these meaningful connections, I might have died.

This experience provided me with some *immunity*, which, in turn, I have endeavoured to inject to my suicidal patients. I learned, not only from books but from (inter)personal experience, that suicide can be prevented: a powerful conviction. A meaningful human connection is a good antidote against despair, and a life-saver. In a way similar to how suicide can be infectious, passion for life can also be contagious (Heyno, 2008; Ezquerro, 2023).

Of course, to be an effective psychiatrist or psychotherapist in the treatment of suicide-risk patients, you do not need to have had a personal suicidal experience. Certainly, you may treat tuberculosis successfully without having contracted the infection. Having said that, in the case of suicide, there can well be a subliminal or unconscious communication which might reassure patients that you know what it is like. And, in feeling understood and wanted as a person, it is easier for them to reengage with the world and become attached to life again.

Before ending this (unplanned) subsection, I would also like to emphasise that some populations are especially vulnerable and require special care. Prisoners and other people who are isolated, experiencing conflict, disaster, violence, abuse or major loss are more at risk than the average citizen. Most alarmingly, suicide rates are disproportionally high amongst groups who experience overt or subtle forms of discrimination; for example, ethnic minorities, migrants and refugees, as well as people with homosexual or bisexual orientation and transgender and intersex persons (Cheung and Zwickl, 2021; Biggs, 2022).

4.4(iii) Some recent developments on suicide prevention

I was very pleased to learn that, in 2013, a WHO's Mental Health Action Plan was agreed for the global prevention of suicide. WHO Member States committed themselves to working towards the global target of reducing the suicide rate in all countries by an average of one third, by 2030.

That was commendable and perhaps not realistic enough; nonetheless, whilst thinking about suicide prevention nobody has the right to say that a plan is too ambitious (see further below).

Indeed, to date, only a few countries have included suicide prevention among their health priorities and only 38 countries have reported having a national suicide prevention strategy (WHO, 2023). Suicide is still illegal and taboo in many countries across the world, which distorts data; only some 80 Member States have good-quality vital registration data that can be used directly to estimate suicide rates and enhance prevention.

I am also glad to say that the British government recently published the first ever cross-government suicide prevention plan (GOV.UK, 2019). The strategy has a distinct focus on addressing the increase in suicide and self-harm among young people, whilst social media companies will be asked to take more responsibility for online content that promotes methods of suicide and self-harm. It also sets out specific actions for local government, the NHS and the criminal justice system:

- every local authority should be putting an effective suicide prevention plan in place;
- every mental health trust should have a zero-suicide ambition plan for mental health inpatients;

- every prison should be putting actions in place to reduce suicides and self-harm, and improve staff awareness and training;
- the specific needs of the highest risk groups, including middle-aged men, should be addressed;
- research on things that can be linked to suicide should improve.

At the time this Action Plan was published, there were over 4,500 suicides per year in England, and around 13 people ended their life every day. Men were three times more likely to die by suicide than women, and suicide was the leading cause of death in men under 50 years of age (GOV.UK, 2019).

The then Minister for Mental Health and Suicide Prevention Jackie Doyle-Price stated:

> As a society we need to do everything we can to support vulnerable and at-risk people, as well as those in crisis . . . Every 6 seconds someone contacts Samaritans volunteers for support, so we know that there is a huge amount to be done to help those struggling to cope.
>
> When we can work in partnership, we can make a bigger impact in preventing suicide, particularly among the hardest to reach high-risk groups such as low-income and middle-aged men.
>
> (Doyle-Price, in GOV.UK, 2019)

In 2017, an excellent ground-roots initiative had been born: the Zero Suicide Alliance, which was co-founded by Steve Mallen, following the suicide of his 18-year-old son Edward; it has obtained government funding, as well as the backing of multiple NHS trusts.

The alliance, which works with businesses, charities and bereaved families, has delivered online suicide-awareness training to several million people. It is part of a global *zero suicide* movement designed to shake up prevention strategies and attitudes at every level of society. Of course, Mallen does not believe suicide can be completely eradicated; however, he asked, if zero isn't the right number to aim for, then what is it?

Part of the zero approach involves providing education and information in all areas of life, from hairdressing salons, schools and other workplaces to late-night taxis, as well as on clifftops and bridges. The Alliance argues that intervening early is infinitely easier, and certainly a lot more economical, than when people are in crisis, let alone when they die by suicide (Usborne, 2021).

As a new development, in the UK, there is an ongoing commitment to create specific suicide bereavement support services in all NHS trusts, as part of a long-term prevention strategy. Indeed, charities and public have welcomed the plan whilst questioning the NHS's ability to deliver, given growing demand and staff shortages.

The admirable Zero Suicide Alliance's effort to involve society-as-a-whole in suicide prevention programmes and attitudes, brings to mind a rare novel,

Travesuras de la niña mala (The Bad Girl), which Mario Vargas Llosa published soon before he won the Nobel Prize for Literature, in 2010.

This literary treasure and most stirring piece of work is one of the most powerful and moving stories I have come across about suicide prevention. In the novel, Vargas Llosa (2006) beautifully describes the despair experienced by one of the main characters, Ricardo, who felt overwhelmed by his emotional problems in the context of a passionate but conflictive relationship of love and attachment, in Paris.

At night, alone and dejected, Ricardo approached Pont Mirabeu from where he was planning to throw himself into the dark emptiness, with the intention of burying his body in the muddy waters of the Seine River. As he climbed to the edge of the bridge, a late-middle-aged *clochard* (a homeless vagabond) appeared out of the blue and grabbed his legs with considerable force, whilst telling him:

> Don't be an idiot!

The young man was stunned and fell down to the dirty asphalt, not into the abyss. The *clochard* immediately put his bottle of vinegary wine into Ricardo's mouth. It was not a *Gran Reserva* of Rioja, but wine nonetheless. As Ricardo was still trying to recover from the shock, his rescuer, just before walking away, shouted at him:

> Don't dare trying to do it again!

Ricardo could not get over his perplexity but, deep inside him, he knew that he would always remember the vagabond's bulging and bloodshot eyes and his rough and croaky, but human, voice. He did not attempt to take his own life again from that very moment.

4.5 The clinical picture

Tim, aged 52, was referred for psychotherapy by his local community mental health team. This was on the grounds of his longstanding personality problems and a recent episode of psychotic depression, which had led to a serious suicide attempt followed by a three-week stay at an inpatient psychiatric unit.

Tim was an only child and a premature birth; he had a diagnosis of mildly generalised brain damage and spent the first three months of his life in hospital. Subsequently, he needed frequent follow-up medical appointments to closely monitor his growth and wellbeing.

His mother (a nurse) had a severe episode of postnatal depression, requiring a long inpatient admission, and early maternal-filial bonding became difficult. Even after recovering from her depression, she was quite disorganised and detached from him and, at times, used threats of killing herself when he misbehaved. In the circumstances, Tim was unable to form any kind of secure attachment relationship with his mother.

His father (a bricklayer) was very strict and religious. He tried to be supportive but was often intrusive and impinged upon most aspects of Tim's life.

In addition, he put great pressure on him around the age of 14 to go to a seminary to become a priest, at a time of conflicted sexual feelings and adolescent turmoil. The attachment relationship with his father had a highly anxious and ambivalent quality.

Overall, during his childhood and adolescence, Tim struggled between maternal detachment and paternal enmeshment. It seems that the only consistent support during his formative years came from his maternal uncle, who lived nearby and visited him quite often; he was also his godfather.

At school, Tim was a late developer but fortunate enough to attract sympathy and care from his teachers (it would appear that he triggered maternal-like attitudes in some of them). With their support, he managed to make reasonably good academic progress and to fit in well within his peer group, particularly with the boys.

However, he never seemed to fulfil his parents' expectations and became a victim of frequent paternal and maternal corporal punishment for not excelling at school.

Tim challenged his father's various attempts to send him to a seminary, but could not cope with the pressure and had a psychotic breakdown at the age of 15. He tried to kill himself by placing his head inside the gas oven at the parental home, following which he was admitted to a residential psychiatric unit for adolescents where he stayed for one and a half years.

At the special care baby unit, he had needed the provision of oxygen inside a warm incubator for his survival. Of course, this might be totally unrelated to the method of his attempted suicide and, indeed, he did not have any conscious memories of that *erased* experience. But I wonder about the possible *inscription* that such an experience may have had on his immature body and brain.

Gradually, Tim made a reasonable recovery. He went back to school and completed his GCSEs but did not pursue his A-levels. Interestingly, he started working first as a porter and then as a storekeeper in a nearby hospital.

It would appear that he had developed an important connection, or *group attachment*, to healthcare institutions; which may partly relate to his previous history of needing special hospital care and, perhaps, also to the fact that his mother was a healthcare professional.

A few years later, Tim obtained a permanent job as a school caretaker. For the first time, he had his own place outside the parental home, although within the school grounds. As during his schooldays as an emotionally insecure, he now felt supported by the school that employed him. However, in the new circumstances, he also developed an additional caring role towards the institution; which had a beneficial effect on him. Receiving and giving care are both good for the brain (see Chapter 1).

Tim, who had previously been unable to form a romantic relationship, became confident enough to start a relationship with one of the school's teaching assistants;

they soon got married, despite his father's strong opposition to it. He was able to sustain an emotional equilibrium and to hold down his job for nearly two decades, until he was hit by an extraordinary sequence of losses within a four-year period:

First, as Tim was infertile, he and his wife applied to adopt a child; but their application was rejected on the grounds of his psychiatric history.

Second, a year later, his wife suddenly left him and started divorce proceedings.

Third, during the divorce proceedings his mother unexpectedly died.

Fourth, his maternal uncle (the only reliable support in his life) died in a car crash the same year.

Fifth, he became unable to cope and started getting into trouble at work, which led to his being made redundant and the loss of his caretaker home at the school.

Sixth, approximately at the same time, his dog, the only *attachment figure* remaining, as he put it, died.

Then, Tim took a massive overdose; he survived, just. Following a three-week inpatient admission to an acute inpatient psychiatric ward, he continued feeling suicidal.

On discharge, he was referred to me for NHS psychotherapy, whilst still being supported with domiciliary visits by a male community psychiatric nurse and a female social worker, until he joined an outpatient group at one of my NHS clinics.

4.6 The therapy group

I interviewed four men and four women, over a three-month period, with a view to starting a weekly psychotherapy group. They presented themselves with a wide range of mental health and personality problems. They came from diverse cultures and had different backgrounds, with ages ranging from 27 to 52 years. Some were married; others were divorced or single. Some had children; others did not.

All were seen at least twice for hour-long individual sessions. Some were seen up to four or five times, as they appeared to need more time to connect with me prior to joining the group psychotherapy programme; Tim (the oldest member) was one of them.

The group was *slow open*. People joined with a view to leaving when they became ready. This decision would have to be negotiated with the other members and with me. In view of the longstanding nature of their problems and the analytic quality of our therapeutic approach, I told them that I expected a minimum time-commitment of one year.

Tim was not the only group member with a history of suicide attempts. Another patient, **Peter**, had tried to kill himself as an adolescent, when his parents split up. He was not as big a suicide risk as Tim; but, during the assessment, he presented with depressive symptoms, including some suicidal ideation. I thought that I would need to be especially alert and keep an eye on both of them, as they might have had the potential to push a new therapy group to the limit of its capacity to contain suicidal anxieties.

The group started in January 2000. The arrival of a new millennium (one of the most widely shared events on our planet) had been a depressing experience for most of the patients, as they felt they could not fully participate in the celebrations, due to their mental health problems. However, starting a new millennium became a common theme in the first session and I tried to inject them with a sense of a new beginning, metaphorically and literally. This idea was well received and appreciated by most; it led to a common wish for moving on together.

It soon became apparent that **Tim** was stuck with himself and unable to look forward to anything. It took him several weeks to report that he was feeling so depressed that, in fact, he had not stayed up to receive the new millennium. He was at home on his own, switched the TV off and took several sleeping tablets, he said, not with the intention of killing himself but with that of disconnecting himself from the world.

I commented that, perhaps Tim was also trying to connect himself in some way with his loved ones who, in dying, had disconnected themselves from him and from the world.

Although most people in the group said that my interpretation made sense to them, Tim looked puzzled and indicated that he did not understand what I meant. **Sylvia** looked at him with sympathy and said that perhaps he was trying to grieve his many losses.

Tim reacted promptly and exclaimed that it had been impossible for him to grieve any of his losses. Group members listened with concern and interest. **Henry** commented that he had read in a magazine that a bereavement lasting more than one year should be considered pathological. Tim replied that he could then understand he had a pathological bereavement.

Peter intervened and said that we were lucky in the UK to have psychotherapy paid by the NHS, for at least one year! He added that, in countries where psychotherapy is not funded by the State, medical insurers would not pay for more than three months in respect of therapy for bereavement.

Indeed, I was conscious that one year was the minimum therapeutic time-commitment agreed with them but did not comment on that. I was more preoccupied about the fact that, in a subtle way, the group appeared to be entering a political debate on health services rather than staying with **Tim**'s pain. I took some risk and said:

> Tim, I do not think that you have a pathological bereavement, but a massive accumulation of big losses which are too painful and overwhelming to bear. We all have a limit to the level of loss we can cope with at any one time.

I was aware that Tim had spent the first three months of his life in hospital as a premature baby, with a diagnosis of generalised brain damage, whilst his mother was recovering from postnatal depression. It seemed clear that his early brain develop-ment was affected by his difficult start in life and, also, his mother's inability to provide a secure attachment for him.

In the circumstances, he became vulnerable to anxiety and depression in the face of separation and loss. He found it hard getting started in the group. After a pause, I added:

> I think, Tim, you need to grieve one loss at a time rather than all the losses at once. Take your time; you can go at your own pace and grieve little by little. And, of course, you can stay in the group for as long as you need to.

Tim said that he felt relieved and reassured to hear that. It was important for him to realise that he was not alone and that he would not be forced to achieve, in a short while, something for which he was still unprepared.

In a later development, as he was talking in the group about his unresolved anger with his father, I linked it with the fact that his father had wanted to force him into the priesthood when he was clearly unwilling and unprepared for it. In the group, he was having an experience that was different from what he had lived at home; this represented an opportunity for him to change.

In fact, following the anxieties of the initial group stages, Tim talked about feel-ing better with himself and became increasingly attached to the group, to the point that he was very much looking forward to coming to the sessions every week.

At one point, he said that the group had become a replacement family for him. Group members were pleased to see Tim making progress, after several months in which he had been so anxious and depressed that could think of nothing to say to them.

During that time in the group, Tim sometimes said he could not go beyond feel-ing that life was not worth it anymore and that he would end up killing himself. However, he was at this time beginning to feel able to help himself and, also, give support and encouragement to other people.

His improved way of communicating in the group gave him confidence to explore the relationship with his girlfriend, with whom he had developed an anx-iously ambivalent attachment pattern.

Tim's community mental health team perceived his improvement as good enough to discharge him from their care. This meant that his female social worker and his male community psychiatric nurse (who had provided *ad hoc* home sup-port) were no longer involved.

In the circumstances, Tim would have to complete his recovery with *only* group psychotherapy. I must confess that I missed the *safety net* that my colleagues had provided. From now on, I had to provide overall management as well as psycho-therapy for him.

Tim continued attending the group impeccably. He was particularly fond of **Carol**, a member who worked as a nurse. She had joined the group following quite a severe episode of post-natal depression, which resonated within him with his mother's history. Carol made a good recovery and, after a year and a half, she started talking about fully enjoying her work and her family life again. She negotiated a period of six months as preparation for her leaving the group, after two years of therapy.

Carol was the first patient who left the group. The other members missed her. Interestingly, most of them felt reassured that they might also become ready in the not-so-distant future, partly encouraged by Carol's complete recovery and partly by rediscovering their own care-giving qualities towards **Rose**, the new member who joined the group to replace her.

However, **Tim** started to experience acute anxiety states and reported arguments with his girlfriend at home, which ended in the break-up of their relationship. He felt again unable to cope and had a wish to live no longer.

I said to him that Carol's departure and the separation from his girlfriend could be getting mixed with the traumatic separations and losses he had experienced in the past.

The group became a lifeline for Tim. Gradually, he was able to work through his feelings about being *abandoned* by Carol and by his girlfriend, and to disentangle what belonged to his recent relationship with them and what to his previous experiences with his mother. He was able to sustain a precarious equilibrium for a further year.

During this time, he sometimes felt on the verge of having another breakdown. The balance was disturbed by the news of his father's late diagnosis of terminal cancer and impending death.

In the group, **Tim** became very distressed and said that he regretted he would not have enough time to repair the ruptures in the difficult relationship he had with his father. I said to him that I wondered if, at a less conscious level, he might have interpreted the sad news as another threat of abandonment – something he was familiar with, looking back to earlier stages in his life.

He responded that he could see where I was coming from. At the end of the session, I told Tim that, if needed, he could phone me at the psychotherapy service before the next session.

A few days after the session, whilst at home, alone, Tim felt unable to cope. He thought about telephoning the psychotherapy service to seek help before the next session, but lost control and stabbed himself in the stomach with a kitchen knife.

As he was bleeding profusely, he just then managed to phone the Accident and Emergency department of his local hospital. He was rescued within a few minutes and, against the odds, survived.

I was asked about the possibility of offering him a voluntary admission to the local inpatient psychiatric unit or, if he declined the offer, to consider a compulsory admission under the Mental Health Act.

I thought that, although he would have been kept safe temporarily, either of these two options would have an unsatisfactory response to his suicide attempt. The social mix and overall environment of an acute psychiatric unit was of little relevance to Tim's current predicament. This time, he did not have psychotic symptoms. The admission would have been too restrictive and potentially traumatic an option for him.

Indeed, he needed a review of his care plan to reduce the suicide risk. With an open mind, I decided to pay him a short visit, whilst he was still at the general hospital recovering from his wounds. I was concerned about his survival and considered that this visit may provide him with a much-needed sense of continuity of care, in the difficult circumstances of his rupture. He very much appreciated the gesture.

It crossed my mind that his recent suicide attempt was possibly a statement about his deeply rooted anger and resentment towards his father, his rage towards his ex-girlfriend for abandoning him and, perhaps, also about his anger with me for not having helped him enough. But I did not dare to share my thoughts with him then; the timing and place would have been wrong. Instead, I said that I looked forward to his return to the group, which happened four weeks later.

On his discharge from hospital, I saw **Tim** for one individual session to review his care plan. I told him that I was exploring the possibility that one of my colleagues in the psychotherapy service might offer him one-to-one sessions alongside the group. He welcomed the idea. I also reminded him to contact the service Monday to Friday between 8.00 am and 6.00 pm, or the emergency numbers outside these hours, if he felt on the verge of losing control again in between the therapy sessions.

After careful thinking, I decided to ask him to sign a document, in which he formally committed himself to make phone contact instead of injuring himself. I did it as a dynamic-administration strategy. I explained to him that I wanted to protect him primarily and, also, protect the service, including myself. I was implicitly suggesting that, behind his suicidal behaviour, there might have been some form of violence towards other people (his father, his girlfriend or the professionals caring for him), as well as towards himself.

In addition, I said to him that, although the destructive elements of his suicide attempts were undeniable and should be kept in mind, I would also like to consider a positive aspect that his suicidal impulse may contain an urge for transformation and new life. He listened to that intently. I was striving to be compassionate, encouraging and hopeful; whilst also recognising Tim's more negative and violent feelings, and trying to help him become more able to allow them into conscious awareness.

On his return to the group, **Tim** shared details and circumstances of his last suicide attempt.

This generated a high level of anxiety in the group, although members tried their best to welcome him back and expressed feelings of being very pleased to see him again. Some talked about feeling unable to cope with an anxiety that, at the next attempt, Tim might *succeed* in killing himself.

Peter, who had made a suicide attempt as an adolescent when his parents split up, tried to be particularly empathetic and supportive. When he joined the group, he was depressed and presented suicidal ideation, following the break-up of his marriage. He and his ex-wife had two children. He explained that, for him, keeping weekly contacts with his children was the best deterrent against suicide, as seeing them grow made his life more meaningful.

I was aware that Tim had wanted to have children, but he was infertile and his application to adopt a child, with his then wife, was turned down on the grounds of his mental health problems. Of course, Peter was trying to be supportive but I wondered if some of his material might be triggering painful memories in Tim's mind.

Peter continued saying that killing himself would be a violent act on his children and he did not want them to go through such a traumatic experience. Peter added that seeing his friends regularly was also of help, and encouraged **Tim** to come out of his isolation and have a social life. Tim thanked Peter and the other members for their support.

At the beginning of the following session, Tim was absent. Previously, on those very few occasions when he had been unable to attend the group, he had left a message. Members started the session expressing their fears that I might announce that Tim had killed himself. Some commented that they could hardly bear their anxiety about it.

After the session, I contacted Tim and he explained that he had fallen asleep after agonising during the early hours of the morning with suicidal thoughts, which he managed to keep at bay. During the next session, he occupied a significantly large proportion of time and space in the group. Members were very sympathetic and supportive, but the anxiety in the room could barely be contained.

It should be noticed, that **Peter** asked me if I or one of my colleagues in the service could offer individual therapy to Tim, in parallel with the group. For me, this was a good example of the meaning contained in the expression that, in the group-analytic approach, we can trust the group.

Tim then said that he had discussed the combined treatment option at his review meeting with me. And I added that we were in the process of identifying a suitable therapist for him. There was a unanimous feeling of approval and relief in the group.

4.7 Individual and group psychotherapy combined

I was glad that one of my junior colleagues, Dr Priya Bajaj, was available to offer Tim weekly individual therapy for one year. Dr Bajaj was a junior psychiatrist in training, with a special interest in psychotherapy. I was her supervisor and educational tutor, with all the pros and cons regarding the possibility of working together in a combined treatment programme for Tim.

I considered that her lack of experience in psychotherapy would be compensated for by her reliability, her caring approach, her willingness to learn and her commitment to protect Tim from harm. She was conversant with group work and a member of one of my weekly supervision groups, together with three other trainees.

Having said that, I was aware that, in addition to the split transference and to the boundary issues inherent in combined treatment, Dr Bajaj and I needed to be mindful about the possible dynamic around our status differential, particularly regarding my role as her supervising consultant. I discussed this reservation with her, and we decided to see Tim for a threesome session with a view to agreeing our proposed care plan with him.

At this joint meeting with Tim, we were upfront about our roles. I explained to him that the individual sessions would be confidential, apart from the fact that Dr Bajaj would discuss the clinical material with me in supervision. He understood and accepted that confidentiality should not be seen as an absolute term, and that there might be occasions when it could be necessary to share some information with other professionals, in order to keep him safe.

I also said to Tim that, in the group, it would be up to him to refer to or elaborate upon the issues brought to his individual sessions. I added that, although he would normally be expected to deal with group issues or difficulties in the group, it would be legitimate to discuss such difficulties in the individual sessions, with a view to eventually resolving them in the group.

Timing was important too. The group met on Tuesdays and I asked Dr Bajaj to see Tim on Fridays, in order to keep the gaps in between sessions as short as possible. He appreciated that.

Prior to commencing the individual sessions, Dr Bajaj was anxious about her role as an individual therapist with someone who did still appear to be stuck with himself and suicidal, after three years of group therapy.

She was principally worried about her ability to contain the suicide risk. We teased this out in supervision. I reassured Dr Bajaj that we would be working as a team to contain the risk, and invited her to ring me immediately after an individual session if she had serious concerns. This was a joint therapeutic enterprise.

At the initial session with Dr Bajaj, one of Tim's first remarks was:

You will obviously know everything about me, so I don't have to repeat things.

It seemed clear that, initially, Tim perceived his individual therapy as an extension of the therapy group, as if he had paused for a few days after a group session and then plunged into another session with *fewer* people and more space.

During the first few weeks, he showed a slight resistance to engage, partly related to the fact that Dr Bajaj's availability was only one year. He said to her that he may need more than twelve months. In supervision, we considered that Tim was already anticipating that Dr Bajaj would *abandon* him in a year's time.

Despite his anticipatory separation-anxiety, the individual sessions were still driven by his strong determination to work through his losses. He greatly appreciated having additional space for this task, showed enthusiasm for the sessions and time-keeping was never a problem. It was almost as if he knew exactly when the glass was full and he would stop just before it reached the verge of overflowing.

In supervision, we discussed that this was different from other very anxious patients who would attempt to push the time boundary of the therapy session. Tim appeared to be reasonably contained in his individual sessions, possibly having internalised the structure and therapeutic time-boundary of the group sessions.

In fact, right from the outset, Tim appeared to cope well with the combined sessions and his suicidal ideation diminished quite rapidly. This had a direct impact on the group as a whole: the level of anxiety about Tim was clearly brought down.

The group continued representing a sort of replacement family for him. He said he considered the group was his main secure base. It was a place where he felt supported and understood and, also, a place where he could give something useful to others, which made him feel better with himself. At the same time, his individual therapy provided him with an additional secure base, which he was able to use creatively to explore new possibilities in his personal and working life.

Outside the two therapies, Tim gradually started to move on from a position of self-centredness to become more able to engage with other people socially. Significantly, he decided to join a training scheme to become a mental health worker, about which he received strong encouragement from his fellow group members. The scheme was set up by the NHS in conjunction with a mental health charity, to ensure that people with a history of mental illness would not be discriminated against, in respect of opportunities to return to paid employment.

Tim also started to explore a relationship with a new girlfriend (Ann) who, like his individual therapist, was significantly younger than him. Ann was, in fact, 25 years his junior.

Anecdotes, feelings and doubts about her emerged more readily in the individual sessions than in the group sessions. Tim had endured a raw deal in the past and all significant intimate relationships had been with dominant women who let him down and, ultimately, abandoned him. So, he ended up having to fend for himself or to seek help from healthcare bodies.

Over the months, Tim became very emotionally involved with Ann. She came from a disturbed family background and he developed a strong caring attitude towards her. At times, it seemed that he was re-enacting some aspects of his past relationship with his mother, who had needed to be cared for on and off. Some feelings of anger towards his parents appeared to resurface, followed by a sense of guilt.

After a while, Tim's sexual attraction towards Ann was no longer reciprocated; he felt rejected once again. This lack of reciprocity hurt him even more deeply after the remark that she made about their age gap:

You could be my father!

Tim's self-esteem and confidence plummeted but he was able to talk about it in both the individual and group sessions. He managed to keep his depressive and suicidal feelings at bay, and began to disentangle what belonged to past rejections or losses and what to the current disappointment.

In the group, he said that he had felt rejected and discriminated against by *the system*, when he and his then wife applied to adopt a child. He reflected that he now was in a relationship with someone who could be his daughter.

Furthermore, Tim started to reflect on his own ageing in the context of his father's life coming to an end. The additional space created by his combined therapy helped Tim deal with separation and loss. He said to Dr Bajaj that it was easier for him to cope with the sense of loss and depression he felt after the group sessions knowing that he would soon have an individual appointment, and vice versa.

This dual, individual and group, attachment helped him assuage his fears about separation and threatened separation, to which he was especially vulnerable.

Despite his sense of rejection, Tim managed to build a friendly enough relationship with Ann which was mutually rewarding. They became reasonably attached to each other and negotiated a situation in which they would be neither too close with, nor too distant from, one another.

Tim felt good with himself as he became able to support Ann emotionally, using the resilience he had developed through his own experience of fighting adversity. At one point, he encouraged her to have therapy for herself; which was a turning point and helped them consolidate their friendship.

The turbulent relationship with his father remained a theme that Tim also needed to work upon in both his individual and group therapy; which he perceived as complementary to one another.

He struggled with the figure of an emotionally intrusive and physically abusive father; and made repeated, frantic, unsuccessful attempts to connect with him right up to his death. He became able to use humour as a reasonable defence whenever he felt plagued with memories of the past, including the paternal abuse and his psychotic breakdowns.

Frequently, Tim's narratives (describing recent contacts with his father) reflected his inner conflicts between an unmet need for secure attachment, for recognition and acceptance, and a need to let go. He had an acute awareness of being inadequate in his father's eyes; he relived the painful experience of being the recipient of his father's anger in every new encounter with him.

At times, this appeared to be the expression of a desperate wish for being connected with his father. At one point, he said to Dr Bajaj that being condemned and ridiculed by his father was more bearable than being abandoned.

When it came, his father's death affected him immensely but he talked about it in the individual and group sessions. This time he did not collapse, nor did he feel suicidal. He was able to create space for grieving his loss.

There was a sense of regret at not having been able to change the relationship with his father before his departure. However, Tim became able to do some work on the *internal* relationship with his father and gradually achieved a sense of reconciliation with him.

As the end of his individual therapy was in sight, Tim did not experience the overwhelming anxiety of previous separations. He coped well with his separation from Dr Bajaj whilst he continued attending the group sessions.

In the group, he talked about feeling hugely sad about her departure, but was also more able to appreciate the good things that life brings every day. Suicide was no longer a preoccupation for him. He was committed to the process of moving on up.

Tim continued his group psychotherapy for a further six months after the individual therapy had ended. He talked of how proud he felt about having successfully completed his training as a mental health worker. He was particularly proud of the fact that he had supported some patients to overcome their suicidal feelings. His trainers were so satisfied with his dedication and performance that a new post of occupational therapist assistant was created. He was invited to apply and got the job!

Group members saw Tim's success at employment, in his mid-50s, as one of the highlights of his combined therapy. He had been out of work for seven years. On his first day at work, he experienced the nervousness of a little boy entering school after being suspended for a long period.

However, he was soon able to put his old fears of inadequacy behind him. His self-effacing manner and diligence won him great accolades from his patients, colleagues and managers.

Meeting his work challenges with increasing confidence and settling down in his new role became a rather stimulating and fulfilling experience for him. His confidence rose and he regained control of his life.

During the ending phase of his four and a half years of group therapy, Tim managed to review and learn from his difficult attachment history and his past crises. His capacity to cope with stress, separation and loss was enhanced. Recognising his vulnerability and understanding its origins made him stronger. He was able to develop his own resources and come to terms with his many ruptures and losses. Life was meaningful again.

4.8 Discussion

I was an adolescent going through an existential crisis when one of my teachers at school gave me a copy of *La Peste* [The Plague] by Albert Camus (1947). Once I started, I couldn't stop reading. I was haunted by a tragic story that contained overwhelming acts of secular humanity and compassion, in the context of a desperate fight for survival in the plagued city of Oran.

I was thinking at the time that life without God would be an absurdity and, yet, I fell in love with Dr Rieux – to my young mind, an atheist saint who put his life at risk to save that of others infected by the disease, in a brutal exercise of awe-inspiring solidarity. At one point in the battle, Rieux thought aloud:

It's an idea that can be laughable, but the only way to fight the plague is honesty.

His interlocutor then asked:

What is honesty?

To which Rieux responded:

> I don't know what it is in general. But, in my case, I know it consists of doing
> my job.
>
> (Camus, 1947)

And Rieux gave himself body and soul to his work as a doctor. So powerful was the
impact of his behaviour on my disoriented adolescent mind that I decided to study
medicine, psychiatry and psychotherapy, in succession.

When Tim was referred to me, some 20 years after I had qualified as a doctor,
I did think (and still do) that helping him not to commit suicide was a large part of
doing my job. To be completely honest, I must confess that, during the four and a
half years I was responsible for his treatment, his suicidality confronted me with
existential questions about human life (Solomon, 2005).

I was deeply affected when I learned that Tim had stabbed himself in the stomach with a kitchen knife.

The method Tim used to try to end his life resonated with the story of Cato the
Younger who, in the year 46 BCE, ripped his own guts out to prevent Julius Caesar
(an immensely powerful, parental-like authority figure) from using him for political gain.

At the time of his suicide attempt, Tim struggled with his unresolved rage
towards the authority of his father. *Mutatis mutandis*, Cato was full of rage towards
Caesar; but ended up killing himself with his own sword. However, he did not
immediately die of the wound . . .

According to Plutarch, whilst being critically wounded, Cato fell off his bed
making such a noise that the servants cried out for help. His son and his friends
came into the chamber and saw him weltering in his own blood, his bowels out of
his body, but still alive.

A physician was urgently called to help him, and would have put in his bowels
and sewed up the wound . . . But Cato pushed him away and, tearing the wound
open, soon expired (Taylor, 1971). Incidentally, two years later, Caesar was assassinated by Brutus and Cassius.

Suicide continues to be a major hazard in mental health, despite the increasing
availability of assessment and treatment methods; which has sometimes generated
feelings of despondency, anxiety and hopelessness amongst professionals, as if its
occurrence were almost random (Kashdan and Roberts, 2011; Chartrand, Sareen,
Toews and Bolton, 2012; Klonsky, May and Saffer, 2016; McLaughlin, McGowan,
O'Neill and Kernohan 2014; Frances, 2021).

One of the big questions in my mind is whether suicidality should always be
considered a mental health problem, or whether mental health professionals should
look at it from a wider existential perspective.

Some people think that the freedom to choose not to live should be a fundamental human right. In one sense, suicide can be seen as a heroic act: having the
courage to take your own life can be quite an undertaking. On the other hand, many

people think of suicide as a coward's way out. In my opinion, it is neither – but the result of an attachment or existential crisis.

I have worked as a doctor, psychiatrist and psychotherapist for over 40 years. My professional ethos cannot support a patient's decision to kill themself. Human beings can recover from trauma; ruptures can be repaired, at least to a significant extent; even the *unbearable* pain of terminal illness can be mitigated.

The bottom line is to live as healthily as possible, for as long as possible, to develop our potentialities meaningfully connected with other people, to the very end.

Significantly, many suicidal patients who end up not killing themselves, or *spoiling* the job, live to develop a new appreciation for life. A good number of them become advocates for organisations that try to prevent other people from committing suicide (Hendricks, 2018).

According to Albert Camus, suicide is the only truly serious philosophical problem. For him, real suicidal acts and suicidal ideation are deeply rooted in the idiosyncratic quality of human existence.

In his essay *Le Mythe de Sisyphe* [The Myth of Sisyphus], Camus (1942a) conceived suicide as a surrender to the realisation that life is an *absurdity*, since we are all *condemned* to death, and so a life without meaning is not a life worth the trouble. He presented suicidality not so much as a reaction to life events, but as a condition of existence that builds within the human psyche over time, eventually pushing the person to abruptly end their suffering.

However, Camus turned the argument on its head and pointed out that, although suicide could be seen as a way of *settling* the meaningless of life, it is an absurd response in its own right because there can be no more meaning in death than in life.

Hence, he suggested, the best response against the absurdity of life (and death) would be the *revolt* of exercising the *freedom* of choosing to live anyway, and doing it with *passion*. This provides human life with meaningful value. If life ultimately has no meaning, then living in the face of that reality gives it meaning. I can certainly buy this argument!

According to Camus, although the creeping (often unconscious) realisation of the absurdity of life can climax in suicide, a more fully conscious realisation of this absurdity can be a buffer that help us keep going. Having the courage to contemplate that which is absurd allows us to realise that it is actually absurd to kill ourselves over the absurdity of life – part of which is the certainty of death.

Brack (2020) suggested that Camus' philosophy implicitly responds to the question *why wait for your time to come when you could choose the time and place of your death*? with a *why not*? Even accepting that living in the face of death can be absurd, suicide in itself can also be an absurdity. So, why not stick around to see what happens?

In *L'Étranger* (often translated as The Outsider; sometimes as The Stranger or even as The Foreigner), Camus (1942b) explored what might make life worth living or otherwise.

He seems to encourage us to face the absurdity of life in a deceptively simple way, with a *smile* on our face: getting out of bed, not giving in to despair, going for a walk by the beach, enjoying the sunshine, playing or watching football, having coffee or lunch with a friend, and embracing the meaninglessness of existence.

According to John Bowlby, existential meaning is enhanced by satisfactory attachment relationships:

> Intimate attachments to other human beings are the hub around which a person's life revolves, not only when he is an infant or a toddler or a schoolchild but throughout his adolescence and his years of maturity as well, and on into old age. From these intimate attachments a person draws his strength and enjoyment of life and, through what he contributes, he gives strength and enjoyment to others.

> (Bowlby, 1980: 442)

Secure attachment promotes the development of a capacity to regulate emotion and mood, as well as an ability to grow confidently in the interpersonal and group context, which reduces suicide risk. On the other hand, accumulated trauma during childhood and adolescence can significantly impair brain and psychosocial development, affecting life quality and increasing suicide risk in the longer term.

Bowlby's views have been validated by modern neurobiology, which provides empirical evidence for one of the basic tenets of attachment theory that early attachment with a primary figure (or figures) providing maternal care and protection impacts significantly upon the maturation of the brain (Schore, 1994; Csikszentmihalyi, 2021).

Tim had a difficult start in life as a premature baby with some degree of brain damage which required special hospital care. The lack of secure attachment with a depressed and aloof mother, and with an intrusive and punitive father, probably indicated that, as a baby and young child, he needed a compensatory early *group attachment* (represented by the regular hospital care and the school support he received).

He sustained a precarious equilibrium but had a first psychotic breakdown, suicide attempt and inpatient psychiatric admission, as he collapsed under the developmental demands of adolescence and the intrusive pressure his father put on him to become a priest, in the absence of maternal support.

Tim just survived and found a role in society as a school caretaker; he was fortunate enough to establish a satisfactory intimate attachment with one of the school's teaching assistants. His new meaningful attachments (interpersonal and group) helped him stay at the coping level for nearly two decades. However, the loss of these favourable life circumstances became mixed with other, past and current, losses. All this together led to his second psychotic episode, suicide attempt and inpatient psychiatric admission.

Tim was referred for psychotherapy and worked hard in his weekly therapy group. However, although he appeared to perceive it as a secure-enough base, the group proved insufficient to contain his despair and suicide risk. In fact, in the face of new adverse events in his life, he committed a third, and deadly serious, suicide attempt by stabbing himself . . . He nearly died.

Whilst Tim was recovering from his wounds at his local general hospital, I found it helpful to read Hillman's (1964) book, *Suicide and the Soul*, in which he referred to the potentially transformative urge of the suicidal act: metaphorically, a part of the self must *die* in order to make room for a new way of being.

For all of us involved in his care, Tim's survival was a huge relief. We were strongly committed to help him develop an ability to reintegrate past experiences in a new light, and to incorporate new attachments and meaning into his life.

This transformative process was facilitated by the introduction of individual therapy, coordinated alongside his group psychotherapy. This combination created a multiple caregiving system, which he perceived as more containing and enabling. Eventually, he became able to develop a more consistent self-regulatory function.

Tim's therapeutic interactions stimulated his brain and its capacities to engage meaningfully with the brains of others. He became more able to engage with the opportunities available in new relationships, including his successful training as a mental health worker. Internalising his combined therapy and helping other people enabled him to help himself.

As part of the process, I had to listen to the anxieties of group members about Tim' suicide risk and protect them from too unbearable a feeling of vicarious despair. One of the crucial tasks of a group-analytic psychotherapist is to protect the group from the impact that individual problems may have on members and on the group-as-a-whole.

Although the group had become a protective secure base for Tim, or a replacement family (as he put it), his needs for a more intimate and nurturing one-to-one attachment became powerfully re-activated. Tim's individual sessions significantly reduced the level of anxiety in the group, and contributed to a more balanced therapeutic climate where new developments became possible again.

The therapeutic outcome for Tim was enhanced through the empathetic engagement with the individual therapist. Previous unmet needs for validation and recognition were reactivated in this relationship, which provided opportunities for him to correct the past negative experiences of being unsuccessful through the eyes of his parents and rejected by them.

The reparative experiences of the individual therapy helped Tim fill in some of the incomplete aspects of his fragile individual self. In a similar way, long-term secure belonging and group attachment helped him fill in some missing aspects of his group-self.

4.9 Conclusion

Suicide is a serious public-health problem with complex clinical and existential dimensions, which often reflects societal pathologies. Suicides are preventable with timely and evidence-based interventions. For effective large-scale prevention, comprehensive and multisectoral strategies as well as national and global plans are needed.

Suicide can be seen as a paradoxical struggle to live without pain at the cost of life itself. Indeed, suicidal behaviour habitually contains both a violence that can destroy life and an urge for new life. From the perspective of John Bowlby's attachment theory, behind any suicidal act there is ultimately a crisis of attachment. Understanding and working through this crisis and its concomitant pre-suicide states of mind are optimal life-savers.

There is ample evidence that severe disruptions in early attachment relationships increase suicide risk in the longer term. The way people grow, the quality of their attachments and their social environment, how they come to see themselves as a person and the roles they adopt throughout their development, have an important effect on lifetime suicidality.

The qualitative and clinical-process research presented in this chapter shows that combined individual and group psychotherapy can be an effective and beneficial treatment modality for patients who are a suicide risk. The reconstruction of patients' interpersonal and group attachment history, and the understanding of its impact on their development and vulnerability, are crucial elements of the therapeutic process. In this case study, the provision of two therapeutic secure bases, within a closely coordinated clinical governance structure, proved vital.

The present clinical study has the important limitation of being a piece of qualitative research, and it is necessary to be cautious about extrapolation. However, this study reinforces the existing literature that recommends combined individual and group psychotherapy as a valuable and effective treatment method for suicidal patients, given the fact that it reduces their chances of being admitted to hospital and of dying by suicide.

The scientific groundings of attachment-based individual and group psychotherapy are in tune with the current imperative for clinical governance and evidence-based interventions.

Note: The clinical material presented in this chapter has followed strict guidelines from the General Medical Council to protect the confidentiality due to patients.

References

Adams GC, Balbuena L, Meng X and Asmundson GJ (2016) When social anxiety and depression go together: A population study of comorbidity and associated consequences. *Journal of Affective Disorders* 206: 48–54.

Aronson ML (1964) Technical problems in combined therapy. *International Journal of Group Psychotherapy* 14(4): 425–432.

Balint M (1961) *Psychotherapeutic Techniques in Medicine*. Mind and Medicine Monograph. London: Tavistock Publications.

Bateman A, Campbell C and Fonagy P (2021) Rupture and Repair in Mentalization-Based Group Psychotherapy. *International Journal of Group Psychotherapy* 71(2): 371–392.

Bateman A and Fonagy P (2019). Mentalization-based treatment for borderline and antisocial personality disorder. In: Kealy D and Ogrodniczuk JS (eds) *Contemporary Psychodynamic Psychotherapy: Evolving clinical practice*. London: Elsevier Academic Press, pp. 133–148.

Battegay R (1986) Specific differences and reciprocal influences of individual and group psychotherapy. *Group Analysis* 19(4): 341–346.

Bedi R, Muller RT and Classen CC (2014) Cumulative risk for deliberate self-harm among treatment-seeking women with histories of childhood abuse. *Psychological Trauma: Theory, Research, Practice and Policy* 6(6): 600–609.

Behr H and Hearst L (2005) *Group-Analytic Psychotherapy: A Meeting of Minds.* London: Whurr.

Bell D (2008) Who is killing what or whom? Some notes on the internal phenomenology of suicide. In: Briggs S, Lemma A and Crouch W (eds) *Relating to Self-Harm and Suicide. Psychoanalytic Perspectives on Practice, Theory and Prevention.* London: Routledge, pp. 25–37.

Berry K, Roberts N, Danquah A and Davies L (2014) An exploratory study of associations between adult attachment, health service utilisation and health service costs. *Psychosis* 6(4): 355–358.

Biggs M (2022) Suicide by Clinic-Referred Transgender Adolescents in the United Kingdom. *Archives of Sexual Behaviour* 51(2): 685–690.

Blackwell D (2021) Anti-science or revolutionary consciousness. *Group Analysis* 54(1): 116–123.

Bowlby J (1973) *Attachment and Loss: Vol. 2. Separation, Anxiety and Anger* (1991 edition). London: Penguin Books.

Bowlby J (1979) On knowing what you are not supposed to know and feeling what you are not supposed to feel. *Canadian Journal of Psychiatry* 24(5): 403–408.

Bowlby J (1980) *Attachment and Loss: Vol. 3. Loss, Sadness and Depression* (1991 edition). London: Penguin Books.

Bowlby J (1984) Violence in the family as a disorder of the attachment and care-giving systems. *The American Journal of Psychoanalysis* 44(1): 9–27.

Bowlby J (1988) *A Secure Base: Clinical Applications of Attachment Theory.* London: Routledge.

Brack CE (2020) Camus and Suicide. *Philosophize.* Available at Camus and Suicide | Chad E. Brack (chadebrack.com).

Briggs S, Lemma A and Crouch W (eds) (2008) *Relating to Self-Harm and Suicide: Psychoanalytic Perspectives on Practice, Theory and Prevention.* London: Routledge.

Brown D (1988) Psychosomatic disorder and the group. Lecture at *The Introductory General Course,* Institute of Group Analysis, London (4 February).

Burrow T (1927) *The Social Basis of Consciousness.* New York: Harcourt.

Burrow T (1958) *A Search for Man's Sanity. Selected Letters with Biographical Notes.* New York: Oxford University Press.

Campbell D and Hale R (2017) *Working in the Dark: Understanding the pre-suicide state of mind.* London and New York: Routledge.

Camus A (1942a) *Le Mythe de Sisyphe* [The Myth of Sisyphus]. Paris: Gallimard.

Camus A (1942b) *L'Étranger* [The Outsider]. Paris: Gallimard.

Camus A (1947) *La Peste* [The Plague]. Paris: Gallimard.

Caparrós N, Ezquerro A, Kaes R, Neri C, Rodrigué E and Sanfeliu I (2004). *Y el Grupo Creó al Hombre.* Madrid: Biblioteca Nueva.

Chartrand H, Sareen J, Toews M and Bolton, J. M (2012) Suicide attempts versus non-suicidal self-injury among individuals with anxiety disorders in a nationally representative sample. *Depression and Anxiety* 29(3): 172–179.

Cheung A and Zwickl S (2021). Why have nearly half of Transgender Australians attempted suicide? Pursuit. Melbourne, Australia: University of Melbourne. Available at   https://pursuit.unimelb.edu.au/articles/why-have-nearly-half-of-transgender-austra lians-attempted-suicide

Cohn HW (1986) The double context: On combining individual and group therapy. *Group Analysis* 19(4): 327–339.

Csikszentmihalyi M (2021) Adolescence. *Encyclopaedia Britannica*. Available at https:// www.britannica.com/science/adolescence

Cyrulnik B (2017) *Psychothérapie de Dieu*. Paris: Odile Jacob.

Cyrulnik B (2018) *Psicoterapia de Dios*. Barcelona, Spain: Editorial Gedisa.

Dluhy M (2007) An empty self: Detached aloneness within the context of individual and group therapy. *Group: The Journal of the Eastern Group Psychotherapy Society* 31(1–2) 17–30.

Durkheim É (1897) *Le Suicide: Étude de sociologie* [Suicide: A Study in Sociology] (1952 edition). London: Routledge and Kegan Paul.

Durkin HE (1983) Developmental levels: their therapeutic implications for analytic group psychotherapy. *Group: The Journal of the Eastern Group Psychotherapy Society* 7(3): 3–10.

Ezquerro A (1989) Group psychotherapy with the pre-elderly. *Group Analysis* 22(3): 299–308.

Ezquerro A (1996) The Tavistock and Group Analytic Approaches to Group Psychotherapy: A Trainee's Perspective. *Psychoanalytic Psychotherapy* 10(2): 155–170.

Ezquerro A (2023) *Apego y Desarrollo a lo largo de la vida: El poder del apego grupal*. Madrid: Editorial Sentir.

Ezquerro A and Bajaj P (2007) Combining individual and group-analytic psychotherapy: When the group is not enough, or is it? *Group: The Journal of the Eastern Group Psychotherapy Society* 31(1–2): 5–16.

Ezquerro A and Cañete M (2023) *Group Analysis throughout the Life Cycle: Foulkes Revisited from a Group Attachment and Developmental Perspective*. London and New York: Routledge.

Fazel S and Runeson B (2020). Suicide. *New England Journal of Medicine* 382(3): 266–274.

Filippi LS (1983) Psicoterapia psicoanalitica combinata, di grupo e individuale, con soggetti borderline. *Archivo di Psicología, Neurologia e Psichiatria* 44(3): 289–298.

Fonagy P and Target M (2007) The rooting of the mind in the body: New links between attachment theory and psychoanalytic thought. *Journal of American the Psychoanalytic Association* 55(2): 411–456.

Ford JD and Gomez JM (2015) The relationship of psychological trauma and dissociative and posttraumatic stress disorders to non-suicidal self-injury and suicidality: A review. *Journal of Trauma and Dissociation* 16(3): 232–271.

Foulkes E (1990) S.H. Foulkes: a brief memoir. In: Foulkes E (ed) *SH Foulkes Selected Papers: Psychoanalysis and Group Analysis*. London: Karnac Books, pp. 3–20.

Foulkes SH (1948) *Introduction to Group Analytic Psychotherapy*. London: Heinemann.

Foulkes SH (1964) *Therapeutic Group Analysis*. London: George Allen & Unwin.

Foulkes SH (1975) *Group Analytic Psychotherapy. Method and Principles*. London: Gordon and Breach.

Foulkes SH and Lewis E (1944) Group Analysis: Studies of the treatment of groups on psychoanalytic lines. *British Journal of Medical Psychology* 20: 175–184.

Frances A (2021) Ten books. *The British Journal of Psychiatry* 218(5): 289–291.

Freud S (1920) Beyond the Pleasure Principle. In: In: Strachey (ed) *The Standard Edition of the Complete Psychological Works of Sigmund Freud* (Vol. 12). London: The Hogarth Press, pp. 1–64.

Garland C (1980) Face to face. *Group Analysis* 13(1): 42–43.

Garland C (1982) Group Analysis: Taking the Non-problem Seriously. *Group Analysis* 15(1): 4–14.

GOV.UK (2019) First ever cross-government suicide prevention plan published. GOV.UK, 22 January. Available at https://www.gov.uk/government/news/first-ever-cross-gover nment-suicide-prevention-plan-published

Green J, Berry K, Danquah A and Pratt D. (2021) Attachment security and suicide idea-tion and behaviour: The mediating role of reflective functioning. *International Journal of Environmental Research and Public Health* 18(6): 3090.

Hale R (2008) Psychoanalysis and suicide: process and typology. In: Briggs S, Lemma A and Crouch W (eds) *Relating to Self-Harm and Suicide: Psychoanalytic Perspectives on Practice, Theory and Prevention.* London: Routledge, pp. 13–24.

Hendin H (1991) Psychotherapy and suicide. *American Journal of Psychotherapy* 35(4): 469–480.

Hendricks S (2018) The meaning of life: Albert Camus on faith, suicide and absurdity. *Big Think.* Available at https://bigthink.com/personal-growth/the-meaning-of-life-albert-camus-on-faith-suicide-and-absurdity/

Heyno (2008) On being affected without being infected: managing suicidal thoughts in stu-dent counselling. In: Briggs S, Lemma A and Crouch W (eds) *Relating to Self-Harm and Suicide: Psychoanalytic Perspectives on Practice, Theory and Prevention.* London: Routledge, pp. 175–186.

Hillman J (1964) *Suicide and the Soul.* Dallas, TX: Spring Publications.

Hillman J and Ventura M (1992) *We've had a hundred years of psychotherapy and the world's getting worse.* San Francisco, CA: Harper.

Hobdell R (1991) Individual and group therapy combined. In: Roberts J and Pines M (eds) *The Practice of Group Analysis.* London and New York: Tavistock/Routledge, pp. 136–147.

Hopper E (2001) Difficult patients in group analysis: The personification of (ba) I: A/M. *Group: The Journal of the Eastern Group Psychotherapy Society* 25(3): 139–171.

Humphrey N (2017) Why Do So Many People Want to Die? *Sapiens,* 21 November. Avail-able at www.sapiens.org/biology/suicide-human-origins/

Humphrey N (2018) The lure of death: suicide and human evolution. *Philosophical Trans-actions of the Royal Society B: Biological Sciences* 373(1754): 30012736. Available at https://doi.org/10.1098/rstb.2017.0269

Jenkins R (2022) Addressing suicide as a public-health problem. *The Lancet* 359(9309): 813–814.

Kafka F (1983) *Stories 1904–1924.* London: Futura.

Kaplan KJ and Worth SA (1993) Individuation-attachment and suicide trajectory: A devel-opmental guide for the clinician. *Omega: Journal of Death and Dying* 27(3): 207–237.

Karterud S, Johansen MS and Wilberg T (2007) Conjoint group and individual psychother-apy in a research trial for patients with severe personality disorders. *Group: The Journal of the Eastern Group Psychotherapy Society* 32(1–2): 31–46.

Kashdan TB and Roberts JE (2011) Comorbid social anxiety disorder in clients with depres-sive disorders: Predicting changes in depressive symptoms, therapeutic relationships, and focus of attention in group treatment. *Behaviour Research and Therapy* 49(12): 875–884.

Kegerreis D (2007) Attending to splitting: The therapist couple in a conjoint individual group psychotherapy programme for patients with borderline personality disorder. *Group: The Journal of the Eastern Group Psychotherapy Society* 31(1–2): 89–106.

Kharsati N and Bhola P (2016) Self-injurious behavior, emotion regulation, and attachment styles among college students in India. *Industrial Psychiatry Journal* 25(1): 23–28.

Klonsky ED, May AM and Saffer BY (2016) Suicide, suicide attempts, and suicidal idea-tion. *Annual Review of Clinical Psychology* 12: 307–330.

Kulawik H (1982) Kombination der dynamischen gruppen psychotherapie mit der psy-chodynamischen einzeltherapie. *Psychiatrie Neurologie und Medizinische Psychologie* 34(4): 222–228.

Ledgerwood DM (1999) Suicide and Attachment: Fear of Abandonment and Isolation from a Developmental Perspective. *Journal of Contemporary Psychotherapy* 29(1): 65–73.

Leenaars AA (1988) *Suicide Notes.* New York: Human Sciences Press.

Leenaars AA (2001) Controlling the environment to prevent suicide. In: Wasserman D (ed) *Suicide and Unnecessary Death.* London: Martin Dunitz Ltd, pp. 259–264.

Levi-Belz Y, Gvion Y, Horesh N and Apter A (2013) Attachment patterns in medically serious suicide attempts: The mediating role of self-disclosure and loneliness. *Suicide and Life-Threatening Behavior* 43(5): 511–522.

Lipsius SH (1991) Combined individual and group psychotherapy: guidelines at the interface. *International Journal of Group Psychotherapy* 41(3): 313–327.

Lizardi D, Grunebaum MF, Burke A, Stanley B, Mann JJ, Harkavy-Friedman J and Oquendo M (2011) The effect of social adjustment and attachment style on suicidal behaviour. *Acta Psychiatrica Scandinavica* 124(4): 295–300.

Lofton P, Daugherty C and Mayerson P (1983) Combined group and individual treatment for the borderline patient. *Group: The Journal of the Eastern Group Psychotherapy Society* 7(3): 21–26.

McLaughlin C, McGowan I, O'Neill S and Kernohan G (2014) The burden of living with and caring for a suicidal family member. *Journal of Mental Health* 23: 236–240.

Mann JJ (2013) The serotonergic system in mood disorders and suicidal behaviour. *Philosophical Transactions of the Royal Society B: Biological Sciences* 368(1615): 20120537. Available at *https://doi.org/10.1098/rstb.2012.0537*

Maratos J (1996) Self through attachment and attachment through self in group therapy. *Group Analysis* 29(2): 191–198.

Miniati M, Callari A and Pini S (2017) Adult Attachment Style and Suicidality. *Psychiatria Danubina* 29(3): 250–259.

Minne C (2008) Violence to body and mind: infanticide as suicide. In: Briggs S, Lemma A and Crouch W (eds) *Relating to Self-Harm and Suicide: Psychoanalytic Perspectives on Practice, Theory and Prevention.* London: Routledge, pp. 139–149.

Navarro D, Marín-Mayor M, Gasparyan A, García-Gutiérrez MS, Rubio G, Manzanares J (2023) Molecular Changes Associated with Suicide. *International Journal of Molecular Sciences* 24(23):16726. Available at https://doi.org/10.3390%2Fijms242316726

O'Connor RC and Nock MK (2014) The psychology of suicidal behaviour. *The Lancet Psychiatry* 1(1): 73–85.

Özer U, Yildirim EA and Erkoç SN (2015) Relationship of suicidal ideation and behavior to attachment style in patients with major depression. *Noro Psikiyatri Arsivi* 52(3): 283–288.

Palitsky D, Mota N, Afifi TO, Downs AC and Sareen J (2013) The association between adult attachment style, mental disorders, and suicidality. *The Journal of Nervous and Mental Disease* 201(7): 579–586.

Pines M (1980) What to expect in the psychotherapy of borderline patients. *Group Analysis* 13(2): 168–177.

Pines M (1996) The self as a group: the group as a self. *Group Analysis* 29(2): 183–190.

Porter K (1980) Combined individual and group psychotherapy: a review of the literature 1965–1978. *International Journal of Group Psychotherapy* 30(1): 107–114.

Rutan JS and Stone WN (1993) *Psychodynamic Group Psychotherapy.* New York and London: The Guilford Press.

Sager C (1960) Concurrent individual and group analytic psychotherapy. *American Journal Orthopsychiatry* 30: 225–241.

Samaritans (2024). Latest Suicide Data. Samaritans.org. Available at www.samaritans.org/about-samaritans/research-policy/suicide-facts-and-figures/latest-suicide-data/

Schermer VL (2009) On the vicissitudes of combining individual and group psychotherapy. *International Journal of Group Psychotherapy* 59(1): 149–162.

Schlapobersky J (2016) *From the Couch to the Circle: Group-Analytic Psychotherapy in Practice.* London: Routledge.

Schore AN (1994) *Affect Regulation and the Origin of the Self.* Hillsdale, NJ: Lawrence Erlbaum.

Segalla RA (1996) The Unbearable Embeddedness of Being: Self Psychology, Intersubjectivity and Large Group Experiences. *Group: The Journal of the Eastern Group Psychotherapy Society* 20(4): 257–271.

Segalla RA (2007) Influences from Kohutian and contemporary theories in the development of a combined treatment model. *Group: The Journal of the Eastern Group Psychotherapy Society* 31(1–2) 107–118.

Shneidman E (1985) *Definition of Suicide.* New York: Wiley.

Slavinska-Holy N (1983) Combining individual and homogeneous group psychotherapies for borderline conditions. *International Journal of Group Psychotherapy* 33(3): 297–312.

Solomon RC (2005) *Existentialism.* Oxford: Oxford University Press.

Stepp SD, Morse JQ, Yaggi KE, Reynolds SK, Reed LI and Pilkonis PA (2008) The role of attachment styles and interpersonal problems in suicide-related behaviors. *Suicide and Life-Threatening Behavior* 38: 592–607.

Taylor LR (1971) *Party Politics in the Age of Caesar.* Berkeley, CA: University of California Press.

Timmerman T and Cholbi M (eds) (2020) *Exploring the Philosophy of Death and Dying: Classical and Contemporary Perspectives.* New York: Routledge.

Turecki G and Brent DA (2016). Suicide and suicidal behaviour. *The Lancet* 387(10024): 1227–1239.

Ulman KH (2002) The ghost in the group room: counter-transferential pressures associated with conjoint individual and group psychotherapy. *International Journal of Group Psychotherapy* 52(3): 387–407.

Usborne S (2021) I don't intend to let my son down twice: the bereaved father trying to end suicide. *The Guardian* (11 August). Available at www.theguardian.com/society/2021/aug/11/i-dont-intend-to-let-my-son-down-twice-the-bereaved-father-trying-to-end-suicide

Van Montfoort R and Thelosen E (1994) Combined individual and group analytic psychotherapy with young psychotics. *Group Analysis* 27(4): 497–503.

Van Orden KA, Witte TK, Cukrowicz KC, Braithwaite, Selby EA and Joiner TE (2010) The interpersonal theory of suicide. *Psychological Review* 117(2): 575–600.

Vargas Llosa M (2006) *Travesuras de la niña mala.* Madrid: Alfaguara.

Wender L and Stein A (1949) Group psychotherapy as an aid to out-patient treatment in a psychiatric clinic. *Psychiatric Quarterly* 23: 415–424.

WHO (2023) Suicide: Key facts. World Health Organization. Available at https://www.who.int/news-room/fact-sheets/detail/suicide

Wong N (1988) Combined Individual and Group Treatment with Borderline and Narcissistic Patients. In: Slavinska-Holy N (ed) *Borderline and Narcissistic Patients in Therapy.* Madison, CT: International Universities Press, pp. 17–45.

Wrath AJ and Camelia Adams G (2018) Self-Injurious Behaviors and Adult Attachment: A Review of the Literature. *Archives of Suicide Research* 23(4): 527–550.

Yakeley J and Burbridge-James W (2018) Psychodynamic approaches to suicide and self-harm. *British Journal of Psychiatry Advances* 24(1): 37–45.

Zulueta F de and Mark P (2000) Attachment and contained splitting: A combined approach of group and individual therapy to the treatment of patients suffering from borderline personality disorder *Group Analysis* 33(4): 486–500.

Arturo Ezquerro: https://orcid.org/0000-0002-9910-4576

Chapter 5

Group cohesion versus group coherency through an attachment lens

Arturo Ezquerro

5.1 Introduction: The politics of uncertainty

Socrates is considered a pioneer of a complex form of *dialectical* teaching from which his disciples learned experientially, as well as intellectually. From a group-analytic perspective, this might be seen as an early form of *therapeutic* group work (Ezquerro, 2010).

The contemporary British philosopher Anthony Grayling examined some of Socrates' strategies in dealing with uncertainty, and wrote about Meno, a young man from Thessaly who was described in historical records as treacherous, eager for wealth and supremely self-confident. With much enthusiasm, Meno visited the master in Athens and was very keen on knowing his view in respect of a crucial query: is virtue teachable?

This question considerably troubled the ancient Greeks, who could not understand why the offspring of virtuous parents were as likely to misbehave as those of non-virtuous parents. During the visit, to Meno's surprise, Socrates replied that he did not know the answer. Meno persisted and was utterly astonished when Socrates confessed that he did not know the answer to the even more crucial question: what is virtue?

Grayling (2002) recounted some of this Socratic dialogue from Plato's work *Meno*:

"Do you know what virtue is?", Socrates asked.

And when the flabbergasted youth replied, "Yes, of course!", Socrates was full of curiosity and responded promptly:

"Wonderful! Please tell me. For a long time, I have longed to find out!"

Needless to say, Socrates swiftly and comprehensively demolished Meno's efforts to define virtue, making him exclaim at last:

"I am thoroughly confused; I don't know what to think".

DOI: 10.4324/9781003271956-6

To which Socrates, with a calmed tone of voice, commented:

"Now that you realise you are confused, we can begin to progress towards understanding".

Some twenty-four centuries later, Gunnison (2003) tuned in with this complex exchange by quoting Henry Miller:

Confusion is a word we have invented for an order which is not understood.
(Miller, in Gunnison, 2003: 58)

This chapter endeavours to study the constructs of *group cohesion* (or cohesiveness) and *group coherency* (or coherence), as they relate to group-analytic psychotherapy and group attachment (see Chapter 1).

Group cohesion has been considered the most frequently studied group process dimension (Marziali, Munroe-Blum and McLeary, 1997; Hopper 2003; Marmarosh, Holtz and Schottenbauer, 2005; Ezquerro, 2010, 2017a, 2020, 2021; Begovac and Begovac, 2013; Tasca, 2014; Marmarosh, 2017, 2020, 2021; Terrazas-Carrillo, Vásquez and García, 2023; Tasca and Marmarosh, 2023).

In the circumstances, we have to formulate an obvious question: is cohesion teachable? Having said that, and paraphrasing Socrates, we will need to ask ourselves what cohesion is in the first place, before we can go any further.

According to the 21st century edition of the *Collins English Dictionary* (2000), *cohesion* is the act or state of holding or sticking firmly together. In physics, it is the force that holds together atoms or molecules; in botany, the fusion of flower parts that are usually separate, such as petals. On the other hand, *coherency* is a logical or natural connection, order or consistency.

Both words have a Latin root, *cohaerere*, meaning to adhere or to be bound. The term cohesion has the more passive connotation of a physical force binding parts together, whereas the term coherency is more evocative of active connectedness and mutual interconnection. In a number of different fields, coherency refers to the quality of being orderly, logically integrated, aesthetically consistent and intelligible.

In physiology, there is a type of coherence that occurs when two or more of the body's oscillatory systems, such as respiration and heart rhythms, become entrained and operate at the same frequency. This is called *cross-coherence* (McCraty and Childre, 2010; McCraty and Zayas, 2014).

In *Overcoming Emotional Chaos*, Childre and Rozman (2002) referred to group coherency as more advanced a position than group cohesion. A coherent group shows a logical, orderly and aesthetically consistent relationship among its constituents, and between them and the group-as-a-whole.

Coherency implies correlations, connectedness, consistency, wholeness and a global order, in which the whole is not constituted by a collection of aggregates but becomes greater than the sum of its individual parts.

It should be noted that Earl Hopper (a psychoanalyst, sociologist and group analyst) did not specifically employ the term group coherency. Instead, he pointed out that the cohesion of groups has been studied in multiple disciplines, including general systems theory, social biology, classical psychoanalysis, sociology, social psychology, group dynamics, group psychotherapy and group analysis.

In fact, Hopper (2003) formulated a fourth basic assumption in the unconscious life of groups, which he termed *incohesion: aggregation/massification* – something that can apply to highly defended, traumatised and, on deeper reading, *incoherent* groups and social systems.

Despite countless publications on the subject, group cohesion (let alone group coherency) continues to defy a precise definition. There is little consensus about the dimensions that best describe the complex phenomena that comprises group cohesion, no matter it is a dominant construct within the specialist literature.

Dion (2000) considered that group cohesion was a *muddled* concept from the outset. Bloch and Crouch (1987) put together a number of statements about group cohesion, which they found in the early group therapy literature, as evidence that the construct was rather blurred:

> esprit de corps, friendly environment, unification of the group, emotional acceptance, emotional support, loss of feelings of isolation, group reassurance, feeling of belonging, group identification, togetherness, permissive environment, the group's tolerance of the patient, the therapist's tolerance of the patient, acceptance by the group and supportive relations.
>
> (Bloch and Crouch, 1987: 99)

Bednar and Kaul (1994) affirmed that there was little *cohesion* in group cohesion research and minimal consensus about the dimensions that best describe the complex phenomena that comprises it. They recommended that the term be dropped altogether. Indeed, this has not happened and it is unlikely that it will happen, since group cohesion is too well established and too convenient a term.

However, it is important to highlight the multidimensionality, complexity and fluctuating nature of this construct, and to be open-minded about the related construct of *group coherency*, as related to but distinct from that of *group cohesion* (Pines, 1986a, 2002).

This state of affairs can bring uncertainty, unpredictability and confusion. Nevertheless, the complexity associated with it may open a window of opportunities for the emergence of new meaning.

5.1(i) Contents and aims of the chapter

Clinicians and researchers have largely categorised *group cohesion* (a basic force in the process of forming a group and keeping it together) as a crucial therapeutic factor and precondition for effective group psychotherapy and group attachment. This chapter offers a complementary view that, in the longer term, a group that only operates at the cohesion level may restrict significantly its own therapeutic potential.

In contrast, the concept of *group coherency* is highlighted as an organising principle that promotes deeper understanding and more mature levels of functioning, which are key to satisfactory relationships, personal growth and group development.

To validate this working hypothesis, the chapter reviews the literature on *cohesion* and *coherency*, from the fields of psychoanalysis, group analysis, group psychotherapy, complexity and attachment theory, and also presents a piece of qualitative clinical-process research from a weekly outpatient group.

The conductor made a mistake, but managed to talk about it in the group, examined his countertransference and learned from it, which helped change the group's complex *modus operandi* from one of undifferentiated cohesion to one of coherency, as members worked through their conflicts and accepted and integrated their differences.

Indeed, coherency is not a permanent state that stays fixed in individuals and groups, but it can be better described as a position that has to be negotiated and re-negotiated on a regular basis. Groups can retreat from *loci* of coherency to more primitive positions where cohesive forces prevail. We all make mistakes and become anxious, even disorganised, at times, but our errors provide opportunities for learning from experience and making necessary changes. This, in turn, enables us to develop new positions of coherency: a life-long task.

The chapter aims to contribute to the theoretical understanding and clinical applications of both *cohesion* and *coherency* from group-analytic and attachment standpoints, including insights from complexity theory, as well as recent developments on ruptures and repairs in group psychotherapy.

5.2 Complexity, cohesion and coherency in group psychotherapy

Surprisingly, I could only find two references to cohesion or coherency in the writings of SH Foulkes, the *father* of group analysis. He did not openly explore the nature of either of these two constructs and, to some extent, appeared to use both terms interchangeably. However, on a closer look, he gave the impression that cohesion is a more basic force which can develop and result in coherency:

> The group, through sharing, can be more tolerant and less afraid . . . than a patient in individual therapy. The group finds strength in its cohesion. It can maintain growing integration . . . finding it easier than does the isolated individual to remain capable of . . . accepting, and indeed helping to lay bare, . . . irrational manifestations.

> (Foulkes 1972: 242)

> The total interactions of the individuals are in fact the result of affinities or disaffinities of individual instincts, emotions, reactions of all sorts, character

predispositions . . . Essentially, this gives the group coherence and meaning for each of the participants, even if each is far from conscious of this.

(Foulkes, 1973: 228–229)

On the other hand, Foulkes did not use the concept of attachment, let alone group attachment, in his theorising. However, he referred to a unifying context whenever "the group associates, responds and acts as a whole" (Foulkes, 1964: 118), as if it were an invisible organism.

Foulkes also postulated "the existence of a group mind in the same way as we postulate the existence of an individual mind" (Foulkes, 1964: 118), and accepted that complexity encompasses the paradigm of human thinking, feeling and relating. This is at the core of group-analytic work, and he put it this way:

> What an enormous complexity of processes and actions and interactions play between even two or three of these people, or these people and myself, or between two in relation to another three, and so on. What enormous complexity, quite impossible to perceive and disentangle even theoretically all at the same time. How is it that they can nevertheless understand each other, that they can to some extent refer to a shared common sense of what is going on?.
>
> (Foulkes, 1973: 227)

With his *trained* intuition Foulkes left the question of complexity open, at a time when the concept of cohesion as an invisible and unifying force that held members together was well extended in the field of group psychotherapy.

Cartwright (1968) proposed a rather generic and unspecific definition of group cohesion:

> the resultant of all forces acting on members to remain in the group.
>
> (Cartwright, 1968, quoted in Bloch and Crouch, 1987: 100)

Of course, that definition was only a starting point. We need to ask ourselves: what are the forces that, in conjunction, determine group cohesion? And what are the consequences of such forces?

Braaten (1991) indicated that, in order to form a cohesive therapy group, it is important to select suitable patients, to have a balanced membership, and to employ effective orientation, training and contracting. In addition, he suggested that group cohesion might be a requisite for resolving group rebellion and conflict, promoting the building of constructive norming and therapeutic culture, and reducing avoidance and defensiveness.

Yalom (1975) initially defined group cohesion as the *attractiveness* of a group for its members, and included it as a major therapeutic factor. According to him, a group has to be cohesive in order to be therapeutic. However, his position was somewhat ambiguous and he later described group cohesion as the

necessary *precondition* [my emphasis] for effective therapy.
                                                            (Yalom, 1975: 50)

He further related cohesion to feelings of valuing the group and belonging *in* the group. He added that cohesion is an agent of change in members' lives through

the interrelation of group self-esteem and [individual] self-esteem.
                                                            (Yalom, 1975: 107)

It became progressively accepted that group cohesion is a complex multidimensional phenomenon. Silbergeld et al (1975) linked it to group affiliation, spontaneity and involvement. Other clinicians (Bloch and Crouch, 1987) related cohesion to acceptance and togetherness with a warm, friendly and supportive atmosphere in the group. Cohesion has also been described as the group counterpart to the *therapeutic alliance* in individual psychotherapy (Marziali, Munroe-Blum and McLeary, 1997).

The distinction between group cohesion as a therapeutic factor or as a requisite for change is obscured by the vague nature of the concept. Most group psychotherapists tend to agree with the idea that some degree of cohesion is required, since there is an obvious need for members to stay together in order to work effectively. This indicates that, on balance, cohesion is better conceived as a *precondition* for change rather than as a therapeutic factor *per se* (Ezquerro, 2017a).

A group must be attractive enough to its members in order that therapeutic factors can operate. An unattractive group may end up with members dropping out of treatment or losing their motivation to work at the required task. On the other hand, an excessively cohesive group may set up boundaries that are too concretely defined and rather rigid or impermeable, which may also interfere with the therapeutic task. The therapist's behaviour can indeed influence the course one way or another (Ezquerro, 2010).

Over the years, a number of analytic authors (Slavson, 1964; Hinshelwood, 1985; Begovac and Begovac, 2013; Ezquerro, 2010, 2020, 2021) have pointed out that group cohesion is not invariably linked to productive therapy: as well as benefits, it can have detrimental effects. When harmony is superficial and members ignore or evade conflict, it may turn out to be non-productive or even anti-therapeutic.

In a bad scenario, cohesion can generate, in some group members, powerful feelings of being trapped or coerced (Hinshelwood, 1985). Indeed, if cohesion is intrinsically a requisite for change, then it is potentially a condition for both therapeutic and anti-therapeutic change.

Research studies are inconclusive in terms of possible direct links between cohesion and positive therapeutic outcome, apart from a significant correlation between cohesion and lower dropping-out rates (Budman, Soldz, Demby and Feldstein, 1990).

In a large quantitative piece of research, Marmarosh, Holtz and Schottenbauer (2005) indicated that cohesion is directly related to curative group factors such as collective self-esteem and hope for the self. These authors also referred to previous studies which showed a significantly positive correlation between group cohesion, liking the group and patients' satisfaction.

The above characteristics contribute to the process of internalising the group in a way that it is perceived by members as a part of themselves. This has also been described as the development of a *group self* that is integral to a balanced *individual self* (Caparrós et al, 2004).

However, being part of a cohesive group does not necessarily mean that members will perceive it as critical to their identity. Some patients may feel positive about their therapy group but, at the same time, regard themselves as unimportant members (Marmarosh, Holtz and Schottenbauer, 2005).

Group therapists have to be aware that, in addition to building a sense of value and liking of the group, it is important to address how members internalise the group and carry it with them in between sessions and after the therapy has ended (Ezquerro, 2010).

From what has been presented so far, I can suggest that, depending on the circumstances, as well as the shape that each particular group takes, cohesion may either enhance or put limitations to the group's therapeutic potential.

In the wake of this debate, Pines (1985, 1986a, 1986b, 1989) made a landmark contribution by advancing the construct of *group coherency*, as a higher-order type of group functioning, distinct from that of group cohesion or cohesiveness. This was a major breakthrough in group-analytic theorising.

Prior to Pines, the concept of group coherency had been absent in the specialist literature by and large. Yalom did not deal with it at all, and Kellerman (1981), who edited a book which provided a comprehensive review of all previous publications on group cohesion, did not index the term coherency either. Other authors, like Foulkes (1973) and Hartman (1981) referred to coherency but mainly treated it as undistinguishable from cohesion.

In contrast to that, Pines (1985) believed that a proper distinction between the two terms had become necessary. In order to approach the subject, he initially looked at the etymology of the word group and found two origins:

The more ancient root is Germanic: *crop* (the gizzard of a bird). The evolution of the word group from crop is that in the crop of an animal there is an agglomeration of substances that have been swallowed and have lost their discrete nature to form an undifferentiated fibrous mass. Here, we can see the image of a primitive group made of individual elements, glued and only partly digested, without showing a higher level of organisation.

Pines (1985) argued that, in a purely cohesive group, elements stick together and partly change by an agglomeration that is shaped into a sort of ball, which has an external boundary but lacks any internal structure. For him, the force that holds this mass together can be termed as *cohesion*, conceived as a unity of material things held together by a physical substance (such as cement, mortar or glue) or by an invisible force such as attraction or affinity.

The second root of the word group comes from Latin: *cruppo*. This term is connected to the notion of grouping as an active process, like in painting or composing. Here, objects are no longer a passive agglomeration but grouped together in order to display a harmony. This leads to a higher form of psychological organisation that has placed them together in order to produce an aesthetic satisfaction.

This second root of group is strongly linked to the concept of *coherency*, as illustrated by Webster's *Dictionary of Synonyms* (1973):

> Coherency usually implies unity, firstly of immaterial, of intangible things, such as the points of an argument, the details of a picture, the incidents, characters and settings of a story; or secondly of material and objective things that are bound into a unity by a spiritual, intellectual or aesthetic relationship, as through their clear sequence or their harmony with one another; it therefore connotes an integrity which makes the whole and the relationship of its parts clear and manifest.

The concept of coherency applied to analytic groups denotes an organisational process at work. This should be part of the group analyst's mind, as a result of their training and therapeutic role.

These organisational principles are gradually internalised by group members who, in turn, become co-organisers of the group. Each member has a double function: being the recipient of the group processes but also an active supporter and vital link in the group structure (Ezquerro, 2010).

5.3 An attachment perspective on group cohesion and group coherency

The literature on attachment has emphasised the evolutionary and universal need that human beings have for significant attachment figures, who provide a protective secure base from which to explore and to grow. A group can come to constitute itself as a subsidiary attachment figure for many people and, for some, as a primary attachment figure (Bowlby, 1969). Indeed, interpersonal and group attachment are key components of healthy psychosocial development (see Chapter 1).

In a chapter on cohesion, interpersonal relationships and attachment in group therapy, Sally Barlow (2013) highlighted the potential benefits of a cohesive group climate. She conceptualised cohesion as a feeling of positive bonding between members with one another and with the therapist, which can be a therapeutic experience in its own right and contribute to improved group processes and outcomes.

Rom and Mikulincer (2003) found that group cohesion significantly moderates the effects of attachment anxiety. Lavy and Granot (2010) and Lavy, Bareli and Ein-Dor (2015) studied this further to find that group cohesion reduces the negative effect of attachment avoidance on socio-emotional functioning.

Gallagher et al (2014) compared the effects of group cohesion on patients with a range of attachment anxiety. It was found that increased group cohesion was significantly associated with symptomatic improvement in those with high levels of attachment anxiety, and less so in people with low levels of such an anxiety or with avoidant attachment patterns.

Using a group climate questionnaire, Jennings, Jumper and Baglio (2021) showed that groups with better overall ratings of therapeutic climate are better at helping members move towards more secure attachment relationships. The interface between attachment and group psychotherapy has been further explored by Leszcz (2017), Marmarosh (2021) and Marmarosh and Tasca (2013).

Flores (2010) argued that, similar to how a securely attached child feels more confident in exploring a strange room whilst in the presence of the mother, securely attached group members will take more risks in exploring their internal world and their relationships with fellow members, if the group environment provides them with a secure base. Such a base can enable members to form a person-to-group attachment, in addition to person-to-person attachments.

However, not even the best secure base can provide a complete and constant sense of security. In the real world, it is more realistic to pursue a base that is facilitating and secure enough. Such a base should not attempt to provide a rigidly controlled environment that sacrifices spontaneity, complexity and diversity, but a creative freedom to explore genuine and ever-evolving relationships.

In a further piece of work, Flores (2017) highlighted that interpersonal emotional engagement accounts for the majority of therapeutic change in group psychotherapy. The growing neuroscience field now provides a body of evidence focused on the positive effect that recurring authentic face-to-face social interaction has on neural processes (see Chapter 1).

According to this evidence, it is crucial to promote the creation of an enriched group environment that enhances opportunities for dependable and mutually trusting engagements among group members – something that has been described elsewhere as *epistemic trust* (Fonagy, Gergely, Jurist and Target, 2002; Fonagy and Allison, 2014; Fonagy, Luyten and Allison, 2015; Fonagy and Campbell, 2017).

From an attachment perspective, the emphasis that the group therapy literature has placed on cohesion should not mean an unrealistically supportive and rigidly safe environment.

Rather, healthy group attachment pertains to creating an environment where personal agency and differences can be safely explored. In turn, this allows for the inevitable conflict that arises in relationships to be addressed.

When there is a threat, real or imagined, the proximity-seeking component of the attachment system is activated. In a therapy group context, this can trigger needs for comfort, protection and cohesive nearness in space, time, or relationship.

Once these needs are met, the group can venture into deeper levels of exploration and operate at a more coherent level again (Ezquerro, 2017a).

However, some patients bring with them a history of major traumatic experiences and highly anxious attachment, which can force them to hold on to more familiar and predictable levels of group cohesion and restrict the quality of their explorations (Ezquerro, 2010).

In an attempt to put together and integrate group-analytic and attachment thinking, we may say that group attachment is secure-enough when members can protest, disagree with and challenge each other and the group therapist without fear of punishment, abandonment or rejection.

This statement may imply that insecure group attachment can reinforce the maintenance of more primitive positions of cohesion, in which conflict and differences are perceived as threatening; whereas secure group attachment nurtures the development of deeper, more sophisticated and higher functioning levels of coherency.

There are indeed cycles and variations in the quality of group coherency, which requires the development of a capacity for self-organisation and regulation by the group-as-a-whole. This implies a synchronised and harmonious order in the relationships between and amongst members, including the leader (McCraty and Zayas, 2014).

In a coherent group, there is more freedom than in a purely cohesive group for individual members to thrive, whilst preserving some degree of cohesion and resonance with shared experiences and common goals.

5.4 A clinical case study

One of the weekly outpatient groups that I conducted in an NHS clinic had been meeting for nine months . . .

Membership had been stable from the beginning, consisting of four women and four men, in their 30s and 40s. They came from different ethnic backgrounds, including white English and second generation Afro-Caribbean, European, Indian and Latin American immigrants.

They all had experiences of early insecure attachments and presented a range of anxiety, affective and eating disorders and relationship difficulties; two of the patients had been sexually abused.

During the early stages, the group could be described as reasonably cohesive. Members appeared not to pay attention to their differences and predominantly looked for things in common. They seemed to develop a capacity for mutual affinity and support. I thought this was appropriate, in terms of group development. Members needed to gain a sense of basic trust, which would gradually enable them to explore conflicts and differences as well.

In the process of forming a new group, a reasonable level of cohesion and harmony is important; conflicts might be temporarily avoided, as members want to ensure the continuity of the group.

However, a cosy or too comfortable an atmosphere in which members obtain gratification but avoid distressing, or otherwise discomforting matters, is counterproductive and can undermine the creative complexities and therapeutic potential of the group (Ezquerro, 2010).

Not long after the group had started, **Susannah** and **Teresa**, briefly mentioned that they had been sexually abused as children; but indicated that they did not yet feel safe enough to explore such a traumatic experience further in the group.

I was aware that one of the men, **Charles**, had a history of conflictive relation-ships with women and a reputation of being a forceful personality. I wondered to what extent gender could be an issue for Teresa and Susannah. Being a man myself, I did not want to force any discussion on sexual abuse and said to them that they could go at their own pace.

5.4(i) Interpersonal and group ruptures

In the tenth month of the life of the group, half way into a session, **Susannah** said that she now felt ready to talk about her experience of being abused as a 13-year-old girl by a 30-year-old man. She explained that she had fallen in love with him and was anxious about losing him, but did not want to have sex because of her age. He forced her to have sexual intercourse without her consent. When she became pregnant, this man ran away.

Susannah stopped eating and attending school. She wanted her pregnancy to come full term, but her mother persuaded her to have an abortion. After this, she hoped that she would be able to put the abuse behind her, but her emotional prob-lems continued on and off. Since then, she did not feel confident enough to form any intimate relationships. More than twenty years later, she was still feeling that she had not come to terms with her experience of being sexually abused.

Several members expressed feelings of support and sympathy to her and of anger towards the young man for having abused her. However, **Charles** made a comment that, surely, she had been seductive. **Susannah** shouted that she was shocked and immediately left the room.

Everyone was openly furious with Charles, except **Teresa** who looked down, with an expression of sadness on her face, but she said nothing. I told **Charles** that, in denying or justifying the sexual abuse, his comment was in itself abusive and invited him to think about what might be behind it.

Charles responded saying that he was sorry and asked me to contact Susannah to give her his sincere apology. He then explained that he had had many negative experiences with women who seduced him and then dropped him. People did not buy his explanation and continued being angry with him. Some commented that he was trying to justify his unacceptable behaviour towards Susannah.

One member, **Rose**, said that she wanted Susannah back in the group and Charles out. Several members nodded. I commented that the angry feelings towards Charles were legitimate and understandable, but added that it would be important to work together, including Susannah and Charles, to try to resolve the conflict and heal the wounds.

After a brief silence, I said to **Teresa** that she was looking sad. She then disclosed that her maternal grandfather had abused her as a child for a number of years, and that she felt terrible with herself for being trapped and not running away from him. People in the room listened to Teresa but did not become actively involved; I felt they were still preoccupied with Susannah's departure.

Timing was difficult anyway, as we were approaching the end of the session. I thanked Teresa for trusting the group and tried to reassure her saying that the abuse was the responsibility of her grandfather, the abusive adult.

In my mind, I also wondered about other adults in her family (her parents and other possible attachment figures) who failed to protect her. However, as time was running out, I simply added that it would be important to continue with her exploration at the next meeting, and that I would also send a message to Susannah.

In fact, after the session, I wrote to **Susannah** inviting her to return to the group and conveying **Charles**' apology and the unanimous wish that people had expressed to see her back. She responded promptly, leaving a telephone message in which she thanked me for the content of the letter but declined to return to the group.

I felt bad with myself for having allowed the group to sit too comfortably on a cohesive frame for several months, easy-going and looking for things in common but not dealing with differences and conflict. Things now appeared to be out of control and I was anxious about the possibility of having some *casualties* for the first time in the life of the group.

The following day, **Susannah** telephoned again and left an additional message in which she requested an individual appointment with me. I was able to offer this to her ten days later, which meant that she did not come to the next group session.

At the start of this session, everyone was in the room except **Susannah** and **Teresa**. I had kept an empty chair for Susannah in the group circle despite her announced absence. I wanted to keep her alive in my mind and in the group's mind. People (including **Charles**) said they were sorry not to see Susannah but glad that she would have an individual appointment with me.

Teresa arrived at this point, sat on one of the two empty chairs and, inadvertently, put her handbag on the chair I had kept for Susannah. Under easier circumstances, I think I would have invited Teresa to explore the meaning of this.

However, it would appear that my *unconscious* anxiety about Susannah's survival might have played a trick on me. Without much thinking, I picked up Teresa's handbag and put it on a chair behind the circle. She immediately stood up, grabbed her handbag abruptly and, without saying a word, left the room slamming the door.

Everyone was astonished. **Rose** said that Teresa's reaction was chaotic and did not make sense to her. **John** commented that Teresa had had a sudden attack of insanity . . .

But I interrupted him and said that I was sorry that I had made a mistake since, in my attempt to protect Susannah's space, I had intruded upon Teresa's space. I added that I should have used verbal communication rather than action, and that I would give my apology to Teresa at the soonest opportunity.

Sylvia intervened to say that I was too hard on myself. She added that she could appreciate that, for a woman, a handbag is a private object. However, she did not think that I had intruded upon Teresa's space and that her behaviour was completely illogical.

At this point, still with some uncertainty, I took the risk of thinking aloud. I said that Susannah and Teresa's experiences of abuse appeared to be significantly different from everyone else's in the group, and that I wondered if, for a survivor of sexual abuse, a handbag could represent an extension of her body.

Several people responded that my comment was unusual but made sense. **Charles** commented that this new insight was helping him understand other people's traumatic experiences better.

5.4(ii) Reparative group work: from cohesion to coherency

At this point, **Teresa** quietly returned to the group, sat on the same chair as before and put the handbag on her lap. Members were surprised but pleased to see her again. I welcomed her back and apologised for having picked up her handbag rather than talking about it.

I also conveyed to her the thoughts I had shared with the group in her absence, with the intention of understanding better the nature of her distress. She replied that the idea of the handbag as an extension of her body made sense to her.

I then commented that I could see a healthy element in her reaction, as she was able to move away from me after I *touched* her body, symbolically – something she had been unable to do as a child when she was sexually abused by her grandfather.

Teresa looked close to tears and said she felt guilty for not having been able to run away from him and for not telling her mother, because she thought her mother would not believe her.

Rose commented that Teresa could now run away as an adult but that, as a child, she could not. Other members (including **Charles**) affirmed that all the responsibility was with her abusive grandfather.

Then it was also possible to look into **Teresa**'s attachment difficulties within her family. Her father left when she was a baby and had no role in her life. Her mother suffered from depression, developed a chaotic lifestyle and neglected her.

People became significantly engaged with Teresa's story in a supportive, reflective and, perhaps, maternal way. And they were also able to reflect on their own attachment histories as neglected children.

Two weeks later, **Susannah** returned to the group and worked through her anger with **Charles** for his insensitivity, which had impacted on her as another abusive experience. This offered her opportunities for a deeper exploration of some of the less conscious aspects of the abuse, and she was able to see more clearly how the abusive adult had sexually exploited her needs for an attachment relationship outside the family, as a vulnerable early teenager.

As has happened to Teresa, Susannah's father had also walked away when she was a small child, leaving her longing for affection and attachment with a father figure.

In later developments, it was possible for **Susannah** and **Teresa** to go beyond their similarities as survivors of sexual abuse. They gradually became able to recognise that, as well as parallels, there were significant differences in their backgrounds and personalities. At one point, they were also able to explore aspects of what had been, until then, a largely unconscious or unspoken rivalry between them.

In addition, **Charles** did some important work on the rather conflictive, arrogant and undeveloped part of his personality – which had prevented him from being in touch with and developing empathy towards other people, especially women.

5.5 Discussion

Coherency originates in our need for survival and for higher levels of communication, differentiation and development. In therapeutic terms, coherency increases the group's self-regulatory capacity; however, it does not evolve in a linear fashion from cohesion but through the gradual internalisation of highly complex interactive processes and attachment relationships (Ezquerro, 2010).

In therapy groups, cohesion and coherency can sometimes be part of a pendulum-like movement, depending on the nature of current stressful circumstances and threats. A coherent group might be exposed to an overwhelming threat and may temporarily retreat into a more defensive or undifferentiated cohesive position.

At other times, a group that appears to be stuck might respond to a gentle push from the conductor, communicate at a more sophisticated level and, in turn, become more creative and coherent.

Freud (1923) made an important distinction between the *coherent unconscious* and the *incoherent repressed unconscious*. In his view, not all that is unconscious is repressed and kept in an incoherent state, but there are aspects of the unconscious ego that form an organised, coherent stratum of the mind. This idea was expanded by Loewald (1980) who linked *coherency* with the process of *internalisation*, as distinct from *repression*:

> What is internalised becomes an inherent part of the coherent ego. What is repressed is split off from the coherent ego.
>
> (Loewald, 1980: 78)

The workings of these processes can indeed be explained in more detail:

> It is of the utmost importance, both theoretically and clinically, to distinguish more clearly and consistently than Freud ever did between processes of repression and processes of internalization. The latter are involved in creating and increasing the coherent integration and organization of the psyche as a whole, whereas repression works against such coherent psychic organization by maintaining a share of psychic processes in a less organised, more primitive state.
>
> (Loewald, 1980: 76)

In terms of attachment theory, there is a vital connection between early human development and the mother-child interaction. In this dyadic relationship, the infant is the lesser organised person who comes to acquire some of the characteristics of the more organised person: the mother or primary attachment figure (Ezquerro, 2017a, 2017b).

According to Bowlby (1973, 1988), for this process to take place, infants need the parent's recognition of their relative uncoordinated needs and urges. What infants introject is the interactive response patterns with the parents; that is the internalisation of an attachment relationship. It is through these processes that the parent or caregiver inserts meaning and coherency into the less organised mind of the infant.

Consequently, it is possible to differentiate cohesion from coherency through the lenses of attachment. Parents and caregivers who are not consistently responsive, or who abuse their children, promote insecure or disorganised attachment patterns.

A highly anxious child, clinging on to the attachment figure, can sometimes be an example of undifferentiated dyadic cohesion, or of *emotional fusion* (Ezquerro, 2010). On the other hand, an abused child who approaches the abusive parent with an averted head provides an image of bewilderment and confusion.

In contrast to these insecure attachment patterns, the child who is securely attached feels confident enough to discover and learn as a separate person, in the knowledge that he or she can return to the parents or attachment figures who provide him or her with a reliable secure base from which to explore.

The quality of relationships in secure attachment is more fluent, harmonious and coherent. The child internalises a mental organisation that helps with the process of regulating the distance. Returning to the secure base at times of need is not regression, but a healthy response in order to maximise survival, to refuel emotionally or to seek protection from an external threat (Bowlby, 1969; Ezquerro, 2017a, 2017b).

Person-to-person attachment is complex enough; person-to-group attachment is even more complex, multidimensional and difficult to comprehend (see Chapter 6). Interestingly, as a construct, *complexity* has been formulated as an emerging science at the edge of chaos (Waldrop, 1994). In the opinion of the Spanish psychoanalyst and group analyst Nicolás Caparrós:

> Chaos is articulated by order and, in a certain way, order is a particular region of an encompassing whole: chaos itself.
>
> (Caparrós, 2010: 259)

Some systems and behaviours might appear chaotic or random at first sight; but *chaos theory* says that, on a closer scrutiny, it might be possible to notice patterns or make links. One of the main premises of this theory is that a minor difference or *attractor* at the start of a process can produce a major change in it as time progresses; even a butterfly can make changes in the weather (Lorenz, 2000).

Regarding the clinical material of this case study, we may say that Teresa's behaviour was not as random as it initially appeared.

Looking at group-analytic psychotherapy through the prism of *complexity theory* (Prigogine 1980, 1997; Mandelbrot, 1997; Stacey, 2001; Maldonado, 2005), one of its prominent features is the unpredictability of the complex behaviours of group members. However, lack of prediction does not imply lack of intelligibility

(Ezquerro, 2010). This latter thought was also spelled out by Stacey (2001) in his article *Complexity and the group matrix.*

In fact, psychodynamic therapies focus on interpretations or explanations that promote change rather than on predictions. Indeed, therapy groups are *dynamic systems* which may have a high sensitivity to *attractors* or small variations in some of their initial conditions.

Maldonado (2005) argued that, in complexity, there are *non-linear logics* which can accommodate para-conscious or difficult to explain phenomena, paradoxes, inconsistencies, impasses and aporias. He referred to these as *logics of relevance*, which require *context* as a crucial part of meaning. In other words, as spelled out in Chapter 6, I am I and my *circumstance* (Ortega y Gasset, 1914).

In connection with this, we may say that Susannah and Teresa's sudden reactions in the group would need to be understood in the context of foreground attractors, against the background of their experiences of childhood sexual abuse, as outlined by Ferenczi (1932, 1949) in *Confusion of the tongues between the adults and the child.*

Matte-Blanco (1988) delved into the question of mental processes and the logic of the unconscious. He described two types of logic: symmetric and asymmetric. The first one is a logic based on similarities; the second one is a logic in which differences are established. Thoughts and feelings contain emerging elements of both and can be included into what Matte-Blanco termed *bi-logic,* a sort of crossroads between different disciplines.

Mutatis mutandis, we may say that well-functioning groups contain emerging *bi-logic* elements of both cohesion and coherency. A remarkable attribute about *bi-logic* is that people from different intellectual backgrounds can gather together and use it as a common ground, within their diversity.

The concept of *emergentism* is deeply rooted in the British philosophical tradition of the early 20th century (Alexander, 1920; Morgan, 1923; Broad, 1925). A property of a system is said to be emergent if it is a new outcome of some other properties of the system and its interactions.

According to Goldstein (1999), emergent phenomena are nascent qualities of a complex system that grows in complexity. Emergent behaviours are associated with novelty or surprise and with the unpredictability of their appearance given a previous state; but are ultimately creations of increasingly coherent structures during the self-organisation process of complex groups and systems.

Self-organisation for its part is a process of attraction and repulsion through which the internal organisation of a system increases its complexity and coherency without the guidance or direction of external resources, as much as it might be possible (Kauffman, 1998).

The above formulations are compatible with a group-analytic perspective, in which the therapist is considered a member and integral part of the group – not an external element. This is consistent with second-order cybernetics (Wiener, 1948; Ezquerro, 2023).

The Foulkesian model advocates the treatment of the group, by the group, including its conductor (Foulkes, 1964). Consequently, the conductor's interventions should not be considered an external resource but rather a part of the group's internal organisation, contributing to its complexity and coherency or otherwise, within what Foulkes (1973) also described as the group-analytic *matrix* (see Chapters 1, 2 and 3).

In an analytic group, an emergent behaviour or property can appear when a number of individuals try to operate in a more complex or coherent fashion. Emergent behaviour is difficult to predict because it is linked to multiple interactions between and amongst members, in combination with their personality qualities and traits as well as their experiences and attachment histories. Matte-Blanco (1975) related this combinatorial potential with unconscious processes which, in his view, have an endless or immeasurable dimension.

Whereas Susannah's abrupt departure was perceived as something logical or understandable, Teresa's behaviour was judged by members as insane, illogical and chaotic. At that stage, the group was predominantly functioning as a closed cohesive system, in which conflict was avoided and differences were overlooked.

After the conductor's intervention, acknowledging his mistake and trying to understand what was going on in the group, and in his mind, members became more open to emerging meanings, connecting Teresa's unpredictable reaction to her past trauma.

Of course, the contribution of the therapist alone is insufficient. In this piece of group-analytic qualitative research, a sequence of interactions and communications was necessary for members to progressively move on from a state of confusion to one of understanding.

After the first nine months, in which the group had mainly operated as a cohesive unit, Susannah felt safe-enough to disclose her sexual abuse. Whereas expressions of sympathy and support to her were predictable responses, Charles' insensitive, outrageous comment was unpredictable; or was it?

In some way, Charles was also manifesting his own unfinished business regarding his relationships with women. At a conscious level, he did not intend to push Susannah out of the group, but he caused an *interpersonal rupture* and she left.

The incident also led to a *group rupture* as it affected the whole group, including its conductor who wanted to repair the rupture by symbolically *protecting* Susannah's place after her departure. In fact, he kept an empty chair for her in her absence.

Group ruptures have been defined as disruptions in cohesion or connection to the leader, individual members or the group-as-a-whole (Lo Coco et al, 2019; Yalom and Leszcz, 2020; Marmarosh, 2021). Ruptures can be subtle and reflect minor tension such as a member interrupting another member. Indeed, they can also be more painful, as expressions of systemic racism, social isolation, class or gender discrimination and other forms of inequality, abuse or violence. But ruptures and their succeeding repair can facilitate change in group psychotherapy.

Interestingly, in this case study, as the group struggled with Susannah's absence, a powerful communication came from Teresa, who sat on her chair whilst placing her handbag on Susannah's chair. By *occupying* two chairs, was Teresa unconsciously expressing some rivalry or a wish to have more individual space to make her own disclosure? Surely, Susannah's disclosure the previous week resonated with Teresa's own experience of sexual abuse.

In turn, by picking up Teresa's handbag and putting it on a chair outside the circle, the conductor did not mean to offend her but he did, causing another rupture!

However, acknowledging his mistake openly and delivering a straightforward apology seemed to induce an emergent type of logic, in which it was possible to progress from the concrete to the symbolic, from confusion to understanding.

The ability to think symbolically helped Teresa look at her traumatic past in a different light. And the group became more able to move on from sameness to an exploration of differences and conflict.

In therapy groups, relatively small stimuli may sometimes lead to great turbulence or change. From the perspective of complexity theory, when a *critical mass* is reached, the group, until then cohesive or disorganised, can organise itself and become more coherent in the face of what, at first, appeared to be contradictory feelings or random behaviours (Thom, 1997; Maldonado, 2005).

In this chapter's clinical case study, apparently small stimuli greatly disrupted the stability of the group, almost to the edge of chaos. However, as the group managed to tolerate unpredictability and work through conflict, a new order was established or recognised. This enabled members to explore their experiences of sexual abuse in a less traumatic way. The group became able to intertwine previously unconnected elements and to achieve a more diverse and coherent understanding; its therapeutic potential was enhanced.

Summing up, the complexity of ruptures and repairs is a crucial component of any therapeutic process.

Indeed, Teresa's handbag was only a metaphor but a powerful one in the context of her childhood sexual abuse, a major rupture which she had been unable to repair. In comparison, the ruptures in the group were smaller and easier to fix up. This process of group reparation injected hope in her mind and in the minds of her fellow members.

According to Bateman, Campbell and Fonagy (2021), the complexities of ruptures and repairs are an essential part of the therapeutic process. Certainly, the *rough and tumble* of human social experience that can be seen in a disorganised (and disorganising) situation is particularly clear and obvious in moments of estrangement. However, when ruptures are tolerated, managed and repaired, the possibility of participating in the ongoing work of social cooperation is opened up for the members involved (Rutan, 2021).

The system of representations that configures the mental activity of each patient in a therapy group can be considered a subsystem that belongs to other higher-order systems, such as the interactions between themselves and the therapist in pairs, in subgroups and as a whole (Cañete and Ezquerro, 2013; Ezquerro and Cañete, 2023). The temporal sequence of members' presences and absences can give a timeless dimension to the group, which helps linking the here-and-now with the there-and-then.

This is in agreement with a thought-provoking insight, formulated by Caparrós (2010), that the irreversible quality of time is reconcilable with repeatable experience.

In his view, the recognition and acceptance of the diverse nature of experiences, images and contradictions of group members can promote a more advanced and coherent understanding. The group-as-a-whole can relate in a freer and more unpredictable way but, at the same time, in more harmonious a fashion with its members.

Stacey (2001) specifically referred to some analogies between complexity sciences and therapeutic groups. For him, under certain conditions of a paradoxical nature, self-organisation may occur without being consciously sought by the group. This gives rise to a new coherence that is not intentional or part of a pre-conceived plan. In this case, emergent elements unfold as a consequence of the group interaction itself.

In the clinical example outlined above, neither had Charles the intention of kicking Susannah out of the group with his abusive comment, nor did Teresa plan to leave her handbag on Susannah's empty chair, nor did it occur to the conductor that relocating Teresa's handbag might be perceived by her as invasive. For a few, intense moments, it was a road to hell.

However, through reflecting, exploring and participating in the mental lives of others, members survived traumatic confrontation and conflict, integrated differences, and developed *group coherency*. As an integral part of this therapeutic process, they co-constructed powerful moments of meeting, in such a way that they felt deeply seen, understood and accepted. This deeper work created a stronger and more genuine sense of solidarity and trust that catalysed healing (Cortina, 2024).

An analytic therapy group is under continuous co-construction. In the early stages, by predominantly looking for things in common, the group may take a cohesive shape within which diversity and complexity can be feared, since they might represent threats to comfort, predictability and stability.

Indeed, complexity and diversity generate uncertainty but also offer a broader range of creative possibilities. Members' openness to these opportunities can generate higher levels of coherency, which enriches the group and increases its transformative potential.

5.6 Conclusion

The literature on group psychotherapy has paid a great deal of attention to the concept of *group cohesion*, to the point of making it the most frequently studied group-process construct. Initially conceived as a crucial therapeutic factor, but later reframed as a precondition for therapeutic change, it has been defined by and large as a conglomeration of forces acting on members to remain in the group.

There is ample evidence that groups which do not hold together, which do not exert a force of attraction or affinity for its members, cannot develop enough of a capacity for the psychological work that is required to make the group a therapeutic tool. There is also substantial evidence that the forces of cohesion can act as resistances to differentiation and growth, putting significant limitations to the group's therapeutic potential and leading sometimes to anti-therapeutic change.

The all-encompassing and imprecise nature of group cohesion *attracted* the *emergence* of the concept of *group coherency*, as a more differentiated, logically integrated and aesthetically consistent construct. Group coherency requires the pre-existence of positive grades of group cohesion, but denotes more advanced and complex stages of group development, in which members become increasingly able to share, accept and work through differences, contradictions and conflicts, including the most painful and difficult aspects of their interpersonal and attachment relationships.

The complexity of this process (sometimes at the edge of chaos) contributes to a larger and deeper range of exploration and meaning, which enhances the group's self-organisation and therapeutic potential. Contemporary attachment literature has in fact pointed out that secure group attachment fosters the development of more sophisticated, self-regulatory and higher functioning levels of coherency, whereas insecure group attachment can reinforce the maintenance of more primitive states of cohesion, in which conflict and differences are feared. In a coherent group, there is more freedom than in a purely cohesive group for members to explore and to grow.

Having said that, group coherency is not a permanent state but an ongoing and life-long developmental task. Groups and individuals can retreat from coherency to more basic cohesive positions. At times, we all feel threatened, become anxious (or even disorganised) and make mistakes; but our errors offer opportunities for learning and so developing new positions of coherency.

Note: The clinical material presented in this chapter has followed strict guidelines from the General Medical Council to protect the confidentiality due to patients.

References

Alexander S (1920) *Space, Time, and Deity. Vol. 1.* London: Macmillan & Co.

Barlow SH (2013) Cohesion, Interpersonal Relationships, and Attachment. In: Barlow SH *Specialty Competencies in Group Psychology*. Oxford: Oxford University Press, pp. 91–111.

Bateman A, Campbell C and Fonagy P (2021) Rupture and Repair in Mentalization-Based Group Psychotherapy. *International Journal of Group Psychotherapy*, 71(2): 371–392.

Bednar R and Kaul T (1994) Experiential Group Research: Can the Canon Fire? In: Bergin A and Garfield A (eds) *Handbook of Psychotherapy and Behavior Change*. New York: Wiley.

Begovac B and Begovac I (2013) Group cohesion and coherency and a threat of loss in the analytic group. *Group Analysis* 46(2): 211–224.

Bloch S and Crouch E (1987) *Therapeutic Factors in Group Psychotherapy*. New York: Oxford University Press.

Bowlby J (1969) *Attachment and Loss: Vol. 1. Attachment* (1991 edition). London: Penguin Books.

Bowlby J (1973) *Attachment and Loss: Vol. 2. Separation, Anxiety and Anger* (1991 edition). London: Penguin Books.

Bowlby J (1988) *A Secure Base: Clinical Applications of Attachment Theory*. London: Routledge.

Braaten LJ (1991) Group cohesion: A new multidimensional model. *Group* 15(1): 39–55.

Broad CD (1925) *The Mind and its Place in Nature*. London: Kegan Paul.

Budman SH, Soldz S, Demby A and Feldstein M (1990) Cohesion, alliance, and outcome in group psychotherapy. *Psychiatry* 52(3): 339–350.

Cañete M and Ezquerro A (2013) Grupo-Análisis y Complejidad. In: Caparrós N y Cruz-Roche R (eds) *Viaje a la Complejidad. Vol. 3: El Psiquismo: Un Proceso Hipercomplejo.* Madrid: Biblioteca Nueva, pp. 434–440.

Caparrós N, Ezquerro A, Kaës R, Neri C, Rodrigué E and Sanfeliu I (2004) *Y el Grupo Creó al Hombre.* Madrid: Biblioteca Nueva.

Caparrós N (2010) El caos, un nuevo espacio para la psicodinámica. *Clínica y Análisis Grupal* 32 (1–2): 253–278.

Cartwright D (1968) The Nature of Group Cohesiveness. In: Cartwright D and Zander A (eds) *Group Dynamics: Research and Theory.* London: Tavistock Publications.

Childre D and Rozman D (2002) *Overcoming Emotional Chaos: Eliminate Anxiety, Lift Depression and Create Security in Your Life.* San Diego, CA: Jodere Group.

Collins English Dictionary (21st Century Edition) (2000) Glasgow: Harper Collins Publishers.

Cortina M (2024, in-press) Book Review of *Group Analysis Throughout the Life Cycle: Foulkes Revisited from a Group Attachment and Developmental Perspective*, by Arturo Ezquerro and Maria Cañete (Routledge). *American Academy of Dynamic Psychotherapy and Psychoanalysis.*

Dion KL (2000) Group cohesion from field of forces to multidimensional construct. *Group Dynamics: Theory, Research, and Practice* 4(1): 7–26.

Ezquerro A (2010) Cohesion and Coherency in Group Analysis. *Group Analysis* 43(4): 496–504.

Ezquerro A (2017a) *Encounters with John Bowlby: Tales of Attachment.* London: Routledge.

Ezquerro A (2017b) *Relatos de apego.* Madrid: Psimática.

Ezquerro A (2020) Brexit: Who is afraid of group attachment? Part I. Europe: what Europe? *Group Analysis* 53(2): 234–254.

Ezquerro A (2021) Brexit: Who is afraid of group attachment? Part II. Democracy: What democracy? *Group Analysis* 54(2): 265–283.

Ezquerro A (2023) *Apego y Desarrollo a lo largo de la vida: El poder del apego grupal.* Madrid: Editorial Sentir.

Ezquerro A and Cañete M (2023) *Group Analysis throughout the Life Cycle: Foulkes Revisited from a Group Attachment and Developmental Perspective.* London and New York: Routledge.

Ferenczi S (1932) Confusion of the tongues between the adults and the child: The language of tenderness and passion. In M. Balint M (ed) *Final Contributions to the Problems and Methods of Psychoanalysis* (1960 edition). London: Karnac Books, pp. 156–167.

Ferenczi S (1949) Confusion of the tongues between the adults and the child: The language of tenderness and passion. *International Journal of Psycho-Analysis* 30: 225–230.

Flores PJ (2010) Group Psychotherapy and Neuro-Plasticity: An Attachment Theory Perspective. *International Journal of Group Psychotherapy* 60(4): 543–566.

Flores PJ (2017) Attachment Theory and Group Psychotherapy. *International Journal of Group Psychotherapy* 67(sup1): S50–S59.

Fonagy P and Allison E (2014) The Role of Mentalizing and Epistemic Trust in the Therapeutic Relationship. *Psychotherapy* 51(3): 372–380.

Fonagy P and Campbell C (2017) Mentalizing, attachment and epistemic trust: how psychotherapy can promote resilience. *Psychiatria Hungarica* 32(3):283–287.

Fonagy P, Gergely, G, Jurist EL and Target M (2002) *Affect regulation, mentalization, and the development of the self.* New York: Other Press.

Fonagy P, Luyten P and Allison E (2015) Epistemic petrification and the restoration of epistemic trust: A new conceptualization of borderline personality disorder and its psychosocial treatment. *Journal of Personality Disorders* 29(5): 575–609.

Foulkes SH (1964) *Therapeutic Group Analysis.* London: Allen and Unwin.

Foulkes SH (1972) Oedipus conflict and regression. In: Foulkes E (ed) (1990) *SH Foulkes Selected Papers: Psychoanalysis and Group Analysis.* London: Karnac Books, pp. 235–248.

Foulkes SH (1973) The Group as Matrix of the Individual's Mental Life. In: Foulkes E (ed) (1990) *SH Foulkes Selected Papers: Psychoanalysis and Group Analysis.* London: Karnac Books, pp. 223–234.

Freud S (1923) *The Ego and the Id. Standard Edition 19.* London: The Hogarth Press.

Gallagher ME, Tasca GA, Ritchie K, Balfour L and Bissada H (2014) Attachment anxiety moderates the relationship between growth in group cohesion and treatment outcomes in Group Psychodynamic Interpersonal Psychotherapy for women with binge eating disorder. *Group Dynamics: Theory, Research and Practice* 18(1): 38–52.

Goldstein J (1999) Emergence as a Construct: History and Issues. *Emergence: Complexity and Organization* 1(1): 49–72.

Grayling AC (2002) Confusion is the beginning of wisdom – Socrates. *The Guardian* (4th May).

Gunnison H (2003) *Hypno-counselling: An eclectic bridge between Milton Erickson and Carl Rogers.* Ross-on-Wye, Herefordshire: PCCS Books.

Hartman JJ (1981) Group cohesion and the regulation of self-esteem. In: Kellerman H (ed) *Group Cohesion.* New York: Grune and Stratton.

Hinshelwood RD (1985) Anti-therapeutic forms of Cohesiveness in Groups. *International Journal of Therapeutic Communities* 6: 133–142.

Hopper E (2003) Incohesion: Aggregation/Massification: The Fourth Basic Assumption in the Unconscious Life of Groups and Group-like Social Systems. In: Lipgar RM and Pines M (eds) *Building on Bion: Roots.* London: Jessica Kingsley Publishers, pp. 198–225.

Jennings J, Jumper S and Baglio C (2021) Using Relationship-Focused Group Therapy to Target Insecure Attachment as a Barrier to Sex Offense-Specific Treatment: A Pilot Study. *Open Journal of Social Sciences* 9(2): 386–408.

Kauffman S (1998) *At Home in the Universe. The Search for the Laws of Self-Organization.* Oxford: Oxford University Press.

Kellerman H (ed) (1981) *Group Cohesion.* New York: Grune and Stratton.

Lavy S and Granot R (2010). Perceived friendship opportunities mediate the association between avoidant attachment and instrumental functioning in teams. A poster presented at the International Association for Relationship Research Conference. Herzliya, Israel.

Lavy S, Bareli Y and Ein-Dor T (2015) The Effects of Attachment Heterogeneity and Team Cohesion on Team Functioning. *Small Group Research* 46(1):27–49.

Leszcz M (2017) How understanding attachment enhances group therapist effectiveness. *International Journal of Group Psychotherapy* 67(2): 280–287.

Lo Coco G, Tasca GA, Hewitt P, Mikail SF and Kivlighan DM (2019) Ruptures and repairs of group therapy alliance. An untold story in psychotherapy research. *Research in Psychotherapy: Psychopathology, Process and Outcome* 22(1): 58–70.

Loewald H (1980) *Papers on Psychoanalysis.* New Haven, CT: Yale University Press.

Lorenz EN (2000) *La esencia del caos: Un campo de conocimiento que se ha convertido en parte importante del mundo que nos rodea.* Madrid: Debate.

McCraty R and Childre D (2010) Coherence: Bridging Personal, Social and Global Health. *Alternative Therapies in Health and Medicine* 16(4): 10–24.

McCraty R and Zayas M (2014) Cardiac coherence, self-regulation, autonomic stability and psychosocial well-being. *Frontiers in Psychology* 5: 1–13.

Maldonado CE (ed) (2005) *Complejidad de las ciencias y ciencias de la complejidad.* Bogotá: Universidad Externado de Colombia.

Mandelbrot B (1997) *Geometria Fractal de la Naturaleza.* Barcelona: Tusquets.

Marmarosh CL (2017) Attachment in Group Psychotherapy: Bridging Theories, Research and Clinical Technique. *International Journal of Group Psychotherapy* 67(2): 157–160.

Marmarosh CL (ed) (2020) *Attachment in Group Psychotherapy.* London and New York: Routledge.

Marmarosh CL (2021) Ruptures and repairs in group psychotherapy: From theory to practice. *International Journal of Group Psychotherapy* 71(2): 205–223.

Marmarosh C, Holtz A and Schottenbauer M (2005) Group Cohesiveness, Group-Derived Collective Self-Esteem, Group-Derived Hope, and the Well-Being of Group Therapy Members. *Group Dynamics: Theory, Research, and Practice* 9(1): 32–44.

Marmarosh CL and Tasca GA (2013) Adult attachment anxiety: Using group therapy to promote change. *Journal of Clinical Psychology* 69(11): 1172–1182.

Marziali E, Munroe-Blum H and McLeary L (1997) The contribution of group cohesion and group alliance to the outcome of group psychotherapy. *International Journal of Group Psychotherapy.* 47(4): 475–499.

Matte-Blanco I (1975) *The Unconscious as Infinite Sets.* London: Duckworth & Co.

Matte-Blanco I (1988) *Thinking, Feeling and Being.* London: Routledge.

Morgan CL (1923) *Emergent Evolution.* London: Williams and Norgate.

Ortega y Gasset J (1914) Meditaciones del Quijote (2014 edition). Madrid: Alianza Editorial.

Pines M (1985) Psychic development and the group analytic situation. *Group* 9(1): 24–37.

Pines M (1986a) Coherency and its disruption in the development of the self. *British Journal of Psychotherapy* 2(3): 180–185.

Pines M (1986b) Coherencia y ruptura en el sentido del self. *Clínica y Análisis Grupal* 10(41): 425–438.

Pines M (1989) The group as a whole approach in Foulkesian group analytic psychotherapy. *Group* 13(3–4): 212–216.

Pines M (2002) The coherency of group analysis. *Group Analysis* 35(1): 13–26.

Prigogine I (1980) *From Being to Becoming: Time and Complexity in the Physical Sciences.* San Francisco, CA: WH Freeman & Co.

Prigogine I (1997) *The End of Certainty: Time, Chaos and the New Laws of Nature.* New York: The Free Press.

Rom E and Mikulincer M (2003) Attachment theory and group processes: The association between attachment style and group-related representations, goals, memories, and functioning. *Journal of Personality and Social Psychology* 84(6): 1220–1235.

Rutan JS (2021) Rupture and repair: Using leader errors in psychodynamic group psychotherapy. *International Journal of Group Psychotherapy* 71(2): 310–331.

Silbergeld S, Koening G, Manderscheid R et al (1975) Assessment of Environment-Therapy Systems: The Group Atmosphere Scale. *Journal of Consulting and Clinical Psychology* 43: 460–469.

Slavson SR (1964) *A Textbook in Analytic Group Psychotherapy.* New York: International University Press.

Stacey R (2001) Complexity and the Group Matrix. *Group Analysis* 34(2): 221–239.

Tasca G (2014) Attachment and Group Psychotherapy: Introduction to a Special Section. *Psychotherapy* 51(1): 53–56.

Tasca GA and Marmarosh C (2023) Alliance rupture and repair in group psychotherapy. In: Eubanks CF, Samstag LW and Muran JC (eds) *Rupture and repair in psychotherapy: A critical process for change.* Washington, DC: American Psychological Association, pp. 53–71.

Terrazas-Carrillo E, Vásquez D and García E (2023) Group Cohesion in Psychoeducational Groups with Latinos: Examining Cultural Correlates. 73(1): 20–43.

Thom R (1997) *Estabilidad structural y morfogénesis.* Barcelona: Gedisa.

Waldrop MM (1994) *Complexity: The Emerging Science at the Edge of Order and Chaos.* New York: Simon and Schuster.

Webster's New Dictionary of Synonyms (1973). Springfield, MA: GC Merriam & Co.

Wiener N (1948) *Cybernetics, or Control and Communication in the Animal and the Machine.* Cambridge, MA: MIT Press.

Yalom ID (1975) *The Theory and Practice of Group Psychotherapy.* New York: Basic Books.

Yalom ID and Leszcz M (2020) *The Theory and Practice of Group Psychotherapy* (6th edition). New York: Basic Books.

Arturo Ezquerro: https://orcid.org/0000-0002-9910-4576

Chapter 6

A case of perverse group attachment

Arturo Ezquerro

6.1 Introduction

At the beginning of the recent COVID-19 pandemic, Sir Paul Preston contacted me to request my professional opinion on a dual filicide, committed by Captain Gonzalo de Aguilera, who killed his two sons in 1964. The murderer was a count, landowner, cavalryman and propaganda press officer for the Francoist army, during the Spanish Civil War.

Captain Aguilera never stood trial and the family tragedy was quickly *buried* without any proper inquiry, having been characterised as the abominable act of a lunatic. Prof Preston (2021a) *exhumed* the case. I looked into it with a rictus of disturbing anxiety, and came to the conclusion that we were dealing with

> a heart-breaking example of a historical figure caught up in an insane moment in history, in which his personal psychopathology interacted with the psychopathology of a violent group, nurtured by colonial and fascist ideology – in the wider context of traumatic national events, resulting in civil war and holocaust.
>
> (Ezquerro, 2021: 279)

I thought that Professor Preston was fighting a good cause in retrospect; I decided to join him and to *take the bull by the horns* . . .

I feel privileged to have developed a warm and loyal friendship with Paul over the years. We met soon after his masterwork *The Spanish Holocaust* was published (Preston, 2012). In 2018, he was knighted by Queen Elizabeth II for his longstanding services to British-Spanish relations. He has devoted some 50 years of his prolific career to the study of contemporary Spanish history, especially the 1936–1939 Civil War and its multiple ramifications and sociopolitical contexts.

Professor Preston's outstanding research (examining the estimated one-million deaths and countless atrocities associated with the war and subsequent Francoist repression) represents an enormous challenge to the unspoken *pact of silence* – under which Spain has lost a significantly large part of its recent historical memory.

When I read Preston's (2021a) draft chapter on the Aguilera case, my first thought was that the two filicides could have been prevented. As a response to his

DOI: 10.4324/9781003271956-7

request for a psychiatric commentary, I committed myself to produce a piece of work that might contain elements of a *psychological autopsy*, but without entering the dangerous territory of delivering a psychiatric diagnosis by proxy.

For the reader interested in the field of criminality and mental health, I would recommend some landmark publications; for example, *Forensic Psychotherapy and Group Analysis* by Dr Estela Welldon (1993), *Forensic Psychotherapy: Crime, Psychodynamics and the Offender Patient*, volumes I and II, by Cordess and Cox (1996a, 1996b), *Forensic Psychotherapy and Psychopathology: Winnicottian Perspectives*, and *Dangerous Lunatics: Trauma, Criminality and Forensic Psychotherapy* by Professor Brett Kahr (2001, 2020).

Looking back, I had learned from John Bowlby (1988) that the internal world of a person is necessarily configured through mental representations of interactions and attachment relationships with significant others and with groups, as well as with the places where the person was born and raised and where he or she lived, studied, worked and loved (or otherwise).

Bowlby (1969) specifically wrote about group attachment and indicated that a school or college, a work group, a religious group or a political group can come to constitute for many people a *subordinate* attachment-figure and, for some people, a *primary* attachment-figure.

Many dictators and other authoritarian or despotic leaders have conspicuously taken advantage of this remarkable human need for group attachment.

Young people and adults struggling with unresolved (personal and collective) trauma are particularly vulnerable and easy prey for consumption by destructive group forces. Hitler's mobilisation of Germany's youth into a disciplined future army, enforcing the doctrine of the Third Reich, was too tragic an example.

In a most despicable fashion, Hitler exploited the needs that young (and not so young) people have for identification with collective ideals, for group belonging, and for group attachment. To quite a large extent, this *perverse* dynamic can resonate with the distressing story of Captain Aguilera, as we shall see throughout this chapter.

6.1(i)   Contents and aims of the chapter

In the circumstances, this chapter examines a constellation of dyadic attachment, family attachment and group attachment experiences (as well as other psychosocial, cultural and political factors) which contributed to the dual filicide perpetrated by Captain Gonzalo de Aguilera. After reviewing relevant literature on filicide, this study employs a combined methodology of historical investigation, in conjunction with psychiatric, attachment-based and group-analytic clinical formulations. In doing so, it takes into account a highly complex context of brutal group dynamics of national depression and exaltation, unresolved trauma, military rebellion, war, dictatorship, genocide and holocaust.

Following on from Bowlby's conception of group attachment, and from key insights provided within the growing discipline of forensic psychotherapy, the chapter scrutinises Captain Aguilera's life circumstances and whereabouts; his interpersonal and group attachment relationships; his world within and around him. This study specifically explores the influence that Aguilera's group attachment history (as well as the cruel ideology and violent group dynamics to which he was exposed) may have had on his personality development, his bizarre thinking and his murderous behaviour.

Finally, a reasoned explanation of what I have elsewhere described as *perverse group attachment* is offered (Ezquerro, 2015, 2019, 2021).

6.2 Filicide: an overview

Filicide is so horrifying and tragic a crime that it defies logical explanation. For parents (and for society by and large) children are an evolutionary-based investment in survival and a powerful symbol of life permanence.

From a DNA perspective on survival, successfully raising a biological child enhances the chance of advancing one's own genetic information.

From a wider group perspective, successfully raising an adoptive, fostered or biological child enhances wellbeing and healthy growth in society, as children represent the future development of any community. Yet, filicide is not a rare occurrence.

Parental mental illness (and the disorganisation inherent in it) is more often than not a major contributing factor, within a complex constellation of cultural, psychological and social stressors.

However, filicide can be such an unpredictable phenomenon that it is frequently the result of more than mental illness and environmental stressors. There can be additional risk factors related to underlying (and fundamentally unconscious) psychodynamic conflicts (Papapietro and Barbo, 2005).

Overall, mothers are more likely to kill their offspring, particularly the neonate, whilst fathers are more likely to kill older children, and nearly one in five filicides corresponds to killings of adult children (Orenstein, 2014). This suggests that filicide is a life-long risk.

A number of studies have indicated that, in some cases, this type of murder can be based on the father's interpretation of the child's behaviour; for example, when the father feels jealous and excluded because the child is more closely *attached* to the mother (Campion, Cravens and Covan, 1988).

The plain reality is that filicide has existed since the dawn of humankind; the problem transcends cultures and eras. In the book of Genesis, God asks Abraham to sacrifice his son Isaac as a burnt offering on Mount Moriah, although stopping short of requiring him to carry this out.

In the ancient classical world, there was legal provision for a father to kill his own children. In fact, Graeco-Roman filicide occurred so regularly that it acquired an almost normative status (Kahr, 1994). And baby girls were openly killed in China by their parents until the early 20th century (West, 2007).

Despite the sacred value attributed to human life by most religions (including Islam, Judaism and Christianity), men and women have continued to commit filicides up until the present time.

In the UK, on average, two children are killed by their progenitors every week. And filicide is the third leading cause of childhood death in the US. Reasons for wanting to end the life of one's own offspring include disability, lack of resources to care for the child, gender, rape, and illegitimacy. Unwanted children are at a higher risk of being killed (Resnick, 1969; West, 2007; Harris and Rice, 2012; Brown, Tyson and Fernandez Arias 2014; Eriksson et al, 2021; Frederick, Devaney and Alisic, 2022).

The classical literature has indeed paid attention to filicide. One of the best-known stories comes from Greek mythology. In Euripides's play *Medea*, Jason (Medea's husband) abandons her to marry Glauce (the daughter of Creon, king of Corinth). Full of rage, Medea avenges her husband's betrayal by killing the children she had conceived with him.

Interestingly, some child-intended fairy tales (such as *Hansel and Gretel*, and *Snow White*) give an underlying filicidal message, as they portray parents who cast their children out into the world with the purpose of making them die.

6.3 Captain Aguilera: the man

Gonzalo de Aguilera was born in Madrid on 26 December 1886, out of wedlock, to an aristocratic Spanish father (Don Agustín de Aguilera) and a commoner English mother (Mary Ada Monro). Being an illegitimate child was a huge social scandal at the time, and caused significant problems in the short and long term.

Aguilera and his mother were not really accepted by the aristocratic paternal family group. This happened in spite of the fact that his mother fabricated a false background for herself, pretending to be the descendant of an aristocratic Scottish family (Preston, 2021a).

Aguilera was, de facto, a hybrid British-Spanish character. However, his greater exposure to the military Spanish culture, his paternal aristocratic background, his friendship with King Alfonso XIII, and the political events in his country of birth pushed him to consider himself primarily a Spaniard with a strong, inflated sense of entitlement.

In order to explore how this might have unfolded, it is necessary to look at a constellation of relationships and roles in Aguilera's nuclear and extended family, as well as his educational, military and wider social environment. I shall start with his father's profile as an uncertain aristocrat.

Don Agustín comes across as an uninspiring character, when compared with other members of the family. Arias González (2013) provides key biographical notes on him. In 1874, at the age of 18, he started training at the Cavalry Academy in Valladolid. He was a poor student and ended being last in his year group, which certainly did not help with his self-esteem. His military career was patchy; he was often on leave for unclear reasons.

In 1876, Don Agustín became the 10th Count of Alba de Yeltes, almost accidentally as he only inherited the title after his three more successful older brothers declined it. This noble status had been originally granted by King Felipe IV in the mid-17th century.

In contrast to Don Agustín, his eldest brother (Don Enrique) was a rather ambitious and high-profile character. He, in fact, became the 17th Marquis of Cerralbo, a more senior position, and amassed a large fortune. He used part of his wealth to create one of the most complete private museums in Spain (in the exclusive Salamanca district in Madrid), which he donated to the State in his will (Arias González, 2013).

Don Enrique never accepted his nephew Aguilera and considered him to be the *black sheep* of the family. Don Agustín had been engaged to marry a very wealthy aristocratic lady but, during a holiday in France, he fell in love with Mary Ada who was working as an English teacher.

Aguilera was seven when his sister *Nena* was born, in 1894. For a child with experiences of illegitimacy and rejection by the paternal family, the arrival of his sister could well have been perceived by him as a threat. To make things emotionally worse for him, the following year he was sent (at the age of eight) to Stonyhurst boarding school in England, where he stayed for the next nine years.

The very year of Nena's birth, Don Agustín had gone to fight as a volunteer in the Cuban War of Independence and was absent from the family for five years, until he was repatriated in 1899, having been held prisoner by the US army for nearly a year, following defeat.

There are good grounds to believe that, as a confused and unhappy child at his English boarding school, Aguilera may have felt abandoned by both his parents and displaced by his sister, who stayed at home (Preston, 2021a).

Soon after his repatriation from Cuba (where death had surrounded him) Don Agustín hurriedly married Mary Ada almost secretly, in 1899, without the royal consent normally granted to members of the aristocracy. As a result, he went through the further social humiliation of losing his title as a Count. That happened at the time Aguilera's puberty at 13.

In 1904, Don Agustín took a ten-year leave from the army. During that period, he spent a lot of time travelling across Europe with Mary Ada and their daughter Nena. This may have aggravated Aguilera's feelings of rejection from his extended paternal family, displacement by his sister and abandonment by his parents.

There is evidence that he was unable or unwilling to form a relationship with his sister; in fact, he was always emotionally detached from her (Arias González, 2013).

Aguilera spent nine years at Stonyhurst boarding school, governed by Jesuits in Lancashire, where his father had also been a student. Like Don Agustín, he was always in the lower part of his year group and left no mark of achievement, although he would later claim to be a gentleman scholar.

However, the reality was that the grades he obtained in 1904 (the same year his father gave up his work for the army) were insufficient for him to gain entry into a British university.

Then, his father sent him to a German university in Bavaria to study science and philosophy – which he did with little academic success (Preston, 2021a).

Bowlby (1973, 1988) referred to the emotional negative impact of English boarding schools on young children, and he quoted the renowned English writer Graham Greene who had written about his experience at boarding school:

> Unhappiness in a child accumulates because he sees no end to the dark tunnel . . . The thirteen weeks of a term might just as well be thirteen years.
>
> (Greene, quoted in Bowlby, 1973: 21)

I can imagine Aguilera may have experienced feelings similar to Greene's. However, the influence of the Jesuits on Aguilera's intellectual development, character and ideology is unclear.

The prolific journalist and president of the British-Spanish Society, Jimmy Burns-Marañón (2016) referred to a sense of isolation expressed by different generations of students at Stonyhurst, a Catholic school in the middle of nowhere, in a quintessentially Protestant country (with a particularity that the head of the Anglican Church is also the head of State), in which Catholics had been persecuted and executed.

Burns-Marañón (2016) also reported the confession his British father (Tom Burns) made that his education at Stonyhurst inspired him to move to Spain as a volunteer to support Franco during the Civil War. Indeed, the Jesuit Order was banned by the Spanish Second Republic in 1932 (Jackson, 1974, 1980).

In contrast to his father, Burns-Marañón stated that the Jesuits influenced him to actively campaign against right-wing dictatorships in Latin America (albeit some 40–50 years later).

According to him, Stonyhurst has shown, over generations, an ethos of openness to the world, a formative education that encourages a free flow of ideas and the development of an attitude of service to others.

6.3(i) Going back to an insecure base

Following his lack of academic success in England and in Germany, Aguilera spent two years of lazy and unproductive life in Madrid, before joining (as his father had done) the Valladolid Cavalry Academy in 1908, aged 21. He was as poor a student as his father had been.

In 1912, Aguilera volunteered to serve in the colonial war in Morocco, maybe, in a quest for adventure and glory (as his father did when he went to Cuba, also as a volunteer). He was exposed to the brutality of the Spanish army upon Moroccan tribesmen, and had to be posted back to Spain the following year (Preston, 2021a). He then lived most of the time in Madrid, where he was a keen polo player and developed a comfortable, uninspiringly privileged lifestyle similar to his father's.

Aguilera's idle routine was dramatically disturbed in June 1916 when, as part of a humanitarian project supported by King Alfonso XIII, he was appointed as a junior military attaché to assist the Spanish Embassy in Berlin, with the task of supporting war prisoners. His secret lover, Magdalena Ruiz, had become pregnant a few months earlier. She stayed in Spain and their son Gonzalo was born in December.

As Aguilera's job in the First World War lasted 18 months, he did not meet his son for the first year of his life and only saw him infrequently from then on. In Germany, he overlapped with the Spanish psychiatrist Antonio Vallejo-Nájera who was appointed in 1917 to do a similar job, conducting inspections of concentration camps (Moreno Calderón, 2017).

Vallejo-Nájera established contact with German psychiatrists, and became interested in *eugenics* and in doctrines of *racial hygiene*. Contemporary eugenics had originally been developed in the UK by Francis Galton, a psychologist, anthropologist and sociologist, at the end of the 19th century.

Galton was a cousin of Charles Darwin and, on a partial reading of the theory of natural selection, came to the conclusion that desirable human qualities were hereditary traits. Darwin disagreed with this interpretation but, following his death in 1882, Galton coined the term *eugenics*; which would later be associated with *genetic determinism* and fascism (Hansen and King, 2001).

Preston (1993) referred in detail to the use that General Franco made of the idea of *organic determinism*. The dictator stated in 1938 that fascism varied according to national characteristics because each nation was an *organism* and each national fascism was the immune system's reaction, a defence mechanism and a sign of wanting to live.

That very year Vallejo-Nájera set up, in Burgos, a psychological research bureau for the inspection of concentration camps. He carried out degrading experiments on republican women and International Brigades' prisoners, with the objective of finding the *red* (communist) gene. He also proposed a link between Marxism and mental retardation (Moreno Calderón, 2017).

The horrors that Aguilera witnessed during the First World War affected him profoundly, but did not prevent him from behaving brutally during the Spanish Civil War.

He would later write that he began to cease being a Christian after the dreadful events he witnessed in Poland, France and Germany, including the first victims of poison gas who coughed up thick bronchial mucus (Preston, 2004, 2021a).

On his return from Germany in November 1917, Aguilera tried to keep his relationship with Magdalena and their son Gonzalo secret from his father. It eventually resulted in yet another social scandal, which mirrored Don Agustín's own experience with Aguilera's mother, Mary Ada, at the time he was born.

Aguilera did not significantly acknowledge his son Gonzalo and could not form a meaningful attachment relationship with him (Arias González, 2013).

A largely unwanted child himself, he did not show feelings of really loving or wanting his son.

In July 1919, Aguilera was part of the unit that escorted King Alfonso XIII during the summer holidays and he was consequently promoted to captain. Don Agustín died in December that year. Alfonso XIII had reinstated his title in 1910, so Aguilera inherited it as the 11th Count of Alba y Yeltes. Like his father, he spent lengthy periods of leave abroad and delayed getting married for some 19 years after the birth of Gonzalo, until 1935, in fact.

Ten years before the wedding, Aguilera's second son (Agustín) was born whilst he was on leave. He would later deny the biological paternity of the child, and did not play any meaningful paternal role with him either (Arias González, 2013). There were hardly any manifestations of father-son attachment.

In 1924, to the delight of his mother Mary Ada, Aguilera (now 38) proposed matrimony to the 22-year-old Livia Falcó (daughter of the Duke Fernán Núñez). The relationship was brought to an end in the summer of 1925 by the intervention of Magdalena. With Gonzalo (now eight) at her side and pushing a pram containing the new-born baby Agustín, she confronted Livia in the street.

She told her that there were three reasons why she could not marry Aguilera: the two children and the pistol that she waived in Livia's face, with which she would shoot her, if she continued to see him. However, Aguilera continued living as if he were a bachelor, all over the place, and would only move in with Magdalena, in Madrid, five years later in 1930. Getting married would take a further five years (Preston, 2021a).

In 1927, Aguilera had passed into the reserve and was seconded to the military household of King Alfonso XIII, with whom he developed a loyal friendship. With the arrival of the Republic, in 1931, the King went into exile and Aguilera retired from the army because of not wanting to vow loyalty to the Republican government. He became friendly with Diego Martín Veloz, a fiercely reactionary landowner from Salamanca, who had many connections with leading military conspirators like General Queipo de Llano.

6.3(ii) A military coup leading to a civil war

Preston (2004) reported that Aguilera did not take a direct part in the military uprising of 1936, although he strongly supported it. Despite volunteering for the nationalist forces, he was disregarded by the military authorities. With the outbreak of the Civil War, he, Magdalena and their two sons moved to Salamanca but his mother, his sister and her family remained in Madrid. On learning about their suffering, Aguilera's visceral hatred of the Republic intensified.

The mastermind of the military coup was General Emilio Mola (Thomas, 1961; Jackson, 1974, 1980; Preston, 2012). He knew Aguilera well and gave him the post of press officer with the task of supervising the movements and reports of foreign correspondents – sometimes serving as a guide, at other times as a censor (Preston, 2021b).

Aguilera was delighted at his new propaganda role, and particularly vociferous in proclaiming that communism was an immense *malignant tumour* which had to be removed.

On the first day of the Civil War, he had actually claimed that (as a pre-emptive retaliatory measure) he had lined up all his labourers, selected six of them, and shot them to teach a lesson to the others – something that, according to Preston (2004), was untrue. However, there is evidence that another landowner had actually killed four of his labourers at random (Preston, 2021a).

Peter Kemp (an English volunteer on Franco's side) noted Aguilera's nickname during the war: *El Capitán Veneno* (Captain Venom). Certainly, Aguilera was well known for making unguarded statements implying that he supported, not only ethnic cleansing but even genocide, on behalf of Franco's group. Harold Cardozo, of the *Daily Mail*, commented that Aguilera's English was so good that he could easily have been taken for a persuasive Englishman.

Preston (2004) emphasised that Aguilera was unashamedly racist and often proclaimed the *patent superiority* of the white man. That was in line with Enrique Suñer's propaganda that the final objective of the war was *strengthening* the race, for which the total extirpation of their enemies would be necessary. Suñer was not an eccentric officer, but a professor of paediatrics and vice-president of the Education and Culture Committee of Franco's government during the war, actively promoting a culture of degrading *racism* and *group violence*.

Only during the Civil War was Aguilera able to transiently experience a sense of belonging as *full* member of a group. His job as an *intellectual* propagandist for the insurgents made him believe he was an authoritative (as well as authoritarian) figure and a champion of what he called the true, legitimate Spain.

His excitement often translated into reckless, para-suicidal driving. The prominent Tory and Catholic convert, Arnold Lunn found Aguilera's driving behaviour a terrifying yet exhilarating experience. He thought it was an expression of indifference to death. Lunn wrote of Aguilera's habit of taking blind corners on the inside, even if it meant being on the wrong side of the road:

> It is difficult on any reasonable theory of chances to explain the fact that Aguilera is still alive. Sooner or later, one would think, he would meet his opposite number on a corner.
>
> (Lunn, in Preston, 2021a: 199)

I can imagine that, during most of the three years of this insane military conflict, Aguilera must have felt on top of the world. However, that illusion faded away after the *moral* certainties of the war happened to come to an end. He was hoping for the return of his King, but Alfonso XIII died during his exile in Rome, in 1941. Two years later, Aguilera's mother died.

Thus, in a short period, he had two major bereavements, in addition to the loss of his grandiose civil-war illusion. And the loss of such as an omnipotent illusion can be as hard, or even harder, than a real loss.

6.3(iii) The aftermath of a devastating war

Preston (2021a) provided an excellent description of Aguilera's life after the war. He retired completely from the army and returned to his estates and his books, but could not reconcile himself to civilian life.

In the 1940s, he received huge fines for declaring himself an enemy of Franco's regime (as the dictator did not reinstate the King) and for failing to declare his wheat production. However, it would appear that some of his aristocratic contacts protected him from getting into more serious trouble.

Interestingly, Aguilera wrote two books. The first, on the *Physics of the Atom*, was published in 1946. Despite his anti-clerical attitudes, he donated all the profits to the Little Sisters of the Poor. This contrasted with his opinions on the poor lower classes, as an inferior race that had to be exterminated!

The second book, *Letters to a Nephew*, was written in the late 1940s and early 1950s but did not find a publisher. It is an autobiographical and idiosyncratic piece of work, in which he elaborated on some of the ideas he had thrown at journalists during the war (Preston, 2004).

Some of his statements were full of misogyny. As a way of illustration, he produced a defence of the medieval chastity belt as a necessary barrier against female promiscuity, and wrote:

> adultery is a crime whose immediate punishment by the death of the guilty pair at the hands of the outraged husband has always been accepted as the natural law.
>
> (Aguilera, in Preston, 2021a: 216–217)

He also wrote he was delighted that a friend had told him that he was *crazier* than Don Quixote for criticising the Catholic Church.

Aguilera did not prosper as a writer and was alienated from his two sons. He lost interest in the administration of his lands and left it to Magdalena. He usually treated his farm workers with consideration and generosity, apart from his eruptions of rage (Arias González, 2013).

He was not a valued figure in Salamanca's high society. He attended *tertulias* (intellectual social-gatherings) and his conversation was considered fascinating, although his irritability did not encourage friendship or intimacy of any kind.

Moreover, he had acquaintances among other landowners but hardly kept any real friends. He stopped opening letters, which led to a face-to-face confrontation with a tax official in Salamanca to whom (pointing at the pistol that he was carrying) he shouted:

> "No one knows what I am capable of doing!".
>
> (Aguilera, in Preston, 2021a: 218)

6.3(iv) The captain's late years resulting in tragedy

As he was getting older, Captain Aguilera became increasingly challenging, unpredictably abrasive and ill-tempered. Arias González (2013) reported that, in 1959, he severed his long-held membership of an exclusive club (the *Gran Peña)* and that he subsequently developed persecution mania.

At some point in 1962, he was visited by one of his tenants. He talked ceaselessly for several hours in an agitated state, jumping from one subject to another in an unconnected fashion. He would stop only for coughing fits or to eat some porridge. The tenant left convinced that they had been in the presence of a total lunatic.

The above could be described as *disorganised speech* or as *flight of ideas* – a pathology that is usually present in manic or hypomanic states and not uncommon in patients suffering from paranoia.

Such people sometimes talk so fast that it can only be possible to catch every other word. They may speak with a disarrayed sentence structure, making it hard to apprehend what they are trying to say.

In addition, they can erratically start and stop sentences or may start a sentence and suddenly jump to another matter, as if they had finished the previous sentence when they had not.

Aguilera's physical and mental health deteriorated rapidly. He contracted pulmonary emphysema, which made him pant continually and breathe agonisingly in the midst of great exhaustion (Arias González, 2013). This may have brought back memories, I can imagine, of the First World War – when he witnessed soldiers dying in agonic rattles, after inhaling lethal poison gas.

Magdalena became seriously concerned by his refusal to allow any decisions to be taken about the running of the estate or the maintenance of the house and, above all, by his talk of suicide. By late 1963, she became so fearful of his violent rages that, for her own protection, she asked her two sons to return to live at the parental home.

Gonzalo and Agustín partly moved back in with their parents and spent as much time as possible watching over their father (Preston, 2021a). Unfortunately, Aguilera never sought or received any form of psychotherapy or psychiatric assistance.

Nevertheless, as things were going from bad to worse, the family discussed the possibility of having him legally incapacitated on the grounds of mental impairment. They put the matter into the hands of a lawyer.

A psychiatrist (José Fermín Prieto Aguirre) and a physician (Emilio Firmat Cimiano) diagnosed him as suffering from paranoia (Arias González, 2013). However, the legal process to have him committed was complex and troublesome.

Preston (2021a) further reported the circumstances leading to the tragedy. Gonzalo and Agustín rearranged the house to provide their father with a separate apartment with his own television and books. They hid all the many guns and knives he possessed.

In connection with that, at the beginning of August 1964, Aguilera (aged 77) wrote to the judicial authorities protesting that he had been kidnapped and imprisoned by his family. On 28 August, his younger son Agustín (aged 39) went into his father's room to look for some papers . . .

At this point, Aguilera complained of sore feet; Agustín knelt to massage his father's feet. Out of the blue, Aguilera rose up and shot him in the chest. Mortally wounded, Agustín staggered out of the room.

Alerted by the sound of the shots, the older son Gonzalo (aged 47) came rapidly. Aguilera shot him too and, stepping over his corpse, went in search of Agustín and found him lying dead at the kitchen's door.

During the Civil War, Aguilera had entertained a theory that all the boot-blacks should be killed. He talked about this to Peter Kemp (1957), who reported it in his book *Mine Were of Trouble*:

> A chap who squats down on his knees to clean your boots at a café or in the street is bound to be a communist, so why not shoot him right away and be done with it? No need for a trial – his guilt is self-evident in his profession.
>
> (Aguilera, 1937, in Preston, 2021a: 212)

None of his two children was a boot-black or a communist; but I can't help wondering about what images might have come to Aguilera's mind when his son Agustín was on his knees massaging his father's feet.

When she heard the gun shots, Magdalena (aged 72) also came out of her room. Aguilera glared at her, whilst slowly reloading his revolver. As he started waving it threateningly, his wife locked herself in another room and, fortunately, managed to escape through a window.

The Civil Guard arrived soon and Aguilera surrendered with no resistance. When the officers asked him about the dual crime, he responded:

> I killed Agustín because he is not my son and, as for Gonzalo, if I hadn't killed him, he would have killed me.
>
> (Aguilera, 1964, in Preston, 2021a: 222)

Aguilera was arrested and taken to the Salamanca's psychiatric sanatorium, where he was detained. On his way to the hospital, as he was animatedly doing some idle talking on a number of different subjects, he commented:

> I'm talking to put what has just happened out of my mind.
>
> (Aguilera, 1964, in Preston, 2021a: 222)

Although some judicial investigations were triggered, Aguilera never stood trial. He remained in hospital reportedly suffering from dementia and severe depression. He was on prescribed drugs for his pulmonary, circulatory and psychiatric problems. He verbally abused the nursing staff (mainly nuns) on a regular basis.

On 15 May 1965, as he had stopped taking his medication, Captain Aguilera died of cardio-respiratory failure in the hospital (Arias González, 2013).

In a personal communication, Paul Preston told me that, as part of his investigation, he asked to see Aguilera's psychiatric file or any legal documents on the filicides, but to no avail. The case was closed.

6.4 A group culture of unresolved trauma, scapegoating and violence

In 1898 Spain was shaken by the humiliating defeat of its armada at the hands of the more technologically advanced navy of a quickly developing and expansionist world power, euphemistically described as *the sausage makers of the United States* (Carr, 2000: 224). As a result, most of the last remnants of the Spanish Empire were lost: Cuba, Puerto Rico, the Philippines and Guam, as well as the Mariana, Palau and Caroline islands.

The military defeat and loss of world imperial status caused a profound trauma to Spain's national psyche. The loss of Cuba was particularly traumatic because of the affinity of peninsular Spaniards with the island, which was seen as another province of Spain (similar to the Canary Islands) rather than as a colony.

For generations, within the Spanish socio-political, intellectual and military culture, the whole episode came to be known as *El Desastre* (The Disaster). The country was sunk into a collective mental state of shame, anger, depression, and unresolved mourning – which led to an existential crisis about the identity and role of Spain, as an impoverished nation in a New World Order.

As it could not be otherwise, a new group of Spanish thinkers, philosophers, artists, musicians and writers would be *baptised* as the *Generation of 1898*! They were all committed to cultural and aesthetic renewal, and associated with a more modern view of life. The group left a significant legacy, particularly regarding a constructive criticism of the Spanish literary, political class and educational establishments.

Salient figures of this generation included writers like Miguel de Unamuno, Pío Baroja, Ángel Ganivet, Azorín, Valle-Inclán, Ramiro de Maeztu, Consuelo Álvarez, Concha Espina and the Machado brothers (Antonio and Manuel), musicians like Isaac Albéniz, Enrique Granados, Pablo Sarasate, Pau Casals and Manuel Falla, as well as painters like Pablo Picasso, Joaquín Sorolla, Ignacio Zuloaga and Santiago Rusiñol.

Noticeably, suicide was a recurrent theme in Baroja's writings. Sadly, Ganivet committed suicide; before killing himself, he wrote:

. . . chained to misery and poverty, we ask ourselves whether all our previous history has been reality or just a dream . . .

Spain has known all the possible forms of glory, and for much of its history has experienced to an excessive degree the saddest glory of them all: we live in a state of perpetual civil war.

(Ganivet, in Burns, 2006: 151)

Much of Ganivet's view was reality-based; he had an intuition that Spain was on the verge of another *Disaster*. Along these lines, Jan Morris (a Welsh historian and travel writer) described how Spain limped into the third decade of the 20th century with one half of her being, for the other half was still lingering wistfully with the *Cid Campeador* and the *conquistadores*:

> She [Spain] was a mess of a country: addled by bitter politics at home – between 1814 and 1923 there were 43 *coups d'état* [and three civil wars]; embroiled in constant wars in the pathetic remnants of her empire, now confined to a few sandy or foetid enclaves in Africa . . .
>
> Conflicted ideologies tortured her – dogmas of monarchy, theocracy, despotism, democracy, socialism, anarchism, communism . . . and in 1936 all this centuries of failure, schism, and frustration gave birth to that ultimate despair, the Spanish War.
>
> (Morris, in Burns, 2006: 152–153)

Indeed, following Napoleon's invasion of the Iberian Peninsula and the subsequent loss of most of Spanish America in the early 19th century, Spain had been going through turmoil and sharp decline. At the beginning of the 20th century, it retained less than a handful of colonies in Africa: Western Sahara, Equatorial Guinea and Spanish Morocco.

At the time of *El Desastre*, European powers were deeply involved in the ignominious *scramble* to carve up Africa, in the age of new imperialism. In 1870, only ten per cent of Africa was under European control; by the outbreak of the First World War, in 1914, this had increased to ninety per cent (Roberts, 2014). Morocco was divided between France and Spain.

The mentality of a deeply humiliated and anachronistic Spanish army was predominantly one of resentment and revenge (Landis, 1972). Scapegoats were desperately needed and new enemies would be identified soon: on the one hand the Rif Berbers (a colonial term to native Amazigh) in northern Morocco and, on the other, the peasants, proletariat and trade unions within Spain herself.

In addition to his feelings of rejection and displacement at home, Captain Aguilera was exposed to the national trauma generated by *El Desastre*: first hand, from his aristocratic paternal family (his father was a cavalry officer fighting in Cuba at the time) and, also, from a wounded country's social unconscious (Hopper, 1996, 2003; Volkan, 2014, 2020; Hopper and Weinberg, 2016; Blackwell, 2023; Penna, 2023).

6.4(i) Vicious repression, racism and genocide

Subsequently, above all during his military career, Captain Aguilera was immersed into a culture of anger, unresolved trauma, resentment, hatred and revenge (Zulueta, 1993).

This was largely manifested by the scapegoating of Moroccan tribesmen (who were massacred during the colonial wars) and of the communists and some ordinary workers, whose legitimate demonstrations and legally-constituted strikes were brutally repressed.

Preston (1993: 11–12) described one of the most disturbing examples of such a ruthless repression. In July 1909, under pressure from both army officers and investors in Moroccan mines, the Spanish government decided to send to the Rif Mountains a brigade of light infantry garrisoned in Barcelona. The reservists were mainly humble working men, many of them with children and the sole breadwinners for their families, whilst the wealthy were able to use their money and influence to hire substitutes.

There were anti-war and anti-colonial demonstrations in Madrid, Barcelona and cities with railway stations from which the conscripts were departing for the new colonial war. This was followed by a general strike called by socialists and anarchists in Barcelona. The repression was ruthless. In reaction, uncontrolled groups attacked police stations, barricades sprang up in the streets and some 80 churches and monasteries were burnt or destroyed.

More than one hundred civilians were killed, as well as eight police officers. Nearly two thousand people would later be tried in military courts for *armed rebellion*. Five were sentenced to death and executed. The episode was described as *the tragic week*. Condemnation in the press at home and abroad was immediate. King Alfonso XIII was forced to dismiss Prime Minister Antonio Maura (Pérez Delgado, 1974).

After these tragic events, the government began repressing dissidents on a larger scale. Unions were suppressed, newspapers were shut down, and libertarian schools were closed. But the workers would not give up and adopted syndicalism as a revolutionary strategy. The European economic crisis at the end of the First World War affected Spain badly. Many factories closed; unemployment soared; peasants and other workers were paid starvation wages, and had to fight for survival.

Anticipating class conflict, especially in light of the then recent Russian Revolution, landowners and other capitalists began a dirty war against unions. Lockouts became frequent; known militants were blacklisted; *pistoleros* (assassins) were hired to kill union leaders.

Anarchists responded in turn with a number of assassinations, including the murder of Prime Minister Eduardo Dato in 1920. Whereas anarchism in Spain had previously been somehow disjointed, solidarity among workers was rapidly developing – which was largely perceived as a collective spirit of revolt.

The period from 1918 to 1921 would be known as the *trienio bolchevique* (Bolshevik triennium). It was eventually crushed by military repression but the consequent constellation of hatreds continued to smoulder on both sides.

The strikes of the triennium had particularly outraged the big landowners who could not forgive the insubordination of labourers whom they considered to be their *property* and almost sub-human (Preston, 2004). A military coup, supported by the aristocracy and by the King himself, put General Primo de Rivera in charge as a dictator for seven years (1923–1930).

The social divisions were hardened after April 1931, when the newly born Spanish Second Republic attempted to implement a comprehensive programme of agrarian reform. This saw landowners flouting the new legislation that governed rural labour, as well as locking out unionised labour, either by leaving land uncultivated or by simply refusing work. As an aristocrat, retired army officer and landowner, Captain Aguilera was on the alert.

During the escalation of this violent climate, he may have recalled previous experiences, in which he was cognisant of sociopolitical violence. Considering his many years of education in England and in Germany, he must have been conscious enough of previous examples of group violence in the wider European colonial context.

Between 1899 and 1902, the British army was involved in the Boer War in South Africa. The military response to the Boers' guerrilla warfare was particularly cruel towards the civilian population: civilian farms were burnt and crops and livestock were destroyed as part of a scorched earth policy, which was justified to protect the *values* of the British Empire (Roberts, 2014). Survivors were forced into concentration camps. About a quarter of the civilian population died of hunger and disease, including many children.

An even more vicious episode occurred between 1904 and 1907, in what has been described as the first *genocide* of the 20th century. Tens of thousands of men, women and children were shot, starved and tortured to death by German troops as they put down rebellious tribes in what is now Namibia. About half of the total Nama population was killed. And, as many as three thousand Herero skulls were sent to Berlin for German scientists to examine for signs that they were racially inferior peoples (Burke and Oltermann, 2016).

Feelings of racial and national superiority were commonplace in the European powers at the time (and, maybe, not so uncommon nowadays). In *Rule Britannia: Brexit and the End of Empire*, Dorling and Tomlinson (2019) actually referred to a widely read English magazine (*Rule Britannia*), which was distinctly popular *across the board* in Great Britain at the turn of the 20th century – when the British Empire was in its prime.

Here, immigrants and foreigners were described as deceitful, effeminate, irreligious, immoral, unclean and unwholesome, with an additional remark that any one Englishman was a match for any seven of them (Dorling and Tomlinson, 2019).

Rule Britannia was widely available during the nine years that Aguilera spent in England (1895–1904). No doubt, he was exposed to that strong feeling of superiority characteristic of English nationalism.

He did, in fact, believe in the supremacy of white northern Europeans over other ethnic groups and, in the autobiographical *Letters to a Nephew*, highlighted the *patent superiority* of the white man in contrast with the *epileptic forms* of the nervous system peculiar to the black race.

Captain Aguilera roughly divided humanity into the "Nordic-European races" and the "Afro-Asiatic masses", and viciously stated that

> the centralist state, as its name suggests, is the most appropriate to rule over the destinies of inferior masses.
>
> (Aguilera, in Preston, 2021a: 216)

Paradoxically, as also reported by Preston (2021b), Captain Aguilera claimed to the American correspondent Edmond Taylor that he was the descendant of a Spanish *conquistador* and a Mexican-Indian princess!

The latter did not seem to have been a northern European, but who cares? Perhaps, aristocrats were likewise a superior race – anyway, at least in Aguilera's mind.

6.4(ii) The terror guns and voices of a perverse group

There is plenty of evidence that Captain Aguilera strongly identified with the ideas and speeches of bloodthirsty Spanish generals such as Francisco Franco, Emilio Mola and Gonzalo Queipo de Llano (Preston, 1993, 2009, 2012). All these sinister characters were closely affected by *El Desastre*, either directly or through experiences within their families and communities.

Francisco Franco was born in 1892 in El Ferrol, a small naval base in Galicia, in north-western Spain, to a relatively upper-class family of several generations of high-ranking officers in the administrative branch of the Spanish navy.

His father, Don Nicolás, developed a comfortable career in the navy and rose as *intendente general* (equivalent to brigadier general). Prior to that, he had been stationed in both Cuba and the Philippines, and gained a reputation for fast living (Preston, 1993).

The young Franco did not want to follow his father's footsteps, and declined to join a navy that had been crippled by the Spanish-American War. Instead, he joined the *Academia de Infantería de Toledo* (Toledo Infantry Academy) in 1907.

After graduating in 1910, Franco served in Morocco and rapidly advanced through the ranks for bravery in combat. In 1926 he became brigadier general at the age of 33, the youngest general in Europe since Napoleon. Two years later he became Director of the General Military Academy in Zaragoza.

In his autobiographical novel *Raza* (Race), published in 1942, General Franco portrayed a naval hero who was killed in Cuba during the Spanish-American War. Franco's father had indeed been in Cuba and, although he was not killed then and there, the more than coincidental links in the novel with him and *El Desastre* are all too obvious.

A few years earlier, Franco had emphatically declared that the Civil War could have

> no other outcome than the triumph of pure and eternal principles over bastard, anti-Spanish ones.
>
> (Franco 1938, in Preston, 1999: 2)

And, at the end of the war, he promulgated the Law of Political Responsibilities:

All the parties and political and social groups which belong to the Popular Front [the political-left coalition that had won the Spanish general election in 1936], the separatist organisations, and all those who have opposed the National Movement are declared outside the law.

(Franco, 1939, in Landis, 1972: 5)

As he seized supreme power as *Generalísimo* (commander in chief of all the armed forces), Franco developed a carefully designed method of *dejar hacer* (turning a blind eye), whilst his subordinates became enmeshed in what Miguel de Unamuno described as

the covenant of blood.

(Unamuno, in Preston, 1999: 55)

Ernesto Giménez Caballero was one of his more fervent admirers and, in the middle of the war, he wrote:

. . . we have seen Franco in the early hours of the morning . . . operating on the living body of Spain with the urgency and tragedy of a surgeon who operates on his own daughter.

(Giménez Caballero, 1938, in Preston, 2021c: 372)

General Emilio Mola was one of the most brutal assassins in the Spanish army. He was born in 1887, in Cuba, where his father had been stationed as a captain in the Civil Guard. His mother, Ramona Vidal, was Cuban. He was brought up in an environment dominated by harsh martial discipline.

The Cuban War of Independence split his family. While his father served in the Spanish forces, his maternal uncle Leoncio Vidal was one of the leading revolutionary Cuban fighters supported by the American army. After the survival anxieties generated by the war, and the mortification of *El Desastre*, the family moved to Spain.

At 17, Mola entered the *Academia de Infantería de Toledo* and developed deeply hostile feelings towards left-wing politicians and civilians. He served in Morocco where he received a military medal, and became a brigadier general in 1927, aged 40. He was made Director-General of Security in 1930, the last man to hold this post before the overthrowing of King Alfonso XIII, with the arrival of the Second Republic in 1931.

According to Preston (2012), Mola fluctuated from wild optimism to suicidal pessimism; which can suggest that he might have suffered from bipolar disorder. He went through phases in which he employed tactics of terror to rip to pieces any possible resistance on the road to power and, also, to *purify* Spain of the noxious elements of the left.

All in all, Mola was directly responsible for the murders of more than forty thousand civilians in the provinces that he controlled in northern Spain, during the first year of the Civil War. One of his first decisions was to order the execution of his chauffeur because he suspected him of sympathising with the Popular Front.

Mola was largely considered the architect of the military rebellion, and in charge of operations in most of northern Spain. On 19 July 1936, the day after the coup, he addressed a meeting of all *alcaldes* (town-hall mayors) of the province of Navarra and told them:

> It is necessary to spread terror. We have to create the impression of mastery, eliminating without scruples or hesitation all those who do not think as we do.
>
> (Mola, 1936, in Preston, 2021b: 242)

Like his fellow conspirators (Franco and Queipo de Llano), Mola regarded the Spanish proletariat in the same way as they regarded the Moroccan tribesmen, as an inferior race that had to be subjugated by sudden, uncompromising violence (Preston, 2012).

He believed that Spain was fighting for its very existence, for the authentically Christian and Spanish civilisation, which was *threatened* by death at the hands of the so-called *anti-Spain*. This term was employed at the time to include any group, idea or institution that did not agree with the rebels' vision of Spain. Marxism, separatism and freemasonry were at the top of the *anti-Spain*.

Mola's hatred of the Second Republic was expressed virulently in a broadcast on 27 February 1937, in which he stated that

> it was born stunted, deformed, bastard; more than a birth, it was an abortion, and as an abortion it was doomed to perish and it perished.
>
> (Mola, 1937, in Preston, 2021b: 242)

In this broadcast, the idea of killing off the Republic seen as a *bastard*, illegitimate child comes across powerfully as a bizarre metaphor. In fact, Aguilera was an illegitimate child who ended up killing his two illegitimate children.

The abominable message of extermination and surgical removal of those perceived as hostile to the rebels' notion of Spain could usually be heard in Mola's broadcasts, again and again.

The execution of trade unionists, members of left-wing parties, elected municipal officials, republican functionaries, school teachers and freemasons constituted what came to be known as *preventive assassinations*, since he believed that the authentically Christian Spanish civilisation was *threatened* by death at the hands of the *anti-Spain* (Preston, 2012).

Another practitioner of massive preventive killings was General Queipo de Llano. Like Mola's and Aguilera's fathers, Queipo was directly involved as a cavalryman in the Cuban Independence War that led to *El Desastre*. It happened that he was in hiding when Cuban rebels, supported by the US army, attacked his garrison; all his group companions were killed. That experience must have left him with a profound survival anxiety and a feeling that either you kill or, else, be killed.

When Queipo subsequently served in Morocco, his response to the Rif's rebellion was that it must be vigorously crushed. Like many officers in the so-called *Africanists* group, he firmly believed in the army's right to intervene in politics as a self-proclaimed arbiter and protector of Spain, not only to defend it from its external enemies, but also from those whom the generals considered internal enemies of the nation.

At the beginning of the Civil War, Queipo was based in Seville and in charge of operations in southern Spain. He gave instructions to annihilate the leaders of Marxist and communist organisations, as well as a number of affiliates chosen at random.

Under Queipo's jurisdiction, more than forty-five thousand civilians were assassinated and he often celebrated his atrocities in nightly radio talks, in which he expanded the notion that any person who had a *red* idea must be killed (Preston, 2012).

Landowners and aristocrats (Aguilera belonged to both groups) knew they were outnumbered by the masses. In fact, they feared to be killed by the masses and many of them thought that to *thin down* the numbers could be justified. A large number of landowners collaborated, financed, or expectantly awaited news of the military plot to overthrow the Republic.

When the Civil War began, they accompanied the rebels' columns and played an active role in selecting victims in captured villages for execution. Rich, aristocratic officers abounded on the rebel side as well, and so were to be found in the press apparatus. Having said that, it is also true that, in the Republican zone, some landowners and aristocrats were at risk of being killed by the local left (Preston, 2004).

According to Preston (2012), the exterminatory objectives of the rebels found an echo on the extreme left, particularly in the anarchist movement. In Republican-held areas, especially in Madrid and Barcelona, the underlying hatreds deriving from misery, hunger and exploitation led to random terror killings of the clergy, wealthy aristocrats, bankers, landowners and industrialists, who were all regarded as the instruments of oppression.

Unlike the systematic murders perpetrated by the rebels throughout the Civil War, the violence of the ultra-left happened despite (not because of) the Republican authorities.

In this context, and within the strategy of pre-emptive massive killing, Captain Aguilera often repeated some of the terrorising messages of Franco, Mola and Queipo. He in fact said to John Whitaker (correspondent of the *Chicago Daily News*):

> It is a race war, not merely a class war. You don't understand because you don't realize that there are two races in Spain – a slave race and a ruler race . . . We've got to kill and kill and kill, you understand?.

> (Aguilera, 1936, in Preston, 2021a: 203)

In addition, Aguilera produced his own *theory* about the problems of Spain:

> You know what's wrong with Spain? Modern plumbing! In healthier times –
> I mean healthier times spiritually, you understand – plague and pestilence used
> to slaughter the Spanish masses. Held them down to proper proportions . . . Now
> with modern sewage disposal and the like, they multiply too fast . . . and you
> can't expect them not to be infected with the virus of Bolshevism.
>
> (Aguilera, 1936, in Preston, 2021a: 178)

In addition, he suggested some *remedies* for the Spanish problems, as reported by
Charles Foltz (correspondent of the *Associated Press*):

> Sewers caused all our troubles. The masses in this country are not like your
> Americans, nor even like the British. They are slave stock . . . Had we no sewers
> in Madrid, Barcelona and Bilbao, all these *red* leaders would have died in their
> infancy instead of exciting the rabble and causing good Spanish blood to flow.
> When the war is over, we should destroy the sewers.
>
> (Aguilera, 1937, in Preston, 2021a: 203)

However, in a number of letters to his wife, Aguilera disclosed a different set of
feelings that revealed key signals about some narcissistic aspects of his personality.
After the fall of Bilbao, he wrote to Magdalena:

> We are already in Bilbao. And do you know who was the first army officer to
> enter the city? Your husband!
>
> . . . Never in my life have so many women kissed me in so little time. It was
> overwhelmingly emotional . . . I went out on the balcony of the Provincial
> Council and the crowd fell silent and I improvised a speech.
>
> (Aguilera, 1937, in Preston, 2021a: 206)

In another letter to Magdalena, he was equally thrilled, as his involvement with the
correspondents conferred on him a degree of celebrity. He wrote:

> You will get a surprise when you hear the radio speaking about me. Almost all
> the papers quote me constantly, especially in France. I have more photos that
> they brought to me yesterday, and I have been in the cinema newsreels and they
> have even seen me in London.
>
> (Aguilera, 1937, in Preston, 2021a: 206)

6.5 An attachment-based psychodynamic and group-analytic formulation

We are ourselves and our circumstances, are we not? This is a simply logical idea;
but it was not so explicitly formulated until the Spanish philosopher José Ortega y
Gasset (1914) spelled it out, in his book *Meditations on Don Quixote*.

Digging into Ortega's reflection *Yo soy yo y mi circunstancia* (I am I and my circumstance), we can conclude that the *circumstance* includes the broader context in which we exist: relationships, family, society, culture, politics and history, as well as our body with its physical characteristics, affecting personality development.

Ortega y Gasset implicitly stated that the notion of a purely individual identity is an abstraction. According to him, the *circumstance* is what connects an individual to a wider reality of others and to the world. And this is a world shaped by personal and sociopolitical history, including interpersonal and group attachments, as well as a social unconscious. At its core, individual lives are ultimately group lives.

Thinking about Captain Aguilera's case, we need to take into account his Spanish background and other *circumstances*.

Spain had built the first global empire on Earth and created the first global trade, as analysed in *The Silver Way: China, Spanish America and the Birth of Globalisation, 1565–1815* (Gordon and Morales del Pino, 2017) and in *Spain: The Centre of the World 1519–1682* (Goodwin, 2016).

These scholars consider that the *circumstance* of having held a world-empire status forged, to a large extent, the character of Spain and many Spaniards. From the 15th century onward, they went to America, Africa and Asia as *conquistadors* and settlers; they killed and destroyed much of the native cultures; they travelled as merchants and diplomats, as missionaries, university professors, linguists, poets and artists. In addition, they campaigned across Europe as feared professional soldiers.

People living in the UK would be very familiar with a widely used saying that applied to the extension of the British Empire, in the 19th and 20th century. The expression "the empire on which the sun never sets" was in fact quite accurate; during that period, literally, there was always a British colony in full daylight at any given time.

Interestingly, this motto was originally coined to describe the dominions of the Spanish Empire during the 16th, 17th, 18th and early 19th century. Of course, for both British and Spanish empires, this was much more than just a geographical concept. Certainly, for Captain Aguilera, it was a disturbing existential issue:

> The 16th century showed the greatness of Spain. The sun did not set in her dominions. It was a unique period of mystics, saints and artists. The *siècle* of the Spanish Empire! Do you now the population of our Fatherland at the time? Twelve million! Who cares if we now kill half of its population [the anti-Spain] if that proves to be necessary to reconquer our empire?.
>
> (Preston, 2021a: 175)

It is beyond the scope of this chapter to study the anatomy, sociopolitical structures and power dynamics of world empires, built through the brutality of invasion and conquest and the subjugation of indigenous populations – which often amounted to slavery and genocide.

Having said that, and as an aid to the present case study, I would like to emphasise that the social unconscious of a country and its citizens is moulded by their origins and history. Captain Aguilera was indeed pathologically nostalgic for the Spanish Golden Age and, like many of his contemporary compatriots, did not find a way to come to terms with new realities.

Some historians (Balfour and Quiroga, 2007; Goodwin, 2016) have suggested that, during its Golden Age, Spain had achieved a rare dynamic equilibrium in which the fierce tensions between Crown, Church and State, between aristocracy and urban oligarchs, town and country, peasants and landlords, found ways to balance one another somehow.

Of course, their perspective does not take sufficient account of *los olvidados*, masses of people (as Aguilera described them) who were exploited, abused or exterminated by inquisitorial, discriminatory and other power-based methods.

We cannot ignore the reality that, gradually, Spaniards found themselves overstretched by religious wars in Europe, and damaged by the rule of decadent monarchs and their venial favourites. Slowly, their world empire began to come apart, only to ultimately collapse at *El Desatre*, as narrated by John Hooper (1995) in *The New Spaniards*, and by Giles Tremlett (2012) in *Ghosts of Spain: Travels through a Country's Hidden Past*.

For the reader interested in understanding the influence of national trauma and war on the personal and social unconscious, I would recommend some key publications: *Beyond the Chains of Illusion: My Encounter with Marx and Freud* (Fromm, 1962), *The Personal Unconscious in Persons, Groups and Societies* (Hopper and Weinberg, 2016), *Dreamtelling, Relations, and Large Groups* (Friedman, 2019) and *From Crowd Psychology to the Dynamics of Large Groups* (Penna, 2023).

In these books, the often elusive (and always challenging) notion of the social unconscious is brought to life and rooted in both interpersonal and group experience. For the individual, the process of becoming aware of the demands of the social unconscious is in itself difficult and painful.

Earl Hopper, a British-American group analyst, sociologist and psychoanalyst, defined the social unconscious in a precise and helpful way, as follows:

> The existence of constraints of social, cultural and communicational arrangements of which people are unaware, in so far as these arrangements are not perceived (not known) and, if perceived, not acknowledged (denied) and, if acknowledged, not taken as problematic (given) and, if taken as problematic, not considered with an optimal degree of detachment and objectivity.
>
> (Hopper, 1996: 9)

Hopper's formulation resonates with that of Erich Fromm, a German-born psychologist, sociologist and psychoanalyst, who fled the Nazi regime and settled in the US:

> By the *social unconscious* I refer to those areas of repression that are common to most members of society; these commonly repressed elements are those

contents which a given society cannot permit its members to be aware of, if the society with its specific contradictions is to operate successfully.

(Fromm, 1962: 88)

Fromm further pointed out that shared unconscious attitudes and emotions remaining unconscious are due to the power of prevailing ideologies, belief systems and prejudices largely sustained by people in positions of power. When ideologies and prejudices that bind social groups together cease to function, the *glue* provided by the social unconscious can become social dynamite and create profound social disruptions, leading to radical changes for better or worse.

Many people, in their struggle to survive, become particularly vulnerable to destructive social-unconscious dynamics, as happened to Aguilera. Unfortunately, he did not have a therapeutic antidote against these destructive forces.

In a broader social dimension, unconscious and unresolved collective trauma can manifest itself in many different ways, involving psychopathology, violence or both – as in the case of perverse group attachment.

6.5(i) Some dynamics of perverse group attachment

Captain Aguilera was a child when the last tangible symbols of the Spanish Empire collapsed in 1898. *El Desastre* was a symbolic death of centuries of national pride.

Some *quixotic* Spanish politicians had decided to embark on a hopeless war, pushing the Spanish fleet in Cuba to follow an archaic principle that *honour without vessels is better than vessels without honour*: long live death! This suicidal attitude would later become the maxim of the Spanish Legion, of which Aguilera would be a fervent admirer.

Anyhow, *El Desastre* became a large part of the conscious mind of Aguilera's aristocratic family and of the unconscious collective mind of his country of birth. Indeed, it constituted a significant part of his own *circumstance*.

As a young child, he may have found it difficult to understand what was going on around him, within and outside the family. On the one hand, he could not form a secure attachment with his basically absent father – who did not seem to have been able to show affection towards him. In fact, Don Agustín did not fully accept him as his son, nor did he provide a good paternal role model for him.

In turn, Aguilera experienced a reverential fear of his decidedly strict father although, *paradoxically*, behaved in many ways like him. He in fact followed in his father's footsteps, both marrying someone from a lower social class and joining the army, as he struggled to develop his own individual and group identity.

On the other hand, from the warm and affectionate nature of the later correspondence with his mother, we may infer that he was loved by her to some extent – though not as securely as she loved her daughter Nena, the favourite child. Aguilera must have resented the ambivalent quality of his mother's love, as well as the fact that he had been displaced by his sister within the family.

In addition, the mother's shame and fabrication of a false class identity (as a reaction to being rejected by the Aguilera clan) surely added to the identity confusion and dissociation of her son. As Preston (2021a) suggested, isn't it ironic that she developed a puritanical hostility towards *illegitimate* children and non-married mothers? These maternal psychological defences were no doubt projected onto her son in various ways (mainly unconscious).

I wonder if Aguilera's compulsive boasting and his erratic snobbery may in part relate to some of the defensive attitudes that he internalised from his mother's chronic shame. In any case, grandiose snobbery was certainly an established group norm within the wider aristocratic, landowning and military contexts to which he was constantly exposed.

In terms of his overall attachment history within his family of origin, and on the evidence available from his biographers, it would be plausible to suggest that Aguilera established insecure attachment patterns with both his parents.

His attachment with his father might have had a hugely *avoidant* quality, whilst the attachment with his mother may have had a predominantly anxious-ambivalent quality. There is also evidence that he avoided any attachment relationship with his sister Nena, as he felt very jealous of her.

In terms of his attachment history within the family that he formed, there is no evidence that Aguilera was able to establish an attachment bond with any of his two sons. In fact, he never felt they were his children. It would appear that he replicated with them the elusive attachment he had experienced with his own father.

There is some evidence from Aguilera's biographers that the quality of attachment with his wife may have had an ambivalent quality too, as it had happened with his attachment to his mother. He often denigrated his wife, who belonged to a lower social class, but turned to her for validation and emotional support.

Within this ambivalence, on some occasions, he perceived his wife as a secure-enough base; which had some resemblance to how he had previously perceived his mother, at times.

Having said that, Aguilera's disorganised, erratic and violent behaviour and, ultimately, his psychotic illness indicate that, during his childhood and adolescence, he may have internalised experiences contributing to an overall disorganised pattern of attachment.

Neither parent provided a consistently secure base for him and his emotional needs were largely unmet. He did not grow as a confident person but created a false self-image (as his mother had done for herself) to impress people around him.

In generic terms, when children develop a disorganised attachment pattern, their caregivers have not created a safe, secure base for them to confidently return to. Instead, they may have established a patchy, neglectful or abusive relationship with the child they were supposed to care for. The child may experience contradictory feelings, wanting to love them, but also being afraid of them – as happened to Aguilera, who was particularly scared of his father.

The hypothesis that Aguilera may have internalised disorganised (and disorganising) attachment experiences is consistent with findings from recent specialist research; for example, Bucci, Emsley and Berry (2017) found that a disorganised attachment pattern is more significantly linked to positive symptoms of psychosis than any other attachment patterns (see Chapter 3).

In terms of his group-attachment history, being an illegitimate and largely unwanted child, Aguilera was not really treated as a full member of the aristocracy. He certainly was not a member of the royal family, but cultivated an idealised personal friendship with King Alfonso XIII, possibly in an attempt to mitigate the pain caused by the rejection of his aristocratic family. This *friendship* further contributed to his inflated sense of entitlement and his snobbery.

For many years, Captain Aguilera desperately tried to develop a military group identity, but was often disregarded by the army, which amplified his feelings of rejection and resentment. It is highly relevant that he was unable to establish any sense of an emotionally secure group attachment experience. At all times, he found it difficult to fit in; besides, he was often rejected by the various groups of which he was meant to be a member.

Against the above background, during the Civil War, Aguilera was given a propaganda role that pushed him to form a *perverse* attachment to a violent group. A person like him, with a mastery of foreign languages and (most importantly) with character traits that were consistent with an emotionally unstable, narcissistic and histrionic personality, was an easy target to become his leaders' spokesman for destruction and death (Cortina, 2022).

Furthermore, Aguilera's explosive and uncontrolled outbursts are consistent with what Bowlby (1973) described as *anger of despair*, which can be overwhelmingly dysfunctional and destructive.

From the outbreak of the war, he surrendered to the excitement of forming a group attachment with the military rebels – which made him feel that he could take revenge and have power over entire groups of other people.

After the war, Captain Aguilera came to be expendable and was gradually ostracised. Alongside this social rebuff, he also became increasingly self-isolating. And the more isolated one is, the greater the risk of developing mental health problems.

As Preston (2021a) highlighted, in later life, he became increasingly self-absorbed and despondent; he claimed to have been surrounded by hypocrisy, lies, envy and trickery; he bitterly reflected that his life had taken place in isolated meditation and bounded by mistrust; he was disgusted that, by dint of opposing the prevailing tide and injustice, he had faced serious personal disadvantage and the sadness of not having achieved much. He felt he was a failure.

From a life-long perspective, Aguilera was a man of sharp and irreconcilable contrasts. He was an outrageous racist, yet he proudly claimed to be the descendant of a *conquistador* and a Mexican-Indian princess. He hated the poor and considered them an inferior race, yet he was fond of the Little Sisters of the Poor and made donations to them.

In addition, he showed compassion for the victims of the First World War, yet he was a vociferous intellectual champion of the atrocities perpetrated by fascist armies in the Spanish Civil War.

Aguilera appeared to have been unable to come to terms with being an illegitimate and largely unwanted child. He hated that fact that he could not develop a meaningful sense of really belonging in a group. He was incapable of working through and integrating the different and often paradoxical elements that shaped his tormented personality, and ended up being at war with himself.

It is not unusual to find some of these contradictions in individuals with a history of major childhood trauma, resulting in mental unintegration or disorganisation. I would summarise his unintegrated conflictive traits, as follows:

His *Spanishness* and his *Britishness*; his aristocracy and his commonality; his elitist education in England and his uninspiring wealthy complacency; his civilian laziness and his military excitement; his mediocrity and his wish for grandiosity; his intellectual aspirations and his disorganization as a landowner; his Christian beliefs and his anti-clericalism; his depressive moods and his manic states; his intermittently generous friendliness towards his peasants and his delinquent tax avoidance leading to dangerous hostility towards tax officials; his hatred of authority figures and his desperate need for role models of paternal authority; his degrading mistreatment of women and his anxious search for affection from his mother and his wife. The list is longer.

(Ezquerro, 2021: 293)

As his physical and mental health deteriorated, Aguilera considered taking his own life. Maybe, his false and patchy sense of emotional security or, if you like, his narcissism *protected* him from killing himself, although he eventually gave up, lost his appetite for life and stopped taking his medication – which accelerated his death.

He certainly frightened his wife Magdalena and lost her as an attachment figure, after which he no longer had any traces of an emotionally secure base.

The return of his two sons to the parental home may have produced within him a feeling of displacement, similar in a way to the feeling of being displaced by his sister Nena when she was born.

I can imagine that he was awfully jealous of both his children, Gonzalo and Agustín, for the close attachment they had with their mother, at a time when he felt abandoned by all.

The pain of feeling abandoned, the anger of being jealous and the shame of perceiving himself as a *no-body* intermingled. Any of these three factors alone can constitute a most dangerous source of violence; their combination might be lethal. For many murderers, it is better to be bad than not to be at all; thus, they can become *some-body* in the eyes of the world.

Fascist regimes portray the enemy as less than human and, in doing so, they weaken the resistance in themselves to killing innocent people and, then, there is nothing to stop them. An ecosystem of uncontrolled group violence and murder (like the one internalised by Aguilera) takes over.

The Spanish Civil War itself was massively filicidal and fratricidal – a holocaust, as described by Preston (2012). Franco and his military machine had, as a target, the systematic killing of those Spaniards they perceived as their enemies, whom they literally called the *bastard* children of their own Fatherland – something that was poignantly mirrored and re-enacted, in some way, by Captain Aguilera. And, like him, the Francoist regime never stood trial.

6.6 Conclusion

Filicide is a complex crime and a life-long risk phenomenon; it is often the result of more than a combination of mental health problems and environmental stress-ors. In order to prevent its occurrence, as much as might be possible, it is crucial to identify at an early stage the risk factors that relate to the underlying unresolved conflicts of the potential perpetrator.

In the case of Captain Gonzalo de Aguilera, there were highly contradictory and conflictive elements in his emotionally unstable personality and in his disturbed mind – which were clearly visible and should have attracted an early psychiatric and psychotherapeutic intervention.

His mental health problems appear to have been a consequence of the cumu-lative trauma caused by distinctly unfavourable individual-attachment, family-attachment and group-attachment experiences.

Within these, maternal ambivalence combined with paternal, extended family and wider group rejections (as a result of being an illegitimate and largely unwanted child) were prominent features – which penetrated deeply into Aguilera's uncon-scious and persecuted him like a ghost throughout his life.

It is noteworthy that Aguilera himself had two illegitimate children, to whom he did not show affection and with whom he could not form any meaningful attach-ment relationship. Illegitimacy was a huge scandal in aristocratic circles at the time he and his children were born. In that context, his group attachment history became extremely difficult.

Captain Aguilera tried to form a secure attachment with a number of groups in his aristocratic, educational, military, landowning, intellectual and monarchic circles, but to no avail.

As a defensive strategy and a way of trying to compensate for his losses, during the Spanish Civil War, he established a *perverse group attachment* to a tyrannical and extremely violent nationalist group – which was struggling to come to terms with the unresolved existential trauma caused by *El Desastre*.

This bloodthirsty, and filicidal, group dynamic had a strong bearing on Captain Aguilera's bizarre thinking and murderous ideation, and further contributed to his emotional instability and mental disturbance.

In later life, as he was increasingly having unpredictable explosions of rage, isolating himself and talking about suicide, Aguilera should have had a proper psy-chiatric consultation and risk assessment, with a view to receiving specialist psy-chotherapy possibly combined with psychotropic medication – which may have prevented the tragic murder of his two sons, especially if he had understood that unresolved grief is a fuel for turmoil and aggression.

Image 6.1 Saturn devouring his son by Goya, Padro Museum, Madrid. Public domain via Casa de la Imagen, Logroño (La Rioja).

Sadly, it is not possible to move the clock back. However, Paul Preston's exhumation of the case (and of the hidden horrors of the Spanish Civil War) provide us with a good opportunity for learning about the impact of unresolved national trauma and for honest group-analytic reflection.

This may in turn help many people confront the ghosts of the past, with a view to achieving a less traumatic sense of closure and to properly healing old wounds – a cause that the author of this chapter very much supports.

Note 1: Goya finished painting *Saturn devouring his son*, in 1823. The previous decade, in March 1812, Spain had produced the first global (transcontinental) Constitution. It represented a complete break with the old absolutist monarchic regime and was considered one the three most liberal constitutions of its time, alongside the French and American constitutions. It applied to mainland Spain, as well as to all the people living in the Spanish territories of America, Africa and Asia. Interestingly, Constitution Square in the town of St Augustine (which was founded by the Spaniards in 1565 and is the oldest city in today's United States) is dedicated to the Spanish Constitution of 1812, rather than to the US Constitution (Chislett, 2013).

Unfortunately, the 1812 Constitution was short-lived. On his return to Spain in 1814, King Fernando VII abolished it and imposed a despotic regime. A successful *pronunciamiento* (coup d'état) by Rafael de Riego, in January 1820, pushed the King to accept the Constitution, but this only lasted three years. In fact, after a tense Liberal Triennium, Riego was executed in November 1823 and the Constitution was abolished again. Some art experts have suggested that Goya's painting may symbolise the return of the autocratic Spanish State killing its own children. But Goya left no clue as to the meaning of his painting and, that very year of 1823, when he finished this dramatic piece of work, he went into voluntary exile in France – where he died five years later.

Note 2: In the prologue of *The Spanish Holocaust*, Paul Preston made an important reflection about his choice for the title of his outstanding work:

> I thought long and hard about using the word 'holocaust' in the title of this book. I feel intense sorrow and outrage about the Nazis' deliberate attempt to annihilate European Jewry. I also feel intense sorrow and outrage about the lesser, but nonetheless massive, suffering undergone by the Spanish people during the Civil War . . . my use of the word 'holocaust' is not intended to equate what happened within Spain with what happened throughout the rest of continental Europe under German occupation but rather to suggest that it be examined in a broadly comparative context. It is hoped thereby to suggest parallels and resonances that will lead to a better understanding.
>
> (Preston, 2012: xi–xii)

Note 3: As I was completing this chapter, I couldn't help thinking about the current 32 military confrontations in the world, including the Dantesque images coming from the Middle East, particularly Gaza. I am deeply concerned about the never-ending Israel-Palestine conflict, in which unresolved collective trauma (transmitted from generation to generation for, at least, over eight decades) appear to continue operating as a fuel that ignites violence, retaliation and beyond-belief destruction.

I postulate that the recent violations of international law and the crimes against humanity, perpetrated by Hamas and by the Government of Israel, can represent a vicious circle of hatred, terror and perverse revenge. I wonder if unresolved trauma from the Holocaust perpetrated by the Nazis might also be contributing to the ongoing Nakba or Palestinian holocaust: the massive killing of Palestinian civilians as well as their violent displacement and dispossession, along with the destruction of their homes, society, culture, identity, human rights and national aspirations.

The above intractable conflict might be seen as too tragic an example of what happens when encapsulated past traumatic experience is reactivated or triggered. In a landmark piece of work, *Encapsulation as a defence against the fear of annihilation*, Earl Hopper (1991) had referred to some of these processes.

Moreover, according to Koh (2021), unresolved trauma can push individual and collective minds to regress to levels that limit their capacity to think about conflict in a manner required for effective peace processes. Traumatised groups tend to choose a particular type of leader who promises to save them from their predicament and, upon failing to do so, finds scapegoats among them or creates external enemies. Sadly, this contributes to the entrenchment of conflict.

I would like to add that, with the permanent settlements of the Neolithic, which (strangely enough) started in the Middle East, new forms of conflict and war were generated to own and defend the land. Attachment to land (which can be seen as a novel manifestation of group attachment) has come to be highly problematical when sacred value is attributed to it (Rozin and Wolf, 2008).

Note 4: A shorter version, containing some 40 per cent of this chapter, was published in: Ezquerro A (2021) Captain Aguilera and filicide: An attachment-based exploration. *Attachment: New Directions in Psychotherapy and Relational Psychoanalysis* 15(2): 279–297. I would like to thank this journal for kindly authorising the reproduction of several parts of the above article.

References

Arias González L (2013) *Gonzalo de Aguilera Munro XI Conde de Alba de Yeltes (1886–1965). Vidas y radicalismo de un hidalgo heterodoxo*. Salamanca, Spain: Ediciones Universidad de Salamanca.

Balfour S and Quiroga A (2007) *España reinventada: Nación e identidad desde la Transición*. Barcelona: Ediciones Península.

Blackwell D (2023) The dialectics of Chat: Privilege, power and institutional racism. *Group Analysis* 56(4): 541–557.

Bowlby J (1969) *Attachment and Loss: Vol. 1. Attachment* (1991 edition). London: Penguin Books.

Bowlby J (1973) *Attachment and Loss: Vol. 2. Separation, Anxiety and Anger* (1991 edition). London: Penguin Books.

Bowlby J (1988) *A Secure Base: Clinical Applications of Attachment Theory*. London: Routledge.

Brown T, Tyson D and Fernandez Arias P (2014) Filicide and parental separation and divorce. *Child Abuse Review* 23(2): 79–88.

Bucci S, Emsley R and Berry K (2017) Attachment in psychosis: A latent profile analysis of attachment styles and association with symptoms in a large psychosis cohort. *Psychiatry Research* 247: 243–249.

Burke J and Oltermann P (2016) Germany moves to atone for 'forgotten genocide' in Namibia. *The Guardian*, 25 December. Available at www.theguardian.com/world/2016/dec/25/germany-moves-to-atone-for-forgotten-genocide-in-namibia

Burns J (2006) *Spain: A Literary Companion*. Mijas Pueblo (Málaga): Ediciones Santana SL.

Burns-Marañón J (2016) *Franciscus: El papa de la promesa*. Barcelona: Stella Maris.

Campion JF Cravens JM and Covan F (1988) A study of filicidal men. *American Journal of Psychiatry* 145(9): 1141–1144.

Carr R (2000) Liberalism and Reaction: 1833–1931. In: Carr R (ed) *Spain: A History*. Oxford: Oxford University Press, pp. 205–242.

Chislett W (2013) *Spain: What Everyone Needs to Know*. New York: Oxford University Press.

Cordess C and Cox M (1996a) *Forensic Psychotherapy: Crime, Psychodynamics and the Offender Patient. Volume I: Mainly Theory*. London: Jessica Kingsley Publishers.

Cordess C and Cox M (1996b) *Forensic Psychotherapy: Crime, Psychodynamics and the Offender Patient. Volume II: Mainly Practice*. London: Jessica Kingsley Publishers.

Cortina M (2022) Our Prehistory as Egalitarian Foragers with Antiauthoritarian Leadership: What These Nomads Can Teach Us Today? In Maccoby M and Cortina M (eds) *Leadership, Psychoanalysis and Society*. London: Routledge, pp. 19–49.

Dorling D and Tomlinson S (2019) *Rule Britannia: Brexit and the End of Empire*. London: Biteback Publishing.

Eriksson L, Arnautovska U, McPhedran S, Mazerolle P and Wortley R (2021) Child and Adult Attachment Styles among Individuals Who Have Committed Filicide: The Case for Examining Attachment by Gender. *International Journal of Forensic Mental Health* 20(1): 63–79.

Ezquerro A (2015) John Bowlby: The timeless supervisor. *Attachment: New Directions in Psychotherapy and Relational Psychoanalysis* 9(2): 165–175.

Ezquerro A (2019) The Power of Group *Attachment. In: Group Analysis North Open Seminar*, University of Manchester, 8 November.

Ezquerro A (2021) Captain Aguilera and filicide: An attachment-based exploration. *Attachment: New Directions in Psychotherapy and Relational Psychoanalysis* 15(2): 279–297.

Frederick J, Devaney J and Alisic E (2022) Adverse childhood experiences and potential pathways to filicide perpetration: A systematic search and review. *Child Abuse Review* 31(3): e2743. Available at https://doi.org/10.1002/car.2743

Friedman R (2019) *Dreamtelling, Relation Disorders and Large Groups: New Developments in Group Analysis*. London: Routledge.

Fromm E (1962) *Beyond the Chains of Illusion: My Encounter with Marx and Freud*. New York: Touchstone.

Goodwin R (2016) *Spain: The Centre of the World 1519–1682*. London: Bloomsbury.

Gordon P and Morales del Pino JJ (2017) *The Silver Way: China, Spanish America and the Birth of Globalisation: 1565–1815*. London: Penguin Books.

Hansen R and King D (2001) Eugenic Ideas, Political Interests and Policy Variance Immigration and Sterilization Policy in Britain and the US. *World Politics* 53(2): 237–263.

Harris GT and Rice ME (2012) Filicide and child maltreatment: Prospects for ultimate explanation. In: Shackelford TK and Weekes-Shackelford VA (eds) *The Oxford Handbook of Evolutionary Perspectives on Violence, Homicide, and War*. New York: Oxford University Press, pp. 91–105.

Hooper J (1995) *The New Spaniards*. London: Penguin Books.

Hopper E (1991) Encapsulation as a defence against the fear of annihilation. *International Journal of Psychoanalysis* 72(4): 607–624.

Hopper E (1996) The social unconscious in clinical work. *Group* 20(1): 7–42.

Hopper E (2003) *The Social Unconscious: Selected Papers*. London: Jessica Kingsley Publishers.

Hopper E and Weinberg H (2016) *The Social Unconscious in Persons, Groups and Societies*. London: Karnac Books.

Jackson G (1974) *The Spanish Republic and the Civil* War (2005 edition). Barcelona: RBA.

Jackson G (1980) *A Concise History of the Spanish Civil War*. London: Thames & Hudson.

Kahr B (1994) The historical foundations of ritual abuse: an excavation of ancient infanticide. In: Sinason V (ed) *Treating Survivors of Satanist Abuse*. London: Routledge, pp. 45–56.

Kahr B (2001) *Forensic Psychotherapy and Psychopathology: Winnicottian Perspectives*. London: Routledge.

Kahr B (2020) *Dangerous Lunatics: Trauma, Criminality and Forensic Psychotherapy*. London: Karnac Books.

Kemp P (1957) *Mine Were of Trouble*. London: Cassell.

Koh E (2021) The Impact of Trauma on Peace Processes. *New England Journal of Public Policy* 33(10): 4. Available at https://scholarworks.umb.edu/nejpp/vol33/iss1/4

Landis AH (1972) *Spain! The Unfinished Revolution!* Baldwin Park, CA: Camelot.

Moreno Calderón F (2017) Antonio Vallejo-Nájera Lobón. *Información y Documentación sobre la Guerra Civil Española*. Available at https://guerracivil3639.wordpress.com/2017/02/18/antonio-vallejo-najera-lobon/

Orenstein D (2014) Analysis: 32 years of U.S. filicide arrests. *News from Brown University*. Available at https://news.brown.edu/articles/2014/02/filicide

Ortega y Gasset J (1914) *Meditaciones del Quijote* (2014 edition). Madrid: Alianza Editorial.

Papapietro DJ and Barbo E (2005) Commentary: Toward a Psychodynamic Understanding of Filicide – Beyond Psychosis and Into the Heart of Darkness. *Journal of the American Academy of Psychiatry and the Law* 33(4): 505–508.

Penna C (2023) *From Crowd Psychology to the Dynamics of Large Groups: Historical, Theoretical and Practical Considerations*. London: Routledge.

Pérez-Delgado R (1974) *Antonio Maura*. Madrid: Ediciones Tebas.

Preston P (1993) *Franco: A Biography* (1995 edition). London: Fontana Press.

Preston P (1999) *Comrades! Portraits from the Spanish Civil War* (2006 edition). London: Harper Perennial.

Preston P (2004) The Answer Lies in the Sewers: Captain Aguilera and the Mentality of the Francoist Officer Corps. *Science and Society* 68(3): 277–312.

Preston P (2009) *We Saw Spain Die: Foreign Correspondents in the Spanish Civil War*. London: Constable and Robinson.

Preston P (2012) *The Spanish Holocaust: Inquisition and Extermination in Twentieth-Century Spain* (2013 edition). London: Harper Press.

Preston P (2021a) El mensajero. In: Preston P *Arquitectos del terror: Franco y los artífices del odio*. Barcelona: Penguin Random House, pp. 171–223.

Preston P (2021b) El asesino del Norte. In: Preston P *Arquitectos del terror: Franco y los artífices del odio*. Barcelona: Penguin Random House, pp. 225–283.

Preston P (2021c) La guerra interminable. In: Preston P *Arquitectos del terror: Franco y los artífices del odio*. Barcelona: Penguin Random House, pp. 347–377.

Resnick PJ (1969) Child murder by parents: A psychiatric review of filicide. *The American Journal of Psychiatry*, 126(3): 325–334.

Roberts JM (2014) *The Penguin History of the World*. London: Penguin Books.

Rozin P and Wolf S (2008) Attachment to land: The case of the land of Israel for American and Israeli Jews and the role of contagion. *Judgment and Decision Making* 3(4): 325–334. Available at https://doi.org/10.1017/S1930297500000899

Thomas H (1961) *The Spanish Civil War* (2001 edition) New York: Modern Library.

Tremlett G (2012) *Ghosts of Spain: Travels through a Country's Hidden Past*. London: Faber & Faber.

Volkan V (2014) *Psychoanalysis, International Relations and Diplomacy. A source-book on Large-Group Psychology*. London: Karnac Books.

Volkan V (2020) *Large-Group Psychology: Racism, Societal Divisions, Narcissistic Leaders and Who We Are Now*. London: Phoenix Publishing House.

Welldon E (1993) Forensic psychotherapy and group analysis. *Group Analysis* 26(4): 487–502.

West SG (2007) An Overview of Filicide. *Psychiatry* 4(2): 48–57.

Zulueta F de (1993) *From Pain to Violence: The Traumatic Roots of Destructiveness*. London: Whurr Publishers.

Arturo Ezquerro: https://orcid.org/0000-0002-9910-4576

Afterword

In *The Power of Group Attachment*, Arturo Ezquerro and María Cañete apply Bowlby's theory to unconscious processes in groups that help us better understand murderous rage, group cohesion, political violence, and the impact of trauma on the individual and the group. It is wonderful to see these authors use Bowlby's work to understand and address group leadership and group attachment. I do not believe there is any book like this, and it is an important resource as we try to navigate political polarization, racism, hate, war, climate change, healthcare inequality, and pandemics (Marmarosh, 2022). If there was ever a time in history that we needed to address the power of groups, now is the time. Immediately, Ezquerro and Cañete warn:

> We are aware that our approach might be perceived as a *huge leap*. Having said that, we are clear that humanity needs a fundamental shift, a radical change, a group attachment re(e)volution . . . (see Chapter 1).

I completely agree. As I read these words, I found myself reminiscing about conversations with colleagues who could not accept the idea of a book bridging attachment theory and group therapy (Marmarosh, Markin and Spiegel, 2013), rejected group as a specialty (Whittingham, Lefforge and Marmarosh, 2021), or rejected the necessity of teaching group dynamics. I appreciate the courage that Ezquerro and Cañete demonstrate as they leap. In my opinion, it is an important leap to take and, like Bowlby, they are successful.

It is a leap to prioritize the group in psychology, psychoanalysis and wider mental health. The focus of psychoanalysis has always been on the individual and, even with the more recent acknowledgement of the social forces within psychoanalysis (Layton and Leavy-Sperounis, 2020), the main form of intervention remains the individual. This is also true for psychology. Most of the major analytic institutes and psychology graduate training programs today in the United States do not emphasize group theory or practice and often, group dynamics and treatment come secondary to individual treatment modalities.

Individual treatment is even prioritized when we have people suffering who cannot get access to mental health care (Whittingham, Marmarosh, Mallow and Scherer, 2023). Many clinics become filled and prefer waiting lists instead of initiating group therapy. It is my belief that the major problems we see within our field, and the traumatic hate we see spreading throughout the world is a direct result of groups and our attachments to them. Understanding how early relationships and systemic forces within the environment shape people and groups helps us consider different interventions that include group treatment.

In the initial chapter, the authors explore the important role groups have played in human evolution and how groups have been critical to human survival throughout history. The authors' description of the anthropological and cross-cultural perspective sheds light on how the secure base provided by group attachment has been as important, if not more important, as the secure attachment to an individual caregiver. Social psychologists have also provided research linking group identities to self-esteem enhancement, self-protection during threat, and emotion regulation (Forsyth, 2014). Given the power of groups to foster exploration, safety, and survival, group therapy might be the treatment of choice for many people, especially those from more collectivistic cultures.

One of the many strengths of this book is that it integrates theory and practice creatively. Not only have the authors addressed examples of theory, historical leaders, and political groups, they have also shared clinical case material from group therapy sessions. In this respect, I want to draw attention to Chapter 5 (on group cohesion and coherency) where the authors explore the fluctuations in cohesion that are necessary for psychotherapy groups to be effective. Their distinction between group cohesion and group coherency and how this reflects the state and stage of the attachment dynamic is particularly enlightening.

They describe how a working group must be able to invite unconscious trauma into the group or it will continue to haunt its members. However, if we invite these hauntings, we need to expect ruptures, and we have to develop the foundation of safety to foster risk and repair. It is through the repair of emotionally traumatizing experiences that members revise the internal working models of themselves, others, and groups (Marmarosh, 2022).

The above clinical example is a powerful one that demonstrates the interrelationship between the leader, the group, and traumatic moments of meeting. It shows how easily the group fragments when past trauma resurfaces through the group process. We all have been in a group when suddenly, past trauma is activated and the ability for the members to feel safe evaporates into thin air. We see this happening in our classes, supervision groups, faculty meetings, and universities. Unfortunately, leaders sometimes don't know what to do. They remain detached during this process or unable to tolerate the chaos that envelopes the group (Marmarosh, 2021).

However, in this clinical example, the leader did not detach or remain silent. The leader called the members to check in, met with them individually outside of the group, saved chairs for them during the session, directly addressed the abusive nature of their statements, tolerated the uncertainty of interventions, and examined countertransference. It is impressive how the leader in this chapter remained a secure base for the group members (Mikulincer and Shaver, 2017).

Most importantly, the leader held onto multiple realities and perspectives and ultimately fostered the repair. Even though the leader was a male with ultimate power, position and privilege in the group – he also retained the ability to reflect on his own identity in the group and how his actions triggered deep trauma in a female member. His ability to be empathic during this painful group enactment allowed the group to contain the dissociated pain and trauma that was lingering beneath the group's surface. The leader's empathy led to the members' empathy, emotion regulation, and insight (Fonagy, Campbell and Bateman, 2020).

All too often in groups, trauma is triggered, and the group suddenly shifts from feeling cohesive to abusive. Often, it is the leader who determines how well the group will survive. In this case, the leader did not become defensive, engage in splitting, or foster a scapegoat to hold the unwanted rage and blame. The group returned to a deeper cohesion (also termed coherency), one that was derived from the knowledge that the group survived and explored unconscious affect related to trauma.

As the unconscious became conscious, the group became more authentic and the cohesion more genuine. The group served as a secure base for the members because the leader fostered trust within the group where cohesion could evolve into coherency. This was a wonderful example of how chaos in a group can lead to a meaningful outcome. It also highlights our need for strong, benign leaders who are trained to understand group dynamics, empathy, and emotion regulation. We need better leaders.

Given the enormous pain and suffering we are seeing around the world, will disorganizing chaos lead to meaningful change? I don't know. But I do know that the next generation needs more tools to cope with group trauma, polarizing ideologies, and emotional pain. We need to do more. Sroufe's (2005) longitudinal research findings suggest that we are always influenced by our attachments, our attachment styles can change, and there is hope.

Mikulincer and Shaver's (2001, 2007) research suggests that priming secure individual attachments can reduce aggression towards people with a different group identity. Group members can treat other group members with more respect, curiosity, and compassion. It is possible that positive group experiences can improve our sense of wellbeing and challenge racism, hatred, genocide, and discrimination. On the other hand, we must also remember that negative group experiences can erode our sense of wellbeing and inflame hatred, outgroup derogation, and aggression. The trauma of poverty, war, and human suffering will have an impact for generations.

It is up to us to join Arturo Ezquerro and María Cañete to advocate for more consideration of group theory and practice. We need more securely attached leaders, more empathy for unresolved trauma, and to give more attention to group training. We all must take a leap and join this "group attachment re(e)volution".

Cheri Marmarosh, PhD, ABBP, CGP, F-APA,
Associate Professor, Professional Psychology Program, The George
Washington University; Professor Director of Research, Center for
the International Study of Spirituality and Mental Health, Divine
Mercy University; Collaborations with McLean Hospital, Harvard
University, and University of Navarra; Editor, *International
Journal of Group Psychotherapy*.
Washington, DC
February 2024

References

Fonagy P, Campbell C and Bateman A (2020) Mentalizing, attachment, and epistemic trust in group therapy. In: Marmarosh CL (ed) *Attachment in Group Psychotherapy*. London and New York: Routledge, pp. 20–45.

Forsyth DR (2014) *Group Dynamics*. Belmont, CA: Wadsworth Cengage Learning.

Layton L and Leavy-Sperounis M (2020) *Toward a Social Psychoanalysis: Culture, Character, and Normative Unconscious Processes*. London and New York: Routledge.

Marmarosh CL (2021) Ruptures and Repairs in Group Psychotherapy: From Theory to Practice. *International Journal of Group Psychotherapy* 71(2): 205–223.

Marmarosh CL (2022) Attachments, trauma, and COVID-19: Implications for leaders, groups, and social justice. *Group Dynamics: Theory, Research, and Practice* 26(2): 85–91.

Marmarosh CL, Markin R and Spiegel E (2013) *Attachment in Group Psychotherapy*. Washington, DC, USA: The American Psychological Association.

Mikulincer M and Shaver PR (2001) Attachment theory and intergroup bias: evidence that priming the secure base schema attenuates negative reactions to out-groups. *Journal of Personality and Social Psychology* 81(1): 97–103.

Mikulincer M and Shaver PR (2007) Boosting attachment security to promote mental health, prosocial values, and inter-group tolerance. *Psychological Inquiry* 18(3): 139–156.

Mikulincer M and Shaver PR (2017) Augmenting the sense of attachment security in group contexts: The effects of a responsive leader and a cohesive group. *International Journal of Group Psychotherapy* 67(2): 161–175.

Sroufe LA (2005) Attachment and development: A prospective, longitudinal study from birth to adulthood. *Attachment and Human Development* 7(4): 349–367.

Whittingham M, Lefforge NL and Marmarosh CL (2021) Group psychotherapy as a specialty: An inconvenient truth. *American Journal of Psychotherapy* 74(2): 60–66.

Whittingham M, Marmarosh CL, Mallow P and Scherer M (2023) Mental health care equity and access: A group therapy solution. *American Psychologist* 78(2): 119–125.

Author index

Subject index

223, 226–227, 230–233; ideological
conflicts 220, 223, 225, 227, 233–237;
interpersonal and group relationships
conflicts 87, 160, 164; 187–188, 192, 197;
intrapsychic conflicts 73, 75–76, 102,
109, 116, 160, 163, 172, 209, 233–234;
military conflicts 2, 54, 214–216,
223–227, 236–237; working through
conflicts 8, 50, 52, 80–81, 201–203
confusion 30, 106, 110, 185–186, 198–201;
see also complexity theory; identity
confusion; uncertainty
Confusion of the tongues between the
adults and the child (Ferenczi) 199
Congo Republic 26
containment, maternal 76; therapeutic 46,
83, 117, 136, 148–149
contemporary foragers/hunter-gatherers
25–27, 32–33; see also pan-forager
model of childcare
continuity and reliability of care 27, 39, 43,
52, 84, 111, 119, 123, 128, 131–132,
135–136, 138, 164, 168, 198; see also
attachment (secure/secure-enough/
healthy)
cooperation 19, 20–21, 31–34; see also
competition; group collaboration/
cooperation; mutual aid
cooperative group breeding 26, 30, 32;
see also group attachment
CORE (clinical outcomes in routine
evaluation) 131
co-therapy 116, 118, 124–125, 132, 134
countertransference 8, 44, 159, 187, 242;
see also transference
COVID-19 pandemic 41–42, 207
creativity 53, 66, 171, 192; see also group
attachment; exploration; survival
crisis: crisis of attachment 9, 148, 154–155,
159, 161, 175, 178; economic crisis 221;
existential see existential crisis; global
see global crisis; see also suicide
critical mass 201; see also complexity
theory
cross-cultural perspectives on attachment
see attachment
Cuba 211–212, 219–220, 223–225, 230
Cuban War of Independence 211, 224–225
cultural acquisition device 28–30; see also
group culture; knowledge and culture
transmission

cultural diversity 28–32, 241
cultural system of meaning 28–29
culture: developing a therapeutic group
culture 43, 89, 125–130, 137–138;
culture and evolution 9, 20–21, 27–32;
native cultures 18, 228; primitive
cultures 18; universal attachment
culture 2–3, 16, 22, 25 see also cultural
acquisition device; group culture
cumulative cultural evolution 20; see also
evolution of the human group
cumulative interpretation 128; see also
interpretations in therapy
cumulative trauma 128; see also trauma

Daily Mail 215
danger 3, 9, 23–24, 31, 54, 119, 129,
157; see also attachment; protection;
proximity-seeking; stranger
The Dark Night of the Soul (Saint John of
the Cross) 69
daydreaming 101; see also fantasy
death anxiety see anxiety
death awareness 157–158
death instinct 104, 107–108, 157
de-cathected energy 101–102; see also
cathected energy
delusions 98, 100, 107, 109–111, 125;
see also hallucinations; pychosis
dementia praecox 71; see also
schizopfrenia
democracy 1, 114–115, 220; see also
dictatorship
denial 75, 80, 89; see also mania
dependency xxii, 23, 75–76; see also
insecure attachment
depression 8, 29, 67, 70–71, 74–75,
81–86, 147, 154, 159, 172, 196, 218;
group psychotherapy for depression 42,
44; mystical account of depression 69;
national depression 8, 208, 219
(see also unresolved collective trauma);
post-natal depression 84, 162,
166–167; psychotic depression 66–67,
70, 120, 162; see also bipolar disorder;
melancholia; suicide
El Desastre [The Disaster] 219–220,
223–225, 230, 234; see also Spanish-
American War
despair 146, 157, 159–160, 162, 176–177,
220, 232; see also anger of despair;

For Product Safety Concerns and Information please contact our EU
representative GPSR@taylorandfrancis.com
Taylor & Francis Verlag GmbH, Kaufingerstraße 24, 80331 München, Germany

www.ingramcontent.com/pod-product-compliance
Lightning Source LLC
Chambersburg PA
CBHW050632280326
41932CB00015B/2619